THE ENDS OF THE EARTH

A SAMPLING OF BOOKS ON SCIENCE BY ISAAC ASIMOV

The Living River

The Wellsprings of Life

Life and Energy

The Genetic Code

The Human Body

The Human Brain

A Short History of Biology

Asimov's Biographical Encyclopedia
of Science and Technology

A Short History of Chemistry

The Noble Gases

The Neutrino

Understanding Physics (3 volumes)

The Universe

Photosynthesis

Asimov's Guide to Science

Jupiter, the Largest Planet

Our World in Space

THE ENDS OF THE EARTH

The Polar Regions of the World

By Isaac Asimov

Illustrations by
Bob Hines

WEYBRIGHT AND TALLEY
NEW YORK

Weybright and Talley
750 Third Avenue
New York, New York

Library of Congress Cataloging in Publication Data

Asimov, Isaac, 1920–
 The ends of the Earth.

 Includes index.
 1. Earth sciences—Polar regions. 2. Polar
regions—Description and travel. I. Title.
QE70.A8 550′.911 74–20326
ISBN 0–679–40123–7

Manufactured in the United States of America

Dedicated to:

J. O. Jeppson,
  fellow writer

CONTENTS

Chapter 1   **Sunlight, Shape, and Movement**   1

The Flat Earth   3
The Tilted Earth   4
The Spherical Earth   8
The Rotating Earth   10

Chapter 2   **The Axis and the Sun**   19

The Tipped Axis   20
The Revolving Earth   23
Solstices and Equinoxes   28
Tropics and Zones   30

Chapter 3   **Discovering the Poles**   35

Myths   36
Travelers   39
The Celestial Sphere   44
The Moving Sun   47
Polestars and Bears   50

Chapter 4   **Past the Arctic Circle**   59

Men of the Arctic   60
The Irish and the Vikings   62
The Southeast Passage   69
The West Passage   72
The Northeast Passage   75

Chapter 5 **To the North Pole** 83

The Northwest Passage 84
Penetrating the Archipelago 87
The Coast of Siberia 92
The Coast of Canada 97
Greenland 101
Across the Sea Ice 105

Chapter 6 **To the South Pole** 111

Skirting the Continents 112
The New Continent 117
The Antarctic Islands 123
The Shores of Antarctica 126
The Interior of Antarctica 130

Chapter 7 **Our Unique Ocean** 135

The Formation of Planets 136
The Formation of Atmospheres 140
The Formation of Oceans 143
The Water Molecule 148

Chapter 8 **The Effect of the Ocean** 155

Temperature Extremes 155
Water Vapor 160
Fresh Water 165
Density 170

Chapter 9 **Ice** 175

The Freezing of Water 175
Sea Ice 179

The Tundra   182
Snow   193
Glaciers   199
Icebergs   207
Planetary Ice Caps   211

Chapter 10   The Polar Ocean   215

Land Life on the Ice Sheets   215
Air Circulation   218
Surface-Ocean Circulation   221
Cold Water   225
Polar Oceanic Life   231

Chapter 11   The Global Magnet   247

Magnetism   247
The Magnetic Poles   251
The Earth's Core   255

Chapter 12   The Magnetic Field   263

The Aurorae   263
Ions   267
Cosmic Rays   271
The Solar Wind   275
Evolution   279
Magnetic Field Reversals   283

Chapter 13   The Ice Ages   289

The Glaciers of the Past   289
Advances and Retreats   294

Sea Level   301
Dust Clouds and Sunspots   306
The Changing Orbit   310
Carbon Dioxide   315

Chapter 14   **The Drifting Continents**   321

The Arctic Ocean   322
The Shifting Poles   326
The Shifting Plates   329
Fossils in Antarctica   339
The Future   344

Index   351

THE ENDS OF THE EARTH

1

SUNLIGHT, SHAPE, AND MOVEMENT

The first geographic fact that most American children learn is that there is a North Pole. They gather that it is snowy and icy there so that travel must be by sleigh. Travel is associated with a night in December so that nighttime and the North Pole seem to go together. And they learn that one sort of animal that lives near the North Pole is the reindeer.

They learn all this, very likely, even before they know that the Earth is round, or where the United States is in relation to other countries, or where they themselves live within the United States. Thanks to the legend of Santa Claus, the North Pole comes first.

Perhaps because of this, Americans grow up taking the North Pole (and its opposite number, the South Pole) for granted, along with its frigid cold, its snow and ice, and its long nights.

Stop and think about the matter for a moment and it might seem puzzling. Most Americans live in areas where there may be snow and ice on occasion, but where conditions, on the average, are quite pleasant. Why should the polar regions be different?

Or suppose you don't think about it in terms of personal, and limited, experience, but consider some hard facts.

Whether the Earth is warm or cold, whether there is ice upon it or not, depends on the Sun, for almost all the Earth's surface heat comes from that body. (A little comes from the Earth's interior, but so little that we can ignore it.)

The Sun, to be sure, is 150,000,000 kilometers* from the Earth and that might make it seem too distant to have much of a warming effect on us. It is, however, a huge body, 1,400,000 kilometers across, and its surface is at a temperature of 6000 C.† The Sun is large enough and hot enough to warm the Earth, even from its great distance, to an average temperature of 14 C.

But 14 C. is the temperature of a pleasant day in the spring or fall. The air is cool but by no means unpleasantly cold, and it is certainly too warm for the snow and ice we associate with the polar regions. For snow to fall and for ice to accumulate, the temperature must fall below 0 C.

An average, however, is only an average. The temperature goes up and down from hour to hour and from day to day and from place to place on the surface of the globe. In some places it is usually considerably above the overall average and in other places considerably below.

---

* Almost the entire world, except for the United States, now uses the "metric system" of measurement. Scientists everywhere, even including American scientists, use it exclusively. To use anything else in dealing with matters involving the whole Earth would be provincial. I will therefore use the metric system and give equivalents in footnotes now and then. The kilometer, for instance, is equal to 0.62137 miles. It is reasonably accurate to say that one kilometer is equal to five-eighths of a mile, and that one mile is equal to 1⅗ kilometers.

† In the United States, we use the Fahrenheit scale (named after the man who invented it) to measure temperature. By this scale the freezing point of water is 32 F. and the boiling point is 212 F. The Celsius scale (named after *its* inventor), which is used by the rest of the world and by all scientists, has the freezing point of water at 0 C. and the boiling point at 100 C. Body temperature, which most of us think of as 98.6 F., is also 37 C., while a pleasant room temperature of 68 F. is 20 C.

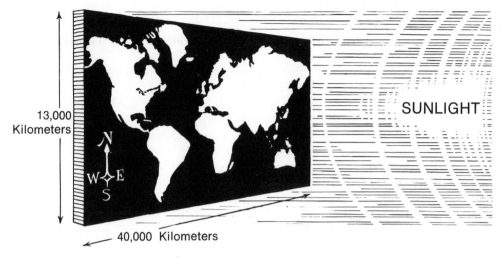

13,000 Kilometers

SUNLIGHT

40,000 Kilometers

Figure 1. The Flat Earth

Why this is so depends upon the Earth's shape and its motions, and one way of approaching it is to see what would happen if the Earth were bathed in sunlight under different conditions. We can begin with a very simple set of conditions and then, one by one, add complications.

The Flat Earth

Suppose, for instance, the Earth were flat. Suppose we imagined it to be a flat, rectangular slab, 13,000 kilometers in one direction and 40,000 kilometers in the other. (The face of such a slab would have a surface area equal to that of the Earth.)

We can call the direction from the center of the slab to one of the near edges "north" and the opposite direction would be "south." From the center to the far edge at the right of the north-south line (as we look at it) is "east" and opposite to that is "west" (see figure 1).

Let us imagine, next, that this Earth slab is placed in such a way that it is motionless with respect to the Sun and that it is exactly perpendicular to the direction of the light rays coming from the Sun. (Let us also suppose that it is the side of the slab toward the Sun that interests us. The other side we can ignore.)

To anyone standing anywhere on such a flat Earth, the Sun will seem directly overhead, that is, at "zenith."

(Strictly speaking, the Sun is directly overhead the central point of the Earth slab. Since the Sun is 150,000,000 kilometers away, even the full 40,000-kilometer width of the slab is insignificant. If you were standing at the extreme edge of the slab the Sun would be displaced from the exact overhead point by only about 1 percent of its own width, something we can certainly disregard.)

If this were so—a flat Earth, motionless, with sunlight pouring directly down upon it without cessation—the Earth slab would get pretty hot, much hotter than the real Earth ever gets. The temperature wouldn't go up indefinitely because some of the heat would be reradiated out into space. Still the Earth slab would surely reach temperatures above the boiling point of water.

We are starting, however, with the simplest possible situation. Now let's begin to add refinements and see how the situation changes.

The Tilted Earth

Suppose the Earth slab is slanted away from the perpendicular to sunlight. It would be useful in taking this into account to use some way of measuring exactly how great the slant may be.

For instance, if we imagine ourselves to be a cosmic giant capable of handling the Earth slab, we could picture turning it about more and more until the side that had previously faced the Sun faced away from it. Then, if we continued to turn it, the slab would finally make a complete turn, and the side that had originally faced the Sun would be facing it once more.

By a convention as old as the ancient Babylonians, such a complete turn is divided into 360 equal divisions, each of which is called a "degree of arc," or, commonly, just a "degree."

Anything which turns completely around, so that it faces its original direction is said to have turned through 360 degrees. A circle marks out an imaginary complete turn if you move your finger around it, so that the circumference of a circle marks out 360 degrees. If you move partway around the circle and that partway is so many 360ths of the circumference, it is that many degrees. If you move halfway around the circle, you have moved 180/360 of the way around, or 180 degrees. A quarter way around is 90 degrees, and 17/360 of the way around is 17 degrees.

It has also been customary, since Babylonian days, to divide each degree into sixty equal parts called "minutes of arc," and to divide each minute of arc into sixty equal "seconds of arc." Usually, these are referred to simply as "minutes" and "seconds." Thus, 17½ degrees can be written as 17 degrees and 30 minutes, and you can easily understand what it is to speak of 19 degrees 24 minutes and 49 seconds. Frequently, one makes such statements more condensed by using the symbol ° for degree, ′ for minute, and ″ for second. Therefore you can speak of 17° 30′, or 19° 24′ 49″. We can also use the simpler decimal notation 17.5° or 19.41°, and so on. I shall use the decimal system whenever possible.

Suppose, then, we tip the Earth slab in the northern direction. That is, we imagine ourselves pushing the northern edge away from the Sun and the southern edge toward the Sun in such a way that the center of the slab stays in the same place. In that case, the *average* distance from the Sun remains unchanged.

If we tip the slab northward more and more, we find that when we've tipped it one-quarter of a complete turnaround (that is, 90 degrees), the slab is lined up parallel to the Sun's rays. It is the edge of the slab that is now facing the Sun.

The same is true if you tip the slab in the southern direction, with the southern edge moving away from the Sun and the northern edge toward it, or eastward, or westward, or, for that matter, in any direction. In no matter which direction you tip the Earth slab, 90 degrees will see it lined up with its edge to the Sun.

(You can try this, in concrete terms, using a playing card, if you have trouble visualizing it in imagination.)

If, in any direction, the slab is tilted more than 90 degrees, the side on which you imagine people to be living faces away from the Sun, and that is of no interest as far as our purpose in this book is concerned. Let us then consider what the situation is if the Earth slab is tilted anywhere up to 90 degrees from the original perpendicular position (which can be called a 0-degree tilt) in any direction.

When a rectangular slab is tilted in any direction, its area in the line of sight decreases. (Try it with a playing card.) By the time it is tilted 90 degrees in any direction, so that it is edge on, the area in the line of sight (neglecting the thickness of the slab—or of the playing card) is zero.

This means that as the Earth slab is tilted, it stops a smaller and smaller quantity of sunlight, until, at a 90-degree tilt, it stops no sunlight at all. The sunlight skims the flat surface and passes by (see figure 2).

Another way of putting it is that as the Earth slab is tilted, a given quantity of sunlight spreads out over a larger and larger area.

Either way you look at it, whether as a given portion of the Earth slab receiving less sunlight or as a given quantity of sunlight spreading over a larger area, the Earth slab receives and must absorb less energy from the Sun, and will not attain as high a temperature. The more the Earth slab is tilted, the cooler it will be.

We can put figures to this. The amount of sunlight received by any fixed area of the Earth slab at a particular angle of tilt

Figure 2. The Tilted Earth

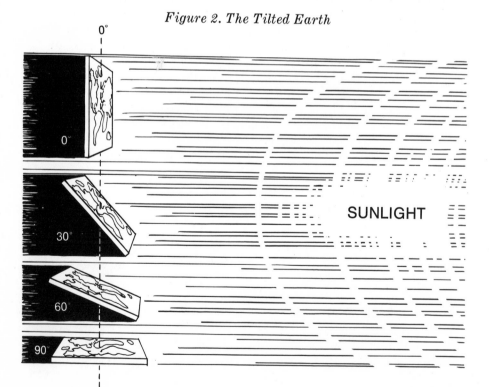

is proportional to what the mathematicians call the cosine of that angle. Exactly what the cosine is need not concern us; its value can be looked up in tables and the cosine for any angle can be obtained. A brief table for every ten degrees would look like this:

angle	cosine
0°	1.000
10°	0.985
20°	0.940
30°	0.866
40°	0.766
50°	0.643
60°	0.500
70°	0.342
80°	0.174
90°	0.000

As you see, the quantity of sunlight received by the slab declines slowly at first as it is tilted. Even after it is tilted 30 degrees, it still receives nearly seven-eighths as much sunlight as when it was untilted. Another 30 degrees, however, and the quantity of sunlight is down to one-half, and with the final 30 degrees it is down to nothing. This is true no matter in which direction the slab is tilted.

If we imagine ourselves standing on the Earth slab, we can tell the amount by which it was tipped, and in which direction, by noting the position of the Sun in the sky. The Sun is at the zenith when the slab is untipped. If the slab is tipped 10 degrees or 20 degrees or 30 degrees, the Sun is observed to be 10 degrees or 20 degrees or 30 degrees from the zenith. If the tipping is northward, the Sun is to the south of the zenith; if eastward, it is to the west; in general, the Sun departs from the zenith in the direction opposite to that in which the slab is tilted.

If the slab is tilted 90 degrees in any direction, then it is edgewise to the Sun, and to someone standing on the slab, the Sun is seen at the horizon. The line of the horizon cuts its glowing circle in half.*

* We assume here, as all through this chapter, for the sake of simplicity, that there are no clouds, mist, or haze to hide the Sun and that there are no unevennesses at the horizon, no mountains, trees, or houses to break it up. We imagine the horizon to be a perfectly smooth and unobscured line.

In other words, the angular measure from the zenith to the horizon, in any direction, is just 90 degrees.

Since the distance of the Sun from the zenith is the measure of the angle of tilt, we can say that the lower the Sun is in the sky—the farther from the zenith and the nearer the horizon—the less heat it is delivering to the spot on which you are standing.

The Spherical Earth

Now let us add a second refinement and abandon the Earth slab, whether tilted or untilted. Instead let's consider a sphere, something which very nearly represents the actual shape of the Earth.

If we imagine a sphere with an extreme width of 13,000 kilometers, we will find it will have a surface area just about equal to that of the slab we were dealing with earlier. And this is, in actual fact, the size of the Earth's sphere.

Let us begin by supposing the sphere to be hanging motion-less in space 150,000,000 kilometers from the Sun. Naturally, only half of the surface of such a sphere receives sunlight. The other half is blocked off from the Sun by the bulk of the Earth itself; it is in the Earth's own shadow. For the while, we will ignore the unlighted, or nightside, of the sphere, and consider only the lighted, or dayside.

On a sphere that is 13,000 kilometers across, any small portion of its surface looks flat and can be treated as though it were flat without any great error. If, for instance, you drew a circle a kilometer across on any portion of the sphere (suppos-ing it to be perfectly smooth and eliminating consideration of mountains or canyons), the line of the circle would be only 6 centimeters* below where it would have been if you had drawn it on a perfectly flat surface. A 6-centimeter difference in a kilometer simply isn't noticeable. (That's why, in fact, it took people so long to realize that the Earth was not flat, but spherical.)

The different portions of the sphere's surface—those dif-ferent little bits of nearly flat areas—are tilted to the Sun's rays by different amounts. The surface of that small area on

* A centimeter is 1/100,000 of a kilometer, or, in our units, two-fifths of an inch.

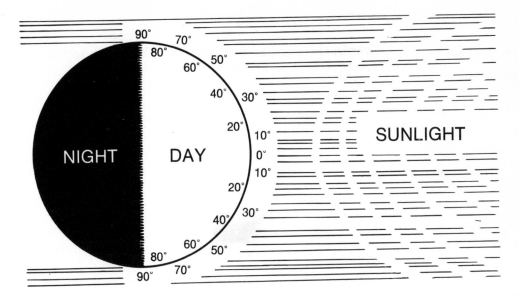

Figure 3. The Spherical Earth

the sphere which is in the very center of the side of the Earth facing the Sun, is perpendicular to the Sun's rays. It is the untilted portion. We can imagine it to be the 0-degree mark, the starting point of our calculations.

If, from the 0-degree point, you were to move in a smooth curve in a given unchanging direction, and travel one-quarter of the way around the sphere—90 degrees—you would come to the dividing line between the day and the nightside of the sphere. At that point, the small area you are standing on is tilted 90 degrees to the Sun's rays, which just skim the surface (see figure 3).

The sphere might, in fact, be viewed as a combination of very many small slabs, each one tilted by a particular amount to the Sun's rays. The amount of tilt is equal to the number of degrees one moves from the 0-degree mark. If you travel 30 degrees in any direction, you will be standing on a slab that is tilted 30 degrees to the Sun's rays, and so on.

You can then tell your position on the sphere by the position of the Sun in the sky. At the 0-degree point, the Sun is, of course, at the zenith—directly overhead. As you travel away from that 0-degree point, degree by degree, the Sun's position gets farther away from the zenith, degree by degree, its motion exactly matching yours but in the opposite direction.

As you travel from the 0-degree point in any direction, the increasing tilt of the portion of the sphere on which you are moving means that that particular area is getting less and less sunlight and must end up at a lower and lower temperature. A motionless spherical Earth is hottest at the 0-degree point and gets cooler and cooler as one moves away from that point in any direction.

At 90 degrees in any direction, no sunlight reaches the surface to speak of (the Sun is precisely at the horizon and its light skims the surface of the sphere) and the sphere is very cold there. (So, of course, is the entire nightside, which gets no sunlight, but we are not taking the nightside into consideration at the moment.)

We have then a sphere in which there is eternal summer (and a good, hot one, too) at the center of the dayside, and eternal winter all around the 90-degree rim.

The Rotating Earth

Now we can add a third refinement. The sphere should not be viewed as motionless, but as rotating. That, after all, is what the Earth is actually doing.

When a sphere rotates without external interference, it does so about a line running through its center. This is its "axis of rotation," or, more simply, its "axis."

A sphere can rotate in a wiggling way so that the axis is always changing, but it takes the application of energy to make that change. The more massive the sphere and the more rapidly it is rotating, the greater its quantity of "angular momentum," and the more energy it takes to alter the position of the axis.

The Earth is so massive a body (6,000,000,000,000,000,000,000, or 6 billion trillion, tonnes*) and rotates so rapidly (a complete turn in 24 hours so that some points on its surface must be moving at 1670 kilometers per hour) that its axis is fixed. Any changes that take place in its direction must be very small, or must take place very slowly, or both.

* One tonne, or "metric ton," is equal to 1.1 of our ordinary American tons.

The axis intersects the surface of a rotating sphere at two points on opposite sides of the sphere. These are the "poles." As it happens, mankind's notion of "north" turns out to be in the direction of one of the poles, and "south" in the direction of the other. We therefore speak of the "North Pole" and "South Pole" of the Earth.

If we compare the concept of a flat Earth with that of a rotating, spherical Earth, we find that the expression "the end of the Earth" has a different meaning in the two cases.

Where the flat Earth is concerned, we have a literal end—a place where one reaches a limit and can step off into space. As a matter of fact, most people, through most of history, visualized such an end to the Earth as actually existing somewhere.

With a rotating, spherical Earth on the other hand, there is no such literal end. Held to the Earth's surface by the pull of gravity, a human being can move indefinitely in any direction

Figure 4. Directions

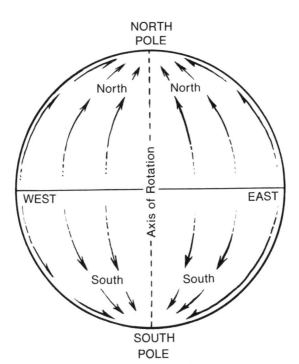

and keep going round and round the planet, retracing his steps eventually perhaps, but coming to no limit beyond which is nothing but space.

Yet the situation is not entirely the same for all directions.

Remember that north is defined as the direction toward the North Pole and south as the direction toward the South Pole. East and west are directions at right angles to the north-south line. We can travel east forever, retracing our steps over and over, but always going east. We can travel west forever on the same terms. Such travel, east or west, can take us in different paths. A person traveling east (or west) from New York City and another traveling east (or west) from Miami can continue to travel east (or west) forever without ever crossing paths.

Going north and south is different. No matter where you start, you are moving in the direction of the North Pole when you move north, and at the North Pole, therefore, all north-ward lines meet. If you imagine a person going north from New York and another going north from Seattle, you will find that the paths they take come closer and closer to each other and finally meet at the North Pole. If they were moving south, the paths would move farther apart for a while, but would eventually begin to come closer and closer to each other and finally meet at the South Pole. This would happen if the two travelers started from any two points on Earth (see figure 4).*

Once you reach the North Pole from any direction, you have gone as far north as you can. If you continue moving in your original direction, whatever that might have been, you pass the North Pole and begin moving away from it and toward the far-distant South Pole. This means you are now going south. From the North Pole, *all* directions are south.

The same is true of the South Pole in reverse. From the South Pole, all directions are north.

The North Pole and the South Pole are the only points on the Earth's surface from which you cannot move in a choice of directions. They are the only points which represent extremes of direction. They are the two unique points on the Earth's surface.

---

* It would be possible to define directions in such a way as to make "poles" anywhere on Earth, but none of those "poles" would be as convenient for use as the poles that are defined by Earth's actual rotation. So though the directions we use are man-made, the definitions are not arbitrary.

Because the North Pole is the farthest north you can go and the South Pole is the farthest south, they can be considered ends of the Earth, if not in the literal sense, then in the directional sense. One is the northern end of the Earth, the other the southern end. It is for this reason that I have chosen to name this book about the poles and the regions about them *The Ends of the Earth.*

Now let's consider the Earth as it turns—

The entire Earth turns about its axis in a single piece, so that any point on its surface makes a complete circle in 24 hours. Since the surface curves, however, some parts of it are closer to the axis than others. The closer a point on the surface is to the North Pole (or the South Pole), the closer it is to the axis and the smaller the circle it makes as it rotates.*

At the North Pole, and at the South Pole, the axis intersects the Earth's surface. Those points on the surface remain fixed as the Earth rotates. The poles are the only points on the Earth's surface that don't mark out circles as the Earth rotates— another way in which the poles are unique.

Any point on the surface of a rotating sphere, except for the poles, does mark out a circle as the sphere rotates. If you consider various points lying on a north-south line, all mark out circles that are parallel to each other, meaning that any of these circles is a fixed distance from any other at all points.

The circles are therefore called "parallels of latitude." "Latitude" is from a Latin word meaning "width" because as one ordinarily draws maps of the Earth on a flat surface, the parallels become straight lines drawn across the width of the map from left to right.

Parallels of latitude differ in length. The farther one travels from the North Pole or from the South Pole, the longer the parallels of latitude get. Naturally, the maximum length will come when you are as far away from *both* poles as possible. That will take place when you are on some point on the surface of the Earth that is equally far from the North Pole and the South Pole.

You can't do better than that. If you try to get still farther from the North Pole, you will be getting closer to the South

---

* If you find this difficult to see in your imagination, use a globe, if one is available. Rotate it slowly and observe what happens to a small piece of paper Scotch-taped to various points on it.

Pole; if you try to get still farther from the South Pole, you will be getting closer to the North Pole. In either case, the parallel of latitude will be a smaller circle than at the midway point.

At just halfway between the poles, the parallel of latitude sweeps out a circle that is the longest that can be drawn on the Earth's surface. The length of that circle is 40,000 kilometers, and it is the "circumference" of the Earth.

The parallel of latitude that is halfway between the poles is called the "equator." From any point on the equator, it is 10,000 kilometers* along the surface due north to the North Pole, or due south to the South Pole.

If you imagine a knife cutting through the Earth all along its equator, you will end with two equal halves of a sphere, two hemispheres. (This is one of the reasons "equator," which comes from a Latin word meaning "equal," is a good name.)

The North Pole would be at the center of one hemisphere, 10,000 kilometers from any point at the cut edge, while the South Pole would be at the center of the other hemisphere. The two halves of the sphere are called the "Northern Hemisphere" and the "Southern Hemisphere" respectively (see figure 5).

Since all parts of the United States are north of the Earth's equator, the United States is in the Northern Hemisphere. Australia, on the other hand, is in the Southern Hemisphere. Africa is partly in the Northern, partly in the Southern Hemisphere.

The equator is an example of a "great circle," one which goes around the full width of the Earth and divides its surface into two equal parts. An infinite number of such great circles can be drawn on the Earth, but all of them are at some angle to the equator. Of all the infinite number of great circles that can be drawn on the Earth, only the equator divides the surface of the Earth into halves in which the poles are centered.

Half the surface of the rotating, spherical Earth is, of course, bathed in sunlight.

We can suppose, to begin with, that the axis is perpendicular to the Sun's rays, so that the North Pole and the South Pole are each located just at the boundary between the dayside and the nightside.

---

* This rather even distance is no coincidence. The length of the kilometer was originally chosen back in the 1790s in such a way as to make it 1/10,000 of the distance along the Earth's surface from the North Pole to the equator.

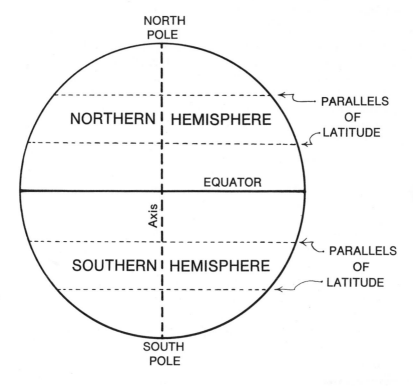

Figure 5. The Hemispheres

The point at the surface which is directly toward the Sun, and which earlier (in the case of the stationary, spherical Earth) we called 0 degrees, moves as the Earth rotates, and marks out a circle all around the Earth. The circle it marks out is the equator. In other words, every part of the equator moves through the point on Earth which is directly under the Sun; every part of the equator gets its chance to be at the 0-degree point. Therefore, we might as well call the entire equator 0 degrees.

In the same way, a point which is 5 degrees north of the equator marks out a circle which we can call "5° north latitude," or, more simply, "5° N." A point which is 5 degrees south of the equator marks out a circle which we can call "5° south latitude," or "5° S."

There are parallels of latitude for every degree and fraction of a degree north or south of the equator, and the parallels of latitude mark out smaller and smaller circles, the higher the degree number. Finally, we come to 90° N. and 90° S. which represent the North Pole and the South Pole, respectively, and they are not circles at all, but mere points—another way in which the poles represent unique spots on the Earth (see figure 6).

The rotating Earth is clearly much milder in temperature than a stationary Earth would be. There isn't a dayside forever baked under the Sun and a nightside forever denied the Sun. Instead each point undergoes a period of day and a period of night, warming and cooling in turn so that there are no spots either as hot or as cold as parts of a stationary Earth would be.*

All points on a rotating Earth of the type described here, one with the axis of rotation perpendicular to the direction of the Sun's rays, would experience 12 hours of day and 12 hours of night, as it turned in its 24-hour period of rotation.

All parts of the Earth would experience a similar cooling tendency during the 12 hours of darkness, as surface heat radiated away into space. All parts of Earth would *not*, however, experience a similar warming tendency during the 12 hours of sunlight. The farther one travels from the equator, either north or south, the more tipped the surface is away from the Sun, and the less heat is delivered to that surface by the Sun. Consequently, it will be warmest at the equator, and will get cooler and cooler as we move away from the equator until it is coldest at the poles.

We can look at this in another way, by imagining ourselves standing on a rotating Earth of the type we are now considering, with the axis perpendicular to the Sun's rays.

If we imagine the Earth to be rotating from west to east (which is what it does), we will see the Sun moving across the sky from east to west. It will rise at the eastern horizon, move across the sky, and set at the western horizon.

If we are standing on any point on the equator, we will see the Sun reach the exact zenith at a time halfway between sunrise and sunset. (That halfway time is "noon.")

---

* There are other factors that minimize temperature extremes—air and ocean currents, for instance—but we need not be concerned with them at this point. They will be mentioned later.

If we are standing on any point on Earth that is *not* on the equator, the Sun will be at its highest point at noon, but that highest point will *not* be at zenith. If we are standing at 30° N., the noonday Sun will be 30 degrees south of the zenith. From any point in the Northern Hemisphere, the noonday Sun will be south of the zenith. The number of degrees the noonday Sun will be south of the zenith will equal the number of degrees we would be standing north of the equator.

The same is true in reverse if we are in the Southern Hemisphere. The noonday Sun will then be north of the hemisphere by the number of degrees that we are standing south of the equator.

In other words, the farther we are from the equator, the lower the Sun is in the sky in general, and the less light and warmth we get.

As we approach the poles, the Sun is very low in the sky

Figure 6. Latitude

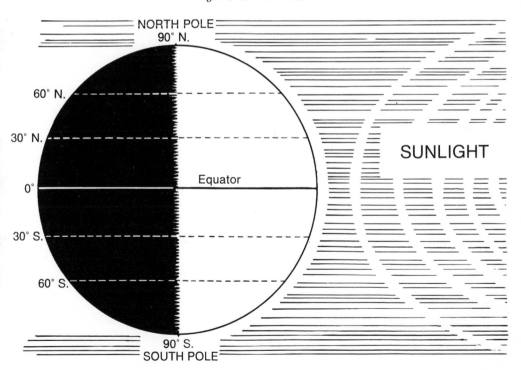

indeed. If we are at 80° N., the Sun will rise in the east and skim the southern horizon. At noon, it will be as high above the horizon as it can get and it will then be 80 degrees south of zenith, or only 10 degrees above the horizon.

At 80° S., the Sun will, in reverse, skim the northern horizon and rise 10 degrees above it at noon before beginning to decline again.

At the North Pole itself (and at the South Pole, too), the Sun will remain at the horizon constantly, merely moving around it, making a complete circle in 24 hours.

2 THE AXIS AND THE SUN

The Earth *is* a sphere and it *is* rotating. We have just been considering a rotating, spherical Earth and, in doing so, we have seen that it is plain the regions about the poles must be the coldest portions of the planet, as indeed they are.

Does this mean, then, that we have worked out the rationale behind the existence and properties of the poles and can pass on to the consideration of other things?

Not yet. Mere coldness is not enough. The rotating, spherical Earth we considered at the end of the previous chapter has, at every point on its surface, a day and night that are each 12 hours long. Yet this, we know, is not so in actual fact. Both day and night vary in length and, in particular, the nights near the poles can be very long—up to six months long.

How can that be?

To explain varying lengths of day and night, we must introduce a fourth complication. The Earth's axis is *not* directed perpendicularly to the Sun's rays as we have heretofore assumed. The axis is at an angle to that direction; it is tipped, and the amount of tipping is 23° 27′. We will not be too far off base if we consider the tip to be through an angle of 23.5 degrees.

The Tipped Axis

Suppose, then, we imagine the Earth to be rotating as before. Instead of having the axis so arranged that both North Pole and South Pole are at the day-night boundary, however, let us have the axis so tipped that the North Pole is 23.5 degrees into the dayside. The South Pole, then, would be 23.5 degrees from the day-night boundary, also, but in the other direction. It would be tipped into the nightside (see figure 7).

As the Earth rotates about its tipped axis, the North Pole continues to remain in place, exposed to permanent sunshine. Anyone standing at the North Pole under those conditions would see the Sun 23.5 degrees above the horizon (just about a quarter of the way up toward the zenith). As the Earth rotated, the Sun would describe a circle in the sky, always remaining the same distance above the different parts of the horizon it passed.

Points near the North Pole would turn in small circles about the tipped axis and would remain always in the lighted portion of Earth. A point at 80° N., for instance (which is 10 degrees from the North Pole), would, when it was on the side of the pole away from the day-night boundary, be 33.5 degrees (23.5 + 10) from that boundary. As it turned, it would eventually move between the North Pole and the day-night boundary and be 13.5 degrees (23.5 − 10) from that boundary.

Anyone standing anywhere on the 80° N. parallel under those conditions would see the Sun making a tipped circle in the sky. It would be 33.5 degrees over the southern horizon at noon, then it would sink as it circled the sky until it was only 13.5 degrees over the northern horizon at midnight, then it would rise again, and so on.

The tipping would be more and more marked as one moved farther and farther from the North Pole. At any point on the 66.5° N. parallel (which is 23.5 degrees from the North Pole), one would reach a point, as the Earth turned, that was 47 degrees from the day-night boundary, then, as the Earth continued to turn, one would describe a circle that would just touch the day-night boundary at the other extreme.

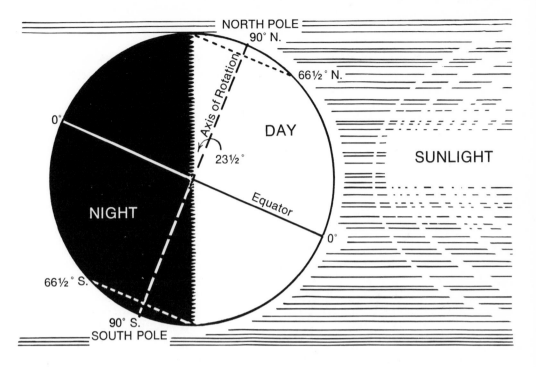

Figure 7. The Tipped Axis

From the 66.5° N. parallel, the Sun would be seen to describe a circle in the sky, in which it was 47 degrees above the southern horizon (just over halfway up to zenith) at noon, and would then swoop down to touch the northern horizon, and have the horizon line bisect the body of the Sun at midnight. Then it would climb back to 47 degrees above the southern horizon again.*

> * At least, that's how it would be if the Earth didn't have an atmosphere. Earth's atmosphere has a tendency to refract (bend) light rays that strike it at an angle. This tendency increases as light strikes it more and more at an angle from the perpendicular, and is at its maximum when light comes from the horizon. When the Sun touches the horizon, the effect of light refraction is to bend the light so that we see it above the horizon by a distance equal to its own width. However, as long as we know that this complication does exist, we needn't concern ourselves further with it for the purposes of this book.

If one is still farther from the North Pole so that one is south of the 66.5° N. parallel, the circle represented by that parallel crosses the day-night boundary. This means that to anyone standing some distance south of 66.5° N. the Sun, as it dips toward the northern horizon, dips below it so that there is night.*

From the astronomic viewpoint, we can consider the entire portion of the Earth north of 66.5° N. as making up the North Polar region. It is the only part of the Northern Hemisphere that can ever see the Sun above the horizon through an entire 24-hour period.

As one progresses south of 66.5° N., under the tipped-axis condition I have been describing, there is both day and night, but day is longer than night. At first, just below the 66.5° N. parallel, the Sun dips below the northern horizon only briefly. The farther south one goes, however, the more prolonged are the dips. Gradually, the length of the night approaches that of the day, and finally, when one reaches the equator, day and night are equal, 12 hours long apiece. (That is another reason why the equator has its name. Day and night are always equal in length there.)

Let us next shift to the South Pole under these same conditions of tipped axis. The South Pole is tipped 23.5 degrees into the nightside of the Earth and remains in position as the Earth turns, so that it does not see the Sun at all. From the South Pole (if one could somehow look through the Earth), the Sun makes a slow 24-hour circle at a constant 23.5 degrees *below* the horizon.

As one moves away from the South Pole, the circle made by the Sun, as it marks out different positions in the sky, tilts. The Sun sinks farther below the southern horizon and marks out a circle that brings it up nearer the northern horizon. If one is far enough from the South Pole, one can begin to see a twilight

---

* Again, the presence of an atmosphere complicates matters a little. Even when, despite refraction, the Sun is seen to dip a bit below the horizon, it continues to illuminate the upper regions of the atmosphere, and the scattering of light up there lends the surface a dim illumination called "twilight." To astronomers, the Sun must be 18° below the horizon before there is no twilight effect at all and true night may be said to exist. That means one would have to be at 48½° N. before the Sun would dip far enough below the horizon for true night to be experienced. Again, this is a refinement we can neglect.

lightening of the sky at the northern horizon as the Sun approaches the uppermost part of its tilted circle.

Finally (disregarding atmospheric refraction), if you are standing at the 66.5° S. parallel, you will see the Sun actually reach the northern horizon and show itself briefly at noon.

Thus, the region of the Earth that is south of the 66.5° S. parallel can be called the South Polar region. It is the only part of the Southern Hemisphere that can ever experience night for a full 24-hour period.

As one continues to progress north from the 66.5° S. parallel, one enters a region where there is both day and night. At first the day is very short as the Sun makes but a brief appearance above the northern horizon at noon. As one continues to travel northward, the day grows longer, and the difference in length between the day and the night diminishes. Finally, when one reaches the equator, the day and night are equal in length, each 12 hours long.

When the Earth's axis is tipped in the fashion described, then, the Northern Hemisphere, as a whole, has more day than night—with continuous day in the North Polar region. The Southern Hemisphere, on the other hand, gets more night than day—with continuous night in the South Polar region.

Under these conditions, the Northern Hemisphere is bound to be warmer than the Southern Hemisphere; the Northern Hemisphere is experiencing summer, we might say, while the Southern Hemisphere is experiencing winter.

Yet this cannot be the permanent condition. The Northern Hemisphere does not experience an eternal summer, nor does the Southern Hemisphere experience an eternal winter. There is an alternation of seasons, and to account for that we must now add one final complication.

The Revolving Earth

In addition to rotating about its axis, the Earth also moves (or "revolves") about the Sun, marking out a nearly circular path, or "orbit," as it does so.*

> * The path is actually an "ellipse," which is a curve resembling a more or less flattened circle. In the case of Earth's orbit, the flattening is very slight, and we can call the orbit a circle without being too far off. Later in the book, we will have to take the noncircularity of the orbit into account.

As the Earth revolves about the Sun, however, the axis of rotation remains fixed in direction. It does *not*, for instance, change its position so that the North Pole always faces into the dayside. On the contrary, since the North Pole is tipped into the dayside at one side of Earth's orbit, it is tipped into the nightside when the Earth moves around to the other side of the Sun, a half year later. It is the turn of the South Pole to be tipped into the dayside that half-year later (see figure 8).

At one side of the orbit, in other words, the Northern Hemisphere is experiencing summer and the North Polar region continuous day, while at the other end, it is experiencing winter and the North Polar region continuous night. The Southern Hemisphere experiences these things in reverse. When the Northern Hemisphere is in summer, the Southern Hemisphere is in winter, and vice versa. When the North Polar region has continuous day, the South Polar region has continuous night, and vice versa.

As the Earth revolves about the Sun with the axis maintaining a fixed position, the position of the day-night boundary relative to the poles slowly shifts. (It must do so if the poles are going to alternate between periods of continuous day and continuous night.)

Figure 8. The Revolving Earth

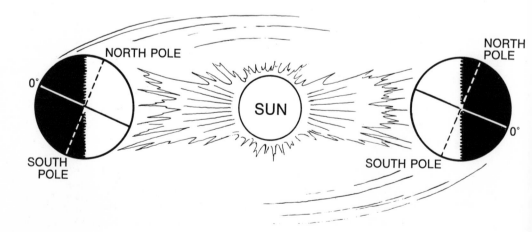

Suppose we imagine the Earth, to begin with, in the position I discussed earlier, where the North Pole is 23.5° into the dayside and the entire North Polar region has continuous day. As the Earth moves in its orbit, the day-night boundary creeps closer and closer to the North Pole.

From places within the North Polar region, you will see the Sun sink closer and closer to the horizon at every point of the circle it makes in the sky. It is marking out a very tight spiral as it slowly sinks downward.

If you are so far from the North Pole that the Sun at midnight is quite close to the northern horizon, it begins to sink below it after a while. The region of continuous day contracts as places closer and closer to the North Pole begin to experience short (and then lengthening) periods of night.

Finally, when the Earth has moved one-quarter of the way around its orbit (taking three months to do so), the day-night boundary touches the North Pole. Everywhere in the North Polar region (and, in fact, everywhere on Earth) day and night are now equal. From the North Pole itself, you would see the Sun (neglecting the effect of refraction) making a complete circle at the horizon, half its disk above and half below the horizon.

As the Earth continues to move in its orbit, the day-night boundary moves past the North Pole, which now begins to experience continuous night. A larger and larger part of the North Polar region is immersed in the continuous night, until, by the time Earth has passed halfway around its orbit, after six months, all of the North Polar region is in continuous night.

Then, as Earth still continues to move in its orbit, the day-night boundary begins to move back toward the North Pole and the situation slowly reverses itself, reaching day-night equality in length over all the Earth at the three-quarters mark in the orbit (after nine months) and back to continuous day over the entire North Polar region after twelve months, when one complete turn in the orbit has been made.

Precisely the same thing happens in the South Polar region in reverse. We start with continuous night (when the North Polar region is experiencing continuous day). The day-night boundary slowly approaches the night-ridden South Pole as it approaches the day-exposed North Pole. When one-quarter of the orbit is passed, the day-night boundary is at the South Pole as well as at the North Pole so that there is day-night equality in both polar regions.

Then, as continuous night creeps over the North Polar region and spreads out farther and farther from the North Pole until the entire region is in continuous night, so, in perfect step, does continuous day creep over the South Polar region and spread out farther and farther from the South Pole until the entire region is in continuous day. Then the situation reverses itself in the south as in the north.

On the whole, then, the situation is the same, *in average*, as it would be if the Earth's axis were perfectly perpendicular to the direction of the Sun's rays and were not tipped at all. To be sure, each polar region has periods of abnormally long exposure to sunlight, but these are balanced by equally long periods of abnormally long deprivation of sunlight.

The same is true, less extremely, for the entire Northern Hemisphere and the entire Southern Hemisphere. Each experiences a summer and winter, but on the average, temperature decreases as one moves northward from the equator, or southward from the equator, and the two polar regions are the coldest portions of the Earth.

We can go through the yearly cycle of change again, this time as it would look to someone standing on Earth's surface. Suppose you were standing at the North Pole and, to begin with, that the whole North Polar region were in continuous day and the North Pole itself were a full 23.5 degrees away from the day-night boundary into the dayside, as far as it ever gets.

At that time, we would see the Sun describe its circle in the sky, 23.5 degrees above the horizon at every point.

As the Earth revolved about the Sun, though, the Sun would slowly sink closer to the horizon as it circled the sky, until, after three months, it would be just at the horizon as it made its circle. It would then continue to sink, disappearing below the horizon, sinking lower and lower for three months, then rising higher and higher for three months, until after a total of six months below the horizon, it would be back skimming the horizon. It would then rise farther and farther above the horizon for three months till it reached its maximum height of 23.5 degrees, and then begin the cycle all over.

All told, the Sun at the North Pole would be above the horizon for six months and below the horizon for six months so that day and night are each half a year long. Precisely the same is true of the South Pole, in reverse. When it is day at the North Pole it is night at the South Pole, and vice versa.*

As one goes farther and farther from either pole, the period of continuous day grows shorter and shorter; so does the period of continuous night. In between the continuous day and the continuous night, there is a period of alternating day and night. After the period of continuous day, there is a succession of short nights every 24 hours. The nights grow steadily longer and finally fade into the period of continuous night. When the long night is over, there is a succession of short days that grow longer and longer and fade into continuous day.

The intermediate period of alternating day and night takes up more and more of the year as one moves away from the poles. Finally, at the 66.5-degree parallel, either north or south, there is only one 24-hour period at one extreme of the Earth's orbit when the Sun remains above the horizon the entire time, and one 24-hour period at the other extreme when it remains below the horizon the entire time. During the remainder of the year there is alternating day and night.

Between 66.5° N. and 66.5° S., the surface of the world everywhere experiences some day and some night (however long or short either may be) in every 24-hour period during the entire year.

We can say, then, that the polar regions stretching beyond the 66.5-degree parallel are those places where there is continuous day for at least one 24-hour period, and continuous night for at least one 24-hour period.

Outside the polar regions, the Sun is *always* above the horizon at noon and *always* below the horizon at midnight. However, the days are longer than the nights during one half of the year and the nights are longer than the days during the other half of the year. The disproportion grows less the more closely one approaches the equator. At the equator, the day and night are exactly 12 hours long every day of the year.

* This description is actually too simple. Atmospheric refraction keeps the Sun apparently above the horizon even when it is slightly below it. And when it is slightly below it, there is still twilight. True deep night endures for considerably less than six months at either pole.

Solstices and Equinoxes

The varying position of the Sun in the sky can be watched throughout the year only outside the polar regions. Only outside the polar regions can the Sun be seen at noon every day (if we ignore interference by mist, fog, and clouds).

Let us suppose, then, we observe the Sun from New York City. Each day the Sun reaches its highest position that it will reach on that day at or near noon.* As seen from New York City, the Sun will each noon be south of the zenith, but not always by the same amount.

At a certain time of the year, the noonday Sun, as observed from New York, may be so many degrees above the southern horizon. The next day it will be a trifle higher at noon, and the next day it will be a trifle higher still.

The noonday Sun will move higher and higher each day, fairly rapidly at first but then more and more slowly, till for a while it moves at a mere crawl and then seems to come to a momentary halt when it reaches a maximum height. This maximum height, as seen from New York City, is about 74 degrees above the southern horizon, which still leaves it 16 degrees short of the horizon.

The noonday Sun then starts sinking from day to day, at first very slowly, then faster and faster. After three months, the rate of sinking reaches a maximum and begins to slow again, slower and slower and slower until, finally, the Sun has sunk to a minimum height as it seems to come to a momentary halt again. This minimum height, as seen from New York City, is only 26 degrees above the southern horizon, or 64 degrees from the zenith.

Then the noonday Sun starts rising again, to repeat the cycle all over.

It takes half a year for the noonday Sun to fall from its maximum height down to its minimum height, and another half a year after that to rise to its maximum height again. This apparent motion of the noonday Sun up and down the sky is a reflection of the motion of the Earth around the Sun.

---

* What we call "standard time" doesn't follow the Sun's movements exactly and "daylight saving time" throws the clock a full hour out of adjustment with the Sun. The Sun must be observed, therefore, without a too-slavish reliance on man-made and man-adjusted time.

The maximum height and the minimum height come at times when the Sun's movement seems to halt momentarily before it changes direction, and the times at which they take place are called "solstices," from Latin words meaning "Sun stand still." The two solstices occur half a year apart. The one at which the noonday Sun reaches its maximum height (as seen from New York City) occurs on June 21 and is called the "summer solstice." The other, at which the noonday Sun reaches its minimum height (as seen from New York City), occurs on December 21 and is the "winter solstice."

The height of the noonday Sun reflects the position of the day-night boundary in the polar regions. As seen from New York City, the noonday Sun's climb in the sky mirrors the movement of the day-night boundary beyond the North Pole so that more and more of the North Polar region is tipped into constant day.

At the summer solstice, June 21, the entire North Polar region is in sunlight. It is the day when points on the 66.5° N. parallel experience their one 24-hour period of sunlight.

The winter solstice, December 21, represents a reverse situation. It is the time when the entire North Polar region has tipped into the nightside. It is the time when points on the 66.5° N. parallel experience their one 24-hour period of nighttime.

In the Northern Hemisphere generally, June 21 is the day when every point experiences its longest day and its shortest night. On December 21, throughout the Northern Hemisphere, every point experiences its shortest day and its longest night.

The situation, as you might expect, is just reversed in the Southern Hemisphere. From New Zealand, for instance, the noonday Sun is always north of the horizon. The farther north it is, the closer to the northern horizon, the shorter the day and the longer the night. Thus, when the noonday Sun moves northward and is high in the sky in New York, it is low in the sky in New Zealand. When it moves south and is low in the sky in New York, it is high in the sky in New Zealand.

It is June 21 that is the winter solstice in the Southern Hemisphere, the day on which the daytime is shortest and the nighttime longest. It is on that day that points on the 66.5° S. parallel experience their one 24-hour period of darkness and all the South Polar region is shrouded in continuous night.

And it is December 21 that is the summer solstice in the Southern Hemisphere, the day on which the daytime is longest and the nighttime shortest. It is on that day that points on the 66.5° S. parallel experience their one 24-hour period of continuous sunshine and all the South Polar region is in continuous day.

As the Sun moves from the June 21 solstice to the December 21 solstice, the long days of the Northern Hemisphere grow shorter and the short nights longer. At the same time, the short days of the Southern Hemisphere grow longer and the long nights shorter. Gradually the disparity in length decreases in both hemispheres and on September 23 the disparity momentarily vanishes. Day and night are each 12 hours long the whole world over.

Then as the sun continues to move on to the December 21 solstice, the disparity in length between day and night begins to grow again in the opposite sense to what it was before. On December 21 the disparity is at a maximum again.

Then as the Sun moves from the December 21 solstice back to the June 21 solstice, the disparity decreases again. A second momentary day on which day and night are equal all over the world takes place on March 20.

The two times at which day and night are momentarily equal in length over the world, on September 23 and March 20, are called "equinoxes" (from Latin words meaning "equal nights"). It is on those days that the day-night boundary passes exactly across the North Pole and the South Pole.

September 23 is the "autumnal equinox" because it starts the season of autumn (in the Northern Hemisphere) and March 20 is the "vernal equinox," from a Latin word for "spring," because it starts the season of spring (again in the Northern Hemisphere).

In the Northern Hemisphere it is spring from March 20 to June 21, summer from June 21 to September 23, fall (or autumn) from September 23 to December 21, and winter from December 21 to March 20. In the Southern Hemisphere, the cycle is reversed, and the time periods just listed represent fall, winter, spring, and summer, respectively.

Tropics and Zones

On the vernal equinox, March 20, when the day-night boundary is passing through the North Pole at one end of the Earth and the South Pole at the other, the Sun must be shining directly down at a point halfway between the two; that is, on the equator.

As the day-night boundary swings beyond the North Pole, placing more and more of the North Polar region into continuous daytime, the noontime Sun, moving farther and farther north, shines directly down on parallels north of the equator. At the summer solstice, June 21, the Sun is shining down directly on the farthest possible point north of the equator, 23.5° N. (At this time, the North Pole is tipped its maximum amount into the daylit portion of the globe—and by 23.5°.)

Then past the summer solstice, the noonday Sun moves southward again, and is again directly over the equator on the autumnal equinox, September 23. The noonday Sun continues to move south until, at the winter solstice, it is shining down directly on the farthest possible point south of the equator, 23.5° S.

Between the parallels of 23.5° N. and 23.5° S., then, the noonday Sun can be either north or south of the zenith depending on the time of the year. At the equator, the noonday Sun is north of zenith for half the year (from March 20 to September 23) and south of zenith for the other half the year (September 23 to March 20) and is exactly at zenith on March 20 and September 23.

As we move north from the equator, the noonday Sun is south of zenith for more than half the year—more and more as we continue still farther north. Finally, when we reach 23.5° N., the Sun barely reaches the zenith at the time it reaches its northernmost point, on June 21, and is south of the zenith at all other times.

As we move south from the equator, the noonday Sun is north of zenith for more than half the year—more and more as we continue still farther south. Finally, when we reach 23.5° S., the Sun barely reaches the zenith at the time it reaches its southernmost point on December 21, and is north of the zenith at all other times.

The two extreme parallels, 23.5° N. and 23.5° S., are called "tropics," from a Latin word meaning "to turn," because at those parallels the noonday Sun reaches the most northerly (or southerly) point of the Earth over which it can shine from the zenith, after which it turns and moves in the other direction.

Each tropic has a separate name arising from the position of the Sun against the starry background.

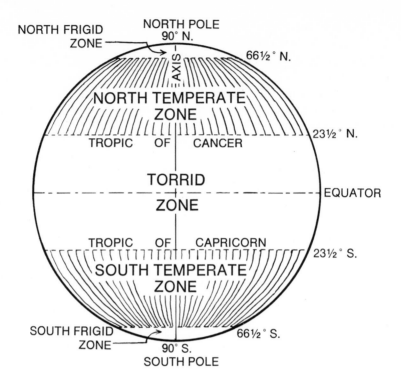

Figure 9. The Zones

In ancient times, the apparent path of the Sun around the sky (actually a reflection of the Earth's revolution about the Sun) was carefully marked off. That path was divided into twelve star-combinations called "constellations," in each of which the Sun remained a month. The entire belt of twelve constellations is called the "zodiac."

On June 21, when the Sun is shining directly down over the northern tropic at 23.5° N., the ancients found it to be entering the constellation known as Cancer (the Crab). For that reason, 23.5° N. is called the "Tropic of Cancer."

On December 21, when the Sun is shining down directly over the southern tropic at 23.5° S., the ancients found it to be entering the constellation known as Capricorn (the Goat). For that reason, 23.5° S. is called the "Tropic of Capricorn."

On the basis of the behavior of the noonday Sun, it is possible to divide the Earth into five "zones" (see figure 9).

Between 23.5° N. and 23.5° S., the noonday Sun will always at two times during the year (or once at exactly those boundary parallels) be at zenith. In this portion of the Earth's surface, which is exactly bisected by the equator, the Sun is more nearly overhead than anywhere else on Earth and the surface is, on the average, least tipped to the rays of the Sun. This region is therefore the warmest part of the Earth and is called the "Torrid Zone" in consequence. Sometimes, in honor of its boundary parallels, it is called the "Tropic Zone," "the Tropics."

At the northern end of the Earth, between 66.5° N. and 90° N., there is a region that experiences a period of continuous day centering about June 21. At the southern end of the Earth, between 66.5° S. and 90° S., there is a region that experiences a period of continuous day centering about December 21. Both these regions (the polar regions) have, on the average, the coldest weather on Earth. They are therefore known as the "North Frigid Zone" and the "South Frigid Zone."

Between the North Frigid Zone and the Torrid Zone (that is, between 66.5° N. and 23.5° N.) lies a region which, on the whole, is neither as warm as the Torrid Zone nor as cold as the North Frigid Zone. Its climate, being between the two extremes, is more "temperate," and it is therefore called the "North Temperate Zone."

From all points in the North Temperate Zone, there is a steady alternation of day and night, as in the Torrid Zone. Unlike conditions in the Torrid Zone, however, the noonday Sun is *never* at zenith in the North Temperate Zone. It is always south of the zenith, coming nearest the zenith at the time of the June 21 solstice.

Similarly, between the South Frigid Zone and the Torrid Zone (between 66.5° S. and 23.5° S.) lies the "South Temperate Zone." There the noonday Sun is never at the zenith either. From the South Temperate Zone, the noonday Sun is seen always to the north of zenith, coming nearest the zenith at the time of the December 21 solstice.

The North Frigid Zone is synonymous with what I have earlier called the North Polar region, while the South Frigid Zone is synonymous with the South Polar region. Whatever the name, it is with these sections at the northern and southern ends of the Earth that this book is concerned.

3
DISCOVERING THE POLES

In the last two chapters, I have described the Earth and have shown what and where the polar regions are, and just what days are like in those regions. It was not necessary to make any actual observations or make any actual measurements to know how the days and nights lengthened and shortened. It was all the inevitable consequence of the shape of the Earth, of the manner of Earth's rotation, the tipping of its axis of rotation, and the manner of Earth's revolution about the Sun.

But then I had the important advantage of knowing all those basic facts about the Earth since childhood and of having been taught the consequences thereof before it ever occurred to me to reason it out for myself.

What about early man, though, who did not know any of the facts to begin with, who did not even dream the Earth was round, for instance? There was no reason why he should have been able to deduce that polar regions must exist and what they must be like before he had ever set eyes on them and while he was still thousands of miles away. Or was there?

Myths

There were, of course, hints. There were clear seasonal variations in the weather, for instance. In some parts of the Earth, there were distinct winters and summers, with winters often a time of cold and starvation. One couldn't avoid noticing that. Nor could one help noticing that in summer days were long and nights short, while in winter days were short and nights long.

Even in the Tropics, where there was no real winter and it was warm all year round, there were dry seasons and wet seasons. There was almost always some yearly change to be noted.

There was, however, no real understanding of such changes, to begin with. As far as mankind was concerned, weather changes just happened. The easiest explanation was that they were the result of the beneficent—or malevolent—or indifferent—will of the gods.

Eventually, though, after the day-to-day variations of rain and sun and warmer and cooler were allowed for, it must have become noticeable that there was a rough periodicity of the seasons. It became possible to predict with certainty that in a certain number of months the land would grow green again— or the drought would come—or the snows fall. The life of the tribe depended on understanding such periodicities and guiding one's behavior by anticipating them, especially after agriculture had been developed.

Once it was understood that changes were not entirely arbitrary, the matter grew more interesting. Why should such periodicities exist? Why should the gods be constrained to make it hot and cold, wet and dry, green and brown in so regular a fashion, when they were all powerful and could do it any other way if they so chose?

Since human beings are restlessly curious and invent a reason if they know none, there were developed various mythical explanations of the seasons.

The myth best known to us is the ancient Greek tale of Persephone, the daughter of Demeter, the goddess of agriculture. Persephone was kidnapped by the love-stricken Hades, god of the underworld, and taken down to his dark domain.

Demeter, grief-stricken, sought Persephone until she finally found her. Then, a compromise was reached. Persephone remained a fixed portion of each year underground with Hades, and then for the rest of the year remained aboveground with Demeter. While Persephone was underground, Demeter did not allow crops to grow—and it was winter. In this fashion, the alternation of summer and winter was explained.

Similar myths were part of the beliefs of almost every agricultural community of primitive times. It was easy to imagine gods who died and were then resurrected in order to explain, or perhaps only to symbolize, the manner in which vegetation died in the fall and was reborn in the spring.

The behavior of the noonday Sun, its slow climb and its equally slow fall, was also noted. It tended to be high in summer and low in winter, an observed fact, but an unexplained one.

In the absence of sure knowledge of why the Sun behaved as it did, and with a consequent lack of confidence in the inevitability of the cycle, in very early times there must have been considerable nervousness about the sinking Sun each year. Would it, on this particular occasion, simply continue to sink, and would it eventually decline below the southern horizon forever? Would light and heat vanish? Would Earth freeze? Would all men die?

There must have been great relief each year at the time of the winter solstice when it was finally determined that the Sun's retreat toward the southern horizon had come to an end once again and that it would be returning northward. The apparent rebirth of the Sun and the assurance that gave that spring and summer would come again and that life would not die were the occasion for wild celebrations that soon became traditional.

The Romans celebrated the Saturnalia at the time of the winter solstice. There was a several-day period of happiness, of revelry, of brotherhood, and gift-giving.

In the time of early Christianity, those who worshiped the god Mithras (a symbol of the Sun) naturally celebrated the winter solstice, choosing December 25 as their "Day of the Sun." As a holiday, it proved so popular that the Christian Church, unable to defeat it, adopted it and gave it its own significance.

What's more, each year begins at January 1, after the end of the celebration of the winter solstice, as though the sure knowledge of the rebirth of the Sun makes it safe to begin a new year.*

However interesting the cycles of the Sun and of the seasons and however important they were to mankind, understanding beyond the mythical came late.

Consider, for instance, the Greek historian Herodotus, who completed his history of the world (as known to him) about 430 B.C. In the fourth book of this work, he says that the Egyptian king Necho (who reigned from 609 to 593 B.C.) had sent out a fleet manned by Phoenicians (the greatest navigators of the ancient world) to circumnavigate Africa. They apparently sailed down the Red Sea and returned by way of the Strait of Gibraltar. When the Phoenicians returned, after three years, they reported having carried through their mission successfully.

Herodotus, although he gives the account, clearly doesn't believe it. In particular, he haughtily refuses to believe one cock-and-bull tale told by the Phoenicians. He says, "These men made a statement which I do not myself believe, though others may, to the effect that as they sailed on a westerly course round the southern end of Libya [Africa], they had the sun on their right—to northward of them."

Herodotus knew that the noonday Sun was always to the south of the zenith in Greece and in all the lands that he had visited (and for his time he was a great traveler). He considered this a law of nature, therefore, and would not believe that it was possible to have the Sun north of the zenith anywhere on Earth.

Yet if the Phoenicians had sailed down the eastern coast of Africa and had then rounded the southern end, sailing westward, they would then have been in the South Temperate Zone and the noonday Sun would indeed always have been to their north at any season of the year.

It is precisely this which makes us confident that the Phoenicians really did the job. Herodotus, for all his travels, had never been out of the North Temperate Zone (and neither had the Phoenicians, probably, before their voyage), and what

* Just the same, January 1 was not always the beginning of the year. The vernal equinox was the beginning in many cultures and that makes sense, too. The autumnal equinox also serves as the beginning in some cases.

he thought was a law of nature was only a local phenomenon.

Had Herodotus or the Phoenicians known the shape of the Earth and understood its motions, they would have seen that the noonday Sun *had* to be north of the zenith if they traveled far enough south. Indeed, they could have predicted it to be so without having budged a step from home.

Since the shape and the motions of the Earth were not then understood, the Phoenicians could not have dreamed of a northward Sun, or reported it, if they had not actually seen it (and with what must have been considerable astonishment, too).

We are pretty sure today, therefore, that those Phoenicians of 600 B.C., despite Herodotus' skepticism, really did circumnavigate Africa, and set a record for daring seafaring that was not surpassed till A.D. 1492, twenty-one centuries later.

Travelers

The Phoenician feat points up the educational advantages of travel. The Phoenicians were ignored, but if they had not been, some careful thought might have shown that the Earth had to be spherical, on the basis of that one observation of a northward Sun.

In fact, even if theoretical deductions as to Earth's shape and motions were left to one side, wide traveling might have involved observations of the manner in which day and night alternated, or did not alternate, and of how their lengths varied from season to season at different places on Earth. In that way, the five zones of the Earth, the two frigid zones, the two temperate zones, and the Torrid Zone, might have been worked out just by traveling and observing. The existence of the poles could have been demonstrated, too, if explorers had gone far enough north and south, just on the basis of the manner of alternation of day and night and without any talk of Earth's shape and motions.

That, however, is not the way it happened.

Unfortunately, travel was difficult in ancient times, and very few people ever traveled far from home. The Phoenician navigators were very much in a minority. Furthermore, through the accidents of history and geography, those people who thought most about the Earth, and traveled most, all tended to travel east and west, rather than north and south.

And it was north-and-south travel that was required if the zones of the Earth were to be worked out.

At the time of the Roman emperor Marcus Aurelius (who ruled from A.D. 161 to 180), the ancient world was at the height of its prosperity. Four large and powerful empires were highly civilized at the time and they stretched across Eurasia from the Atlantic Ocean to the Pacific. Reading from west to east, they were the Roman, the Parthian, the Indian, and the Chinese empires.

These lands all lay between 10° N. and 50° N. The entire stretch of territory, save for the southern parts of India, was in the North Temperate Zone, and all of it without exception was north of the equator. Although the stretch of civilization was some 11,000 kilometers east and west, it was only about 1500 kilometers north and south.

The ancients, therefore, were less aware of the zones of the Earth than one might think, considering the extent of the world's civilized areas.

Even with limited traveling, it might be supposed that some hints would reach the civilized nations concerning the unusual conditions to the north and the south.

The Greeks of Herodotus' time, for instance, knew that Egypt, which lay to the south of Greece, was generally warmer than Greece, and that the Sahara Desert, which lay not far south of the southern shores of the Mediterranean Sea, was hot indeed. The Greeks also knew that when the wind blew from the north it brought cold weather with it. There was, therefore, an association of cold with the north and heat with the south.

This was not necessarily seen as an inevitable consequence of the Earth's shape and motions, however. There was no feeling that there was steadily increasing heat as one went south, and steadily increasing cold as one went north.

The ancient Greeks believed that well to the south of Egypt was the land of Ethiopia, which they pictured as a kind of paradise beloved by the gods. It is at least so described in Homer, with no indication of blistering heat.

As for the north, the Greeks, right up through the time of Herodotus, felt that there was a land in the Far North that was warm and paradise-like. They called the land "Hyperborea" ("beyond the north wind"). Herodotus speaks of the Hyperboreans as though they really existed.

Any area of uncomfortable warmth or cold might, therefore,

be purely local. The Greeks had a mythological explanation of the Sahara Desert, for instance. They said that the Sun god had a son named Phaethon who persuaded his father to let him drive the chariot of the Sun. The god gave in, but, with Phaethon at the reins, the flaming horses went out of control. The chariot of the Sun moved out of its accustomed path and approached the Earth, cutting a swath of blistering heat across northern Africa. It was this that baked the Sahara Desert into the Earth and burned the African peoples dark. The only thing that saved the Earth was Zeus's hasty decision to kill Phaethon with a thunderbolt.

Yet there are signs that rumors from a distance did reach the ancients, especially rumors of most unusual situations in the Far North. After all, even in very early times, there was trade with peoples of northern Europe, notably for amber which was found on the shores of the Baltic Sea. The Phoenicians early sailed out of the Mediterranean Sea and into the Atlantic Ocean, where they turned north and voyaged as far as the British Isles in search of tin. (They kept the route secret, however, in order to preserve a tin monopoly, so that their travels did not add to the sum of man's knowledge—which would have been worth far more than tin.)

By such trade and from such voyages, vague word of cold and ice, of long nights and long days, may have reached the southern lands. Consider the *Odyssey*, for instance, the Greek epic poem dealing with the wanderings of Odysseus. It was supposedly written by Homer in the ninth century B.C., and received its present form in the sixth century B.C.

At the opening of the eleventh book of that poem, Odysseus is telling of his adventurous wanderings. He is sailing westward to the Strait of Gibraltar, beyond which is the ocean. He says of his ship:

"All day long her sails were full as she held her course over the sea, but when the sun went down and darkness was over all the earth, we got into the deep waters of the river Oceanus, where lie the land and city of the Cimmerians, who live enshrouded in mist and darkness which the rays of the sun never pierce neither at his rising nor as he goes down again out of the heavens, but the poor wretches live in one long, melancholy night."

That surely sounds like some vague rumor of the long polar night. And, on the other hand, notions of the Hyperboreans might have arisen out of the distorted tales of the long polar day.

The first explorer whom we know by name and know to have sailed in the direction of the polar regions was Pytheas, of the Greek city of Massilia (on the site of the modern Marseille).

About 320 B.C., he repeated Odysseus' feat of sailing beyond Gibraltar and then headed northward. He wrote two accounts of his journey, but they do not survive. Mostly, we know of what he said through references in other writers, some of whom quoted him only to sneer at his statements as a pack of lies. Yet to us, with our greater knowledge of geography, Pytheas' accounts, like those of the circumnavigating Phoenicians, bear the ring of truth.

Pytheas explored the coasts of western Europe, and seems definitely to have reached Britain and to have circumnavigated it. He described the manner in which the Britons threshed grain indoors because the weather was too uniformly miserable to give them much of a chance of threshing grain outdoors (something that was easily possible in the warm and sunny lands of the Mediterranean). Pytheas also described drinks they made of fermented grain (beer) and honey (mead).

Pytheas apparently traveled north of Britain and was puzzled by the extreme difference in the lengths of day and night, greater than the difference in the more southerly lands of the Mediterranean. He also made note of the large tides, something that was new to an inhabitant of the nearly tideless Mediterranean.

He either experienced the matter himself or listened to the words of those he encountered, for he announced that there was a land to the north where the Sun never rose at all and where the lengthening night stretched out until it endured through the entire 24-hour period of the day.

The most northerly land he reached he called "Thule," but nobody knows what land it was that he called by this name. It may have been the Shetland Islands, or Iceland, or the Scandinavian peninsula. In any case, in later days, it was widely supposed that Thule was the farthest reach of land there was to the north; that beyond it lay only mists and ice. It was therefore called "Ultima Thule" ("Farthest Thule").

Pytheas' observations were not followed up. The Romans eventually extended their empire to the southern reaches of the island of Britain, but they went no farther. They were not

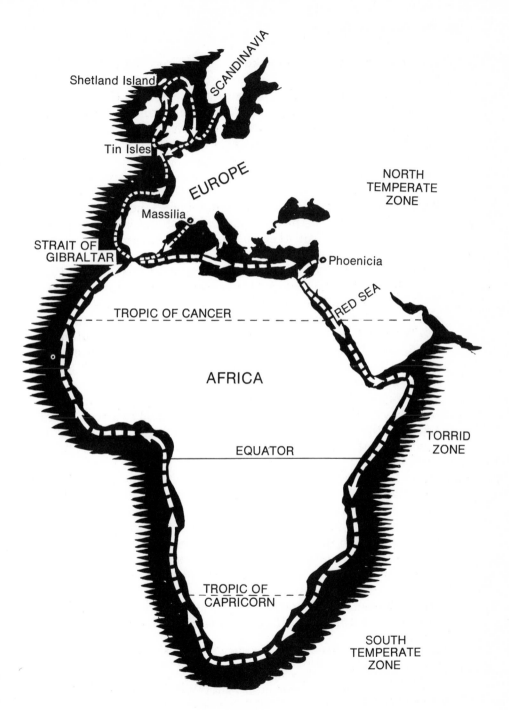

Figure 10. Voyages of the Phoenicians and Pytheas

explorers merely for the sake of exploring, and they did not attempt to go farther north (see figure 10).

If there were some in the ancient world who got a better notion of the Earth than was possible through the limited explorations of the ancient travelers, that came about through the observations of the stars, rather than of the Earth itself.

The Celestial Sphere

When early man studied the heavenly bodies, he was bound to note the Sun first. Its motions, east to west and north to south, were complicated, but even more so were the motions of the Moon, which changed its shape as well as its position with respect to the Sun and the stars. Among other heavenly bodies, there were five starlike objects (which we now call Mercury, Venus, Mars, Jupiter, and Saturn) which moved in a fashion more complicated than even the Sun and the Moon. These were the "planets," so called by the Greeks from a word meaning "wanderers" because of their apparently irregular motions.

If we leave these planets out of consideration, there remain some six thousand stars, altogether, visible to the unaided eye under perfect conditions (though, of course, only half of them are above the horizon at any one moment). These stars maintain their position relative to each other, night after night, generation after generation, so that they were called the "fixed stars."

The fixed stars move all in one piece, as though a solid sky were moving, with the stars part of that sky, stuck here and there as though they were tiny, luminous thumbtacks.*

The sky and the fixed stars move in a very simple fashion. They move from the eastern horizon to the western horizon and then back to the eastern horizon in 24 hours.

This, of course, is simply an apparent motion. The Earth turns on its axis, west to east, under a motionless sky. The Earth's motion is so smooth and gentle, however, that we don't feel it, as we turn with it. To us the Earth seems motionless,

---

* Actually, as we know today, the stars are Sunlike bodies spread through all of space at enormous distances from each other and from us. They are all moving, but they are so far from us that their motions result in such small changes in their apparent positions that it takes centuries to detect even slight shifts with the unaided eye.

and it is the sky we see turning in the opposite direction, east to west, in 24 hours.*

The apparent east-to-west motion of the sky, since it is only a reflection of the real west-to-east motion of the Earth, must be about the Earth's axis. If, then, the Earth's axis is extended (in imagination) in both directions, it will eventually intersect the sky at points called the "celestial poles." There is, at one end of the sky, the "North Celestial Pole" and, at the other end, the "South Celestial Pole."

Just as, in the course of the Earth's rotation, points on the surface of the Earth make smaller and smaller circles the closer they are to the poles, so the stars in the sky make smaller and smaller circles (in the opposite direction) the closer they are to the celestial poles. And just as the poles on Earth's surface do not move in the course of the Earth's rotation, so do the celestial poles in the sky remain unmoving in the course of the sky's apparent rotation.

It was far easier for early man to study the sky than to study the Earth. Only small portions of Earth's surface could be seen at one time, and even the greatest ancient travelers saw only somewhat larger, but still small portions of Earth's surface. Anyone, however, could see half of all the visible stars at a glance.

It followed, therefore, that while no one could tell what the shape of the Earth was from simply looking about, and while ancient mankind simply took the easy way out of assuming it was flat, it was easy to tell that the sky at least was a sphere. We call it the "celestial sphere" from a Latin word for "sky."

By studying the motion of the stars, the ancient astronomers could tell they pivoted about the point that was the North Celestial Pole. That at least was in an easily visible portion of the sky even though the Earth's North Pole was off in the mysterious distance with its very existence unsuspected.

Since Greece is some 50 degrees from the Earth's North Pole, the North Celestial Pole would be 50 degrees from the zenith,

---

* The ancients, mistaking appearance for reality, assumed the Earth was *really* stationary and that the starry sphere *really* rotated. There is no use sneering at them for this. It was an honest and natural mistake and one that all of us would make today if we did not know our senses were not to be trusted in this respect—thanks to the painstaking work of generations of thinkers on whose shoulders we now stand.

or 40 degrees above the northern horizon, nearly halfway to zenith. The South Celestial Pole would be at the opposite point of the celestial sphere. That meant it was 40 degrees below the southern horizon.

Since neither celestial pole moved as the sky rotated, the North Celestial Pole was always to be marked off in the visible sky (as seen by the Greek astronomers) while the South Celestial Pole was never visible. Yet the Greek astronomers knew the unseen pole existed. It may have been the first case of the discovery of something you did not see, and could not see, simply because that existence could be surely deduced from what was known.

The ancient astronomers could also work out the existence of a line around the sky midway between the celestial poles, and this is called the "celestial equator." Parallels of latitude could be worked out in the sky between the celestial equator and the celestial poles. Indeed, the system for marking off a sphere in this way, and with circles at right angles to the parallels (these other circles being "meridians of longitude"), was worked out in the sky before it was worked out on Earth.

It was from observing the position of the North Celestial Pole in the sky as observed from different places on Earth that the Greeks may have received their first hints as to the actual shape of the planet.

As one travels northward, the North Celestial Pole rises higher in the sky. (If one traveled to the North Pole, which no ancient Greek ever did, of course, the North Celestial Pole would be at the zenith.)

As one travels southward, the North Celestial Pole sinks lower in the sky. (If one traveled to the equator, which no ancient Greek ever did, as far as we know, the North Celestial Pole would be at the northern horizon, while the South Celestial Pole would have risen to the southern horizon. If the traveler went still farther south, the North Celestial Pole would sink below the northern horizon, while the South Celestial Pole would rise higher and higher above the southern horizon.)

This apparent motion of the celestial poles would not take place if the Earth were flat, but only if the Earth's surface were itself curved, at least in a north-south direction. Other pieces of evidence (the way in which ships disappeared hull first as they put off to sea, and the shape of the Earth's shadow during an eclipse of the Moon) made it clear that the Earth's surface curved equally in all directions and that the Earth, like the sky, was a sphere.

The first person we know by name who seems to have maintained that the Earth was a sphere was Philolaus, a Greek philosopher who was born in Tarentum in southern Italy. He may have come to this conclusion about 450 B.C.

Philolaus' statements may not have been very convincing at first, but about 320 B.C. the Greek philosopher Aristotle summarized all the evidence in favor of the spherical shape of the Earth and since his time no educated man in the Western world has doubted it.

The Moving Sun

The Greek astronomers could, and did, study the changing position of the Sun against the starry heavens. To be sure, the Sun blanked out all the stars in the heavens when it was in the sky, but by observing the stars as they appeared at midnight, one could calculate the position of the Sun in the other half of the celestial sphere.

Thus, the Greek astronomers observed that the Sun was exactly at the celestial equator at the vernal equinox, March 20, and was then entering the constellation of Aries, the Ram. It then slowly moved northward and eastward along the celestial sphere, until at the summer solstice, June 21, it entered the constellation of Cancer, the Crab, skimming the 23.5 ° N. parallel as it did so.

The Sun then moved slowly southward and eastward till it was back at the celestial equator at the autumnal equinox, September 23, when it was entering the constellation of Libra, the Scales. It continued to move slowly southward and eastward till at the winter solstice, December 21, it entered the constellation of Capricorn, the Goat, skimming, as it did so, the 23.5° S. parallel. It then moved slowly northward and eastward till it was back at the celestial equator at the vernal equinox.

Astronomers following these motions of the Sun, equating them with the changing lengths of day and night, and knowing the Earth was a sphere, could work out the existence of the various zones on Earth, much in the way I did in the previous chapter. It doesn't matter whether you assume the Earth is moving around the Sun, or the Sun is moving around the sky.

The arguments end up in the same place: with an Earth possessing a Torrid Zone, two temperate zones, one north and one south, and two frigid zones, one north and one south. It can be reasoned out, either way, that the frigid zones must be, on the average, cold; that they must experience long days during one half the year and long nights during the other. It can even be reasoned out that two poles exist, at which there must be a six-month day and a six-month night in alternation.

All this follows primarily from the fact that the Earth is a sphere, and we might argue that the first man to believe the Earth was round must have believed it had poles. Yet we cannot give the credit to Philolaus, for his championing of the round Earth did not include its consequences.

It was the greatest of the Greek astronomers, Hipparchus, who, about 130 B.C. (three centuries after the time of Philolaus), showed a clear understanding of the consequences of the spherical shape of the Earth. He was the first, in fact, to divide the Earth into its five zones. As a result, it can be fair to say that it was Hipparchus who discovered the poles of the Earth in the sense that he showed they must exist.

Had Herodotus lived three centuries later than he did, he would have known of Hipparchus' work and he would not have doubted the testimony of the Phoenician navigators. He would have known that the noontime Sun *had* to be to the north of the zenith if the Phoenicians had gone far enough south, and he would have taken their observation as evidence that the continent of Africa jutted beyond the equator and, very likely, beyond the Tropic of Capricorn.

Hipparchus' writings are lost, but about A.D. 150, a Greek astronomer, Claudius Ptolemaeus (usually known as Ptolemy in the English-speaking world) summarized Greek astronomy, particularly Hipparchus' findings, in a great textbook, which survived through all the dark times afterward.

Ptolemy made a map of the known world, which placed all the lands known to the ancient people of the Mediterranean world into the Northern Hemisphere (see figure 11). Ptolemy knew there was a Southern Hemisphere and suggested that there were probably continents there, too, but naturally he had no evidence concerning their existence.

These possible southern continents remained in the imagination of Europeans for fifteen centuries. Eventually, they were sought for, but not until some centuries had passed in which

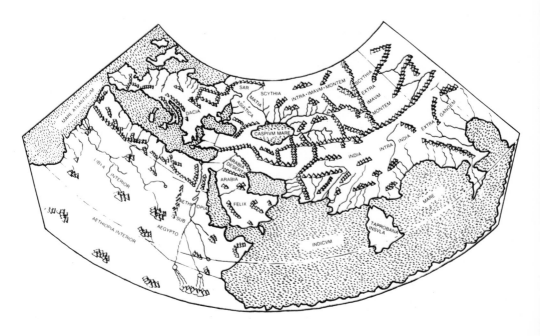

Figure 11. Ptolemy's Map

there was a general belief that the Torrid Zone might be so hot as to be impassable; and that the Earth might be forever divided into two inhabited portions, north and south, with no interconnections. (The Phoenician circumnavigation of Africa had disproved that, but no one took that tale seriously through most of those fifteen centuries.)

Ptolemy made two mistakes that were of importance. In the first place, he was wrong about the size of the Earth. As long ago as 250 B.C. (four centuries before Ptolemy), a Greek geographer, Eratosthenes, had measured the shadow cast by the Sun at different places on Earth at the same time, and had used that to calculate that the Earth was a sphere 40,000 kilometers around at the equator—which is correct.

About 80 B.C., however, another Greek astronomer, Posidonius, using similar methods, arrived, erroneously, at the smaller figure of a 29,000-kilometer circumference. Ptolemy (fortunately, as it turned out) acepted the smaller figure.

Furthermore, Ptolemy overestimated the distance from the Atlantic coasts of Europe to the Pacific coasts of Asia by way of the land route from Spain eastward to China. Therefore when he made a map showing the width of Europe and Asia in terms of meridians of longitude, people imagined it wrapped around the Northern Hemisphere of a globe that was only 29,000 kilometers in circumference and found that the two ends of the continent approached each other rather closely. If one sailed west from Europe across the Atlantic Ocean, it could be argued, one ought only to cross less than 5000 kilometers of ocean before reaching the eastern coasts of Asia. If there were islands in the Atlantic, one might be able to make the journey in smaller stages.

No ancient actually tried to sail off westward and check this. Indeed, after Ptolemy's time, there was a decline in astronomy and in science generally. It was not till some thirteen centuries after Ptolemy's death that the crossing of the Atlantic gap was put to the test.*

Polestars and Bears

When I say that the Greek astronomers followed the changing position of the North Celestial Pole as one moved northward and southward, I am perhaps oversimplifying matters a bit.

There is nothing to mark off the North Celestial Pole as a point from the rest of the sky. If it was a matter of locating it precisely and measuring its position from this point on Earth and from that point, the ancients might not have managed.

If there had happened to be a bright star at or very near the North Celestial Pole, the job would have been much simpler. It would be noticed that a particular star remained fixed in place the whole night long, night after night. With attention riveted on that star, it would become clear that other stars revolved about it. The existence of a North Celestial Pole would virtually force itself on the attention of stargazers and life would have been easier for them.

As it happens, anyone studying the night sky today would

* Had navigators known that Eurasia was narrower than Ptolemy had thought, and that the Earth was larger; had they known that to reach China by sailing west from Spain was a matter of 20,000 kilometers at the shortest, and not 5000, the events of A.D. 1492 would surely not have taken place—at least not in that year. Ptolemy's errors were influential indeed, therefore.

find that there *is* such a star in the sky near the North Celestial Pole. It is a second-magnitude star, only about one-thirtieth as bright as the very brightest star, Sirius, but still bright enough to be easily seen. It is only 1 degree from the North Celestial Pole so that in the course of 24 hours it makes a little circle about the celestial pole that is 2 degrees in diameter, or only four times the width of the full Moon.

This star is not motionless, but its motion is so small that it seems, to the casual observer, to be virtually in the same place at all times. It is variously called the "North Star," the "Pole Star," and "Polaris." (There is no comparably bright star anywhere near the South Celestial Pole.)

Unfortunately, however, the ancient Greeks did not have the advantage of Polaris, for the axis of the Earth does *not*, after all, point in the same direction forever, and the North Celestial Pole does not remain in the same spot in the sky forever.

I said, earlier in the book, that the Earth was so massive, and rotated so quickly, that the axis could only change its position very slightly or very slowly. Well, there is a very slow change caused by the fact that the Earth is not exactly a sphere.

If it were an exact sphere, all straight lines passing through the center of the Earth from one surface to the opposite surface—all "diameters," in other words—would be exactly equal in length. This is not so. The "equatorial diameter," a straight line drawn from one point on the equator through the center of the Earth to an opposite point on the equator is 40 kilometers greater than the "polar diameter," a straight line from the North Pole, through the center of the Earth, to the South Pole.

The difference is not much in a total diameter of 12,700 kilometers, but it leaves a small bulge in the equatorial regions. The Moon's gravitation attracts this bulge and the Earth is forced to wobble slowly in its rotation. The axis remains tilted at 23.5 degrees, but it twists so that the North Pole moves in a slow circle. So does the South Pole (see figure 12).

Naturally, the North and South Celestial poles make similar circles in the sky, circles 47 degrees across. It takes a long time to mark out that circle—25,800 years—so if you note the position of the North Celestial Pole from year to year, especially with the unaided eye, you won't notice any change in your lifetime.

This motion of the Earth's axis affects the entire celestial

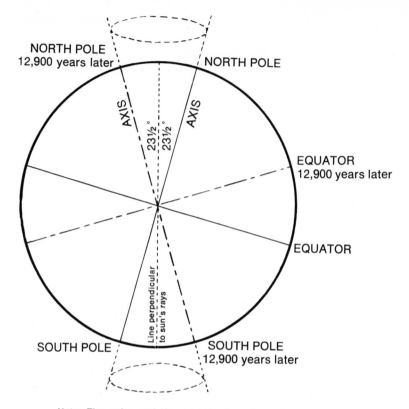

Note: The poles and the equator do not wander over an essentially stationary earth. They remain put with respect to the earth; it is the whole earth that wobbles.

Figure 12. The Precession of the Equinoxes

sphere. As the position of the North Celestial Pole slowly shifts in one direction and that of the South Celestial Pole in the other direction, the position of the celestial equator also shifts. The Sun, at the vernal equinox, crosses the celestial equator at a point slightly different from that which it would have reached and crossed if the Earth's axis didn't move.

Each year the Sun crosses the celestial equator about $\frac{1}{71}$ of a degree farther west than the year before. This wouldn't be noticeable to an astronomer observing the situation with his unaided eyes. It mounts up from year to year, however. After seventy-one years, the difference is a full degree, or nearly twice the width of the Sun, and that would certainly be noticed. In fact, after 2150 years, the Sun would be entering a different constellation at the vernal equinox.*

The first to notice the slow but steady shift of the position of the vernal equinoxes was Hipparchus. Since each year the Sun reached the celestial equator about 18 minutes before it would have done so if the axis had remained steady (that is, the actual time preceded what it should have been), Hipparchus called it "the precession of the equinoxes." The slow motion of the axis, which produces this effect, is still called that today.

As the North Celestial Pole marks out its circle in the sky, it nowhere passes so close to so bright a star as it does to Polaris. Even though it is now only 1 degree from Polaris, the precession of the equinoxes is still carrying the North Celestial Pole toward the star. In 2100, the North Celestial Pole will skim by Polaris at a distance of only one-half degree, and then it will start moving away again.

There are only two other reasonably bright stars that the North Celestial Pole approaches in its circular motion. One is Thuban, which is the brightest star in the constellation of Draco, the Dragon. It is only one-quarter as bright as Polaris and it approaches to only about 3 degrees of the North Celestial Pole at its closest. Thuban was the polestar back in 2500 B.C. or so, when the pyramids were being built, and its direction was used as a guide in the construction of some of them. That early in history, however, astronomers were not ready to deduce from its change in position with north-south travel that the Earth was a sphere.

At the other side of the circle marked out by the North Celestial Pole is the very bright star, Vega, in the constellation of Lyra, the Lyre. It is the fourth brightest star in the sky, over six times as bright as Polaris, but it never approaches closer than 5 degrees to the North Celestial Pole. Even so, a bright

---

* In Greek times, the Sun was in the constellation of Aries, the Ram, at the vernal equinox. Now it is in the constellation of Pisces, the Fish. Not too long in the future it will shift to Aquarius, the Water Carrier. Astrologers, however, still work with the system used by the Greeks and imagine the constellations not to have shifted with respect to the Sun. That is just one of the many pieces of nonsense out of which astrology is composed.

star like Vega would make a good North Star despite its rather uncomfortable distance. Unfortunately, the last time it was that close was about 12,000 B.C., before any but the most primitive astronomy could possibly have existed.

Our fortune in having Polaris so close to the North Celestial Pole is strictly our own, then. Even so short a time ago as when Columbus discovered America, Polaris was 3.5 degrees from the North Celestial Pole.

At the time when the Greek astronomers were working out the spherical nature of Earth, Polaris was more than 25 degrees from the North Celestial Pole and there was no worthwhile North Star at all. The ancient Greeks did not have our convenient marker and had to work out the movement of the North Celestial Pole without it.

That the advance of geographic knowledge continued anyway was the result of the fact that the Greeks had something almost as good as a North Star—

As the stars circle the North Celestial Pole, those close to it make small circles—circles too small to intersect the northern horizon. That means those stars remain in the sky all night long every night. Since the North Celestial Pole is 40 degrees above the northern horizon, as seen from Greece, any star within 40 degrees of it never sets but is always in the sky. (On the other hand, any star that is within 40 degrees of the South Celestial Pole never rises and is always invisible from Greece—barring such changes as the precession of the equinoxes brings about.)

As one travels north, the North Celestial Pole rises higher above the horizon and a larger circle of stars remains above the northern horizon at all times. (At the North Pole, the North Celestial Pole is at the zenith, and all the stars in the Northern Celestial Hemisphere circle sideways, remaining constantly above the horizon, while all the stars in the Southern Celestial Hemisphere remain always below the horizon.)

As one travels south, the North Celestial Pole sinks toward the horizon and smaller circles of stars remain above the horizon in the north and below the horizon in the south. (At the equator, the two celestial poles are at opposite horizons, and all the stars, without exception, rise and set.)

It is, therefore, the manner in which the "circumpolar stars" (those that circled the celestial pole without setting) behaved that was the key to the curvature of the Earth's surface, rather than observations of the North Celestial Pole directly.

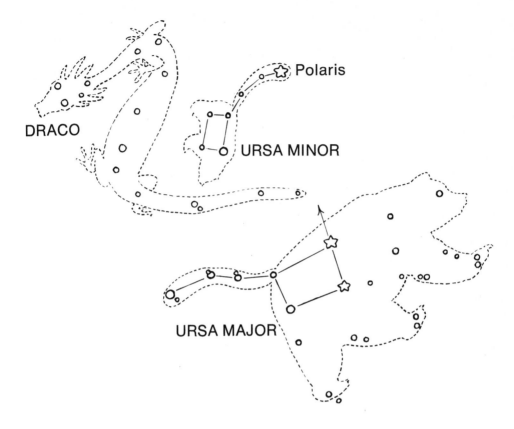

DRACO

Polaris

URSA MINOR

URSA MAJOR

Figure 13. The Big Dipper and the Celestial North Pole

But were those circumpolar stars noticeable enough to make a dent on the observer? Yes, indeed, for among them is a particularly noticeable combination of stars—the seven stars that make up what we call "the Big Dipper" (see figure 13).

The seven stars are all quite bright and their pattern is very distinctive. Anyone looking at the sky from the latitude of Greece (which is just about that of New York City and its surrounding region) was bound to see the Big Dipper every night and at all hours of the night.

Even casual observation would show that the Big Dipper moves in a circle and its varying positions could be used as a kind of nighttime clock. Thus in Shakespeare's *Henry IV, Part One*, a carrier (the equivalent of a modern truck driver), getting up at night to put his wagon on the road, says, "Charles' Wain [the Big Dipper] is over the new chimney, and yet our horse not packed."

Once the motion of the Big Dipper was carefully studied, the center about which it rotated could be marked out. Probably it was through the observation of the Big Dipper that the North Celestial Pole was discovered. Fortunately for astronomers, the North Celestial Pole, as it moved in response to the precession of the equinoxes, has been skimming along the Big Dipper through all the history of civilization. For that reason, though the North Celestial Pole has changed its position considerably, the Big Dipper has remained circumpolar and has continued to mark out the pole by its stately daily circle in the sky.

Some people think that the Phoenicians were the first people who learned to use the Big Dipper as an unfailing indication of the direction of north, since it is always in the sky and always in the northern quadrant. Knowing north, all the other directions are known, and this may have helped the Phoenicians develop the daring to launch out into the open sea, instead of hugging the shore. And in the *Odyssey*, Homer has Odysseus use the Big Dipper as a guide in navigation, too.

The Big Dipper is part of a larger constellation of stars in which the imaginative Greeks saw the figure of a bear. We still call the constellation "Ursa Major" today, using the Latin phrase for "Great Bear." Another constellation, including seven dimmer stars, also in a dipper arrangement, but more tightly spaced, is "Ursa Minor" ("Little Bear"). The final star in the handle of the Little Dipper is Polaris.

To the Greeks, the word for bear was "arktos," and it was that word which they applied to those constellations that remained forever in the northern part of the sky. To refer to the northern direction, therefore, the Greeks would say "arktikos," the direction "of the bear." *

It is because of this old Greek way of speaking that we still call the Far North of the Earth's sphere "the Arctic" today. In fact, almost no one speaks of the North Frigid Zone, or even of the North Polar region. It is almost always of the Arctic that

---

* It is sometimes argued that the Greeks spoke of the north in relation to bears because they had heard rumors of the existence of polar bears. We can't rule this out altogether, but it is unlikely. After all, we must allow for coincidence, too.

we speak. The 66.5° N. parallel that bounds the North Frigid Zone is therefore called "the Arctic Circle."

The Greek astronomers knew that, on the opposite side of the Earth from the North Frigid Zone, there had to be a South Frigid Zone with similar properties. The South Frigid Zone was on the opposite side of the Arctic, and the Greek word for "the opposite side" is "anti." The southern end of the Earth is therefore called "the Antarctic," and the 66.5° S. parallel that bounds the South Frigid Zone is "the Antarctic Circle."

4 PAST THE ARCTIC CIRCLE

In the previous chapter, I explained why we could argue that the Greeks, and Hipparchus in particular, discovered the poles. By that line of argument we could date the discovery of the poles as no later than 130 B.C., and possibly as long ago as 450 B.C.—twenty-one to twenty-four centuries ago.

Yet this sort of theoretical discovery of places that are conceivably within physical reach seems unsatisfactory. It is not knowing that Mount Everest has a peak that counts, but the actual climbing of the mountain and reaching that peak.

What we usually mean by geographical "discovery," then, is the footsteps and eyesight of an actual person, venturing out onto a portion of the Earth's surface that no one before has ever trodden or seen. ▾

Generally, though, we show unconscious racism by supposing that the only people who count in geographic discovery are western Europeans of our own culture. For instance, Columbus discovered America, we will all agree, but, in doing so, we ignore the fact that there were already people in the Americas who had been there for thousands of years and whose ancestors had certainly discovered the land long before Columbus.

In defense of the traditional view, however, we might argue that though much of the Earth was already inhabited in prehistoric times, most of the inhabitants, here and there, made little or no deliberate attempt to learn more of their planet's surface than their home and its immediate surroundings. It was generally the people of civilized lands who ventured outward for the purpose of learning and mapping as much of the Earth's surface as they could reach. It is this deliberate search that we might refer to as exploration and discovery.

Whether they were explorers or not, the Arctic regions were already inhabited (albeit thinly) long before men from the civilized southern lands ventured so far north. It may even be that men had walked past the Arctic Circle thousands of years before the Greeks had discovered the necessity of polar regions on Earth.

Men of the Arctic

Some 25,000 years ago, for instance, there were tribes in what is now Siberia, who hunted the mammoth, an elephant-like beast now extinct, coated with shaggy hair to enable it to withstand the frigid temperatures. In pursuit of the mammoths, these Siberians found their way northward and eastward into what is now Alaska. From that place, over the next 15,000 years, men migrated into every corner of the American continents (till then untenanted by human beings), and it was those migrants whose descendants were the American Indians.

In the process of coursing over Siberia and entering Alaska, those prehistoric tribesmen may have crossed the Arctic Circle here and there. If so, they were the first human beings to enter the Arctic—long before what we consider "civilization" had arisen anywhere on the face of the Earth.

By the time Europeans penetrated Siberia in comparatively modern times, they found tribesmen there, still living lives much as their ancestors had done, except for the fact that the mammoths were long since gone. They live there still, even today, although nowadays civilization, both for good and for evil, has transformed their lives.

There are about 25,000 Samoyeds nowadays in northwestern Siberia, about 250,000 Yakuts in north-central Siberia, and about 25,000 Tungus in northeastern Siberia. Not all of these Siberian people live north of the Arctic Circle, of course.

In Europe, the inhabitants of the Arctic shores are the Lapps, who have lived in the area since at least 100 B.C. or so. There are about 36,500 Lapps living in northern Scandinavia now.

None of these Arctic peoples of Eurasia are, however, as thoroughly adapted to the cold world of the Far North as are the Arctic people of North America.

About 1000 B.C., there were the beginnings of another invasion of North America from Asia. The invaders reached the Aleutian Islands first, a chain of islands swinging in an arc from southwestern Alaska to Siberia. These are not truly Arctic since they are well south of the Arctic Circle. Indeed, some of the islands are south of the 52° N. parallel, and are as far south as London and Berlin. These invaders, however, or allied groups following them, eventually passed through the Aleutians, or leapfrogged them and made their way into northern Alaska.

The new invaders were more clearly related to the people of eastern Asia than the American Indians are. The former have the characteristic eyelids and facial structure of what we call the Mongolian type.

In two respects, conditions had changed in northern North America between the periods of the two Asian invasions. At the time of the original entry of the ancestors of the Indians into Alaska, all of northern North America, except for portions of the Pacific, had been buried in ice (something we'll get back to later in the book) and did not offer any reasonable chance of colonization. The first invaders had therefore been pushed southward by the icy facts of geography.

By 1000 B.C., when the second invasion was under way, however, the ice was mostly gone, at least in summer, and the northern coastline was in its present shape. The Arctic coastline of North America was still not exactly a tempting living area, but it was not the unutterably bleak land it had been some thousands of years before.

Secondly, the earlier invasion had been of tribesmen whose chief food had been land mammals. In search of those they had inevitably made their way southward where the climate was warmer, the vegetation more lush, and the animal herds more numerous.

The newer invasion was of people who had developed techniques for the hunting of sea animals—seals, walruses, birds, fish—perhaps because southern areas were already occupied and it was necessary to learn how to live where they were or die. Sea animals were far more numerous off the Arctic shores than land animals could be on those shores, so that the new hunters tended to cling to those shores and even to flourish there surprisingly well.

These Arctic inhabitants living off the sea are known to us as Eskimos. This word was coined in 1611 by a priest who heard them referred to by neighboring Indians as "eskimantsik," a word meaning "eater of raw flesh."

By A.D. 1, the Eskimos' methods of wresting a living out of the Arctic shores and of protecting themselves efficiently against the cold were well developed, and they began spreading out over the northern rim of North America. By A.D. 1000 they had reached the eastern borders of that rim and were crossing over into Greenland.

These intrepid Eskimos were certainly the first human beings to venture along the Arctic shores of the New World (several centuries before Columbus) and to this day remain the most well-adapted inhabitants of the Arctic. About 70,000 of them live there today, some 10,000 in Canada, 15,000 in Alaska, 45,000 in Greenland, and even about 1200 in eastern Siberia.

The Irish and the Vikings

At the time the Eskimos were taking over the Arctic shores of North America, southern Europe and neighboring lands enjoyed a high civilization under the Greeks and Romans. While the Roman Empire flourished, there was no thought of an invasion of the Arctic or even of exploring in that direction. Matters were too comfortable in the south.

It was only after the Roman Empire had come to an end—in the western provinces at least—that Europeans began venturing into northern lands they had not hitherto occupied. And, oddly enough, the first Arctic explorers were from regions that had not been part of the Roman Empire.

Though much of the island of Britain had been ruled by Rome for three and a half centuries, Ireland had remained outside the imperial bounds. Yet after Rome's western dominions had fallen apart, Ireland came to experience a kind of golden age of culture. Between A.D. 500 and 800, Ireland advanced in learning while the rest of western Europe was falling into decay and darkness.

Christianity had come to Ireland at the beginning of this period, and communities of monks preserved learning. Some of these monks deliberately searched for isolation in order to be less annoyed by worldly matters, and in their search they penetrated farther north than any civilized people had done before.

When the Roman Empire was at its height in the second century A.D., its realm in Britain reached briefly into what is now central Scotland, attaining a latitude of 56° N. The Irish monks went beyond that.

One of them was Saint Brendan, who, about 550, took to the sea and sailed northward, duplicating some of the feats of Pytheas of Massilia, nearly nine centuries before. He seems to have explored the islands off the Scottish coast, the Hebrides to the west, together with the Orkney and the Shetland islands to the north.

Of these islands (all part of the kingdom of Great Britain today), the Shetland Islands are the most northerly. They represent one of the bodies of land that some have suggested as representing Pytheas' land of Thule. The Shetland Islands are a group of some twenty-one inhabited islands with a total area of 1400 square kilometers* of windswept, treeless land, with a population today of about 6000. The northernmost tip of the islands is at 60.8° N.

It is possible that Saint Brendan went still farther north, reaching the Faeroe Islands, about 320 kilometers northwest of the Shetlands. The Faeroe Islands are just about as numerous as the Shetlands, and just about as large in total area. They lie a little farther to the north, however, reaching an extreme of 62.4° N.

By reaching the Faeroe Islands, it is possible that Saint Brendan went beyond Pytheas' farthest reach northward. If so,

---

* One square kilometer is equal to 0.386 square miles, or roughly three-eighths of a square mile.

Saint Brendan set a northern record for the penetration of a European explorer.

Saint Brendan's voyage was remarkable enough for its time but in later years it was much magnified. In 800 a fictional account of his voyages was published and proved very popular. On the basis of that, it was even claimed eventually that Saint Brendan had reached the American continent. This is totally unlikely and yet one statement in the tale has the ring of truth. Mention is made of a "floating crystal castle." Surely no one could mention such a thing unless he had seen an iceberg and, if so, this is the first mention of an iceberg in world literature, as far as we know.

It is possible that Saint Brendan, or, more likely, other Irish monks who followed in his footsteps, reached a still larger and more northerly island. About 795, the Irish wanderers may have reached the island we know as Iceland, some 480 kilometers northwestward from the Faeroe Islands. Iceland is about 103,000 square kilometers in area.

The Irish undoubtedly landed on the southwestern shores of the island at 64° N., but its northernmost points are almost exactly at 66.5° N.—almost precisely at the Arctic Circle.

Considering how far north it is, Iceland is surprisingly mild in temperature (for reasons we will come to later). Both Iceland and the Faeroe Islands were unoccupied when the Irish landed, and in the case of neither island was the occupation permanent. The Irish may have remained a hundred years, but eventually they either died off or left. When the next seamen came (*not* Irish), the islands were empty again.

These new navigators were Scandinavian rovers from Norway and Denmark—the so-called Vikings.

The Vikings were not really an Arctic people but lived in southern Scandinavia well below the Arctic Circle, roughly in the latitude of Scotland. Their ancestors had arrived there about 3000 B.C. They were able to carry on agriculture in their Scandinavian homeland, but that was far enough north to make it a risky and marginal procedure. In periods of relatively good weather, population increased; but then, in the inevitable periods of worse weather, it was either starve or leave the country in search of food and land elsewhere.

Beginning about A.D. 780, mild weather had increased the Scandinavian population to the point where many felt it wise to seek their fortune elsewhere. For a period of about 250 years, Viking sea raiders terrorized all the coast of western Europe. Vikings occupied most of Ireland and Scotland, reducing them to savagery. They badly ravaged the Anglo-Saxon kingdoms that had been established in Britain after the withdrawal of the Romans and which were to form the nation of England. They pillaged the coasts and rivers of what are now France and Germany. They even penetrated the Mediterranean.

Much more to the point of this book, however, they sailed out into the open northern ocean. Sometimes they were driven westward by storms; sometimes they went in deliberate search of new lands they could loot or in which they could settle.

They reached the Faeroe Islands, for instance, in the ninth century and established the first permanent colony there. If any Irish had reached the islands previously, they were gone when the Vikings came (or were killed if any had lingered). The Faeroe Islands have remained Scandinavian ever since, first under the rule of Norway. Norway and Denmark were combined under a single monarchy in 1380, and when the two nations separated again in 1814, the Faeroe Islands remained a dependency of Denmark.

Today, seventeen of the Faeroe Islands are inhabited, and its population is just under 40,000. After World War II, the Faeroe Islands sought independence. This was denied them but, since 1947, they have had self-government under the Danish monarchy.

The Faeroe Islands were only a stopping place for the Viking seamen. A Norwegian exile, Ingolfur Arnarson, went farther. In 874, he landed in Iceland. Again, any Irish who had ever been there had gone and the island was unoccupied. The Vikings established a permanent and flourishing colony that was based on a fishing economy.

During the early centuries of its existence, Viking Iceland maintained the pagan Norse religion even after the homeland was being rapidly Christianized. As early as 930, Iceland developed a kind of constitution and legislature, an approach to democracy that was unique in the Europe of the time. Christianity finally penetrated Iceland about 1000, but even then the conversion was peaceful and orderly, and the older beliefs gave way gracefully. The Icelandic "sagas," tales written before 1300, are a better source of knowledge concerning Viking pagan beliefs than anything that can be found in Scandinavia proper.

Iceland's history, like that of the Faeroes, consisted of a connection first with Norway, then with Denmark. In 1918, Iceland became an independent, self-governing state which, however, acknowledged the king of Denmark as king of Iceland as well. In 1944, even this link was broken and Iceland became a completely independent republic. Its population today is about 210,000. Its capital is at Reykjavik, where Arnarson had first settled. Reykjavik is at 64.1° N. and is the most northerly national capital in the world. It is, however, by no means Arctic and is 260 kilometers south of the Arctic Circle.

In its first centuries, Iceland was a nucleus for voyages and explorations still farther west.

From the mountaintops in northwestern Iceland one can dimly make out land on the horizon (about 120 kilometers to the northwest), and in that part of the island there lived Eric Thorvaldsson toward the close of the tenth century. He was generally called Eric the Red, from the color of his hair.

In 982, Eric was exiled for some offense, and he decided to use a three-year period of outlawry placed upon him, to go exploring westward. He reached the distant island at last at a point well to the south of the portion one could see from his home, but even so he found its coast choked with ice and couldn't manage a landing. He followed the coast southwestward till he reached a cape he could sail round and then he followed the western coast northward. This southwestern coast (about 550 kilometers west of Iceland) was less bleak, and Eric judged it capable of supporting a colony.

By 985, Eric was back in Iceland drumming up colonists for his new land. In order to do so, he outrageously oversold its good qualities, even to the point of calling it Greenland, a name it still bears today.

Greenland is the largest island in the world, 2,200,000 square kilometers in area, which makes it nearly a quarter as large as the United States. The long axis of the island is north and south and most of it lies within the Arctic Circle.

That northern part remained unknown to the Vikings, however. The southernmost 650 kilometers are south of the Arctic Circle, and it was only the land just west of the southern tip that Eric the Red intended to colonize. The southernmost tip of Greenland, now known as Cape Farewell, is at 59.8° N., which is 750 kilometers south of the Arctic Circle and about 500 kilometers farther south than Reykjavik. Eric's planned colony was very little north of Cape Farewell, at 60.7° N., at about the latitude of such flourishing northern cities as Oslo, Helsinki, and Leningrad.

However, as we shall see, latitude is not the only thing that determines climate, and Greenland is far bleaker than either Norway or Iceland. Still, Eric found volunteers to settle the new land and in 986 he headed west with twenty-five ships. Fourteen ships arrived and a colony was founded. There the Viking colonists hung on, for the climate, a thousand years ago, appears to have been somewhat milder than it is now (there were vineyards in England then) and the coastal strip was marginally endurable.

In fact, the colony persisted for over four centuries. Shortly after 1100 it was converted to Christianity and had its own bishop. At the height of its success, about 1200, as many as 3000 Vikings may have dwelt on the island.

While the Greenland colony existed, it served, in its turn, as a base for explorations still farther west. About 1000, Leif Ericsson, a son of Eric the Red, led a party to a landing somewhere on the North American continent, perhaps on the island of Newfoundland. For some years, Vikings attempted to found a colony in what they called "Vinland" (the exact location of which is uncertain) but that proved ephemeral.

Unlike Iceland and Greenland, the lands farther west were not empty. They were already populated with people the Vikings called "Skrellings" and who were, presumably, Indians. The Indians were hostile and this posed a greater barrier to colonization than Greenland's harsh weather. In the end, troubles among themselves and with the Indians finally wore out the Vinland colonists and those who survived returned to Greenland.

Greenland's continued existence depended on constant communication with Iceland and Norway, and on constant infusions of new settlers. In 1349, however, the Black Death, a vast pandemic of the plague, which had been devastating Europe, reached Scandinavia and Iceland, and the economy shrank there as it did everywhere. The link with Greenland grew more tenuous, and the last ship sailed from Norway to Greenland in 1367. In addition, the Earth underwent a slight cooling trend and Greenland's climate, very poor at best, became so bad as to make agriculture virtually impossible.

Then, too, the Eskimos who had been working their way eastward along North America's Arctic shore had reached northern Greenland at just about the time the Vikings had reached southern Greenland. Slowly, the Eskimos worked their way southward, and when they finally reached the Viking settlements, their hostility may well have added to the troubles of the Greenland colonists.

About 1415, the Greenland colony came to an end and the vast island was left to the Eskimos.

In all their adventures westward, the Vikings had not penetrated north of the Arctic Circle, neither in Iceland, Greenland, nor Vinland. They may have done so in other directions, however.

About 870, even before Iceland had been reached, a Viking named Ottar (according to old records) sailed northward out of sheer curiosity. He said he wanted to see how far north land existed and whether that far northern land was populated.

Apparently, he succeeded in rounding the northern end of the Scandinavian Peninsula, reaching and passing what we now call North Cape, the farthest northern reach of the European continent. North Cape is at 71.1° N., about 200 kilometers north of the Arctic Circle. Assuming the account to be true, this is the first significant crossing of the Arctic Circle by sea and it represents the then-record northward penetration by a European.

Ottar sailed beyond North Cape, where the coast trended southeastward along what we now call the Kola Peninsula, and then entered the White Sea, the first European to do so.

The Vikings penetrated even farther north than North Cape, too. In 1194, according to some old records, Vikings came across an island they called "Svalbard." This is usually identified with an island group better known to us as Spitzbergen. Even the southernmost point of Spitzbergen is at 76.6° N. and is 450 kilometers north of the Arctic Circle. The total area of the Spitzbergen islands is about 63,000 square kilometers.

About 950 kilometers farther east, the Vikings may have encountered the pair of islands now known as Novaya Zemlya (Russian for "new land"). Novaya Zemlya has an area of 83,000 square kilometers and is somewhat farther south than Spitzbergen, so it is Spitzbergen that must represent the farthest northern reach of the Viking explorers (or of anyone else up to that time).

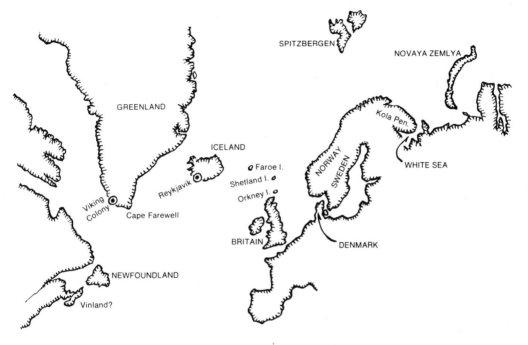

Figure 14. The Viking Explorations

However, no colonies were established, and when the Viking tide receded, the islands remained empty and unknown. Iceland remained the outermost permanent extension of Viking culture (see figure 14).

The Southeast Passage

The nations of Europe that lay west and south of Scandinavia recovered from the damage done by Viking raids, and after A.D. 1000 quickly grew wealthier and more powerful. (Indeed, some of the most powerful elements were Normans, descendants of the Vikings who had settled in northern France and who, at their peak in the twelfth century, ruled not only in most of France, but also in England, in Sicily, in southern Italy, and in parts of the Holy Land.)

The European nations had no desire at that time to explore northward, for their eyes were fixed on the East. During the twelfth and thirteenth centuries, they had sent armies eastward to fight in the Holy Land against the Moslems, and they then gathered their first notions of the wealth of Asia and of the desirable products that were to be found there—silk and spices, for instance.

In the last half of the thirteenth century, an Italian family named Polo spent thirty years in China. In 1296, they returned to Italy, and one of them, Marco Polo, wrote a book of his travels which was immensely popular and which further fascinated the west Europeans with the gorgeous East.

The Polos were able to make the journey to China and back because at that time a vast Mongol Empire had been briefly established through all of Asia and eastern Europe. In the fourteenth century, however, the Mongol Empire broke up and the lands east of Europe were in the hands of various peoples hostile to the west Europeans.

Some Europeans began to think of ways in which one might reach the Far East ("the Indies") by sea, bypassing the land approaches controlled by enemies. There seemed three possible routes to the Indies by sea. We might call them the Southeast Passage, the Northeast Passage, and the West Passage.

All three had disadvantages. The West Passage, taking advantage of the sphericity of the Earth, involved a direct westward sail across the Atlantic. Ptolemy said that a mere 5000-kilometer sail (considerably less in distance than the overland trip eastward) would take a navigator to the east coast of Asia. Marco Polo's data seemed to support that. The trouble was that no one had ever taken the trip and there was no great eagerness to chance a voyage into the unknown.

The Northeast Passage would involve sailing around the northern rim of Europe and Asia. Nobody knew how long that would be, but by the fifteenth century, Europeans knew enough of Scandinavia and its surrounding waters to be certain that the Northwest Passage would involve considerable cold, ice, and hardship.

That left the Southeast Passage around the southern rim of Africa. That would carry ships southward toward the Torrid Zone, which many suspected to be intolerably hot. On the other hand, Africa might not extend very far southward. Ptolemy's map showed Africa ending short of the equator, and no one took seriously Herodotus' tale of the Phoenician navigators taking three years to go around Africa and reaching the South Temperate Zone. It seemed possible that ships might slip around Africa without much trouble.

On the whole, then, the Southeast Passage seemed most promising, and the natural place from which one might start was Portugal. That nation was at the extreme southwest of Europe and was nearest the Atlantic coast of Africa, down which one must sail to start the Southeast Passage.

A Portuguese prince, Henry (called "the Navigator"), a younger brother of King Duarte I, undertook the project. In 1420, he founded a center for navigation at Sagres, at the extreme southwestern tip of Portugal. This became a haven for experienced navigators, a place where ships were built according to new designs, where new aids to navigation were devised and tested, where crews were hired and trained, and where expeditions were carefully outfitted.

A slow but careful probing of Africa's Atlantic coast followed, and this was the beginning of the great Age of Exploration in which west Europeans opened all the world and, inevitably, brought it under their own domination.

It was slow at first. By the time Prince Henry died, in 1460, the Portuguese ships had not reached more than one-fifth of the way around Africa. Continued exploration quickly showed that Africa extended far farther south than Ptolemy had dreamed. On the other hand, it showed that the Torrid Zone, while hot, was not unbearably so and that it was indeed passable.

By 1487, the Portuguese navigator Bartholomeu Dias reached the southern tip of Africa, and by 1497, another Portuguese navigator, Vasco da Gama, went around Africa at last and reached India. It was on Da Gama's voyage that the length of the trip and the monotony of the sailors' diet finally managed to deplete the crew of vitamin C and bring on the first attack of shipboard scurvy, something that was to plague mariners for two and a half centuries.

Thus, the Southeast Passage worked (see figure 15). It was long, but it was practical, and Portugal built up the first European overseas empire in Africa and Asia. It is an empire which was the last European overseas empire, as it was the first, and which came to an end only in the 1970s.

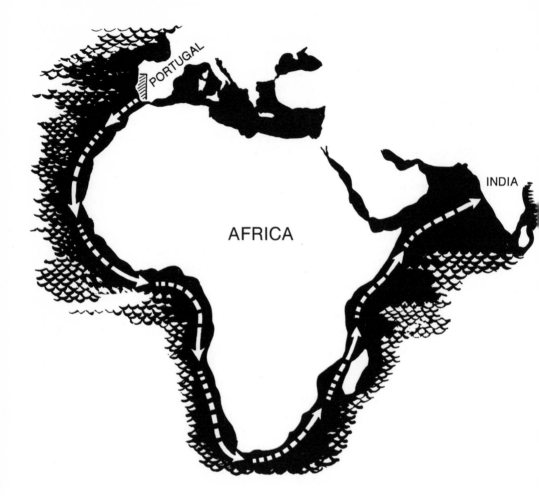

Figure 15. The Southeast Passage

The West Passage

It took the better part of a century to prove the Southeast Passage was practical, and even as it was near its final success, an alternate passage was attempted. Christopher Columbus, a native of Genoa, Italy, knew his Ptolemy and his Marco Polo and was convinced that the West Passage was far more practical than any other. He persuaded King Ferdinand II and

Queen Isabella I of Spain to finance an expedition that was to sail directly west across the Atlantic Ocean.

On August 6, 1492, he set sail and on October 12, 1492, he landed on an island off the eastern shores of North America. It is this which usually counts as the "discovery of America," not because Columbus was the first man to see the continents, or even that he was the first European to do so, but because he was the first European to do it under such circumstances that Europeans never lost sight of it again.

Columbus was convinced that he had reached the east coast of Asia, but, of course, the Earth was larger than Ptolemy had thought and Asia was 20,000 kilometers west of Europe, not 5000. These lands Columbus had discovered proved to be new continents whose existence neither Ptolemy nor any other ancient had suspected, and beyond which was a second ocean far larger than the Atlantic. It was only by passing this second ocean that the Far East could be reached.

The first to maintain this view—that what Columbus had discovered was a "New World" and that two oceans, not one, lay between Europe and Asia—was an Italian navigator, whose Latinized name was Americus Vespucius.

Vespucius presented his view in 1504, and in 1507, a German geographer, Martin Waldseemüller, accepted it and published a map showing the new continent as existing by itself. He proposed that it be named "America" in honor of the man who recognized its existence and this was accepted. It turned out, actually, that America was two continents connected by a narrow isthmus, so we have "North America" and "South America."

In order to get to Asia by the West Passage, then, one had to get past the Americas, by sailing around them either by the north or by the south. In place of the West Passage, there were two possibilities now, a Northwest Passage and a Southwest Passage.

The first to bypass the Americas and reach Asia after crossing the second ocean was a Portuguese navigator, Ferdinand Magellan, who was working in the pay of Spain. In 1519, he left Spain, worked his way around the southern tip of South America and then entered the second ocean, which he named the "Pacific Ocean." In a 100-day voyage across unbroken sea, he and his men barely lived to reach islands off the east coast of

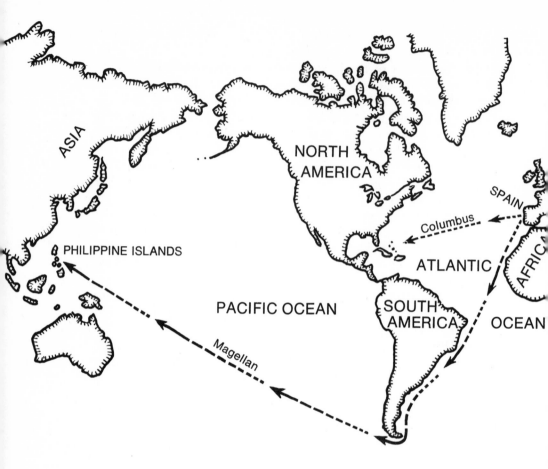

Figure 16. The Southwest Passage

Asia (which were eventually named the "Philippine Islands" in honor of King Philip II of Spain).

By reaching the Philippine Islands, Magellan showed that the Southwest Passage was possible (see figure 16). It was far longer than the Southeast Passage, but it could be traversed. In 1521, Magellan died in the Philippine Islands, but those who were left continued westward. Finally, a single ship, with eighteen men aboard, under the leadership of Juan Sebastián del Cano, arrived back in Spain on September 6, 1522.

This was the first circumnavigation of the globe. It had taken three years and it finally showed, beyond any doubt, that the

Earth was 40,000 kilometers in circumference, as Eratosthenes had calculated eighteen centuries before.

Of the four possible sea routes from Europe to the Far East, then, two had been carried through successfully. Of these the Southeast Passage was under the control of Portugal and the Southwest Passage was under the control of Spain. In the sixteenth century, they were the dominating sea powers of the world.

New nations, however, were rising, and they aspired to power at sea and to the wealth that came with trade and commerce. The chief of these were England (hitherto a minor kingdom on the rim of Europe) and the Netherlands, which was a province of the Spanish Empire and was trying to establish its independence.

England and the Netherlands were not yet in a position to dispute massively the dominance of Spain and Portugal. Though they might raid the sea-lanes and inflict pinpricks on the Iberian giants, it was clear that if they wanted to engage in trade on a major scale they would have to find new routes to the Indies.

That meant either the Northeast Passage or the Northwest Passage, with all the dangers of Arctic voyaging that that might entail.

Thus, it came about that the first explorations of the Arctic that served to bring it permanently into the consciousness of mankind as a whole were carried through by England and the Netherlands, not out of any curiosity about the Arctic itself (how they wished it would go away) but out of a desire to reach the Far East.

The Northeast Passage

Let us consider the Northeast Passage first, since it was the first to be undertaken and the first to show results (though not those expected).

In 1553, England outfitted three ships under Sir Hugh Willoughby and sent him off northeastward in search of the Far East. The ships rounded the northern edge of Scandinavia, as Ottar had done seven centuries before. In doing this Willoughby crossed the Arctic Circle and may be said to have discovered the Arctic in the same sense that Columbus discovered America. Willoughby was not the first man to do so, or even the first European, but he did it for the first time under circumstances that meant the Arctic would never again recede from the consciousness of civilized man.

Willoughby's ships continued about 1000 kilometers eastward, nearly to Novaya Zemlya, before deciding that it was too late into the winter season to continue. They turned back. Two of the ships with Willoughby in charge found a harbor on the Kola Peninsula along the Arctic shore just east of Scandinavia. They spent the winter there but died of the cold.

The third ship, under Richard Chancellor, fortunately for itself, had been separated from the other two in a storm and had made its way past the edge of the Kola Peninsula into the White Sea, as Ottar had once done. In Ottar's day, however, the shores of the White Sea were uninhabited by anyone but occasional Lapps. Now Richard Chancellor found the seaport of Arkhangelsk, a Russian town.

The Russians were as delighted to see him as he was to see them. He was taken overland to Moscow where he was greeted by the Russian czar, Ivan IV ("the Terrible"), who was plainly eager to open trade relations with England. In this he was successful. In 1555, a private corporation was formed in London (popularly called "The Muscovy Company") to carry on trade with Russia. During Chancellor's effort to return to England, however, his ship went down and all aboard were drowned.

The English sometimes referred to Chancellor's voyage as "the discovery of Russia" and for a long time persisted in thinking of it as primarily an Arctic nation, since Arkhangelsk was its one seaport. However, Russia's existence was well known for centuries before Chancellor's voyage.

Russia, indeed, was active in exploration of the Arctic long before England and, through the accident of its geography, was to remain among the foremost in Arctic exploration right down to the present.

Russia had had a northern center from the beginning. One of its important cities when it first entered the stage of history was Novgorod, about 200 kilometers south of modern Leningrad. At 58.5° N. it was well south of the Arctic Circle but it was still as far north as the northernmost tip of Scotland.

About 860, Novgorod fell under the rule of Swedish invaders who called themselves Rus (whence the name, Russia, for the entire nation). These went on to capture Kiev far to the south, and for nearly four centuries the chief center of Russian power was in what is now the Ukraine.

Kievan Russia was destroyed by a Mongol invasion in 1240, but Novgorod retained a very precarious independence during a period when Mongols dominated Russia for nearly three centuries. Novgorod's prosperity depended on trade. Its greatest resource was furs, which it sold in return for products its rude civilization could not produce.

In their search for furs (and perhaps in their eagerness to place additional kilometers between themselves and the Mongols), the Novgorod trappers penetrated northward to the Arctic shoreline, reaching the White Sea in the thirteenth century, 400 years after Ottar had first glimpsed it. The Novgorod trappers explored the coastline east to the Ural Mountains. All of the northern third of what we now call "European Russia" was Novgorod territory, though very thinly held, by 1400. It represented the first time that any Arctic land had been made an integral part of a civilized nation.

South of Novgorod, however, the Mongol hold was weakening and the ruler of "Muscovy" (the regions around the city of Moscow) was growing stronger. In 1380, the ruler of Muscovy, Dmitri Donskoi, defeated the Mongol army and destroyed the legend of its invincibility.

For decades more, the struggle between Muscovy and the Mongols continued, with Muscovy growing continually stronger. Ivan III ("the Great") of Muscovy, who came to the throne in 1462, initiated a policy of cautious annexation of surrounding principalities, and after two wars with Novgorod, that city and its vast northern appanage were annexed in 1478. This represents the birth of modern Russia, with Moscow as its capital, and Ivan III ruled what is now the northern half of European Russia, including the Arctic coast.

Ivan III took the title of "czar" (the word is a distortion of "Caesar"), and in 1480 beat back the Mongols who had made their last attempt to take Moscow. His grandson, Ivan IV, took the offensive against the Mongols in 1552, drove them back and took over the entire course of the Volga River down to the Caspian Sea.

It was in the midst of this victorious campaign that Ivan IV (only twenty-three at the time and, as yet, far from the bloody tyrant he became in later years) greeted Richard Chancellor and established trade relations with England.

The Netherlands was not far behind England. In the 1560s and 1570s, Dutch navigators also reached the Kola Peninsula and also brought their ships into Arkhangelsk. What's more, since the English, content with their early success, were willing to remain at Arkhangelsk and go no farther outward in the Northeast Passage, the Dutch attempted to fill the void.

Nearly half a century after Chancellor's success, a Dutch navigator, Willem Barents, far outdid Chancellor in exploratory feats, if not in commercial success.

In 1594, Barents left Amsterdam with two ships, rounded Norway, and sailed eastward across the stretch of sea that lies to the north of European Russia and of which the White Sea is merely an inlet. It is now called the "Barents Sea" in his honor.

He also reached the island of Novaya Zemlya, where Ottar and Willoughby had been before him, and sailed along its shores to its northern tip. This northern tip is at 77° N. and represented the most northerly penetration by any European since the time of the Vikings.

On a second voyage, in 1596, Barents headed north from Norway's northern shore, and discovered Bear Island, a small piece of land (only 185 square kilometers in area) 390 kilometers north of Norway. Beyond that, 240 kilometers farther north, he spied Spitzbergen, which he mistakenly thought was part of Greenland. This time Spitzbergen did not slip out of European consciousness ever again, so Barents might be looked upon as its effective discoverer.

For many years Spitzbergen remained a kind of international territory, serving as a center of the whaling industry. English, French, Dutch, Danish, Norwegian, and Russian whalers were active there right into the twentieth century. It was not till after World War I that an international conference undertook to make a national territory of it. They awarded it to Norway, which took formal possession in 1925. It still has no year-round population though up to 3000 people—miners, trappers, and others—come there seasonally from towns in Norway and the Soviet Union.

After Barents reached Spitzbergen, he turned east and visited Novaya Zemlya a second time. Though farther south than Spitzbergen, it is colder and less desirable. It consists of two long islands separated by a narrow channel, plus a number of small ones. No one really wanted it and it has remained Russian. It was only in the late 1800s that the Russians tried to place permanent settlers on it, and there are a few hundred people living there now.

Barents' second visit to Novaya Zemlya was an unlucky one for him but epoch-making. He rounded the northern edge and then found he could go no farther through the ice. A cold spell trapped him in the Arctic winter. Like Willoughby, he was going to be forced to remain where he was through the winter.

He had with him sixteen crewmen and a cabin boy. They all built a ramshackle but serviceable house out of driftwood, made beds, made a steam bath, hunted foxes and what other animals they could find, and did their best to stay warm and keep fed. They suffered from scurvy, Barents himself quite badly, and the cabin boy died, but the amazing thing is that they survived the winter, and when the ice broke up and ships could move again, all but the dead cabin boy were ready to go with them.

Barents and his crew had wintered at 76° N., the first Europeans to survive an Arctic winter so far north. Barents himself died soon after they had all set off in two small boats, but the rest reached the Kola Peninsula and safety.

After Barents' voyages, however, attempts to complete the Northeast Passage ceased to have any point to west Europeans. It was clear that it was not a practical route by which to reach the Far East. For the Russians, however, it was another matter altogether. They alone could take a similar route by land; and by land, at least, the weather was less harsh and there was an ample reward in the form of furs. It had been the search for furs, after all, that had carried the hunters of Novgorod to the Arctic shores and as far east as the Ural Mountains in the first place.

In 1581, the Stroganovs, a Russian family that had founded their wealth on furs, employed a Cossack named Yermak Timofievich to explore eastward beyond the Urals. Off went Yermak, and he and his band had no difficulty in conquering a Mongol kingdom just east of the Urals. Its capital was named Sibir and from that town the name Siberia came to be applied to all of northern Asia.

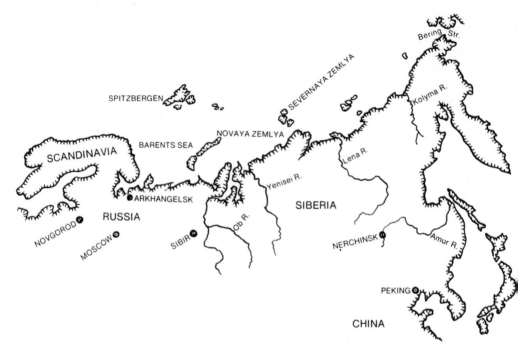

Figure 17. The Northeast Passage

Where Yermak went, other traders followed, pressing eagerly eastward with little effective opposition from the thinly spread primitive peoples in their way. With extraordinary quickness they penetrated to each of the succession of great rivers that cut northward through Siberia to the northern shore.

They began at the Ob River, just 400 kilometers east of the northern Urals. By 1610, they had reached the Yenisei River, 1100 kilometers farther east, and by 1636, the Lena River, 1600 kilometers beyond. By 1644, the Kolyma River was reached, representing yet another 1300-kilometer trek eastward.

The main thrust of the eastward advance was carried out well to the south of the Arctic Circle. Indeed, the modern Trans-Siberian Railroad follows the old explorers' route. However, each river they reached was, quickly enough, followed to its ice-choked mouth, while small boats skirted the shoreline in the area. In this way, the Siberian Arctic was explored farther and farther east.

In 1648, a Cossack named Semyon Ivanov Dezhnev took his ship eastward from the mouth of the Kolyma River, and, having traversed still another 1800 kilometers eastward, he came to the end of Siberia and slipped through a narrow strait (later to be called Bering Strait) into the Pacific Ocean.

In less than seventy years, Russia had stretched its dominions eastward thousands of kilometers across the full width of Asia and gained a land it still retains today (see figure 17).

The Russian explorations showed several things. The northern shore of Russia and Siberia never dipped southward but extended eastward for many thousands of kilometers while remaining north of the Arctic Circle every inch of the way. This means that the Northeast Passage was not a matter of bulldozing one's way through a section of the Arctic and then finding it clear sailing the rest of the way. It meant Arctic, Arctic, Arctic, with only the Bering Strait offering a hole southward.

It was clear then that the Northeast Passage was utterly impractical. Nobody would plunge through all those kilometers of ice-choked water if any alternative at all existed.

On the other hand, if the northern shores of Asia nowhere dipped southward to lead men to the shores of China by a shortcut, neither did they rise northward to envelop the North Pole. All along those thousands of kilometers of Siberian shore there was an unbroken continuation of the same ocean that bathed northern Scandinavia. There seemed to be no North Polar continent. Instead it began to appear that a sizable body of water enveloped the North Pole, and people began to speak of the "Arctic Ocean."

The Russians did, by the way, reach China, but it was not an entirely peaceful feat. When the Russian hunters and traders reached the Amur River in southeastern Siberia, they found the Chinese in possession. The Chinese were not disposed to give way, and Russia could not make its full power felt that far from home. In 1689, Russia and China signed the Treaty of Nerchinsk, at a town on the Amur River about 1350 kilometers north of Peking and 5600 kilometers east of Moscow.

By the terms of that treaty, Russia agreed to withdraw from territory claimed by the Chinese. This was only a temporary solution, however. Russian power in the Far East continued to grow and China's power continued to weaken. Today Nerchinsk and its surrounding territory are part of the Soviet Union and so are other areas that had been under Chinese domination at the time of the treaty.

5

TO THE NORTH POLE

But if the Northeast Passage was impractical, what of the Northwest Passage? If one could not pass around the northern rim of Eurasia, what of the northern rim of North America?

The Spaniards had concentrated most of their exploratory efforts in the warmer latitudes, and in the sixteenth century almost everything north of Florida was an open question. There might be sea passages leading to the Pacific almost anywhere.

To be sure, the Italian navigator John Cabot (an Anglicized version of his name, for he sailed in the pay of England) had touched Newfoundland in 1497. Then, too, the Portuguese navigator Gaspar Corte-Real had spied the coast north of Newfoundland, in 1501, and gave it the Portuguese name, "Labrador," that it still carries. (The word means "slaves," and it came about because Corte-Real picked up some Eskimos and carried them off as slaves.)

These sightings, however, were scarcely dots on the map. Almost anything might exist, almost any hope be fulfilled.

The Northwest Passage

It was the French who made the first attempts at finding a Northwest Passage. In 1524, they outfitted an expedition under an Italian navigator, Giovanni da Verrazano. On March 1, he reached what is now the coast of the United States at Cape Fear. This put him at what is now North Carolina, well north of the Spanish settlements in Florida.

He worked his way northward, reaching New York Bay on April 17 and entering the harbor. He then continued up the coast and poked his ship's nose into Narragansett Bay. Finally he worked his way up to Newfoundland and then returned home. It was clear that North America was a good, solid piece of land at least as far north as Newfoundland. Any search for the Northwest Passage would have to start at Newfoundland and work north.

A French navigator, Jacques Cartier, came west in 1534 and investigated Newfoundland in greater detail, with his two small ships. Between Newfoundland and Labrador, he found an opening which is now called the Strait of Belle Isle, went through it, and came into what seemed a wide inlet of the ocean. Since he entered it on August 10, the day dedicated to Saint Lawrence, he called it the Gulf of St. Lawrence and it still bears that name.

He thought the Gulf of St. Lawrence might be a strait that led into the Pacific Ocean and on to China (and it was perfectly reasonable to think so). As he moved westward, however, the gulf narrowed and narrowed until it looked like a river. He did not give up hope and on a second expedition, when he was stopped by some rapids, he named the area "La Chine" ("China"), a name it still keeps as Lachine—but the name wasn't the place.

He was in the St. Lawrence River and the route did not lead to China. It did, however, lead to a group of great lakes that represented the greatest single body of fresh water anywhere in the world. As a result of Cartier's exploration and of the French explorers who followed him, France seized hold of large stretches of North America along the St. Lawrence River and the Great Lakes, a region that Cartier himself had first given the name of Canada when he misunderstood something the Indian inhabitants had said to him. The French held this region for over two centuries.

If, then, there was to be a Northwest Passage at all, Cartier's expedition demonstrated that it would have to be farther north than Labrador. Considering Labrador's frigid climate, this meant that the Northwest Passage, like the Northeast Passage, might well involve Arctic waters. And yet perhaps there would only be a short voyage through the cold water and then a southward curve into more pleasant latitudes. It was worth looking for.

The first major attempt to move north of Labrador in search of the Northwest Passage was made under English auspices in 1576. Heading the expedition was Martin Frobisher, who sailed to North America with three ships and a crew of thirty-five men. Only one of these ships, with eighteen men aboard, actually completed the crossing.

Frobisher explored the coast of Labrador, then ventured northward. He crossed a strait and reached a large island, the fifth largest in the world, in fact. Both the strait (Hudson Strait) and the island (Baffin Island) are now named for English explorers who did their work a generation after Frobisher.

Frobisher penetrated the southernmost of two large inlets into the southeastern coast of Baffin Island in the hope that this was the beginning of the Northwest Passage. He sent five men forward with a party of Eskimos, hoping they would be guided to the Pacific, but they never returned. Frobisher then returned, and the inlet is called Frobisher Bay in his honor. It reaches as far north as 63° N.—still well south of the Arctic Circle.

Frobisher, and those English explorers who followed him, laid the basis for an English claim to the territories north of French Canada. The territorial disputes that followed in the north, and farther south, too, where the English had established colonies on what is now the eastern coast of the United States, beginning in 1607, continued for nearly two centuries. They ended finally in 1763 in a complete victory for England, or, as it was officially called by then, Great Britain.

The British hold was shaken in the 1770s by the revolt of its southern colonies and the final establishment in 1783 of an independent United States of America.

Canada, however, lying north of the United States, continued to be British, and expanded, as the United States did, until it, like the United States, stretched from the Atlantic Ocean to the Pacific Ocean.

As Canada grew, Great Britain wisely decided not to make its control too tight, and, in 1867, Canada was made a "dominion" within the British Empire, with virtually complete control of its own internal affairs. In 1931, it was recognized (along with other dominions) as equal in every way with Great Britain, politically. Since then it has been an independent country, united with Great Britain only by sentiment and by virtue of recognizing the powerless monarch of Great Britain as the powerless monarch of Canada as well.

Baffin Island, which Frobisher discovered, has an area of 475,000 square kilometers. It is a typically bleak Arctic land, however, with a population today consisting of about 3400 Eskimos. It is part of a large group of islands called the "Arctic Archipelago," or "Queen Elizabeth Islands." Baffin Island, by itself, makes up about a third of the area of the entire archipelago, which consists of a dozen sizable islands and many smaller ones, with a total area of 1,400,000 square kilometers. All of the archipelago (which was to be slowly and painfully explored over the next three centuries) is now part of Canada, which took formal possession of it between 1908 and 1910. All of it, except for the southern third of Baffin Island, is north of the Arctic Circle.

Frobisher's attempt to find the Northwest Passage, in those days of the very first exploration of the archipelago, was aborted by the fact that he came across rocks that glittered yellow and that he took to be gold ore. He brought it back, and at once England experienced a gold fever. Frobisher went back for more, and both he and his English sponsors forgot the Northwest Passage in their interest for more gold. In his second voyage with a much better equipped expedition, Frobisher brought back 200 tons. Then, in 1578, Frobisher led still a third expedition of sixteen ships to Baffin Island. This time storms intervened and Frobisher was forced to return empty-handed.

It was just as well, for by then it was ascertained that the "gold ore" from the northern island was iron pyrites (popularly known as "fool's gold," without a speck of real gold anywhere in it). Frobisher's fool's gold was eventually used for road repair.

On his third voyage, on June 20, 1578, Frobisher caught a glimpse of the southern tip of Greenland, from which, a century and a half before, the last Viking colonists had disappeared. Earlier explorers, notably Corte-Real had also glimpsed it, but it was only after Frobisher's report that the large icy island was never lost to view again. Frobisher, then, might be regarded as its effective discoverer.

There were no attempts to colonize Greenland after its rediscovery and small wonder, for it had become an even more unattractive piece of real estate than it had been in Eric the Red's milder century. The only nation that had any interest in it at all was Denmark (which then included Norway) and that out of pure sentimental memory of the old Viking colony.

In 1721, a Danish missionary, Hans Egede, visited the southwestern coast about where the Vikings had once existed, and worked with the Eskimos there. (He was disappointed at finding only Eskimos, with no sign of anyone who might have been descended from the Vikings.)

From then on, Denmark-Norway continued to maintain close relationships with the Eskimos of Greenland. In 1814, when Norway and Denmark separated, Greenland, like Iceland and the Faeroes, remained under Danish sovereignty. At first, Denmark claimed only southern Greenland, but in 1916 Danish sovereignty over the entire island was recognized. In 1953, it was declared an integral and equal part of Denmark (as Alaska is of the United States).

During World War II and afterward, the United States became and remained extremely interested in Greenland as a military base. This, more than anything else, has brought the Greenland Eskimos into the current of modern civilization. The influx of modern amenities, and of modern medical techniques, has lowered the Eskimo death rate, while leaving the birth rate high. The Eskimo population in Greenland, which was 23,000 in 1950, was 45,000 twenty years later.

Penetrating the Archipelago

Some years after Frobisher's voyages, with the fool's gold fiasco over, the English regained stability and returned to the quest for the Northwest Passage.

The new search was spearheaded by an expedition under John Davis. In 1585, he sailed to Baffin Island and, knowing that Frobisher Bay was a blind alley, went farther north and entered a second inlet, now called Cumberland Sound. It, too, proved to be a blind alley, with its northern tip almost exactly at the Arctic Circle.

In a second voyage, in 1587, Davis moved up the western coast of Greenland and, for the first time, a European ventured beyond the Arctic Circle in the Western Hemisphere. This expedition also represented the first real examination of the island by Europeans since the Vikings. Davis made contact with Eskimos and had his men play instruments and dance for their amusement. The Eskimos were delighted and friendly.

The narrow stretch of water lying between Greenland and the southern portion of Baffin Island, through which Davis passed on this journey, is called Davis Strait in his honor. He went nearly 1600 kilometers up Greenland's western coast, reaching 72.7° N., which lay 650 kilometers north of the Arctic Circle.

It was clear, though, that going up the Davis Strait and exploring the shores of Greenland and Baffin Island simply took the ships farther and farther north. What was needed was a seaway westward, and this Davis did not find, so that the search for the Northwest Passage ended in failure again.

It was Henry Hudson who found the westward seaway that Davis had missed. He was an English navigator who, in 1607, was following up the discoveries of Barents in connection with the Northeast Passage. He examined the eastern coast of Greenland as far north as 73° N. (a little farther north than Davis had ventured up the western coast of the island), found nothing of use, sailed northeastward to Spitzbergen, and then back home.

On his return voyage, he came across a small island, about 375 square kilometers in area, which lay nearly 500 kilometers east of Greenland and about the same distance north of Iceland. He named it after himself, but it didn't keep the name. A Dutch whaler landed there in 1614 and it is now known as "Jan Mayen Island" after him. Like so many other bits of Arctic territory, no nation was in a hurry to take it over. In 1929, however, it was formally annexed to Norway.

Hudson tried to find his way through the ice that blocks the Northeast Passage on each of two more journeys and failed.

Then, in Dutch employ, he tried for the Northwest Passage instead. In 1609, he sailed up a river that entered the sea well north of the brand-new English colony at Virginia, hoping that it might prove to be the sea passage through North America.

It wasn't, though Hudson followed the river 250 kilometers upstream before the gradual shallowing of the water convinced him that it was indeed a river and not a strait. We now call the river which he explored the "Hudson River." As a result of this portion of his voyage, the Dutch laid claim to the area and established a colony and a dominion over the river that lasted for half a century before the region fell to England.

Sailing back to the Netherlands with his report, Hudson was stopped in England and was prevented from working for the Dutch any longer.

In 1610, he tried again, with one ship and a crew of nineteen. He went farther north this time and was in the pay of the English once more. In June of that year he noticed something that both Frobisher and Davis had overlooked.

South of Frobisher Bay, there is a sea passage westward that both Frobisher and Davis had crossed without concern, but to Hudson it didn't look like a mere inlet. He thought it might prove to be a strait lying between Labrador and Baffin Island and that it might be worth exploring.

He sailed into the inlet and made his way westward through considerable ice, to the dissatisfaction of his crew. It proved, indeed, to be a strait, and it is as "Hudson Strait" that it is marked on maps now.

The strait led him farther and farther westward, and, after he had traveled more than 650 kilometers, another inlet that looked like more than an inlet beckoned. It opened southward and that was precisely what Hudson wanted. If he could round the Arctic shore of North America by way of Hudson Strait (which wasn't even truly Arctic, since its northernmost point was at 63° N., well below the Arctic Circle) and then head into more southerly, warmer waters that would carry him the rest of the way to China, he could ask no more.

Alas, it was not to be. What he had entered was merely an inlet after all, an enormous one which we now call "Hudson Bay" in his honor, but one that came to an end. Hudson spent three months in the bay, exploring the eastern shore and reaching the southern portion (a smaller inlet known as "James

Bay" in honor of James I, who then ruled England) in November.

James Bay, lying between 50° and 55° N., was in precisely the stretch of latitude in which England lay, but it was far colder than England. There, in James Bay, Hudson was frozen in for six dreary months. When the ice broke in June 1611, he wanted to continue exploring the western shore in the hope that he might find a passage farther westward, but his crew had had enough. Hudson was set adrift with his son and seven loyal crew members and presumably all died of cold and hunger. (Eight of the mutineers finally reached England and were tried for murder, but there is no record of the results of the trial.)

Other English explorers took up the investigation of Hudson Bay where Hudson himself had left off, and by 1630, its shores were known in detail. England claimed those shores and placed fur-trappers' bases upon them. This "Hudson's Bay Territory" served as the nucleus for its eventual Canadian empire.

In 1612, the English explorer Thomas Button, in exploring Hudson Bay (and, like Hudson himself, being frozen in for the winter), discovered a large island in its mouth. This island, 31,000 square kilometers in size, was named Southampton Island, after the earl of Southampton (better known as a patron of William Shakespeare). It lies south of the Arctic Archipelago and is, in fact, despite its typically Arctic weather, entirely south of the Arctic Circle, as is all of Hudson Bay.

Another great English navigator to tackle the problem of the Northwest Passage was William Baffin. In 1615, he piloted a ship up Davis Strait. Since Hudson Bay was proving useless, Baffin ignored Hudson Strait and decided to probe farther northward.

As he traveled northward through Davis Strait, it widened into a section of the ocean now called Baffin Bay. He reached a point at 78° N., only 1300 kilometers from the North Pole, and was the first to explore the northern coasts of Baffin Island, which is so named in his honor.

North of Baffin Island, he sighted another considerably smaller island, 35,000 square kilometers in area, which is now known as Devon Island. Between the two lay a narrow stretch of water that Baffin named Lancaster Sound, after one of the backers who had financed his expedition.

North of Devon Island was a much larger one, which was eventually named Ellesmere Island in 1852, in honor of Francis Egerton, earl of Ellesmere, who was a writer, a member of Parliament, and a patron of artists. Between Devon Island and Ellesmere Island was a second narrow stretch of water, which Baffin called Jones Sound, after a second backer. Then,

Figure 18. The Northwest Passage to 1650

between Ellesmere Island and Greenland was still a third narrow stretch of water, leading northward, and this Baffin called Smith Sound after a third backer (see figure 18).

Baffin decided that all three sounds were mere inlets and blind alleys and that there was no way out of Baffin Bay, which was a cul-de-sac altogether. Actually, he was wrong. All three were straits, though in view of ice conditions, they were scarcely comfortable waterways.

Baffin's unfavorable report on Baffin Bay caused the English to give up on the Northwest Passage, even as Europeans generally were giving up on the Northeast Passage.

Besides, the two passages had lost their significance even if they had existed. For one thing, as the seventeenth century progressed, Spain and Portugal declined in power and no longer offered any significant threat to England and the Netherlands on the oceans. Indeed, both England and the Netherlands became the most important maritime nations in the world, and each could, and did, use the Southeast Passage and the Southwest Passage freely.

Then, too, the North American continent was being colonized for its own sake by the English and Dutch and French, as well as by the Spanish and Portuguese. North America became increasingly important to Europe, and had value in itself, and was no longer merely an obstacle to be skirted.

It followed, then, that, after about 1650, Arctic exploration no longer involved a desperate attempt to find a way to China. Such exploration as followed served to appease the curiosity of explorers and scientists, rather than the cupidity of merchants. Naturally, it proceeded at a slower pace.

Some overland exploration continued, however. An Englishman, Samuel Hearne, in search of copper mines, trekked from Hudson Bay northwestward in 1771. He walked more than 2000 kilometers and reached the Arctic shore of North America at the mouth of what he called (hopefully) the Coppermine River.

The Coast of Siberia

The first Arctic expedition intended solely to increase knowledge was sponsored by Russia.

In 1682, a ten-year-old boy had come to the throne as Peter I (eventually to be known as "the Great"). Under him, Russia was brought into the mainstream of European history. Peter ruled over an immense realm, thanks to the activities of the Russian fur trappers, but those fur trappers had reported only sketchily of their explorations. They were interested in furs, not reports. It occurred to Peter, therefore, to have the shores of his new realms accurately surveyed and mapped so that he could find out, for one thing, whether the report of Semyon Dezhnev, three-quarters of a century before, was correct, and that Siberia was not, after all, connected with North America.

In 1724, Peter I placed Vitus Jonassen Bering (a Danish mariner who had long served in the Russian navy) at the head of the projected expedition. Peter died the next year, but Bering carried on with the support of Peter's widow, who now ruled as Catherine I. Traveling overland for 8000 kilometers, Bering made his way from St. Petersburg to Kamchatka, a large peninsula jutting southward from far eastern Siberia. There he built ships and began a sea exploration intended to settle whether Siberia came to an end or not.

He explored the coasts of Kamchatka and followed the southeastern shore of Siberia till he came to its end at what is now the Bering Strait. This was named for him rather than for Dezhnev, whose sketchy report had proved of uncertain value. However, the easternmost point of land in Siberia is "Cape Dezhnev."

Unfortunately, cloudy weather prevented Bering from seeing the land on the other side of the strait, and he did not realize quite how narrow it was. At its narrowest point, it is only 85 kilometers wide, and it is that short distance that separates Asia and North America. This line of narrowest separation straddles the 66° N. parallel and is just south of the Arctic Circle.

On his return, Bering spotted a pair of small islands in the Bering Strait. He named them the Diomede Islands. The larger is called "Big Diomede" and the other "Little Diomede."

In later expeditions, Bering charted portions of Siberia's northern shore and also explored the sea to the south of Bering Strait, a stretch of water now known as "Bering Sea" in his honor. He discovered the Aleutian Islands, which swing across the southern border of the Bering Sea in a great arc.

Bering also landed on the North American continent in 1741, becoming the first European to reach what is now Alaska. That same year, however, he died on Bering Island, the westernmost of the Aleutian chain, only 240 kilometers off the Kamchatka shore. Bering Island and a few neighboring ones make up the Komandorskie Islands (Russian for "commander," which is also in honor of Bering).

On the basis of Bering's exploration, Russia claimed the possession of the Aleutian Islands and of Alaska. The Russian grip expanded slowly until it corresponded with the present boundaries of Alaska by the mid-nineteenth century. However, Alaska was too far from home to govern effectively, and its existence offered possible problems with the growing power of the United States.

In 1867, the United States bought Alaska from the Russians for $7,200,000. It was organized as a United States territory in 1912 and in 1959 it became the forty-ninth state of the Union. Included in its territory are most of the Aleutian Islands, though the westernmost Komandorskie Islands remain Russian. The boundary cuts right through the Bering Strait and between the two Diomede islands. Big Diomede is Soviet now, and Little Diomede is American. This means that at that point a 3-kilometer stretch of water is all that separates the two strongest nations on Earth.

The northern third of Alaska lies north of the Arctic Circle, so that since 1867 there has been Arctic territory that is American. It had been explored by Russians before the sale, and the northernmost point of Alaska (and of the United States) was reached by them. It is Point Barrow, which lies at 71.26° N., just a few kilometers farther north than North Cape, the northernmost point of Norway (and Europe), which is at 71.17° N.

Others besides Bering explored the Siberian coast. Under the leadership of S. Chelyuskin, Russian explorers finally managed, in 1743, to go around the Taimyr Peninsula, which juts northward out of the center of the Siberian shore and is icebound throughout the year.

Ships couldn't round the Taimyr through the ice, but Chelyuskin rounded it by sledge and the northernmost point of the peninsula is "Cape Chelyuskin" in his honor. Nor did anyone else repeat Chelyuskin's feat for another century and a half.

Cape Chelyuskin is at 77.75° N. and is considerably farther north than either Point Barrow in Alaska or North Cape in Europe. It is only 1400 kilometers south of the North Pole and is the most northerly point of *any* continental area in the world. The only land that lies nearer the North Pole than Cape

Chelyuskin does are parts of islands, notably, among those already discovered at the time of Chelyuskin's expedition, Spitzbergen, Greenland, and Ellesmere Island.

There remained Arctic islands to be discovered farther south than the Cape Chelyuskin high point, too. About 725 kilometers east of the Taimyr Peninsula is a group of islands lying north of the Siberian coast. These were first sighted in 1770 by a Russian fur merchant named Lyakhov. As a group, these are known in English as "New Siberian Islands" and all are now part of the Soviet Union. The largest and most northern of these is Kotelny Island, whose northernmost point is at 76.3° N. The two southernmost islands of the group are called the Lyakhov Islands after the discoverer.

A non-Russian also added to knowledge concerning Siberia at about this time. In 1778, the British explorer Captain James Cook sailed through the Bering Strait under atmospheric conditions that allowed him to see both sides of the strait, the American as well as the Asian. For the first time, the close approach of the two continents was fully described.

Scraps of land off the coast of Siberia continued to be discovered for another century and a half. Thus, an island north of the east Siberian coastline had been reported by a Russian explorer, Ferdinand Petrovich von Wrangel. He was repeating rumor and, in 1823, he failed to find it himself. The island in question was finally spotted by an American whaler, Thomas Long, in 1867, and the first actual landing was by an American naval officer, Calvin Hooper, in 1881. He called it "New Columbia," and it is only about 5000 square kilometers in area.

The island is only 150 kilometers off the Siberian shore. That and its general undesirability made neither the United States, nor any other nation, desirous of disputing the possession of it with Russia. Russia laid claim to it in 1916, and in the 1920s the Soviet Union (as Russia came to be called after the Russian Revolution of 1917) occupied it, together with a few small nearby islands. It is now known as "Wrangel Island" after the man who never saw it.

In 1871, a new attempt was made to navigate the Northeast Passage (which had never yet been carried out entirely by sea because the uncircumnavigable Taimyr Peninsula stood in the way). This was led by Julius von Payer and Karl Weyprecht of Austria-Hungary (a nation not generally active in Arctic

exploration). They attempted to make their way around
Novaya Zemlya and, in exploring the waters between that
island and Spitzbergen, they came upon islands, on August 30,
1873, which had hitherto evaded all eyes. It was an archipelago
of about 21,000 square kilometers in area.

They called it Franz Josef Land after the ruler of Austria-
Hungary. The northernmost island of the group lies at 82° N.,
which makes it farther north than Spitzbergen and represents
the farthest northward reach of any land in the Eastern
Hemisphere. It lay unclaimed for fifty years and it was not till
1928 that the Soviet Union, which had been exploring the
islands, announced its annexation.

The Swedish explorer Nils Adolf Erik Nordenskjöld was the
first to navigate the Northeast Passage entirely by ship,
between 1878 and 1879. To be sure, he was frozen in when he
rounded Cape Chelyuskin (which he reached for the first time
since Chelyuskin's original feat). But he remained through the
winter, then went on when the ice broke, forcing his way
through.

The last important bodies of land in the Arctic were
discovered in 1913 when a Russian explorer, B. Vilkitski,
discovered three fairly large islands (13,000 square kilometers
each) north of the Taimyr Peninsula, separated from it by what

Figure 19. The Siberian Arctic

is now called Vilkitski Strait. The three islands were named "Nicholas II Land" after the Russian czar. After the Russian Revolution, they were renamed "Severnaya Zemlya" ("Northern Land"), and each of the three islands received good Communist names. Reading from north to south the islands are Komsomolets Island ("Communist Youth"), October Revolution Island, and Bolshevik Island.

With that, the outline of the land areas of the Soviet Arctic was complete (see figure 19).

The Coast of Canada

In the non-Russian Arctic, activity at the time was greatest in the Spitzbergen region, where in the seventeenth and eighteenth centuries, whalers had gone enthusiastically to work at their senseless massacre of whales that produced nothing for which there were not perfectly adequate substitutes. In the end they brought about the virtual destruction of some species of the great northern whales.

William Scoresby was an English whaler who made his fortune at the trade. In the hunt for the poor giants, Scoresby explored the east coast of Greenland, where the largest inlet on that coast, just above the 70° N. line, is called "Scoresby Sound" in his honor. The land to its north is "Scoresby Land." Scoresby sailed north of Spitzbergen and on May 25, 1806, reached the latitude of 81.5° N., a new record. He had come to less than 970 kilometers from the North Pole.

Partly to search out further haunts of the whale, and partly out of a desire to chart the Canadian coastline, the British government took up the search for the Northwest Passage in the nineteenth century at the point where Baffin had left it nearly two centuries before.

The leading spirit in this was John Barrow, a world traveler who had been in China and South Africa. He persuaded the British government to offer 20,000 pounds to anyone completing the Northwest Passage and 5000 pounds to anyone reaching a latitude of 89° N. (It was in Barrow's honor that Point Barrow, the northernmost point in Alaska, was named.)

In 1818, the first expedition of the nineteenth century searching for the Northwest Passage sailed into Baffin Bay. It was under John Ross, and second in command was William Edward Parry. Ross, retracing Baffin's trip, reached Lancaster

Sound, which bounds Baffin Island on the north. It seemed to Ross that he could make out high land blocking the sound in the distance and, like Baffin before him, he came to the conclusion that Baffin Bay was a dead end.

Parry was not so sure Lancaster Sound was worthless. He returned to Baffin Bay the next year with an expedition of his own. He pushed his way into Lancaster Sound and found that it was indeed a strait. He continued on for nearly 650 kilometers to what is now called Melville Island, one of the westerly islands of the Arctic Archipelago.

By that time, Parry had gone far enough west to win a 5000-pound reward offered by the British government for the first person penetrating past 100 degrees west longitude. The tier of islands north of Baffin Island (of which Melville Island is the largest) is named "Parry Islands" in his honor.

Parry wintered on Melville Island, then tried to continue on through the body of water that lay south of Melville Island, and that is now called "McClure Strait." The ice stopped him and he turned back. He had crossed half the northern coast of Canada, and what he did not know was that he had almost made it. Had he gotten through that last channel and had the ice not stopped him, he would have been past the archipelago. Nothing but ice (bad enough) would then have lain between him and the Bering Strait passage to the Pacific Ocean.

In 1820, Parry returned to the Arctic challenge, and tried to make his way around the southern shore of the northwestern end of Baffin Island. He remained there for two winters but could not get through the very narrow, ice-choked "Fury and Hecla Strait" as he named it (after his two ships).

In 1824, Parry tried a third time. This time it was north of Baffin Island again, but instead of continuing westward, he turned south after emerging from Lancaster Sound through the Prince Regent Inlet (named for the son of George III who by then was reigning as George IV). It didn't seem promising and he turned back.

Then, in 1833, John Ross tried again. This time it was a private venture, financed by Felix Booth, who had made his money in the liquor business. Ross sailed through the Prince Regent Inlet and into a gulf that lay on the other side of Fury and Hecla Strait. Ross called it the Gulf of Boothia after his sponsor. Unfortunately, it proved to be a dead end to the west, being bounded by the Boothia Peninsula.

Boothia Peninsula, as it turned out, represents the north-ernmost stretch of the continent, reaching to an extreme of 71.74° N., about 60 kilometers farther north than Point Barrow, but falling 265 kilometers short of the mark of Cape Chelyuskin.

Between them, Parry and Ross had mapped much of the eastern half of the Canadian Arctic, but the Northwest Passage had not yet been penetrated to the end.

The next attempt was made by John Franklin. While Parry and Ross had been charting unknown areas by sea, Franklin had been doing the same by land. He headed expeditions that in 1820 and 1825 had mapped almost the entire Arctic coast of Canada, a stretch of about 1600 kilometers, from Hudson Bay to the Mackenzie River. At times he and his men had to live on lichens and leather, but most of them survived. Now Franklin intended to try exploring by sea. With two ships and 129 men he sailed westward from Great Britain in 1845. He had the best and strongest equipment up to his time; the ships were propeller-driven steamships and had hot-water-heated cabins.

He followed Parry's trail, going north of Baffin Island and entering Lancaster Sound, and then he disappeared. He was not heard of again.

The loss captured the imagination of the English public and from then on, for fourteen years, expedition after expedition sailed to the Canadian Arctic, not primarily to explore, but to find out what had happened to Franklin. Altogether about forty separate expeditions went out in search of Franklin in those fourteen years. Four of them were sent out by Franklin's wife, who resorted to spiritualism in the hope that the spirits might prepare maps to guide the navigators.

Of course, those who searched for Franklin could not help but do a bit of exploration as well. The Scottish explorer John Rae, while on the track of Franklin, discovered in 1847 that the Boothia Peninsula was the farthest north piece of continental land in North America. He was also the first to get word from Eskimos concerning Franklin and, in 1853, he obtained objects that were clearly relics of the expedition. He won a 10,000-pound prize for this. In the course of further explorations, he reported on Victoria Island (named for the British queen), which is the third largest island of the archipelago. (Ellesmere Island is second largest.) He also explored the considerably smaller King William Island to the east of Victoria Island. Rae

was the first European to recognize the value of adopting an
Eskimo way of life for survival in the Arctic.

It was an expedition under Francis Leopold McClintock that
finally uncovered the details of the sad end of the Franklin
party. In 1859, the members of the expedition found skeletons
on King William Island. This lies southwest of the Boothia
Peninsula, so Franklin had evidently gotten past that hurdle. A
journal was found in which the details of the sad end were
given. They had been penned in by ice and had had to abandon
their ships. They struggled southward and in the second
winter, Franklin died. Still plodding away, the rest of the party
died of cold and scurvy as they walked through their third
winter. Not one survived. The frozen remains of thirty of the
men were eventually found.

In the course of the search for Franklin, the coastlines of
most of the islands of the Arctic Archipelago were worked
out—11,000 kilometers of them.

It was also in the course of the search for Franklin that the
first American expedition into the Arctic was launched in 1850.
It was financed by a New Bedford, Massachusetts, merchant,
Henry Grinnell, and the western peninsula of Devon Island is
named Grinnell Peninsula in his honor.

And yet again in the course of the search, a British naval
officer, Robert John McClure, had attempted to tackle the
matter of the Northwest Passage from the other end. He went
through the Bering Strait northward in 1850, then sailed
eastward. He came upon Banks Island, the westernmost island
of the archipelago, and discovered the Prince of Wales Strait
that lay between it and Victoria Island to its southeast.

McClure (after whom McClure Strait was named) was forced
to abandon his ships on the northern shore of Banks Island, but
this was just across the strait from Melville Island, which had
been reached by Parry. Between them, then, Parry and
McClure had demonstrated that the Northwest Passage existed, in the sense that one could trace an all-water route from
Europe to Asia around the northern shores of North America
(see figure 20).

McClure, who had added the last link, was knighted in 1854.
He and his crew shared a 10,000-pound prize for the feat. It
was plain, however, that the victory was not very meaningful.
The ice and the tortuous channels among the islands of the
archipelago made the Northwest Passage impractical.

The Northwest Passage was not navigated in its entirety until the Norwegian explorer Roald Amundsen accomplished it in leisurely fashion between 1903 and 1906.

Greenland

The greatest prize among the Arctic islands was, however and beyond all doubt, Greenland. Larger than all the other islands

Figure 20. The Canadian Arctic

put together, it was almost continental in size. In fact, it is always called Green*land*, never Greenland Island.

It had been known continuously since the late sixteenth century, and by the late nineteenth century, after three hundred years, it was still only part of the coastline that was known. It had never been circumnavigated, no one knew how far north it extended, and its interior had never been seen by the eyes of man.

The west coast was best known. The southern part was sprinkled with Danish settlements, while to the north English and American explorers were probing.

As early as 1818, Ross on his expedition into Baffin Bay had reached what came to be called Hayes Peninsula, jutting westward out of northwestern Greenland and bordering the northern shore of the bay. He noted Eskimos living there at a latitude of 77° N. and named the southwestern tip of the peninsula Cape York. (It was at Cape York, almost as near the North Pole as is the northern rim of Taimyr Peninsula, that the United States established an air force base during World War II. Rather appropriately it was named Thule, in honor of the mysterious far northern land discovered by Pytheas—and the air base is a truer Ultima Thule than anything Pytheas could possibly have reached.)

An American explorer, Elisha Kent Kane (who had helped in the search for Franklin), was the first to work his way northward into Smith Sound, between 1853 and 1855. There, between Greenland and Ellesmere Island, he found a widening of the passage which is now called Kane Basin and which bounds Hayes Peninsula on the north. He reached 80.6° N. before ice prevented him from going farther.

Another American explorer, Charles Francis Hall (who had also been involved in the search for Franklin), lived among the Eskimos for two years, adapting himself to their ways. In 1871, he went northward with a well-equipped naval vessel and the blessing of Congress. He had luck with the ice and managed to push past Kane Basin into the narrow waters that lay between northern Ellesmere Island and Greenland and reached 82.2° N., a new northerly record. It was clear that both Ellesmere Island and Greenland reached considerably farther north than any other piece of land known at the time.

Hall died shortly after going into winter quarters, but his crew managed to get away to safety in the spring of 1872.

The eastern coast lagged behind, as it always had since Viking days. In 1869, however, the Germans organized a great Greenland expedition for the specific purpose of tackling that east coast. It was commanded by the German explorer Karl Christian Koldewey, who had already cut his teeth by leading the first German expedition into the Spitzbergen area. (Germany was then in the process of becoming unified into a modern nation and was beginning a 70-year period during which it was to be the strongest military power on Earth.) With him was the Austrian Julius von Payer, who a few years later was to be one of the discoverers of Franz Josef Land.

Koldewey followed the eastern coast northward, reaching 77° N. in 1870. There he explored a small peninsula jutting out of the eastern shore at that point and called it Germania Land. Its southeasternmost projection he called Cape Bismarck after the Prussian chancellor who completed the unification of Germany in that year.

The Danish explorer Ludvig Mylius-Erichsen explored still farther north in 1906 and 1907 (and ended by being one of the numerous Arctic explorers who died of cold, hunger, and exhaustion in the course of his explorations). He discovered Northeast Foreland, which is a peninsula jutting out of northeastern Greenland at about 82° N., and which represents the most easterly part of the island.

The interior of Greenland represented a more difficult challenge than even the coasts, for it was entirely covered by ice.

The Danish explorer Jens A. D. Jensen made the first significant penetration of the ice. Beginning on the southwestern shore at 62.8° N. (below the Arctic Circle), he moved about 70 kilometers inland in 1878, reaching an icy height of about 1.5 kilometers above sea level.

Later explorers went both farther north and farther inland. Nordenskjöld in 1883, reasonably fresh from his triumphant completion of the Northeast Passage, penetrated 130 kilometers at 68.3° N. and was the first to explore the interior of Greenland north of the Arctic Circle. Then the American explorer Robert Edwin Peary penetrated 160 kilometers into Greenland at 69.5° N. in 1886. He reached a height of 2.2 kilometers above sea level.

In 1888, the Norwegian explorer Fridtjof Nansen achieved a kind of climax to these efforts by becoming the first to cross the

Figure 21. Greenland

ice and to travel overland from one coast of Greenland to the other. He did this, on snowshoes and skis, east to west at 64.4° N., a line somewhat below the Arctic Circle, where Greenland is about 520 kilometers wide. At one point on this trip, Nansen found himself 2.7 kilometers above sea level.

In 1892, Peary explored the ice northward and found the limit of its extension at about 82° N. Farther northward was a bare and barren stretch of land which is now called Peary Land. There was some question at first as to whether it might not be an island lying north of Greenland, but the Danish explorer Knud J. V. Rasmussen showed, in 1912, that it was an integral part of Greenland.

As the twentieth century opened, then, the northernmost

extensions of those most far northern of all far northern lands, Ellesmere Island and Greenland, were worked out. They did come to an end; they did not extend to the North Pole and beyond (see figure 21).

The northernmost point of Ellesmere Island (Cape Columbia) is at 83° N., which is 235 kilometers closer to the North Pole than Cape Chelyuskin is. As for Greenland, its northmost point, at the northern end of Peary Land, is Cape Morris Jesup (named for an American banker and philanthropist who financed Arctic expeditions). Cape Morris Jesup is at 83.63° N., about 25 kilometers farther north than Cape Columbia is.

As it turned out, Cape Morris Jesup has the unusual distinction of being the northernmost piece of land in the world. It lies 725 kilometers from the North Pole.

Across the Sea Ice

There was no way of telling by sea voyages alone, of course, whether there was any land closer to the North Pole than the northern tip of Greenland was. Men could sail only so far north and then the ice would stop them, for most of the Arctic Ocean is covered by a permanent layer of sea ice.

In the Eastern Hemisphere, the ice extends down as far as 71° N. In the Western Hemisphere, ships can sometimes penetrate as far as 84° N. through the channel between Ellesmere Island and Greenland. There are, however, at least 7,500,000 square kilometers of the northernmost portion of the North Polar region inaccessible to surface vessels.

William Scoresby, who had explored the Spitzbergen region in 1806, was the first to recognize this fact, and he suggested that any attempt to reach the North Pole itself be carried through on sledges. The first to translate this into an actual attempt was William Parry, who, in 1827, set out from northern Spitzbergen on sledges and reached a latitude of 82.75° N.

As the nineteenth century wore on and more and more of the Arctic lands were explored, there came about an increased desire to reach the North Pole. If it accomplished nothing more, the person who carried it through would have the glory of being the first to stand at the northern end of the world, a feat that might later be duplicated but never surpassed.

In 1875, the British explorer George Strong Nares was

tracing the northern shores of Ellesmere Island (and the channel between that island and Greenland is now known as Nares Strait) and reached as far north as one could get. Various members of the expedition then ventured out over the ice by sledge, and one of them, Albert Hastings Markham, reached 83.33° N., a new record.

In 1881, an American explorer, Adolphus Washington Greely, followed in Nares' tracks, hoping to beat the record. He did—by 6 kilometers, to 83.40° N.—but was trapped in the ice. Relief expeditions were bungled and in the end, only seven of the twenty-five on the expedition survived. Greely himself was among the survivors and he lived on to 1935, dying at the age of ninety-one.

Meanwhile, an even more spectacular disaster involved another American explorer.

George Washington de Long decided, in 1879, to try for the North Pole from the Eastern Hemisphere. He was financed in the attempt by James Gordon Bennett, the publisher of the *New York Herald*, who eight years before had won a vast publicity coup by sending Stanley to find Dr. Livingston in Africa.

At the time there was the feeling that Wrangel Island, whose southern shore was the only part explored, might be the southern tip of a sizable piece of land that might stretch well northward toward the North Pole. De Long intended to go by ship as far north as he could along the Wrangel shores and then sledge the rest of the way to the pole.

Unfortunately the Arctic ice extends farthest south at just about the region De Long was going to tackle. De Long's ship was trapped in the ice on September 6, 1879, near a small island to the east of Wrangel, which he named Herald Island for his backer's newspaper. The trapped ship drifted helplessly westward north of Wrangel Island (which De Long was thus able to establish as a small piece of land after all).

After drifting till June 1881, the ship broke up near the New Siberian Islands and De Long and his crew made it on foot to the Siberian shore, but most of them, including De Long, died. Only two out of the crew of thirty-two survived.

The venture was not wholly in vain, however. The fact was that the ship drifted, thousands of kilometers, not only to the New Siberian Islands, but farther west still after the remnants had been abandoned. Parts of it were located a year or two later on the shore of southwestern Greenland. It had clearly drifted right across the Arctic Ocean—another piece of evidence that there might well be unbroken sea north of the land already discovered.

It occurred to Nansen (who had been the first to cross the Greenland ice) that a ship, specially constructed to withstand the ice, might deliberately let itself be trapped in ice in such a way as to let itself be carried across the North Pole. After all, if one places a ruler across the Arctic Ocean from the New Siberian Islands, where De Long's ship broke up, to the western coast of Greenland, where relics were found, the straight line passes very near the pole.

In 1893, Nansen put his plan into effect. He built a vessel, the *Fram* ("Forward"), which was designed to resist being crushed by ice, rising upward when pressed from both sides. With support from the Norwegian government, Nansen took his ship to the New Siberian Islands near where De Long's ship broke up and deliberately drove the *Fram* into the ice.

The ship drifted toward Greenland, but (alas) not in a straight line. After moving northward to 80° N., it began to drift west of north, never attaining a northward position much in excess of the 85° N. mark, and then curving southward again west of Spitzbergen, where it arrived in 1896.

On March 14, 1895, when it was clear that the *Fram* was beginning to drift southward, Nansen and a companion left the ship and started northward on dog sleds. They shot bears and walruses, living on the meat and blubber, Eskimo-fashion. They reached 86.22° N. on April 8, 1895, before being forced to turn back (and wintering in Franz Josef Land where they spent eight months in a crude stone hut). It was a new northern record. Nansen had come to within 420 kilometers of the North Pole and had gotten back without losing a man.

Nansen's measurements showed the Arctic Ocean was deep and that it seemed to be getting deeper as one went northward. That made it seem clearer that there was no likelihood of significant quantities of land beyond what was already known, and further exploration became little more than a race for the pole.

Peary was most active in this race. He decided to use the northern reaches of Ellesmere Island as his base, since it was the farthest north one could go by surface vessel through open water and would leave him the shortest distance (less than 800 kilometers) for sledging over ice.

In 1905, his first major attempt from Ellesmere Island brought him to 87.10° N., just 320 kilometers from his goal, before he was forced to turn back. It was a new record, of course, but he wasn't satisfied.

In 1908, he returned to Ellesmere Island for another attempt. He let his ship freeze into the ice on the north shore of the island, then prepared for his push with the aid of 225 Eskimos who cooperated fully.

In late February 1909, Peary started with a large party, including 24 men, 133 dogs, and 19 sledges carrying 6500 pounds of supplies. Depots were established en route, with some of the party dropping off at each depot. Finally Peary, his dog-sled driver, Matthew Hensen (a Black), three Eskimos, and some dogs made the final dash from the northernmost depot. According to the report he brought back, he reached the North Pole on April 6, 1909.

There he slept off exhaustion for 3 hours, then stayed 30 hours more, taking soundings through the ice to get an idea of the ocean depth and taking notes on the weather. He then returned, following his own tracks in the other direction and making use of the depots built on the trip northward. By April 25, he was back on his ship.

The increasing success of Arctic exploration was due to the fact that explorers gradually consented to dress and live Eskimo-style and to use dog power, rather than man power, in pulling sledges.

Vilhjalmur Stefansson, a Canadian-American born of Icelandic parents, carried Eskimo methods to the logical end. From 1906 on, he learned to live for long periods without relying on outside help—and to do so comfortably. He helped remove some of the aura of horror concerning the Arctic which had arisen as the result of the nineteenth-century disasters. From 1913 to 1918 he mapped large areas of the still unexplored portions of the Canadian Arctic, discovering the last remaining bits of land in the archipelago. In 1918 he set up the first scientific station on an ice floe drifting in the Arctic Ocean. For eight months he and his party observed the ice and tides while floating some 650 kilometers.

But then came a development that made all previous

exploratory techniques obsolete. Man ceased to be entirely dependent on surface transportation. The airplane, indifferent to the nature of the surface—whether land, water, or ice—and much faster than any other kind of travel, reduced the difficulties tremendously.

In May 1925, Amundsen and the American explorer Lincoln Ellsworth flew in two airplanes from Spitzbergen to a point at 87.7° N., 260 kilometers from the pole. They landed there and managed to get one of the planes to take off again so that they returned safely. Not only could a point so far north be reached with unprecedented ease, but from the planes a much more panoramic view of the surface could be seen than was conceivably possible from the surface.

Figure 22. The Arctic

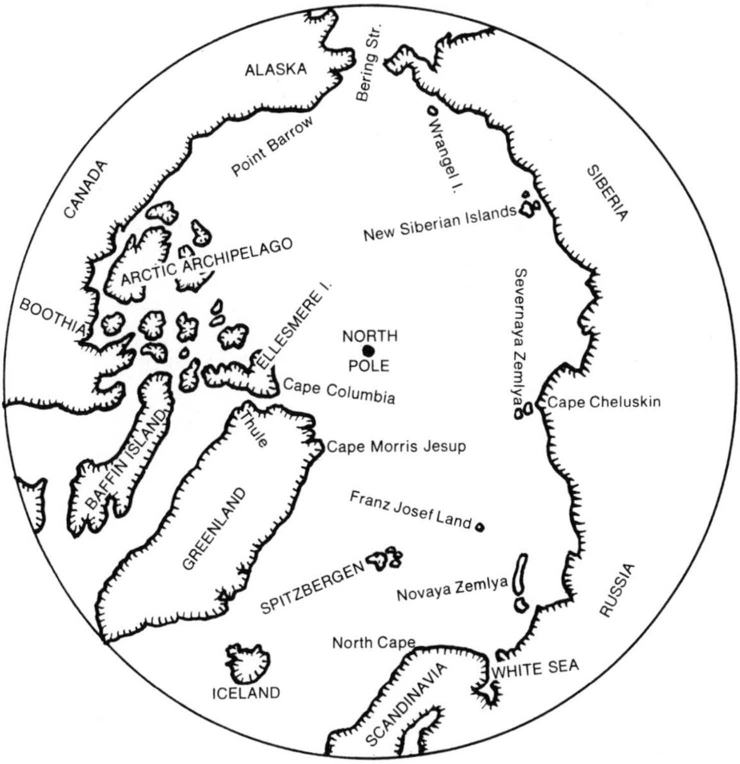

Later flights by both planes and dirigibles amply confirmed the suspicion that there was no significant land that had not been discovered by 1914 (when Severnaya Zemlya had been discovered north of Cape Chelyuskin).

The first to cross the Arctic Ocean by plane was an Australian explorer, Hubert Wilkins, who had been with the Stefansson 1913–1918 expedition in Canada. On April 15, 1928, he and Carl Ben Eielson took off from Point Barrow, Alaska, and flew directly across the Arctic Ocean to Spitzbergen, a distance of 3400 kilometers, in 20.5 hours.

On May 9, 1929, the Americans Richard Byrd and Floyd Bennett flew from Spitzbergen to the North Pole and back in a nonstop flight that lasted only 15 hours. If the shades of earlier explorers who had spent weary, tortured months to gain a few miles could have foreseen that such things would someday be possible, how chagrined they would have been.

If airplanes could fly above the ice, submarines could swim below it. In 1931, Wilkins began to make attempts to go under the ice with a decrepit submarine he had managed to salvage and which he called *Nautilus*. He failed, but in 1958 a nuclear submarine (also called *Nautilus**) traveled from the Bering Strait to the waters west of Spitzbergen. The underwater voyage moved by a route that took the submarine exactly over the North Pole and under the ice.

As far as simple map-extending exploration is concerned, then, nothing in the Arctic remains to be done (see figure 22).

---

* This is not such a coincidence as might be thought. Jules Verne made use of a submarine he called *Nautilus* in his very popular *Twenty Thousand Leagues Under the Sea* which had been published in 1869. After that, *Nautilus* always seemed a natural name for submarines.

TO THE SOUTH POLE

hile the Arctic was penetrated and the North Pole was reached after four centuries of exploration, what about the Antarctic regions?

These were discovered, in theory, by the Greeks, of course. If the Arctic existed, the Antarctic had to exist as well. The Greeks, however, were far closer to the North Pole than to the South Pole, so the first attempts poleward, as by Pytheas, were bound to be north rather than south.

This was true of all the ancient civilizations that flourished in the days of ancient Greek astronomy. The Roman Empire lay entirely in the North Temperate Zone, for its southernmost extension was at Syene in Egypt (the modern Aswan) which is at 24° N., some 65 kilometers north of the Tropic of Cancer.

The Persian Empire and the Chinese Empire were also in the North Temperate Zone. The contemporary Indian civilization, the most southerly of them all, had half its area in the Tropic Zone, but even it didn't reach the equator. The southern shores of the island of Ceylon, the farthest southward extension of ancient Indian civilization, are at 6° N., about 630 kilometers north of the equator.

As for that part of the ancient world which we know best—the Greek and Roman civilizations rimming the Mediterranean Sea—we can say that all their works were entirely limited to the Northern Hemisphere. No Greek and no Roman, as far as we know, ever ventured as far south as the equator. There was, of course, the Phoenician expedition that Herodotus spoke of, that seems to have circumnavigated Africa. They (who were neither Greek nor Roman) represent the farthest southward venture of civilization prior to modern times.

Skirting the Continents

In 1488, the Portuguese navigator Bartholomeu Dias finally duplicated the Phoenician feat of two thousand years before, by reaching the southern tip of Africa. Since he brought the area permanently to the consciousness of the world generally, he may be considered the effective discoverer of South Africa. In the course of his voyage, Dias passed completely through the entire width of the Tropic Zone and penetrated the South Temperate Zone, for southern Africa extends 1200 kilometers southward past the Tropic of Capricorn.

There is a cape beyond which the steadily southward trend of the African shoreline changes to eastward rather sharply. Dias called it "Cape of Storms," since he came upon it only after a storm had driven him far out of his planned course. John II of Portugal, however, on receiving the report, jubilantly renamed it Cape of Good Hope (which it still bears) because the eastward turn of the coastline gave good hope that the continent of Africa had now been successfully skirted and that the Southwest Passage to India would soon be successfully completed—and so it was, only nine years later.

The Cape of Good Hope is not, nevertheless, actually the southern tip of the continent, for though the coastline runs eastward, it bellies a little southward, too. The true southernmost point of Africa is at Cape Agulhas, which lies 160 kilometers east of the Cape of Good Hope and extends some 65 kilometers farther south.

Cape Agulhas is at 34.87° S. This is not really very far south, for all that it represented an astonishing record for 1488. Cape

Agulhas is no nearer the South Pole than Chattanooga, Tennessee, is to the North Pole.

At the time there was no push to explore farther south than Cape Agulhas. Africa was merely in the way of navigators who were heading for the Far East. It was enough to round it as quickly as possible—and that was it.

So unimportant did Africa, or at least its southern tip, seem to European traders that it was not till 1652, more than a century and a half after Dias' voyage, that a European settlement was established on the southern tip of Africa, the first "far south" region to be discovered. The settlement was by the Dutch who, at first, used it only as a way station for ships sailing on to the Far East.

The Dutch remained in control until the time of the Napoleonic Wars; then, in 1814, the area was ceded to Great Britain. Dutch settlers retreated northward, and friction between the Dutch Boers and the British culminated in the Boer War from 1899 to 1902, in which the British were narrowly victorious. In 1910, the Union of South Africa was made a self-governing dominion under the British monarch, and, in 1961, it withdrew from all connection with Great Britain and declared itself a republic.

The population of South Africa now includes about 4,000,000 people of European descent who dominate the country, and some 14,000,000 Blacks and 2,000,000 other non-Whites, who are dominated.

Yet if the discovery of the southern tip of Africa led to nothing, immediately, in the way of Antarctic exploration, there remained a newly discovered continent which also stretched down into the Southern Hemisphere, and which, too, it seemed desirable to skirt.

In 1517, a disaffected Portuguese navigator, Ferdinand Magellan, suggested to the Spanish king, Charles I (better known as the German emperor, Charles V), that the Portuguese monopoly of Far Eastern trade by way of the Southeast Passage might be broken by way of a Southwest Passage around the southern edge of South America. Of course, no one knew how far south South America extended or where along its coasts a sea passage through the continent might be found. That was for Magellan to discover, and that he undertook to do.

Magellan left Spain on September 20, 1519. He probed his way down the eastern coast of South America, investigating every sizable inlet in the hope that it would prove to be an ocean passage across the land barrier.

On December 13, 1519, Magellan probed the Bay of Rio de Janeiro and found it to be a dead end. He edged on southward to the Rio de la Plata, on which the city of Buenos Aires now stands, but that merely led into two rivers. That was a blow, for the Rio de la Plata is already at the latitude of Cape Agulhas, so that South America clearly extended southward farther than Africa did.

Magellan had no choice but to move farther southward, and on October 21, 1520, he finally came to an inlet that seemed promising. He made his way through it under horribly stormy conditions—550 kilometers of torture—and then came out into the open ocean at last, under conditions of such calm that, with tears running down his cheeks, Magellan called it the "Pacific Ocean" ("peaceful"), the name it bears to this day.

The most southerly point reached in this first voyage was that passage through the narrow strait at the southern end of South America, a passage known as the Strait of Magellan ever since.

The Strait of Magellan runs generally from the northeast to the southwest, and South America reaches its most southerly point at the southern tip of the Peninsula de Brunswick, which juts down about midway in the passage. The southern tip is at 53.92° S., which means that South America extends 2100 kilometers farther south than Africa does, reaching to within about 4000 kilometers of the South Pole. This is as near the South Pole as Edmonton, Canada, is to the North Pole.

The narrowing southern end of South America south of the 40° S. mark, about 800,000 square kilometers in area, is called Patagonia (Spanish for "big feet," because the Indian inhabitants were reported to have them).

Patagonia proved even less interesting to Europeans than the southern tip of South Africa had been. South Africa had, at least, a pleasant climate much like that of Europe, while Patagonia is a relatively barren and chilly windswept plateau that is sparsely populated even today.

Yet Patagonia is in the same southern latitude as Europe (or northern United States/southern Canada) in the northern latitude. Patagonia's climate is colder and less pleasant than that of Europe or of New England, even though it is a relatively narrow land with the mitigating effect (as we shall see in later chapters) of ocean on both sides. This was the first indication that as one went toward the Antarctic the climate grew colder faster than if one went toward the Arctic.

The Spaniards did not bother to colonize the unattractive Patagonian region, though they laid claim to it, of course. The southernmost Spanish colonies were just north of the 40° S. line, both on the Atlantic and Pacific coasts. In the 1820s, the American colonies of Spain and Portugal won their independence, and two nations were formed north of Patagonia— Argentina in the east and Chile in the west. The boundary between the two was the Andes Mountain range, the position of which meant the existence of a broad Argentina and a narrow Chile.

In the last half of the nineteenth century, both nations expanded southward, warring against the Indian inhabitants, and in 1881 they agreed to allow the line of the Andes to serve as the boundary down the remaining length of the continent. At very nearly the tip of South America, however, the boundary line turns eastward so that the entire northern shore of the Strait of Magellan is Chilean territory.

Another indication of the Antarctic chill is an island group supposedly first discovered by a deserter from the Magellan expedition. They are located in the Atlantic Ocean about 480 kilometers east of the Strait of Magellan. These consist of two chief islands, East Falkland and West Falkland, separated by the narrow Falkland Sound. Each island is about 6000 square kilometers in area.

The Falkland Islands straddle the 52° S. line, yet the climate is very much like that of the Orkney Islands north of Scotland which straddle the 59° N. line. It was not till over two centuries after their discovery that anyone tried to colonize these islands. There was then about seventy years of dispute between the British on the one hand and the Spaniards (later the Argentinians) on the other. In the end, Great Britain won out and in 1833 took over the islands. They are still British today and have a population of less than 3000.

The Strait of Magellan is a strait precisely because there is land on both sides. South of South America, then (as was not true of the case of Africa), there was land. Magellan's expedition discovered it and called it "Tierra del Fuego" ("Land of Fire") because watch fires were seen on it as the ships passed. It bears the name to this day.

At the time, no one knew anything about Tierra del Fuego, and no one really cared. It was assumed (on no evidence whatever, except that the Greeks had so speculated) to be part of another continent. No one went to look, however, because the Strait of Magellan represented the route of the Southwest Passage and that was all that was wanted of it. The land on either side was important only as obstacles.

Toward the end of 1577, however, the English navigator Francis Drake set off to work his way up the Pacific Coast of South America in search of loot. (In the end he took his ship around the world for the second circumnavigation, and was the first leader of such an expedition to live to see its completion.)

Drake made his way through the Strait of Magellan some nine months after he had set sail and emerged at the Pacific end on September 6, 1578. He was then struck by a violent storm that drove him southward quite against his will. It drove him, in fact, sufficiently far south for him to see that Tierra del Fuego was an island and that south of it there lay open ocean. That stretch of open ocean is known as Drake Passage in his honor to this day. (Once land was discovered still farther south it came to be called, sometimes, Drake Strait.)

Drake sighted the southern shore of Tierra del Fuego, but that was not properly explored till 1616, when Dutch navigators, Jakob Le Maire and William Cornelis Schouten, came that way. They named the southernmost point of Tierra del Fuego Cape Horn.

Tierra del Fuego is an archipelago of many islands and its total area is about 75,000 square kilometers. The easternmost island of the archipelago, lying southeast of the Strait of Magellan, is Isla Grande de Tierra del Fuego. It is by far the largest island in the archipelago, with an area of about 50,000 square kilometers, and oddly enough it is shaped like a horn. That, however, is not the origin of the name Cape Horn. The cape was named for the town of Hoorn in the Netherlands. In fact, Cape Horn is not part of the shores of the large island but is found on Horn Island, a very small island about 75 kilometers south of the large one. Cape Horn is at almost exactly 56° S. and is thus as far south as Edinburgh, Scotland, is north.

Once it was discovered that Tierra del Fuego was an island, it roused even less interest and was left severely to itself two and a half centuries after the voyage of Le Maire and Schouten. And yet, Tierra del Fuego was remarkable at the time of Magellan's voyage as the southernmost piece of territory in the world that possesses a permanent population. More surprising still, it holds that distinction even today!

It was not till the 1880s, when sheep were introduced into Tierra del Fuego and gold was discovered there, that Argentina and Chile grew interested in the archipelago and partitioned it. Argentina now rules over the eastern portion of the large island, that portion east of the Atlantic opening off the Strait of Magellan. Chile has the rest, including the entire southern shore of the strait. This means that anyone passing through the Strait of Magellan has Chilean territory on either side from the Atlantic to the Pacific. Cape Horn is Chilean, too, so that Chile is the southernmost of the world's independent nations.

The New Continent

Through the sixteenth and seventeenth centuries, the only continental masses known to exist south of the equator were the southern third of Africa and the southern two-thirds of South America.

The only other important land masses lying south of the equator, as far as Europeans knew, were certain large islands. There was Madagascar off the southeast coast of Africa, for instance, which lay south of the equator in its entirety. Then there were certain large islands off southeast Asia which actually straddled the equator; and the largest of which (known now as New Guinea) lay entirely south of the equator.

These latter were called the East Indies by Europeans. The islands were civilized, well populated, and rich in products that Europeans desired. When European traders reached them in the early sixteenth century, they quickly gained control over the islands. The Portuguese were first, beginning in 1511, but they were replaced by Dutch traders in 1602.*

* The islands became known as the Dutch East Indies and remained so till they won their independence after World War II and became the nation of Indonesia. Indonesia has a total area of 1,900,000 square kilometers and a population of 125,000,000. The Dutch are completely gone, but the Portuguese still have a remnant of their four-and-a-half-century-old empire in the form of the eastern half of the small island of Timor. Portuguese Timor is 15,000 square kilometers in area and has a population of 600,000.

The Dutch were naturally interested in extending their control and in finding new areas for trade. Ships had ventured into the waters south of the East Indies. A Spanish navigator, Luis Vaez de Torres, had sailed through the South Pacific in 1602 and had explored the southern coast of New Guinea. Those waters are called Torres Strait in his honor.

Torres had missed seeing any of the very large body of land that lay immediately to the south of Torres Strait. Later navigators, however, came back with vague reports of land, and in 1642 the governor-general of the East Indies, Anton Van Diemen, sent an exploring expedition southward under Abel Janszoon Tasman.

Tasman had amazingly bad fortune. In the course of a 10-months' voyage, he managed to sail all around the largest piece of land in that part of the world without actually sighting it. He did explore its northern shores in a second voyage, in 1644, but details of that second voyage are fragmentary. Other reports followed and eventually the Dutch named the body of land New Holland.

English navigators (notably Captain James Cook) explored it more systematically and brought all its shores into the light of knowledge. It was eventually named Australia, from the Latin word for "south."

The name is apt, for it was indeed the southern continent, being the largest body of inhabited land to lie entirely south of the equator. The northernmost point of Australia is Cape York at 10.70° S., just 75 kilometers south of New Guinea, with Torres Strait between. The southernmost point is Southeast Cape in the southeastern portion of the continent, which is at 39.13° S. It is as far south as Cincinnati, Ohio, is north.

Australia is the smallest of the continents, with an area of 7,700,000 square kilometers, considerably less than that of Canada or the United States. Yet it is rather too large to suffer the indignity of being called an island. It is three and a half times as large as Greenland, the next largest continuous body of land.

Australia was, of course, populated at the time of the European discovery of the continent. The population of aborigines may have been as much as 350,000 at the time of discovery. It is down to 40,000 now with about 40,000 more individuals of part-aboriginal ancestry.

In 1788, the British established a colony (an involuntary one composed of convicts) on Australia's southeast shore. By 1829, the whole continent was claimed by the British. In 1901, Australia achieved dominion status and self-government, and now has a population, almost entirely of European descent, of 12,500,000.

Australia extends farther south than Africa, though not nearly as far south as South America. There is, however, additional land near Australia that is located farther south. It was these other smaller bodies of land that Tasman managed to discover when he missed Australia itself.

Sailing eastward well to the south of Australia, Tasman skirted the southern coast of an island lying to the southeast of that continent. He did not circumnavigate it so he didn't know it was an island. He called it Van Diemen's Land in honor of the governor-general of the East Indies, and it retained that name till 1853 when it came to be called Tasmania in honor of the discoverer. That name it retains.

Great Britain took over Tasmania in 1803, and it was made part of the Dominion of Australia in 1901. Tasmania's southernmost point, also called Southeast Cape, lies at 43.67° S., as far south as Marseille, France, is north. Tasmania has an area of 71,500 square kilometers and a population of 400,000. When Tasmania was first occupied by Europeans, there were people akin to the aborigines of Australia already in occupation. They are all gone, wiped out. The last Tasmanian died in 1876.

Farther to the southeast of Australia, Tasman discovered two closely spaced islands, each of which was larger than Tasmania. They were called New Zealand after the Dutch province of Zeeland. They keep the name to this day. The outline of the coasts of the islands was plotted by Captain Cook in 1769. He was the first to circumnavigate the islands.

Of the two large islands of New Zealand, one is north of the other and is called North Island. The other is South Island. The British established their first settlement in New Zealand in 1840 and claimed sovereignty over both islands. New Zealand was given dominion status in 1907 and now has a population of 2,900,000. There were about 50,000 Maoris living in the islands before the coming of Europeans; the number is now 175,000 and still going up.

The southernmost point of South Island is 46.67° S., about as far south as Geneva, Switzerland, is north. There are, however, several small islands south of South Island, most of which are controlled by New Zealand. The southernmost, the Macquarie Islands, about 1350 kilometers east of Tasmania, are Australian territory. Their southernmost point is at 54.8° S., almost but not quite as far south as Cape Horn.

Yet even as Australia was being discovered, there was not one real effort to reach, let alone explore, the Antarctic regions of Earth. This may seem strange when one thinks that the Arctic regions had been probed and poked at for two centuries by that time.

Remember, though, that the Arctic regions were not being explored for their own sake but merely as part of a search for routes to the Far East. The southern routes to the Far East had been found without the need to involve the Antarctic regions and that was that.

Yet there was another mysterious goal that glittered before the eyes of Europeans—that of a large southern continent, populous and rich, somewhere in the southern oceans.

The Greeks had speculated on a great southern continent designed to balance the known land in the Northern Hemisphere but had no evidence at all as to its existence. The geographers of early modern times took the speculation seriously and drew in a southern continent ("Terra Australis") on their maps. This continent filled in the entire southern third of the globe, covering all the Antarctic, with its shores waving completely around the South Temperate Zone. Tierra del Fuego was considered an outpost as were the shorelines dimly reported south of the East Indies.

As time went on, geographic knowledge grew and the boundaries of the speculative southern continent shrank. Tierra del Fuego turned out to be a small island. Australia turned out to be of continental size and was even given the name of the imagined continent, but it did not satisfy. It was smaller than had been looked for and it was rather barren, too.

Yet hope did not die.

All the land that had been discovered south of the equator by the beginning of the eighteenth century amounted to about 18,000,000 square kilometers (see figure 23). This was only one-third of the known land north of the equator. Could the Southern Hemisphere have so little land, when the Northern Hemisphere had so much (see figure 24)?

Suspicion centered on the Pacific Ocean. The known shores of the Americas, of Asia, and of newly discovered Australia

Figure 23. The Southern Hemisphere, 1720

enclosed a body of water which, if it were empty, would have an area of some 165,000,000 square kilometers; more, by a good margin, than the total known land area on Earth. It didn't seem possible that all that area would be blank water. Surely there must be some important and undiscovered land area in all that vastness.

Actually, there was not. The Pacific Ocean was indeed all that vast and all that empty. It was littered with small island groupings, variously given such names as "Melanesia" (from Greek words meaning "black islands" because they were inhabited by dark-skinned people), "Micronesia" ("small islands") and "Polynesia" ("many islands").

Put together, all these islands in the Pacific Ocean (about 10,000 altogether) make up nearly 1,000,000 square kilometers of land. This is not bad in total, since it is half again as large as Texas, but the land is scattered in tiny pieces over an ocean

Figure 24. The Northern Hemisphere

covering nearly a hemisphere and makes up not much more than 0.5 percent of the sea in which they are set.

These islands were not waiting there, empty, to be found by Europeans. The East Indian islands and Australia were inhabited 10,000 years ago at least. From the East Indian islands as a base, people had explored outward, reaching island after island.

The last stages were the most difficult. Even before the Vikings were making their daring voyages along the northern rim of the world, the Pacific Islanders ("Polynesians") were making far longer voyages. For the time and equipment available, the Polynesians may have been the most daring and successful navigators of all time.

By A.D. 1000 the Polynesians had occupied an enormous Pacific triangle of which the corners were New Zealand in the southwest, the Hawaiian Islands in the north, and Easter Island in the east. Their primitive ships had taken them crisscross over some 14,000,000 square kilometers of ocean.

The Antarctic Islands

As the eighteenth century opened, the truth about the Pacific Ocean and the land south of the 55° S. mark of Cape Horn was still unknown to Europeans. To them, the vision of the southern continent, filling the Antarctic regions and bulging up into the Pacific Ocean, still glistened.

In 1738, a French naval officer, Pierre Bouvet de Lozier, headed southward in the first voyage specifically designed to uncover such a continent. He probed south of the southern tip of Africa and sailed through more than 1500 kilometers of ocean along the 55° S. line. This was no farther south than Belfast, Northern Ireland, is north, yet the seas were ice choked. This was another sharp indication that Antarctic conditions were considerably more severe than Arctic ones.

All Bouvet uncovered was a small island (still called Bouvet Island in his honor) about 2600 kilometers south of the southern tip of Africa. It is at 54.43° S., and it is not as far south as Cape Horn, so that it did not establish a record for land farthest south. (The island is under Norwegian sovereignty today.)

Bouvet's negative findings did not kill hope either. The Scottish explorer Alexander Dalrymple published accounts of discoveries in the South Pacific and upheld the notion of a southern continent.

Another attempt at finding it was therefore made a generation after Bouvet. Another French navigator, Yves Joseph de Kerguelen-Tremarec, set out in 1771 and found another island, now known as Kerguelen Island. It was about 4000 kilometers southeast of the southern tip of Africa.

Kerguelen Island is about 5700 square kilometers in area and is surrounded by about 300 islets, averaging three-fourths of a square kilometer apiece. It is not as far south as Bouvet Island, being at only 49.5° S., yet even though it is no farther south than Prague, Czechoslovakia, is north, such is the influence of the Antarctic that the island is subpolar in climate, contains snowfields in the central area, and has as a rather apt alternate name, "Desolation Island." It was annexed by France in 1893.

Even as Kerguelen was setting out on his voyage, a far greater navigator than he was also on the ocean. This was the English navigator James Cook, who has already been mentioned a few times in this book. He has made so remarkable a name for himself as an explorer that he is universally known as Captain Cook and his first name is almost forgotten.

Between 1768 and 1771, on the first of three great voyages, Captain Cook sailed across the South Pacific Ocean and explored the coasts of Australia, New Zealand, and New Guinea, placing them all firmly on the map.

Then, in 1772, he set off on a second expedition in search of the southern continent. He searched what we might call the South Pacific thoroughly and made it plain that no southern continent other than Australia existed anywhere in the South Temperate Zone. In a third voyage he scoured the Pacific north and south and died at last on the Hawaiian Islands. It was he who finally demonstrated the fact that the Pacific Ocean was empty except for small islands, a number of which he discovered.*

On his second voyage, Captain Cook pushed so far southward that he finally crossed the Antarctic Circle. He and his crew were the first men in history—not merely the first Europeans, but the first human beings of any kind—to make that crossing. The Arctic Circle was crossed in prehistoric times by early Siberian inhabitants and was crossed by Europeans in the days of the Vikings, nine centuries before Cook's time. Nothing of the sort could be said of the Antarctic Circle. It remained unviolated until January 17, 1773, when Captain Cook's ship made the first crossing.

Cook made two other crossings in the course of his journey, and his most southerly penetration took place on January 30,

* Captain Cook was the first to make use of citrus fruits for his men and to diversify their diet, so that the scourge of scurvy was no longer a necessary accompaniment to long voyages.

1774, when he reached 71.17° S., as far south as the northern tip of Norway is north. He was then only 1820 kilometers from the South Pole, which was, of course, a record. Throughout his voyage he was stopped by ice and he never saw any actual land.*

It was clear to Cook that if there was land beyond the ice floes he struggled among, it could only be a polar mass, bleak and uninhabitable. Sadly, he announced that if any southern continent existed, it wasn't worth discovering, for it could have no value to man. (If he meant that the land could not be settled and farmed, he was right. There are, however, other kinds of values.)

In the course of his Antarctic probings, Captain Cook discovered South Georgia Island, about 1750 kilometers east of Tierra del Fuego, and also the South Sandwich Islands, running in an arc east and southeast of South Georgia Island. All were eventually annexed by Great Britain.

South Georgia Island is about 3750 square kilometers in area and is about as far south as Cape Horn.

The South Sandwich Islands are farther south than Cape Horn and represented the first land to be discovered south of the 55° S. line. The southernmost of the small islands of this group is (appropriately) Thule Island, and it is at 59.43° S., as far south as Oslo, Norway, is north.

One consequence of Captain Cook's explorations was that the Antarctic waters were shown to be rich in seals and whales. Ships ("sealers" and "whalers") went south to prey on those mammals, and new discoveries were made in consequence.

Thus, a British officer, William Smith, discovered the South Shetland Islands in October 1819. These are directly south of South Georgia. It is as though there is a ridge leading east from the pointed tip of Tierra del Fuego which marks out a great arc, first south and then west, with the upper peaks of this ridge showing above the ocean level as islands. The arc would lead us from Tierra del Fuego east to South Georgia, then along the South Sandwich group in a southward curving arc, and finally to the South Shetland group at the southwestern edge of the arc. (Between the South Sandwich and South

---

* It was a combination of this voyage and Magellan's that inspired Samuel Taylor Coleridge to write "The Rime of the Ancient Mariner" twenty years later.

Shetland groups are the South Orkney Islands, discovered in 1821.) The South Shetland Islands run down to 63° S., as far south as Reykjavik, Iceland, is north.

The Shores of Antarctica

There was no necessity that the ridge extending from Tierra del Fuego to the South Shetland Islands should end there. All those islands existed north of the Antarctic Circle, but there might yet be land farther south if the ridge turned southward.

In 1820, three voyages by ships captained by men of three different nationalities produced signs of that more southerly land.

The British naval commander Edward Bransfield charted the South Shetland Islands, then went farther south to 64.5° S., and on January 30, 1820, may have seen land there. The waters between the South Shetland Islands and the land to the south are still called Bransfield Strait in his honor.*

Later that year, on November 16, 1820, a 21-year-old American sealer, Nathaniel Brown Palmer, in command of a small sloop that was part of a larger fleet, definitely sighted land south of Bransfield Strait.

The land sighted by Bransfield and by Palmer is part of a long, thin arm of land that is clearly part of the ridge that runs down the Andean backbone along the western shore of South America, through Tierra del Fuego, around the island arc, and to the newly discovered land.

The British considered it to have been discovered by Bransfield and called it Graham Land in honor of James R. G. Graham, first lord of the admiralty in 1820. The Americans insisted on priority for Palmer and called it Palmer Land. It was not till 1964 that they came to an agreement on the matter. The neutral name "Antarctic Peninsula" was agreed on by the two.

The Antarctic Peninsula is a gently curving, S-shaped piece of land about 1500 kilometers long, the most northerly point of

---

* Over and over, Antarctic explorations occur in January and February, which to northerners seem an odd time to explore polar regions. Remember, however, that the seasons are reversed in the Southern Hemisphere and that in the Antarctic the days are longest and summer is at its height from December through February.

which is at 63° S., or 480 kilometers north of the Antarctic Circle. The northern, mostly sub-Antarctic portion of the peninsula is now known as Graham Land, while the southern Antarctic portion is Palmer Land.

Was the Antarctic Peninsula a long island or was it part of a larger landmass? There was considerable belief at first that it was an island separated from nearby land by a strait so ice choked as to seem solid. It was not till the 1930s that the decision was reached that the Antarctic Peninsula was indeed part of a larger landmass. And yet, as we shall see, there still remains room for argument.

On February 7, 1821, an American sealer, John Davis, actually set foot on the Antarctic Peninsula, though this fact was not known till the log of his ship was discovered and studied in 1955. Davis expressed the opinion in the log that the land was part of an Antarctic continent, which put him well in advance in the correctness of his opinions as well as in the record of his deed.

The Russians, meanwhile, who were naturally involved in Arctic exploration in view of their geographic position, interested themselves in the Antarctic as well, and they were the third nation in the field. In 1819, the Russian czar, Alexander I, sent the Russian explorer Fabian Gottlieb Bellingshausen southward with specific instructions to circumnavigate the South Polar region farther south than the latitudes reached by Captain Cook nearly half a century before.

Bellingshausen followed orders. He did not sight any continental landmass, nor did he actually reach Cook's southernmost point any more than Bransfield, Palmer, or Davis had. However, in the course of his journey, he came across a small island about the size and shape of Manhattan which he named Peter I Island. The interesting thing about the island is that it was at 68.8° S., or 240 kilometers *south* of the Antarctic Circle. It was the first piece of truly Antarctic land ever discovered.

He also discovered a much larger piece of land just west of the base of the Antarctic Peninsula. He named it for the Czar and thought it was part of a continental landmass. In this case, though, the land did indeed turn out to be an island attached to a larger body by means of an ice-choked strait that looked solid. It is now known as Alexander I Island, and it has an area of 43,000 square kilometers, which makes it the largest island in the world lying south of 55° S.

Peter I Island is now under the rule of Norway. Alexander I Island, in common with the rest of the landmass in the South Polar region generally, is under no commonly recognized dominion. For a long time various nations divided the South Polar region into sectors with boundaries radiating from the South Pole. Many of these sectors overlapped and none of them was generally recognized.

The South Polar region has, to all intents, always been treated as international in character. This was recognized officially in 1959 when the five southernmost nations—Argentina, Chile, South Africa, Australia, and New Zealand—together with seven northern nations that had been active in Antarctic exploration—the United States, Great Britain, the Soviet Union, France, Japan, Belgium, and Norway—signed a treaty pledging to use the region only for scientific and nonmilitary purposes.

Bellingshausen prepared excellent reports of his voyage, and the stretch of ocean he explored west of the Antarctic Peninsula is called Bellingshausen Sea in his honor. The Russians, however, disappointed at the failure to report more in the way of land than he did, didn't publish his findings for ten years. Yet it is possible that Bellingshausen did actually see the continental landmass and mistook the sight of ice-covered land for ice-covered sea. At least the Soviet Union claims Bellingshausen to be the discoverer of the continent, as opposed to the British claim for Bransfield and the American claim for Palmer.

Since the issue can probably never be settled to everyone's satisfaction, it might be best to award the honor to all three as a threefold, independent discovery of the continent in 1820.

An English whaler, James Weddell, found a stretch of ocean that extended farther south than anything explored before and on February 20, 1823, reached a mark of 72.25° S. before winds and ice turned him back. This represented a new southward record, and Weddell had approached to within 1800 kilometers of the South Pole.

The inlet into which Weddell had sailed lies east of the Antarctic Peninsula and is now known as Weddell Sea in his honor. Weddell himself thought the sea penetrated all the way to the South Pole, though ice would prevent a ship from sailing farther south than he had. This, however, turned out not to be so. The southernmost reach of Weddell Sea is at 76° S., and at that point there is a shoreline that is still fully 1350 kilometers from the South Pole.

All the discoveries of the 1820s in the neighborhood of the Antarctic Circle were made in the general area south of Tierra del Fuego. In 1831, the first sighting of Antarctic land on the other side of the world in the general area south of Madagascar was made. In that year, the English navigator John Biscoe saw a shoreline about a hundred kilometers north of the Antarctic Circle and he called it Enderby Land after the owners of his vessel. He saw it from a distance though. Ice prevented him from actually reaching it.

In 1840, the French explorer Jules Dumont d'Urville sailed south from Australia and spied a shoreline near the Antarctic Circle, indeed almost exactly upon it, which he named Adélie Land after his wife. This coastline lies south of Tasmania.

At almost the same time, an American explorer, Charles Wilkes, was exploring a long stretch of coastline between Enderby Land and Adélie Land, a coastline that followed the curve of the Antarctic Circle with surprising exactness. This stretch of coast, lying south of the Indian Ocean, is now known as Wilkes Land. Wilkes, on returning, was the first to proclaim that all the isolated discoveries of the previous twenty years could be fitted together to indicate the existence of a South Polar landmass of continental size.

To be sure Davis had thought this when he landed on the Antarctic Peninsula twenty years before, but that had been intuition only. Wilkes had a careful exploratory voyage to back him up, and he might be said to be the effective discoverer of the *continent* as opposed to this patch or that of land. A natural name for the continent was Antarctica.

An even more notable Antarctic journey was then made by the Scottish explorer James Clark Ross, who was the nephew of the Arctic explorer John Ross, and who had done notable work himself in the Arctic.

In January 1841, he entered an inlet into Antarctica in a region that lay, generally, south of New Zealand. The new inlet is called Ross Sea in his honor. At its western shore, which Ross named Victoria Land after the British queen, is a line of mountains he called Prince Albert Mountains after her husband, the prince consort.

Ross sailed south into Ross Sea, till he found himself stopped by a towering wall of ice, 200 to 300 feet high. This turned out to be an ice shelf, a thick layer of ice which had not been formed directly by freezing of seawater (if it were, it would be much thinner) but had been formed on land and had been extruded out onto the ocean. The result was a huge extent of thick ice filling most of Ross Sea. This Ross Ice Shelf, as it is called, covers an area roughly the size of France.

At the point where Ross encountered the ice shelf, there was a piece of land, now known as Ross Island. On it, Ross discovered, on January 27, two volcanoes, which he named Mount Erebus and Mount Terror after his two ships. Mount Erebus, the taller of the two, was active and 3.7 kilometers high.

To the east of Ross Island, the open sea extended somewhat farther south than to the west. This inlet Ross called McMurdo Bay after the mate of the *Terror*.

Ross sailed along the Ross Ice Shelf for about 700 kilometers before returning to Tasmania. In 1842, he visited Ross Sea again and achieved a new southern mark of 78.15° S., 1150 kilometers from the South Pole.

If the Ross Ice Shelf were imagined as having disappeared, it would be seen that the Ross Sea extended much farther south, farther south, in fact, than any other portion of the world's ocean. At its farthest, it is at 86° S., less than 500 kilometers from the South Pole. In such an exposed sea, another island would appear along its western shore, matching Ross Island on its eastern. This western island, the larger of the two, was eventually named Roosevelt Island.

It was clear by the mid-nineteenth century that the South Pole, unlike the North Pole, was on land and was surrounded by land; and that there was no Antarctic Ocean that was clearly delineated by surrounding landmasses as there was an Arctic Ocean.

To be sure, the waters that rim Antarctica are generally referred to as the Antarctic Ocean, but geographically that is merely the cold southern ends of the Pacific, Atlantic, and Indian oceans, all running together, so to speak. There are arbitrary ways of marking off the Antarctic Ocean, and we will speak of those later.

The Interior of Antarctica

As the end of the nineteenth century neared, ships and men had been nosing round and about Antarctica without any actual landing having been made. There had been the landing of Davis, to be sure, but the fact that this had happened remained unknown, and, in any case, his landing had been made north of the Antarctic Circle. Even counting Davis, there was no actual Antarctic landing upon Antarctica.

In the Antarctic summer of 1894–1895, however, a Norwegian whaler commanded by Leonard Kristenson visited Victoria Land on the rim of the Ross Sea and there, on January 23, 1895, a party alighted and stood on Antarctica.

One of that party of the first men ever to stand on Antarctica south of the Antarctic Circle was the Norwegian Carsten E. Borchgrevink. He returned in 1898 and, with nine other men, wintered in Antarctica, the first ever to do so. Borchgrevink penetrated to the Ross Ice Shelf and found it farther south than it had been in Ross's day.

Until that moment, all Antarctic exploration had been conducted by ship. Borchgrevink put on skis and set off on the very first attempt to penetrate southward by land transportation. On February 16, 1900, he attained a southern mark of 78.8° S., breaking Ross's record after sixty years.

It now became routine to send out sledging expeditions southward over the South Polar land, as over the North Polar ice-covered sea. The ambition arose to reach the South Pole in this way. One of those most on fire to do so was the British explorer Robert Falcon Scott.

Scott entered Ross Sea and named the land at its western end Edward VII Land after the just-crowned king of England. He and his colleagues then sledged over the Ross Ice Shelf and on December 13, 1902, reached 82.28° S., only 800 kilometers from the South Pole.

One of his colleagues, Ernest Shackleton, made another try for the South Pole in the Antarctic summer of 1908–1909. On January 9, 1909, his party of four men managed to reach 88.38° S., only 155 kilometers from the South Pole, each man dragging his own sledge. They were forced to turn back once it was clear that to travel farther would mean their food supply would not last the return journey. They did manage to show, though, that the South Pole was to be found on a high plateau.

All was set now for the final push. Two candidates were in the field. One was Scott and the other was Amundsen, who had made his mark as a polar explorer and had been the first to traverse the Northwest Passage completely.

Amundsen prepared with the utmost care and made use of dog sleds and plenty of dogs. There were fifty-two dogs at the start, and Amundsen went rolling along the ice, with plenty of food. He left on October 20, 1911, and as he proceeded, he killed and fed the weaker dogs to the stronger ones, saving the food supplies he had brought for the human members of the expedition. In this way, there was no danger of being forced to turn back because of threatened vanishing of the food supply as in the case of the Shackleton attempt where there had been no dogs and each man had pulled his own sledge.

Amundsen reached the South Pole on December 14 and the expedition was back on January 21, 1912, with twelve dogs still surviving and working and plenty of food still left and no human casualties.

Scott's attempt was less carefully organized, did not depend so much on dogs, and was plagued by misfortune. The last 650 kilometers was made by man-hauled sledges only. Scott and four companions reached the South Pole on January 17, 1912, and found Amundsen's marker there. It had taken them 69 days to reach the pole (it had taken Amundsen 55) and they were worn out. On the voyage back, all five were caught in a 9-day blizzard that was the final straw, and all died of cold on or about March 29.

Meanwhile, the German explorer Wilhelm Filchner explored Weddell Sea and found in its southern reaches an ice shelf as large as the Ross Ice Shelf. This second ice shelf is now called the Filchner Ice Shelf.*

The two ice shelves, with a total area of 930,000 square kilometers, are on opposite sides of the continent, and if they are ignored, Ross Sea and Weddell Sea approach each other with just a 1000-kilometer stretch of land lying between as an isthmus connecting two parts of Antarctica.

The two parts, East Antarctica and West Antarctica, are quite unequal in size. West Antarctica, which lies south of the American continents, possesses an irregular coastline and the Antarctic Peninsula, and is the smaller, making up about one-third of the continent. It is therefore also called Lesser Antarctica. East Antarctica, or Greater Antarctica, has a

---

* Germany was little involved in Antarctic exploration, though under the Nazi regime ships were sent out in 1938 and 1939. A section of the Antarctica coast was named Neu Schwabenland ("New Swabia") by that expedition.

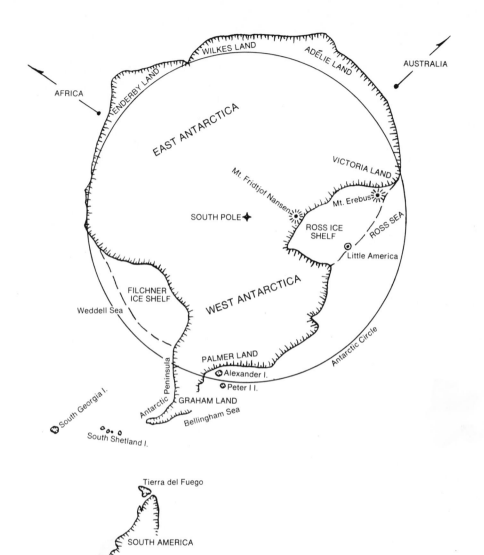

Figure 25. Antarctica

nearly semicircular shoreline running along the Antarctic Circle almost exactly and lies south of Africa, Asia, and Australia.

Crossing the isthmus and running along the eastern shores of Ross Sea and Weddell Sea is Antarctica's most prominent mountain range, the Transantarctic Mountains. One of its peaks, just at the southernmost reach of Ross Sea, is Mount Fridtjof Nansen, which is named for the polar explorer. It is the tallest peak in Antarctica, with its height 5.8 kilometers above sea level.

In the years immediately following the reaching of the South Pole, the British-Australian explorer Douglas Mawson mapped much of the Antarctica coast, and ten years later took care of the rest. The first air flight over Antarctica was made on December 20, 1928, and that heralded the coming of the air age and the enormous simplification of the problem of exploration.

In 1929, the American explorer Richard Evelyn Byrd flew from the Antarctica shore to the South Pole and back in one day, covering a round-trip distance of 2600 kilometers. He established a base he named Little America on the edge of the Ross Ice Shelf near Roosevelt Island. In 1934, Byrd wintered alone in a tiny base 200 kilometers south of Little America. It was the first wintering by any man in the Antarctic interior.

In 1935, Hubert Wilkins and the American explorer Lincoln Ellsworth attempted a trans-Antarctica flight and managed one that was 3700 kilometers long. In 1939, an expedition headed by Byrd mapped 350,000 square kilometers of Antarctica by means of plane flights. And finally, in 1957, a party under the leadership of Vivian Fuchs successfully crossed the continent by land, as part of a vast international program of Antarctic exploration.

And then the exploration of the Antarctic regions, geographically at least, was just about done (see figure 25).

7

OUR UNIQUE OCEAN

ow that the discovery of the polar regions of Earth, both north and south, has been described, let us take a quick overview of each.

The area of the Earth's surface north of 66.5° N. is about 21,000,000 square kilometers. It is bounded by the Arctic Circle, which is, at all points, about 2600 kilometers from the North Pole. The area of the Earth's surface south of 66.5° S. has the same dimensions and differs geometrically only in that it is the Antarctic Circle and the South Pole that are involved.

The total area of both polar regions taken together is 42,000,000 square kilometers, which is twice the area of the Soviet Union, or four and a half times that of the United States, or one-twelfth the area of the entire globe.

But there are differences. The Arctic area has as its core the Arctic Ocean, which has an area of 14,300,000 square kilometers. In other words, the Arctic is two-thirds water at the center and one-third land at the periphery.

The Antarctic is curiously opposite to the Arctic in this, as well as in name and in geographic position. The Antarctic also has an area of about 21,000,000 square kilometers, but it has a central continent, Antarctica, which is about 13,100,000 square kilometers in area, only slightly less than the area of the Arctic Ocean. The Antarctic is two-thirds land at the center and one-third water at the periphery.

What other differences are there?

Let us consider the Arctic again. Begin at Iceland and (imagining ourself looking down at the North Pole) let our eye move in a clockwise direction. We will see the northern two-thirds of Greenland, the northern regions of Canada and Alaska, then the northern third of the Soviet Union, and the northern portions of Finland, Sweden, and Norway. (Finland and Sweden are the only two nations with Arctic territory that have no coastline on the Arctic Ocean.)

Well over 2,000,000 people live in the lands above the Arctic Circle, and towns exist there. The most northerly town of note in North America is Barrow, Alaska, which at 71.26° N. has a population of about 2100. The most northerly town of note in the Eurasian half of the Arctic is Hammerfest, Norway, at 70.65° N., with a population of about 7000.

The largest of all Arctic cities is Murmansk, U.S.S.R., at 68.98° N., with a population of about 310,000.

The population within the Antarctic Circle, however (except for people present, temporarily, at scientific bases), is precisely zero. There are no towns in the Antarctic and no people.

Why is it that the North Polar region is a harsh, but habitable land, while the South Polar region is a frozen sterile waste? Is it because the Arctic is mostly water and the Antarctic mostly land? To find out if that can be the answer, let's consider water and the role it plays on Earth—and to understand how unique that role is, let's start at the beginning.

The Formation of Planets

Astronomers have decided on the basis of what they have learned about the composition of stars and of the gas and dust in the space between the stars, that the most common types of atoms in the universe are hydrogen atoms (the simplest and smallest of all) and helium atoms (next simplest and smallest). About 90 percent of all the atoms in the universe are hydrogen. Another 9 percent are helium.

Together, then, hydrogen and helium make up 99 percent of the atoms in the universe. All other kinds of atoms (and 103 other varieties are known at the moment) make up somewhat less than 1 percent of all the atoms in the universe.

Under conditions that exist on planets, atoms tend to group themselves into more or less tightly bound combinations called molecules. Since helium atoms are among the few that steadfastly resist combination and exist only separately, they can be ignored as far as molecules are concerned. Indeed, because of the tendency of helium atoms to remain single and uncombined, helium is present on a planet such as Earth only in traces.

Hydrogen atoms tend to combine in pairs, and, since hydrogen atoms are so preponderantly common in the universe, we should expect that the most common molecules to be encountered will be those made up of two hydrogen atoms apiece. Molecular hydrogen of this sort is symbolized by chemists as H_2 for perfectly obvious reasons.

The third most common type of atom is the oxygen atom. For every oxygen atom in the universe there are nearly 2000 hydrogen atoms, astronomers estimate, and about 150 helium atoms. Nevertheless, oxygen atoms, though so rare in comparison to those two, are next most common. Everything else is rarer still.

Oxygen atoms tend to combine in pairs, too, so that the oxygen molecule is made up of two atoms apiece and such molecules are written O_2. It is not likely, though, that oxygen molecules are frequently formed in the universe at large. Two oxygen atoms are not likely to combine unless, while moving about in space, they happen to collide. However, hydrogen atoms are so much more common that it is thousands of times as likely that an oxygen atom will strike a hydrogen atom than that it will strike another oxygen atom.

Oxygen atoms and hydrogen atoms will combine with each other. The most stable combination, under planetary conditions, is one in which an oxygen atom will combine with two hydrogen atoms. The result is the formation of a three-atom molecule, H_2O. Water is made up of molecules such as this, and H_2O is the formula of the water molecule.

A substance made up of molecules which, in turn, are made up of more than one kind of atom, is called a compound. It is clear that water must be the most common compound that can exist under planetary conditions.

Based on this consideration alone, it would seem not at all strange, then, that Earth should have so much water on it; an ocean of water, in fact. We might hastily conclude that any planet would have an ocean of water on it. If we did, we would be wrong—so let's continue.

After oxygen, the next most common atoms are neon, nitrogen, and carbon. Neon atoms, like helium atoms, remain single, so we can forget neon. Nitrogen atoms and carbon atoms will combine with hydrogen atoms. Each nitrogen atom combines with three hydrogen atoms to form a compound called ammonia (NH_3), and each carbon atom combines with four hydrogen atoms to form a compound called methane (CH_4).

After these three, the next most common atoms are silicon, magnesium, and iron. Silicon atoms tend to combine with oxygen atoms to form silicon dioxide (SiO_2). This combines further with magnesium atoms and other atoms, too, to form a mixture of what are called silicates. The rock and soil of the Earth's crust consist chiefly of silicates, for instance. Iron atoms can be included among the silicate molecules, but there is so much iron present that some iron atoms can combine among themselves to form iron metal.

Atoms hold together within molecules by chemical forces that are often very strong indeed. Molecules can in turn be held together by chemical forces that are sometimes as strong as those within molecules, sometimes weaker, and sometimes very weak indeed. Molecules are also held together by gravitational forces that are much weaker than chemical forces but that affect all molecules nearly alike.

When molecules are widely separated in space, the gravitational attraction is exceedingly minute and suffices to bring them together only excessively slowly. As they come together, however, the gravitational attraction (which increases with decreasing distance between objects) becomes steadily more intense, and planets form out of scattered fragments, dust, and individual molecules.

Under the influence of the gravitational attractions, dense material sinks to the center of the planet as it forms or even, very slowly, after it forms. Less dense material forms a shell about the center, still less dense material, a shell about that, and so on.

Of the common materials in the universe, iron is the densest, so it is likely to be at the center of planets, together with its sister elements, nickel and cobalt, which are much like iron in properties but are less common. The mixture is likely to be 90 percent iron, 9 percent nickel, and 1 percent cobalt. This is sometimes called the nickel-iron core of a planet.

Around the nickel-iron core is a shell of silicate, about that a shell of water, methane, and ammonia, and about that a shell of hydrogen and helium.

If a planet were made up of material as it exists generally in the universe, you would expect about 99 percent of the planet to be made up of hydrogen and helium. There would be a relatively tiny nickel-iron core, surrounded by a tiny shell of silicate, surrounded by a tiny shell of water, methane, and ammonia, and finally a vast outermost shell of hydrogen and helium.

The four largest planets of the solar system—Jupiter, Saturn, Uranus, and Neptune—may indeed be built up something in this fashion. Jupiter, about which we know the most, and which is 316 times as massive as the Earth, is thought by many astronomers to be so rich in hydrogen as to consist of virtually nothing else.

Yet this is not the way the Earth is formed. There is comparatively little hydrogen on Earth. What happened to it?

The Earth formed considerably nearer the Sun than Jupiter did. Earth was therefore at a higher temperature as it formed. Temperature does not affect the manner of collection of those substances whose molecules are held together by strong chemical forces. These include iron and the silicates.

The condition is different for those molecules that are held by only weak chemical forces or virtually none. These must depend largely or even almost entirely on gravitational pull to do the work, and the effectiveness of gravitational pull depends on temperature. The higher the temperature, the faster molecules move; and the faster they move, the harder it is for the gravitational pull to do the job.

Water, ammonia, methane, helium, and hydrogen have molecules that are held together by only weak chemical forces, and therefore collect chiefly under the pull of gravitational forces. If the temperature is too high, they are not collected but tend to fly away from the gathering planet, so to speak. They make up the "volatile" (from a Latin word meaning "to fly") portion of a planet. The iron and silicates are involatile materials.

The outer planets are far from the Sun and, presumably, were quite cold at the time they were forming. The molecules of the volatile materials moved sluggishly and were easily captured by the gathering involatile core. The more of the volatiles added to the planet, the stronger the total gravitational pull and the easier it was to add still more volatiles. There was a "snowball effect," and in the end huge planets were formed, with tiny involatile cores compared to the vast accumulation of volatile material in the outer shells.

When a planet is forming closer to the Sun and is warmer, its involatile core cannot hold on to the more rapidly moving molecules about it. The inner planets are therefore considerably smaller than the outer ones, since they are made up of involatile matter largely, and the atoms of which the involatile matter is composed are a lot less common than are those of which volatile matter is composed.

Naturally, then, Mars, Earth, Venus, Mercury, and the Moon are much smaller than the giant outer planets.

The Formation of Atmospheres

While a small, warm planet cannot hold on to volatile matter in the vast amounts large, cold planets can, it may hold on to some. Exactly how much each will hold on to depends on just how small and how warm it is. If it is small enough or warm enough or both, it will hold on to just about none. There will then be nothing more than the minutest trace of volatile material attached to it. In particular, it will have no perceptible layer of gases held to its surface by gravity; it will have no atmosphere to speak of.

Tiny bodies such as meteoroids or asteroids are made up entirely of involatile material: iron, rock, or a mixture of both. They have no atmosphere.

Even the Moon, which is 3500 kilometers in diameter, is not large enough to develop a gravitational field strong enough to hold volatile material. It has no atmosphere. It is merely a ball of rock, lacking, in all probability, a nickel-iron core.

Mercury is larger than the Moon, being 5000 kilometers in diameter. It is also much warmer than the Moon, though, since it is at only a third the distance from the Sun that the Moon is. It, too, consists entirely of involatile material, though it differs from the Moon in probably having a sizable nickel-iron core.

Mars is larger still: 6750 kilometers in diameter and is cooler, being farther from the Sun than the Earth is. It manages to hold on to a thin atmosphere.

Of the inner worlds, Venus and Earth are the largest, Venus having a diameter of 12,200 kilometers, and Earth a diameter of 12,757 kilometers. Both have gravitational pulls capable of retaining a fairly thick atmosphere (though not, of course, anything like those that the giant outer planets can drag in).

Even though it is cooler than Mercury and even though it is larger than the Moon, Earth's gravitational pull could not hold the lighter volatiles, hydrogen and helium. Those were never collected. It could, however, collect the heavier ones: ammonia, methane, and water. (Each of these has hydrogen atoms as part of the molecule, so some hydrogen atoms were preserved indirectly.)

In the outer regions of the solar system, such an atmosphere would be stable, and the atmospheres of the outer planets would contain ammonia and methane (and presumably water, too) in addition to hydrogen and helium. There is one smaller world out there: Titan, a satellite of Saturn, which is large enough and cold enough to have a detectable atmosphere, and that atmosphere contains methane.

In the inner regions of the solar system, such an atmosphere is not stable. The more energetic portions of the solar radiation are energetic enough to break up some of the molecules in the atmosphere. Not enough reach the outer planets to do much there, but it is a different story in the inner regions.

The ultraviolet light of the Sun will break up water molecules it may encounter in Earth's upper atmosphere and produce hydrogen and oxygen. The hydrogen formed will drift out into space, as Earth's gravitational pull is not strong enough to hold it.

The oxygen, however, can be held. It is an active substance that combines with many of the other substances it will encounter. It will combine with ammonia, for instance, to form nitrogen and water, and it will combine with methane to form carbon dioxide and water.

The net change is this. Out of a methane/ammonia/water atmosphere, you form a carbon dioxide/nitrogen/water atmosphere.

Once all the methane and ammonia are gone and carbon dioxide and nitrogen are formed instead, what happens? There is still water in the atmosphere and water molecules are still split up. Will this continue till all the water is gone? No. As the water molecules continue to split up, and the hydrogen that is formed continues to leak away, the oxygen accumulates. It has no further ammonia or methane to combine with. Radiation from the Sun, however, converts the oxygen into a more energetic form called ozone. Whereas ordinary oxygen is made up of molecules containing two oxygen atoms apiece (O_2), ozone molecules contain three (O_3).

Ozone is unstable and breaks down almost as quickly as it forms, but there is always some that has formed and that has not yet had time to break down, and this forms a sparse ozone layer high in the atmosphere. On Earth, the ozone layer is about 25 kilometers above Earth's surface.

Ozone is not transparent to ultraviolet light, but absorbs it instead. The ultraviolet light of the Sun, absorbed by the ozone in the upper atmosphere, cannot pass through to split up more water molecules. As a result there are no further atmospheric changes produced by ultraviolet light and the carbon dioxide/nitrogen/water atmosphere is stable. Mars and Venus both have carbon dioxide/nitrogen/water atmospheres.

Earth, however, does not. On Earth, another element of instability was introduced. Life developed and green plants evolved which possessed the capacity of photosynthesis; that is, a process where the Sun's energy was used to split up water molecules. The hydrogen that was produced in this way was combined with carbon dioxide to form plant tissue and the oxygen was allowed to escape into the atmosphere.

Green plants did this not by using ultraviolet light which could not get through the ozone layer, but by using the less energetic *visible* light which *could* get through the ozone layer.

As plant life spread over the world, more and more of the carbon dioxide was consumed and combined with hydrogen, and more and more oxygen was liberated, until now Earth's atmosphere is oxygen/nitrogen/water.*

* It also contains a little carbon dioxide—0.03 percent of the whole—on which plants maintain their existence, and which

Such an atmosphere is unique in the solar system, and depends entirely on the fact that the Earth is neither too large nor too small, neither too hot nor too cold, and that it has the type of environment that made it possible for life to develop and to evolve a photosynthetic mechanism. The result is that Earth is the only body in the solar system to have an atmosphere containing a great deal of oxygen.*

If Earth's atmosphere is unique in a way that is most convenient for oxygen-breathing organisms such as ourselves, it is by no means the only unique aspect of Earth as a world. We will find another if we pass on from the general chemical makeup of planets to their physical structure.

The Formation of Oceans

All simple substances can exist in one of three physical states at planetary temperatures: solid, liquid, and gas.

Any particular substance can be in any one of these forms and can change from one to another depending on the temperature. If the temperature is low enough, it is solid. As the temperature rises, it reaches a particular value (the "melting point") where the solid becomes a liquid; at a still higher temperature (the "boiling point"), the liquid becomes a gas. The melting point and boiling point are, of course, different for different substances under different conditions.

In considering melting points and boiling points, it is convenient to use a temperature scale first introduced by the British physicist Lord Kelvin. By this scale, the zero is placed at

---

doesn't shrink further because animals constantly combine oxygen with their food and form carbon dioxide which they breathe out.

* It may be that elsewhere in the universe, circling stars other than our Sun, there are other planets of intermediate size and temperature on which there developed life, photosynthesis, an Earthlike atmosphere. There are arguments that can be constructed that will lead to the conclusion that there are hundreds of millions of such Earthlike planets in our own galaxy alone, and equal numbers in all the others of millions of galaxies. However, we have no direct evidence concerning such other-star planets; we can only argue that they must exist. The only planets we can study directly are those in our own solar system and among these, Earth's atmosphere is unique.

the lowest possible temperature ("absolute zero") where matter lacks energy altogether. Absolute zero is 0 K., where the K. stands for Kelvin, of course. Absolute zero is 273 degrees below the freezing point of water, which is 0 C.; absolute zero is therefore −273 C.

To convert the Celsius scale to the absolute scale, one must add 273 to the former. Thus, the freezing point of water is 0 C. and is therefore 273 K.; the boiling point of water is 100 C. and therefore 373 K; comfortable room temperature is 20 C. and therefore 293 K., and so on.

Now let's consider the various substances that can be found in quantity on planetary bodies: hydrogen, helium, nitrogen, oxygen, methane, ammonia, carbon dioxide, water, silicates, and iron. How can we characterize each with respect to the solid/liquid/gas forms it may take up?

Of the ten substances listed, the first two are very low boiling under conditions existing on Earth's surface. Helium has a boiling point at 4 K. and hydrogen at 20 K. Such temperatures are never attained on Earth under natural conditions. Consequently, hydrogen and helium are always gases at earthly temperatures and, indeed, at temperatures of any planetary surface. Even distant Pluto has a temperature of about 45 K., which is enough to keep any hydrogen and helium upon it in gaseous form.

Even at temperatures high enough to keep a substance gaseous, it is possible to compress it (without changing the temperature) into liquid or solid form. On the giant outer planets, which may be made up chiefly of hydrogen (and which are therefore called "gas giants"), hydrogen may be a gas only at the outskirts of the planet (the "surface") we see in a telescope. As one penetrates deeper and deeper below that gas surface, the gas gets denser and denser under the pressure produced by the weight of upper layers. Eventually, the pressure may well force the gas into liquidity or even solidity.

So far, though, we are just beginning to know enough concerning conditions on the gas giants to be able to work out the details of what goes on in the depths. Let's omit the four outer planets from further consideration, therefore, and concentrate on the many other bodies in the solar system.

Of the ten common planetary building-block substances, silicates and iron are high melting. They remain solid to temperatures of 1800 K. and up. With such melting points, a body composed of silicates, iron, or both will retain a firmly solid surface even when quite close to the Sun. As was explained earlier in the chapter, any body that is quite hot, quite small, or both consists *only* of high-melting substances.

Now we have left six building-block substances of intermediate melting points: nitrogen, oxygen, methane, ammonia, carbon dioxide, and water.

Of these, nitrogen, oxygen, and carbon dioxide exist only on the inner planets: all three on Earth, and nitrogen and carbon dioxide only on Mars and Venus. Of these three, nitrogen has a boiling point of 77 K and oxygen one of 90 K. Temperatures on Mars, Earth, and Venus are always above these marks so that where these substances occur on these planets it is always in gas form.

Passing on to carbon dioxide, it is unusual in being one of those substances that don't melt and boil in the ordinary way under surface conditions. At a temperature of 195 K., solid carbon dioxide turns directly into a gas instead of melting into a liquid. This conversion of solid into gas directly is called "sublimation." (Liquid carbon dioxide can be made to form if carbon dioxide gas is placed under pressure.)

The surfaces of Venus and Earth are always at a temperature higher than 195 K., so that on those two worlds carbon dioxide always exists in nature as a gas. The surface of Mars is cold enough, however, for carbon dioxide to exist as a solid.

So far, then, seven of the ten planetary building blocks exist as either always gases or always solids or (in the case of carbon dioxide) as sometimes a gas and sometimes a solid. We have come across nothing, so far, that can exist under planetary conditions in the liquid state, and the only possibilities left are methane, ammonia, and water.

Methane has a melting point of 91 K. and a boiling point of 112 K.; ammonia has a melting point of 195 K. and a boiling point of 240 K.; and water has a melting point of 273 K. and a boiling point of 373 K.

On Pluto, or on any member of the solar system lying outside the orbit of Pluto, the surface temperature is low enough for each of these substances to be in solid form. We are familiar with solidified water, which we call ice. The solid forms of methane and ammonia (and for that matter of other low-boiling substances such as oxygen, nitrogen, carbon dioxide, and so on) are also glassy and brittle. Such solids may be lumped together as ices, and we can speak of ammonia ice, methane ice, or even water ice.

Far out beyond the rim of the visible solar system, it is possible that there is a shell of very many small bodies averaging a kilometer or two across that are made up almost entirely of ices, with or without a silicate/iron core. Occasionally, such a body takes up an orbit that brings it into the inner solar system. The heat of the Sun then vaporizes the ices, creating a haze about the object, and, sometimes, this haze is swept outward into a tail. The result is a comet.

In the form of a solid ice, volatile substances can cling to a planetary surface more firmly than they would as gases. The atoms and molecules of frozen volatiles are held together by chemical forces and don't depend on gravitational pull to remain on the planetary surface. Thus, a body that lacks a gravitational field strong enough to retain more than a trace of atmosphere may be cold enough to retain some volatile matter as surface ice.

Observations made by astronomers in 1972 have led them to believe that some of the large satellites circling Jupiter— perhaps all four of them—possess ices on the surface even though they lack any but the thinnest of atmospheres. The layers may not be very thick and they may not cover the entire surface, but they seem to be there.

If we omit the gas giants, we can say that methane, ammonia, and water, if they exist on any world beyond the orbit of Mars, are likely to exist only as solids. On Mars, Earth, and Venus (the only bodies of the inner solar system containing appreciable quantities of volatile substances), methane and ammonia, if they existed, would always be in the form of a gas. One outer world, Titan, the largest satellite of Saturn, contains an atmosphere made up largely of gaseous methane.

In the search of a planetary liquid, then, we have reduced ourselves to one substance and one only—water.

The surface temperature of Mars is cold enough to keep water permanently in the solid form and this is true also of any object beyond the orbit of Mars (excepting the gas giants, which may be made up of hot liquid hydrogen under huge pressures). Venus, on the other hand, has a surface so hot that on it water can only exist in the form of a gas.

That leaves Earth as the only body in the solar system with a temperature range in which water is a liquid. This means that the Earth is the only world we know of that has an ocean. Leaving out of account the gas giants, the other bodies of the solar system, as far as we know, consist of gas only (the Sun, for instance), of solids only (the Moon, for instance), or of solids and gas.

What's more, water is the only substance that can form a planetary ocean on worlds that are not gas giants. There are other liquids at Earth temperature, such as petroleum or mercury, and there are substances that can be liquid at the high temperature of Mercury or the low temperature of Pluto, but these substances occur in comparatively small quantities and would not make an impressive collection of material even if it were all collected in one spot. Only water, as a major planetary building block, can exist in such copious quantities as to form an *ocean*.

It might be argued that ammonia could form an ocean on a world somewhat colder than Earth, since ammonia is nearly as common as water in the cosmic mix out of which the planets were formed. Ammonia is a liquid at a temperature between 195 K. and 240 K., so let us say that the average surface temperature of a planet is 205 K. (or −68 C.). At such a temperature, water would exist as a hard-frozen solid, and we can imagine an ocean of ammonia, sparkling dimly in the light of a distant Sun incapable of delivering enough heat to boil that ocean.

There is a catch, however. If a planet is large enough to have a gravitational field capable of retaining sufficient ammonia to form an ocean, and is cold enough for that ammonia to remain liquid, then it is large enough and cold enough to retain a good deal of hydrogen and helium. This added hydrogen and helium would raise the strength of the gravitational field and would start the snowball effect going. In short, any planet we can imagine with the properties necessary to form an ammonia ocean would build up into a gas giant.

No, we must have a temperature high enough to keep the snowball effect from taking place if we are to end with a planet other than a gas giant; and at such a temperature the only substance that can be present in large enough quantity to form an ocean is water.

Furthermore, the temperature and size of the planet must be just right. A little too small and not enough water is gathered for an ocean; a little too large and the snowball effect might start; a little too cold and the water may be present only in solid form; a little too warm and the water may be present only in gas form.

It is difficult to decide just how tight the requirements are for the development of a world ocean such as Earth has, but we know certainly that Earth is unique in the solar system and is the only small body with an ocean, just as it is the only one of any size with an oxygen-containing atmosphere in which oxygen is a principal ingredient.*

The Water Molecule

Just because an ocean of water is unique to the Earth does not mean that it *necessarily* has an important effect upon the Earth or that our planet, and the polar regions in particular, might not be much the same if there were only a little water or none at all.

Clearly, though, the *chance* that water might have some important effect would be the greater if there were a large amount of water than if there were a little. How much water is there, then, on Earth?

It would seem that there is a great deal of water, since the ocean covers a total of 360,000,000 square kilometers, or 70 percent of the entire surface of the Earth.

And it is a unique ocean in another sense, since it is a single ocean. Earth has only one.

We have names, to be sure, for different portions: Atlantic, Pacific, Indian, and Arctic. These names, however, merely mark off those portions that are partially (only partially) enclosed by the continents. The Atlantic Ocean is separated from the Pacific, in part, by the Americas; and from the Indian, in part, by Africa. The Indian Ocean is separated from the Pacific, in part, by Australia. The Arctic Ocean is separated from the Atlantic, in part, by Greenland.

Despite the separations, the oceans are all interconnected,

* Of course, as in the case of the oxygen atmosphere, there may be worlds circling other stars that have water oceans. It may even be that water oceans and oxygen atmospheres go together. Still, we can as yet know of these other-star worlds only as conjectures.

and the water in any one of them can flow without total hindrance into any of the others.

It was not till 1497, when the Portuguese navigator Vasca da Gama sailed around Africa and reached India, that Europeans could be certain that the Atlantic Ocean and the Indian Ocean were parts of a single body of water. And it was not till 1522 and the completion of the first circumnavigation of the world that Europeans discovered beyond doubt that all the major bodies of water were interconnected and that Earth was covered by a single ocean into which the continents were set as large islands.

And, of course, what we see of the ocean is only the top of it. On the average, the ocean is 3.7 kilometers deep, and there are places where it is over 11 kilometers deep. The total volume of the ocean is about 1,250,000,000 cubic kilometers.* Its total mass is about 1,350,000,000,000,000,000 (1.35 million trillion) tonnes.

It would seem, then, that we would have to agree that the ocean is enormous and that on the basis of sheer size might possibly be expected to have an important effect on the Earth and on the polar regions.

Yet all that mass of ocean, that more than a billion billion tonnes, though it is unimaginably huge on a human scale is, after all, only a little over 1/4000 (or 0.023 percent) of the total mass of the Earth. Viewed that way, the ocean becomes small, a negligibly small layer of dampness surrounding our mighty planet. If you made your way down to the very deepest part of the ocean, you would only be 1/580 of the distance to the center of the Earth—and all the rest of that distance would be first silicates and then nickel-iron.

And is that small layer of water, then, sufficient to make any real difference?

Oddly enough, if we want evidence that it does, we must look not outward at the size and depth and mass of that water, but inward into the tiny water molecule, far too small to make out under the best microscope.

Molecules consist of groups of atoms held together by chemical forces. Each atom contains a tiny central object, the atomic nucleus, that contains most of the mass of the atom. The atomic nucleus carries a positive electric charge. In each atom

---

* A cubic kilometer is equal to 0.24 cubic miles.

there are very light particles called electrons on the outskirts, each carrying a negative electric charge. The atoms making up a molecule hold together by sharing electrons.

In low-boiling substances—the volatile materials we have been speaking about—the different molecules are held together by weaker forces than the electron sharing that holds atoms together within the molecules. Such molecules are easily separated so as to make solids turn into liquids, and easily separated still further so as to make liquids turn into gases.

All things being equal, different molecules of similar size are separated with roughly equal ease and therefore have similar melting points and boiling points. The size of molecules is measured by what is called "molecular weight," and, as it happens, three of the important volatiles that go into the making of a planet are similar in this respect. Methane has a molecular weight of 16, ammonia one of 17, and water one of 18. From that alone, it would be expected that the melting points and boiling points would be higher for ammonia than for methane, and still higher for water—but not by much.

Yet this is not so. The melting points of methane, ammonia, and water are 91 K., 195 K., and 273 K. respectively. The boiling points are 112 K., 240 K., and 373 K. respectively. In both properties, there is a sharp rise in going from methane to ammonia, and from ammonia to water, a rise that cannot possibly be accounted for by the difference in molecular weights. Something else must be involved.

Consider the methane molecule first. It is made up of one carbon atom and four hydrogen atoms (CH_4). The carbon atom is at the center and the four hydrogen atoms surround it in a completely symmetrical manner. The carbon atom shares two electrons with each of the hydrogen atoms and the sharing is more or less equal. This means that the positive electric charges of the four atomic nuclei and the negative electric charges of the eight shared electrons are all quite evenly distributed over the entire molecule. No part of the molecule has more than its fair share of electric charge.

This is not quite the case with the ammonia molecules, each of which consists of one nitrogen atom and three hydrogen atoms (NH_3). The ammonia molecule is shaped like a shallow tripod, with the nitrogen atom on the top and the three hydrogen atoms located at the ends of the three feet. The nitrogen atom has a somewhat stronger attraction for electrons than the hydrogen atoms do, so it has more than its fair portion of the total of the six electrons it shares with the three hydrogen atoms.

Since the electrons shift toward the nitrogen atom, they more than neutralize the positive electric charge in the nitrogen atomic nuclei. The nitrogen atom, at the top of the tripod, has a slight surplus of negative electric charge. The three hydrogen atoms at the bottom of the tripod, with less than their fair share of the electrons, cannot altogether neutralize the positive electric charge on their atomic nuclei. They are left with a slight surplus of positive electric charge.

The nitrogen is at one end of the molecule and the three hydrogen atoms are at the other, so that the molecule as a whole has a slight negative electric charge at one end and a slight positive electric charge at the other end. There is a negative pole at one end, in other words, and a positive pole at the other. The ammonia molecule is therefore "polar." Methane, on the other hand, without any concentration of surplus charges in any part of its symmetrical molecule, is "nonpolar."

The difference is enormous. As it happens, opposite electric charges attract each other. Ammonia molecules, therefore, tend to orient themselves so that the positive pole of one is adjacent to the negative pole of another. The force of attraction between these two poles holds the two molecules together somewhat more strongly than would be the case if there were no polarity.

Now imagine a quantity of methane and a quantity of ammonia at absolute zero, 0 K. At such a temperature the substances lack any kinetic energy (energy of motion) and all the atoms and molecules are essentially motionless. Under such conditions the molecules are frozen in place and form part of a solid.

If we imagine the temperature rising, the various atoms and molecules begin to move more and more rapidly, and vibrate from side to side about their positions more and more energetically. Eventually, the vibration is energetic enough to cause the molecules to pull loose from whatever forces are holding them together and the substance melts. The molecules can now slip and slide over each other freely, which is why a liquid flows. Nevertheless, even in a liquid the molecules remain in contact.

At some still higher temperature, the molecules gain enough energy to break contact with each other and to move about in complete independence. The liquid boils at that point and becomes a gas.

The forces holding the molecules of solid methane in place are very feeble, since methane is nonpolar in nature. When solid methane is heated, the molecular movement produced by a temperature of 91 K. is enough to pull the molecules out of place and cause the solid methane to melt to liquid methane.

Although the molecules of solid ammonia are only slightly more massive than those of solid methane and should break out of their fixed place at roughly the same temperature, they don't because of the extra stickiness (so to speak) of their molecules due to the force of electric attraction that comes of polarity. A temperature of 195 K. (more than a hundred degrees additional, as compared with methane) is required to produce enough movement to pull the ammonia molecules out of place and cause the solid ammonia to melt.

The same thing happens at the boiling point. A temperature of 112 K. is enough to pull the molecules of liquid methane completely apart and cause it to boil and become a gas. To overcome the stickiness of the ammonia molecules, nearly 150 additional degrees of temperature are required, and liquid ammonia boils and becomes a gas at 240 K.

And what of water? It is made up of molecules composed of an oxygen atom attached to two hydrogen atoms. These atoms are arranged in V-shape, with the oxygen at the vertex and the hydrogens at the end of the two arms. The oxygen atom has an even stronger attraction for the electrons than the nitrogen atom has. Its end of the molecule has a larger negative charge, and the hydrogen-atom end a larger positive charge, than is the case with ammonia. Water molecules are even more polar than ammonia molecules are, and therefore "stickier."

It is for that reason that, although water molecules are only a little larger than methane molecules, water has a melting point 180 degrees higher than methane, and a boiling point 260 degrees higher.

It is entirely because of the strongly polar nature of the water molecule, and of its considerable stickiness, that water remains liquid at such a high temperature, so that an ocean is possible on a planet with a temperature like that of Earth.

Let's consider next what we mean by temperature.

As heat pours into any substance, the molecules that make it up move more and more rapidly and possess more and more energy of motion. The average energy contained by the moving molecules is measured by us as "temperature." If two different objects are at the same temperature, the moving molecules of each contain (on the average) the same energy. If one object is at a temperature higher than that of another, the moving molecules of the one at higher temperature contain (on the average) more energy than the one at lower temperature.

It might seem reasonable to suppose that a given amount of heat always produces the same temperature in different substances, but that is not so. Some kinds of molecules are, for one reason or another, more difficult to accelerate to speedier and more energetic motion than are other kinds. It will take more heat to bring one substance to a particular temperature than another.

Suppose we begin with one gram* of each of a variety of different substances and measure the amount of heat required to raise the temperature of each from 14.5 C. to 15.5 C. This amount of heat is called the "specific heat," and it is different for each different substance.

One reason for a high specific heat can be that energy is needed to overcome the attraction for each other of neighboring molecules. (It would take more energy to make billiard balls move about at a given speed if they and the billiard table had been smeared with honey.) It is not surprising then that water has a considerably higher specific heat than most other substances.

The specific heat of water is about five times as high as the specific heat of the Earth's rocky crust. If a quantity of heat pours down upon a stretch of bare rock and upon a stretch of ocean, both may absorb equal amounts of energy, but that energy brings about a considerably greater temperature rise in the rock than in the water.

On a hot day, then, the ocean remains considerably cooler than the land does, even though both are exposed to the same degree of sunlight.

It works the other way around, too. If rock and water lose the same quantity of heat, this is reflected in a considerably

---

* A gram is a small unit of weight in the metric system, equal to 1/28.3 of an ounce.

larger temperature drop in the rock than in the water. On frigid days, the ocean remains considerably warmer than the land does.

What it amounts to, then, is that, when portions of the Earth's surface rise and fall in temperature in the course of the change between day and night and between summer and winter, the ocean changes less than the land does.

There is also this to consider. The solid crust of the exposed land surface of the Earth cannot transfer heat very easily. If a portion of it grows particularly warm, the heat it contains travels only slowly from itself into neighboring regions which are less warm. Similarly, if a portion of the solid crust grows particularly cold, heat will move into it from other warmer portions only very slowly. Rock has a low "heat conductivity."

The conductivity of water is nearly twice as high as that of rock. In addition, liquid water can flow, as solid rock cannot. Currents exist in the ocean, and, as portions of the ocean water flow through other portions, heat is carried along, too, so that warm portions of the sea tend to heat the cold portions, and the latter tend to cool the warm portions.

For all these reasons, then—high specific heat, high heat conductivity, and the ability to flow—the oceans react differently to gain and loss of heat than land does.

The matter of gain and loss of heat is restricted to the surface of the Earth, for it is the surface only that is exposed to sunlight and the surface only that absorbs energy from it, and it is the surface only that loses energy to space. The fact that the ocean forms so small a part of the total Earth is therefore irrelevant; what is important is that it covers so much of the surface.

You can see that the Earth as a whole would react differently to gain and loss of heat if there were no ocean at all, and that, assuming there is an ocean, particular portions of dry land would behave differently in this respect, depending on the nature and distance of neighboring portions of the ocean.

THE EFFECT
OF THE OCEAN

From the discussion in the previous chapter, we can see that, from purely theoretical considerations, we ought to expect that the relatively even-temperatured ocean would exert a moderating influence on the temperature of the land surface of the Earth. It is the Earth's air conditioner, so to speak.

If there were no ocean, the temperature of the Earth's surface would, we should suppose, be considerably higher by day than it actually is, and considerably lower by night than it actually is, considerably higher in summer than it actually is, and considerably lower in winter than it actually is.

There is no reason, however, why we ought to consider this a purely theoretical matter. This fact is amply evidenced by observation.

Temperature Extremes

Suppose we consider the Moon, for instance, which is, on the average, exactly as far from the Sun as Earth is. Unlike the

Earth, however, the Moon lacks an ocean. As a result, its daytime temperature rises in places to just over 100 C., or just enough to boil water, while at nighttime the temperature drops to − 155 C., or almost cold enough to liquefy methane. No spot on Earth's surface is ever as warm as the Moon's surface can get, and no spot on Earth's surface is ever as cold as the Moon's surface can get.

Of course, the Moon rotates so slowly that its day and its night are each two weeks long. In addition, it lacks not only an ocean but also an atmosphere, and an atmosphere, too, exerts a moderating effect on temperature. Conditions on the Moon, therefore, cannot be considered a true picture of what Earth would be like if the ocean were absent and if nothing else were changed.

But then suppose we consider Earth itself.

If the ocean has a mitigating effect on temperature extremes, it is reasonable to suppose that this effect would make itself felt more on those portions of the land surface near the ocean. The farther a portion of land is from the ocean, the more the oceanic effect would be diluted by distance. If a portion of land were thousands of kilometers from the ocean in all directions, it might almost be as though that portion of land were part of an oceanless world.

Therefore (all other things being equal), the temperatures of continental shorelines ought to show less variation from day to night and from summer to winter than the temperatures of continental interiors at the same latitude.

And this is precisely so. We speak of the "oceanic climates" of islands and coastlines where temperature variations are relatively small, and the "continental climates" of the interior where variations are relatively large.

It follows, then, that the coldest temperatures on Earth are not necessarily to be found at the North and South poles, where they would be if the Earth were of uniform structure over its entire surface. Rather, the coldest temperatures would more likely be found at some areas in the polar regions that are far removed from the ocean and therefore not subject to its moderating influence.

Another reason why land, rather than water, would see record low temperatures involves the matter of altitude. The atmosphere serves as a heat reservoir. The atmosphere grows less dense with altitude, and therefore (at least for the first 20 kilometers) temperatures drop with height. The ocean surface is always at sea level (something that is implied by the very term "sea level"), but on land there are elevations in places of up to 8 kilometers above sea level.

Instantly, you can see that the Antarctic, which is mostly land, would be expected to experience greater cold than the Arctic, which is mostly water.

Yet we need not expect that within Antarctica the coldest temperatures should be experienced at the South Pole. The South Pole, after all, is not centrally placed in the continent, but is nearer ice-free ocean than some other parts of the continent are. The South Pole is, indeed, just about on the line that divides Lesser Antarctica from Greater Antarctica, and it is the latter that represents the real continental block and

Figure 26. Antarctic Cold

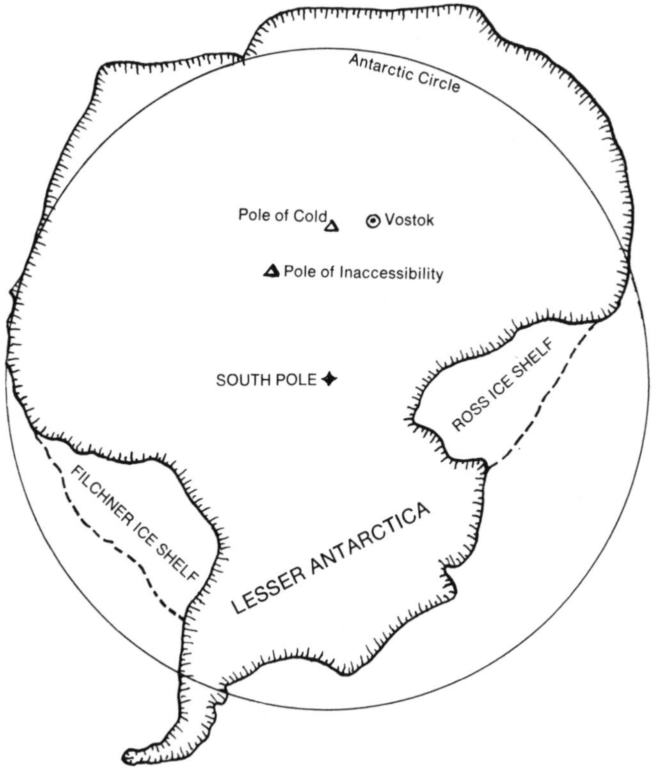

within which we should expect to find the coldest temperatures.

The Antarctic "Pole of Cold" is located at 78° S. and 96° E., and in its neighborhood there are to be recorded the coldest temperatures in the Antarctic and, therefore, in the world (see figure 26). This is 1300 kilometers from the South Pole and should, on strictly geometric principles, be a little warmer than the South Pole. It is, however, somewhat farther removed from the moderating influence of the ocean than the South Pole is, and is also 700 meters higher above sea level.

At the Soviet Antarctic station known as Vostok, which is only 240 kilometers from the Antarctic Pole of Cold, temperatures as low as − 88 C.* were recorded, that record low having been recorded on August 24, 1960.

Temperatures as low as this cannot possibly be expected so close to the North Pole, since that is located in the midst of an oceanic body of water. To find low temperatures in the Arctic, you have to find some sizable body of land as close as possible to the North Pole. The largest body of land in the North Polar regions and hence the one which is most likely to combine a high northern latitude with a considerable separation from the moderating influence of the ocean is the Eurasian continent. It is somewhere in the interior of the polar areas of Eurasia that we would expect to find really low temperatures.

Nor would we be deceived in that expectation. The coldest northern temperatures are to be found in the eastern portion of Siberia. The village of Oymyakon in eastern Siberia recorded a temperature of − 71 C. in January 1964, a record low for the Northern Hemisphere. We can't really say it is a record for the Arctic, for Oymyakon is not really in the Arctic, geographically. It is at 63.27° N., or 320 kilometers *south* of the Arctic Circle and 2900 kilometers from the North Pole (see figure 27).

Since continental climates, thanks to the lack of the moderating influence of the ocean, tend to temperature extremes, we might expect that the summer is hot as the winter is cold in these places we have just cited.

In Siberia, this is so. There is, for instance, the town of Olekminsk, which is about 825 kilometers west of Oymyakon,

---

* For those used to thinking in terms of Fahrenheit, it is worth bending the metric rules of this book to give this temperature as − 127 F.

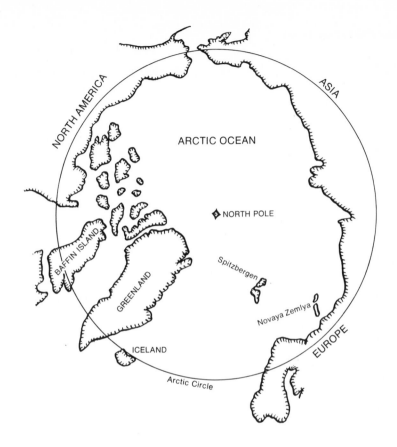

Figure 27. Arctic Cold

about 720 kilometers *south* of the Arctic Circle, and some 1100 kilometers from the nearest body of ocean water. There the temperature can be as low as − 60 C. in the winter and as high as 45 C. in the summer.* This range of a hundred degrees is the greatest temperature range in the world. There are few places on Earth that are hotter in the summer; and there are few places that are colder in the winter.

And can we expect the same of the Antarctic cold spots?

No! The Antarctic cold spots, unlike the Siberian ones, are cold spots *only*. Whereas Oymyakon in Siberia has an average

---

* Again, I can't resist the dramatic effect of the Fahrenheit scale. The temperature range is from − 76 F. to 113 F.

January temperature of −50 C., its *all-year* average is near 0 C. because of the balancing effect of the hot Siberian summer. At the Antarctic Pole of Cold, however, the *all-year* average is −58 C.

In other words, Antarctica has a Siberian winter all year long and rarely does the temperature anywhere in Antarctica at any time of the year climb above the 0 C. mark.

If we are concerned with something that approaches Antarctica in the North Polar region, we have to leave Siberia and turn to Greenland. On the coast of that large island, especially in the southwest, there is considerable warmth. On the southwestern tip, which is, of course, 400 kilometers south of the Arctic Circle (but not farther south than some of the frigid/torrid places in Siberia), the temperature in July averages about 10 C. Even on the northwest coast, only 1350 kilometers from the North Pole, the July average is about 5 C.

It is in the Greenland interior, far from the ameliorating ocean, that the lowest all-year temperature averages are to be found. There an all-year average of −29 C. is to be found.

Although Greenland does not match Antarctica for sheer all-round frigidity and does not attain the temporary depths recorded in the Siberian winter, it is clear that Greenland and Antarctica have something in common that Siberia doesn't share. It is something that gives all three abysmally low winter temperatures, and keeps Greenland and Antarctica, *but not Siberia*, frigid in the summer as well.

What it is that allows Greenland and Antarctica to develop low temperatures during the long polar night but keeps them from building up high temperatures in the long polar day we will come to later. Before we can make proper sense of that as-yet-unconsidered factor, we must continue to consider the properties of water.

Water Vapor

Many of the molecules making up the rocky crust of the Earth are polar in nature; they have an excess of negative electric charge at one end of the molecule, an excess of positive at the other end. Solids made up of such polar molecules often, but not always, tend to break up into electrically charged fragments called "ions" when immersed in a polar liquid. These ions, some carrying a negative electric charge because they include an excess of electrons, and some carrying a positive electric charge because they possess an electron deficit, tend to distribute themselves intimately and evenly through the liquid. The solids "ionize" and "dissolve."

Water, as a strongly polar liquid, exerts this dissolving effect on many polar solids. Water is a good "solvent," but even the best solvent can only dissolve a fixed amount of a particular solid before becoming saturated; that is, holding all the solid it can.

In the case of the various silicates that make up the crust of the Earth, the level of saturation is extremely low. All the water in the ocean can dissolve only an imperceptible fraction of those silicates. The result is that the rocky crust remains undissolved (it is "insoluble") and virtually untouched despite all the soaking the ocean can give it.

Some nonsilicate components of the crust, however, can dissolve to quite a substantial degree before the water becomes saturated with them. Ordinary salt, for instance ("sodium chloride" is its chemical name), is quite soluble. When water has dissolved all the sodium chloride it can, the mixture that results is about 35 percent salt.

We cannot expect to have an ocean on Earth without having it dissolve materials out of the Earth's crust, and we must expect, therefore, to have the liquid in the ocean contain something besides water. Since sodium chloride is the most common of the soluble constituents of the Earth's crust, the ocean is, not surprisingly, quite salty.

There isn't enough salt in the Earth's crust to saturate the vast volume of water in the ocean, but there is enough to fill it to about one-twelfth saturation. The ocean is, in other words, about 3.45 percent, by weight, dissolved matter, and about four-fifths of this is dissolved sodium chloride.

This means that if the ocean were imagined to be boiled away, it would leave behind some 50,000,000,000,000,000 (50 thousand trillion) tonnes of solid matter which had been dissolved in that ocean. If all of this could be evenly spread over the fifty United States, it would make a heap two and a half kilometers high. Since about 80 percent of that solid matter is salt, we can say there are about 40,000,000,000,000,000 (40 thousand trillion) tonnes of salt in the ocean.

But how did the salt get there? As the Earth was shaped and the ocean took on its present form, did it already have its salt content? Or did the ocean begin as a body of water without dissolved materials ("fresh water") and did it slowly dissolve the salt out of the solid crust beneath it and the continental shores on both sides of it?

Or is there a third alternative? Did it start as fresh water and did it gain its salt by more than a passive soaking of the land it directly bordered? Let's see.

One way of converting a liquid to a gas is to heat it to its boiling point, for then the molecules have enough energy of movement to break away from each other altogether.

The molecules in a liquid do not, however, all have the same energy. Some have more than others through the chance of collisions and of energy transfers. Even at temperatures well below the boiling point, some molecules will have enough energy to break away from the rest, and form a gas.

This gas, formed at temperatures below the boiling point, is a "vapor." Water will "vaporize" and turn into "water vapor" even at ordinary temperatures. This happens before our eyes, when we watch a puddle gradually dry up and disappear even though the water in the puddle is quite cool and can by no stretch of the imagination be considered to have boiled away.

Ought we not to expect, then, that the ocean ought to vaporize, dry up, and disappear as the puddle did?

No, not really. Just as molecules in liquid water can occasionally break away to form vapor, molecules of water vapor may happen to lose energy and, if they strike the water surface, they will stay there. In other words, while water molecules in the body of liquid water are leaving as vapor, molecules of vapor are also returning to the body of liquid water.

If a quantity of liquid water is enclosed with a limited volume of air, some of the water will vaporize and some of the water vapor will return. Eventually, an equilibrium will be set up. Water molecules will be leaving the body of water, and returning, at the same rate. The water will therefore vaporize only to some certain extent and no further.

If the water vapor formed from the puddle were kept in the neighborhood of the puddle, then the puddle would only dry slightly and no more. It is only because the wind carries off the water vapor as fast as it is formed so that it never has a chance to return that the puddle vaporizes and vaporizes indefinitely till it is completely gone.

If the air happens to contain a great deal of water vapor for one reason or another—we say that such air is "humid"—then the wind accomplishes nothing by blowing away the vapor arising from the puddle. Other vapor molecules take the place of those blown away. It is for that reason that, on humid days, we have difficulty getting damp objects to dry.

Suppose we consider the ocean as an enormous puddle. The wind can't really blow the water vapor away, for wherever it blows the vapor (except over that minor portion of the Earth's surface which is land), that vapor remains more or less in contact with the ocean.

For that reason, the ocean can only vaporize to a small extent, to the point where an equilibrium is reached between vapor molecules leaving the ocean and other vapor molecules returning to the ocean.

The nature of that equilibrium depends on the temperature. The higher the temperature, the greater the average energy of the water molecules, and the greater the percentage of them that will have enough energy to vaporize. What's more, the smaller will be the percentage of water vapor molecules possessing a sufficiently small amount of energy to return to the water. As the temperature rises, then, the equilibrium shifts in favor of the vapor form, and the greater the amount of liquid which must vaporize before the equilibrium is reached. (At the boiling point, of course, all the liquid must vaporize.)

The average temperature of Earth's surface is 14 C. At that temperature, if we imagined the ocean to vaporize to the equilibrium point, the water vapor produced would make up about 1/17,000 of the weight of the water in the oceans.

In one way, this is a great quantity. It means we can expect the water vapor in Earth's atmosphere to weigh a total of almost 1,000,000,000,000,000 (a thousand trillion) tonnes. If all of it were condensed into liquid water, it would form 45,000 cubic kilometers of water, enough to cover the fifty United States with a layer of water 7.5 meters deep.

In another way, it isn't much at all. If we assume that at any given time 1/17,000 of the ocean is in vapor form, it is clear that the quantity of liquid water present in the ocean is just about as much as it would be if there were no vaporization at all. The loss of 1/17,000 of itself (0.0006 percent) is trivial.

And yet it is trivial only in the matter of weight. As far as its effect on the Earth is concerned, that water vapor, small as it is in comparison with the Earth's liquid water supply, is of enormous importance.

After all, although the average temperature of the Earth's surface is 14 C., that is not the temperature at every point. Nor is it the temperature of any given point at all times. When and where it is warmer than average, there is more water vapor in the air (all things being equal otherwise), and when and where it is colder than average, there is less water vapor in the air.

Thus, a given spot may be quite warm during the day so that considerable vapor builds up in the air. At night the temperature may drop so far that vapor leaves the air, condensing into water droplets on suitable surfaces. One wakes in the morning to find dew on the ground which, in the course of the morning as the Sun climbs higher and the temperature rises, vaporizes again.

A similar process goes on over the Earth generally, and on an enormously enlarged scale.

Thus, vast quantities of liquid water are converted into vapor over the various parts of the ocean, and some of this can be carried high into the atmosphere where the temperature is considerably lower than it is at the water surface. A condensation process takes place high in the air then, and tiny droplets of liquid water form.

The droplets of liquid water absorb light, and collections of them are visible from Earth's surface as clouds high in the air. We all know by personal experience that there are usually clouds in the sky. (At least this is so in the more densely populated portions of Earth's surface.) Sometimes, in fact, clouds blanket all the visible sky.

When Earth is viewed from satellites outside its air blanket, it is seen to be largely obscured by clouds at all times; in fact, though, the cloud cover is never as unbroken or as thick as it is on Venus, where all the water in what might have been its ocean is present as water vapor.

Under certain conditions, the water droplets in the clouds collect into larger and larger drops until the point is reached where they are heavy enough to fall despite the effect of air resistance (which serves to keep particularly small droplets in the air indefinitely). We then have rain.

The complex pattern of temperature difference on Earth, plus the equally complex pattern of ocean currents and wind, together with certain other variables in addition, makes it very difficult to predict just when and where and in how much quantity rain will fall. That, however, does not matter as far as the overall balance of liquid water in the ocean and water vapor in the air is concerned. On the whole, the amount of water that leaves the ocean as vapor and the amount of vapor that returns to the ocean, either molecule by molecule or as huge collections of molecules in the form of raindrops, balance. The net result is that the ocean only evaporates to a tiny extent and no further.

One inevitable consequence of rain, however, is that a certain portion of it does not fall directly on the ocean surface, but falls instead on the land surface of the Earth. It is estimated that 120,000,000,000,000 (120 trillion) tonnes of rain water fall on the land surface of the Earth each year. This is enough water to cover the entire land surface of the Earth, if it stayed there, to a height of about 1.5 meters.

Of course, it doesn't stay there. It soaks into the ground and makes its way downhill, under the pull of gravity. This groundwater collects into swamps, ponds, lakes, rivers, and in almost all cases finds its way back to the ocean. And in doing so, as we shall see, it makes it possible for the ocean to become, and to stay, salty.

Fresh Water

The fact that the ocean does vaporize to some extent has an important effect on Earth's climate. The difference between an ocean that converts 1/17,000 of itself into vapor and one that converts none of itself into vapor is an enormous one.

First, the partial vaporization of the ocean serves to produce clouds in the higher and cooler portions of the atmosphere, and these clouds reflect sunlight far better than bare land and sea surface do.

The bare silicate surface of the Moon and of Mercury makes it possible for those bodies to reflect only about 0.06 of the sunlight falling upon them. (This fraction of light reflected is the "albedo" of a body.) Earth, however, with its cloud layer, has an albedo of 0.30. (The figure for Venus, with its thicker and unbroken cloud layer is 0.59, twice that of Earth, and ten times that of the Moon.)

The fact that the ocean vaporizes, then, keeps the Earth, on the whole, cooler than it would otherwise be, since clouds reflect a substantial portion of solar radiation.

The act of vaporization itself absorbs energy. It takes energy to pull the sticky molecules of liquid water apart and convert them into the separated molecules of water vapor. The energy used for pulling those molecules apart is entirely consumed in that act; it does not go into making the molecules move more quickly. Thus, the water vapor that forms out of liquid water contains more energy than the liquid water does even though both liquid and vapor are at the same temperature.

The energy required for vaporizing water is quite large. It is about 580 times as great as that required to raise the temperature 1 degree. In fact, so much energy is required for vaporizing water that, if water is encouraged to evaporate by a current of dry air over it (to take the vapor away as quickly as it is formed), heat will be withdrawn from the remaining liquid in order to be consumed in the process of vaporization, and the temperature of the water will drop. It is the evaporation of perspiration on our bodies that keeps us from overheating, for instance. (We all know the effect upon ourselves of hot and humid days when there is so much vapor in the air that our perspiration cannot evaporate properly and the natural cooling effect of that perspiration is lost.)

The evaporation of the ocean in tropical areas prevents the ocean's temperature from going up as far as it otherwise would.

To be sure, all this heat is returned to the atmosphere when the water vapor is condensed to liquid again, so that the absorption of energy is not permanent. However, energy is absorbed, by and large, in the warmer portions of the Earth's surface, where vaporization proceeds rapidly, and is given off again, by and large, in the cooler portions, where condensation proceeds rapidly.

The effect of the vaporization of the ocean, then, is not only to keep the Earth cooler than it would otherwise be, by means of clouds, but also to distribute the heat, transferring it from warmer regions to cooler ones, and making the planetary climate more equable than it would otherwise be.

One vital point to keep in mind concerning the vaporization of the ocean is that it is only the water that vaporizes. The salt and the other dissolved substances are not volatile and cannot vaporize at the natural temperatures of the ocean surface.

Consequently, when the water vapor condenses into clouds, dew or rain, the liquid water that forms is *only* water, to a high degree of purity. (There is bound to be some dust and extraneous substances gathered from the air so the purity is not quite perfect, but it is good enough.)

The water that reaches the land surface as a result of rain, then, and appears as groundwater, swamps, lakes, and rivers, is fresh water as opposed to the salt seawater of the ocean.

The fresh water on land is constantly flowing back to the sea, but it is as constantly being replenished by further rainfall, so that the amount present on land at any given time reaches a fairly constant figure. The total quantity of liquid fresh water on land is a considerable quantity by human standards. It comes to about 450,000,000,000,000 tonnes, or about 110,000 tonnes for each man, woman, and child on the planet.

On the planetary scale, it is not much. It represents only about 1/2800 of the water in the ocean.

This small proportion of the Earth's total water supply which is in the form of liquid fresh water on the land is, however, of vital importance to us. Life originated in the ocean and some 80 percent of it still lives in the ocean and is adapted to seawater. Some forms of life adapted themselves to fresh water, on the other hand, and came to live in the lakes and rivers, on land exposed to rainfall, or in the air above such land.

We ourselves are descended from freshwater ancestors and we can drink only fresh water. Furthermore, the nondrinking uses to which we put water in our homes, on our farms, and in our industries in almost every case require fresh water and cannot make do with salt water.

There is, and can be, no shortage of water on our water-soaked planet, but there can be a shortage of fresh water. Such a shortage can take place from time to time almost anywhere when the rains fail and there is a period of drought. As the human population rises and the uses of fresh water multiply, there is the strong possibility that the shortage can become much more widespread and intensive, and this is something we will bring up again in connection with the polar regions later in the book.

The liquid fresh water on the land does not remain as pure, while percolating through the soil, as it was while it was drifting in the atmosphere or falling as rain. Granted that most of the constituents of the land are highly insoluble, there is always a little solution of various substances taking place. By the time fresh water has percolated through rock and soil and has reached the ocean, dissolved material (mainly salt, of course) makes up about 0.01 percent of its bulk.

Such water is only 1/320 as salty as the ocean. It is not salty enough to bother us.* It can be drunk, or used for irrigation, or for industrial purposes.

However, this very slightly salty fresh water keeps flowing into the sea by way of many rivers, and the trifling amount of salt added to the sea in this manner mounts up. It is estimated that all the river water carries nearly 3,000,000,000 tonnes of solids into the ocean each year. This large-sounding amount isn't much on an oceanic scale, of course. It is less than a fifteen-millionth of the solids already present in the ocean.

Yet, as year after year passes, the added solids mount up, little by little.

About two hundred years ago, geologists hadn't the vaguest notion of how old the Earth might be. They felt an answer of sorts might be obtained if it were supposed that the ocean was fresh to begin with and that it had turned as salty as it is now through the steady addition of river salt.

As you see, if the rivers carry to the sea each year less than a fifteen-millionth of the ocean content of salt, it should take a little over 15,000,000 years for the ocean to become as salty as it is today starting from scratch.

Figures in the millions of years seemed an enormous figure for the age of the Earth to the geologists of two centuries ago, but today we know that it is a considerable underestimate. Better means of determining Earth's age yield a now widely accepted figure of some 4,700,000,000 years.

There are several reasons why gauging the increasing saltiness of the sea is unsatisfactory as a method for measuring the age of the Earth, or even the age of the ocean. For one thing, we cannot possibly be sure that rivers deliver a constant quantity of dissolved matter to the ocean each year. Changes in the conformation of the continents and in the presence and location of mountainous areas make it quite certain that the quantity must vary radically and uncertainly over geologic periods of time.

---

* In fact, absolutely pure "distilled water" tastes flat and rather unsatisfactory.

Secondly, the ocean can lose dissolved matter as well as gain it. Shallow arms of the sea can sometimes be pinched off in the course of geologic ages. The pinched-off sections may slowly evaporate, leaving behind dissolved matter in huge thicknesses. The salt mines that are found here and there on land were once parts of the ocean.

It may be, then, that the dissolved matter shuttles back and forth between ocean and land, and that the ocean may, in the very long run, remain at a constant level of saltiness.

Naturally, over the short run, the ocean may vary a bit in saltiness and may be a little more salty or a little less salty than average now and then. Whether the ocean at the present moment is above average in saltiness, below average, or just about average is not known.

Undoubtedly, the ocean varies from the average in saltiness less than it might because of its huge size. It takes a great deal of solid matter to be added, or subtracted, to make even a tiny change in the overall percentage of dissolved matter in the ocean.

What could happen if the ocean were not as huge as it is can be seen in some places on Earth. There are regions in the continental interiors where the fresh water, collecting on the land surfaces, does not drain back into the ocean. It collects, instead, in troughs which are blocked off from the ocean by higher elevations on all sides. There the water collects as an inland sea.

These inland seas receive river water, but they do not lose that water by drainage into the ocean. Instead they lose water only by evaporation and that makes a crucial difference. If a lake loses water by river drainage into the ocean (as the Great Lakes lose their water by drainage through the St. Lawrence River), then both water and dissolved materials are carried away. If a lake loses water only by evaporation, then only the water leaves while the dissolved material remains.

Over long periods of time, then, rivers bring small quantities of dissolved matter into these landlocked lakes, and the dissolved matter stays and accumulates. Because the lakes are far, far smaller in volume than the ocean is, the dissolved matter builds up to surprisingly high values in relatively short periods of time (short, that is, as compared with Earth's history).

The largest such landlocked body of water is the Caspian Sea on the borders of the Soviet Union and Iran. The Caspian Sea, about 400,000 square kilometers in area, receives the water of the Volga River and, except for evaporation, keeps it. Its salt content is now about 1.3 percent, so that it is nearly two-fifths as salty as the ocean. That it has only reached such a level of saltiness shows that it is a relatively young body of water.*

In bodies of water still smaller than the Caspian Sea, the results are even more extreme. The Great Salt Lake, in Utah, which is 4000 square kilometers in area, and the Dead Sea, between Israel and Jordan, which is 1000 square kilometers in area, have a salt content that is 25 percent and more.

Density

Other important effects of the ocean (effects that, as we shall see, strongly influence the polar regions) arise out of the density of water and the way in which it varies. By the density of a substance, we mean the weight† of a particular volume of that substance.

Thus a cubic centimeter‡ of water weighs 1.0 grams. (This is no coincidence. The metric system of measurements is deliberately designed in this way.) We can therefore say that the density of water is 1.0 grams per cubic centimeter. A cubic centimeter of aluminum, however, weighs 2.7 grams, while a cubic centimeter of platinum weighs 21.4 grams. Therefore, the density of aluminum is 2.7 grams per cubic centimeter and that of platinum is 21.4 grams per cubic centimeter.

One ought not to say that platinum is heavier than aluminum, and that aluminum is heavier than water (though many people do), since a large aluminum ingot will be considerably heavier than a small scrap of platinum, and a bathtub full of water will be heavier than the aluminum ingot. You can say,

---

* Under present conditions, the Caspian Sea is losing water by evaporation faster than it is gaining it from the rivers that flow into it. Its area is therefore shrinking and that helps increase its concentration of dissolved solids a little faster than would otherwise be the case.

† It would be more correct at this point to use the term "mass," but it will be simpler to follow the line of argument, and no real harm will be done, if I let the term be "weight" here.

‡ A cubic centimeter is equal to 0.061 cubic inches, or about one-sixteenth of a cubic inch.

however, that a given volume of platinum is heavier than the same volume of aluminum, which, in turn, is heavier than that same volume of water. In other words, platinum is denser than aluminum, and aluminum is denser than water.

The density of a solid determines whether it will float on a particular liquid or not.

Suppose you put a certain solid onto the surface of a particular liquid. It will sink, pushing some of the liquid aside to make room for itself. It pushes that liquid aside through the force of its own weight.

The liquid, which has a tendency to return to the place from which it was evicted, pushes upward on the sinking solid (an effect called "buoyancy"). The greater the amount of liquid displaced, the greater the amount of buoyancy, since that is related to the weight of the displaced liquid. As the solid sinks into the liquid, then, displacing more and more of the liquid as it sinks, the solid's weight decreases as the buoyant push upward increases.

Suppose the solid has a higher density than the liquid has. By the time the solid is completely submerged, it has displaced exactly its own volume of the liquid. The buoyant force, equal to the weight of the liquid displaced, is less than the weight of the solid. The displaced liquid and the displacing solid are equal in volume, and the solid, being denser, is heavier. All the buoyancy of the liquid will not cancel all the weight of the solid, so that gravity will continue to pull the solid downward even after it is completely submerged.

In short, if a solid has a higher density than a liquid, the solid will sink in that liquid. It will not float.

On the other hand, suppose a solid has a lower density than a particular liquid. Before the solid is entirely submerged, the volume of liquid it has displaced, though smaller than its own volume, has a weight equal to that of the solid. The buoyancy then neutralizes the entire weight of the solid and it can sink no more. It remains floating.

In short, if a solid has a lower density than a liquid, it will float on that liquid and will not sink. It can easily be shown that if the density of a solid is a certain fraction of the density of a liquid, that solid will float with that fraction of its volume submerged. If the solid has nine-tenths the density of the liquid, for instance, it will float with nine-tenths its volume submerged and the other tenth above the liquid surface.

Thus, iron, which has a density of 7.86 grams per cubic centimeter will sink in water, which has a density of 1.0 grams per cubic centimeter. Iron will, however, float on mercury, which has a specific gravity of 13.5, and what's more, will float with over two-fifths of itself above the surface of the mercury.

(To be sure, a large ship made primarily of iron will not sink in water, but that is because the iron is turned up on all sides and encloses a large volume of air within. As the ship sinks in the water, it displaces a volume equal not only to the iron of which its hull is made, but to the air contained within the hull. The density of the iron *plus* air is less than that of water. If the ship springs a leak so that water can replace the air, or if it capsizes, it will sink soon enough.)

The density of any given substance is not constant under all conditions. It varies, for instance, with temperature.

Consider a solid or liquid. In such substances the molecules are in contact and are vibrating about some fixed positions in the solid, or moving about over and past each other in the liquid.

As the temperature goes up, the motion becomes more violent and there is more jostling, so to speak. Each molecule requires a little more room in consequence. As the temperature rises, then, the same weight of substance is spread over a little more room, and a given volume contains slightly fewer molecules and weighs less. The density therefore decreases as temperature goes up and increases as temperature goes down.* This is true of gases, too, as well as of solids and liquids.

The change in density with temperature is not great. Let us take water as an example and consider it first at a temperature of 4 C. At that point its density is just 1.0000 grams per cubic centimeter. As the temperature rises, the density decreases. At 14 C. it is 0.9993 grams per cubic centimeter; at 24 C. it is 0.9973 grams per cubic centimeter; and at the boiling point of 100 C., its density is 0.9583 grams per cubic centimeter.

What it amounts to is that very hot water is only a little over

---

* We measure temperature most commonly by the change in density of mercury. As temperature goes up, the density of mercury goes down and a given quantity takes up more room so that the narrow thread of mercury in the thermometer rises. It falls when the temperature decreases.

4 percent less dense than very cold water, and the water on the surface of a tropic sea may be only 3 percent less dense than the water on the surface of a polar sea.

Can such small differences matter? Yes, they can.

Imagine a body of ocean water off the coast of New England as the winter deepens. The surface of the water loses heat to the frigid winds sweeping across it and drops a few degrees in temperature. The water underneath the top few meters of the sea does not drop in temperature, since it is protected by those few meters from contact with the cold wind. Therefore the surface of the ocean becomes colder than the lower layers and very slightly more dense.

That very slightly is enough. The surface layer, being more dense than the lower layer, cannot float on the lower layer but drops through it. It is replaced by slightly warmer and less dense water from below. The new water cools off in its turn and sinks.

In short, as a result of the change in the density of water with changes in temperature, the cooling of the surface of the water sets up a kind of vertical mixing and circulation.

Imagine, next, the surface of a tropical sea which is warming under the Sun. The upper meters of the surface grow warmer and less dense. The warmer water does not sink, of course. The less dense it is, the less capable it is of sinking.

As it warms and grows less dense, however, it takes up more room than it did so that it spreads out over adjacent areas of the ocean, areas that are subjected to less warmth.

In short, the uneven heating of the surface of the ocean as between the tropical regions, the temperate regions, and the polar regions, and as between the surface and the depths, helps to set up both horizontal and vertical currents that keep the ocean well mixed at all times—thanks to the small changes in density with temperature.

These currents, both horizontal and vertical, are of essential importance to life, and, as we shall see, the polar regions play a particularly important role in this respect.

ICE

In the previous chapter, I referred to the Earth's supply of liquid fresh water. This liquid fresh water represents, however, only a minor portion of the total freshwater reserves of the planet. Indeed, the total quantity of fresh water on Earth is equal to 45 times that of the liquid water in the soil and in the lakes, rivers, and swamps.

To see why this is so, let's continue further with our discussion of the properties of water.

The Freezing of Water

So far, I have discussed the conversion of water from the liquid form to the gas either by boiling or vaporization, and from the gas to the liquid by condensation. But something happens at the other end of the temperature scale, too. Liquid water can be converted into the solid form by freezing, and the solid can melt back into liquid.

This change takes place, in the case of water, at 0 C., which can be considered either the freezing point of water or the melting point of ice. The freezing point of water is well below the average temperature of the Earth's surface, so that it is not surprising that some 98 percent of the Earth's water supply is in liquid form. Outside the Tropics, though, it is quite common for the temperature to drop below the freezing point from time to time and the farther toward either pole we go, the more frequently do subfreezing temperatures occur.

In the United States, particularly in the northern half, we expect to see water solidify every winter. A puddle of liquid water will, for instance, solidify into ice as the temperature drops and, of course, will melt again into liquid when the temperature rises once more.

In this respect, water certainly does not seem unique. Any liquid will freeze into a solid form if the temperature is dropped sufficiently. Yet water is different, in this respect, from almost all other substances in one all-important quality—and that involves the matter of density, which we were discussing at the conclusion of the previous chapter.

In general, the density of a liquid continues to increase as the temperature drops, all the way down to the freezing point. Then, when the liquid freezes, the solid form usually has a substantially higher density than the liquid form, for as the molecules take up fixed positions, the arrangement is more compact than when all are sliding around every which way. For instance, the density of liquid hydrogen is 0.071 grams per cubic centimeter and that of solid hydrogen is 0.076 grams per cubic centimeter.

Suppose this density change were true of water (as it is of almost every liquid) and let us see what would then happen. Imagine a lake of water exposed to subfreezing winter weather. The upper layer of water would cool, grow denser, and sink. Warmer water from below would replace it on the surface, would then cool in its turn, and would sink. Little by little, every bit of water would cool further and further until all the water was at the freezing point.

Now the upper layer of water, directly exposed to the cold air, would freeze. Crystals of ice would appear, and, since these would be denser than liquid water (in the case we are imagining), they would sink to the bottom. More and more ice would form and sink. The ice would accumulate on the bottom and pile up until finally the entire lake would be solid ice from top to bottom, assuming that the cold weather continued long enough.

Eventually, the winter would pass and the spring would come. The temperature would then rise above the freezing point of water and the ice on the surface would begin to melt. Water would form over the surface of the ice and would form a thicker and thicker layer as more and more of the ice melted.

The thicker the layer of water, however, the harder it would be for heat to penetrate and reach the still-frozen ice below. If the lake were small and shallow, all of it would melt eventually. If the lake were sizable and deep, the bottom layers could stay frozen throughout the entire summer, since the upper layer would insulate them against heat gain. The liquid water would itself stay pretty cold where it was in contact with the ice. Long before the bottom ice could melt, it would be winter again and the cold upper layer of water would freeze again quickly. If the lake had not frozen solidly the winter before, it would certainly do so now.

This would happen to the ocean, too, and the Earth, even though it were just as close to the Sun as it is now and though it had the same summer with the same quantity of heat pouring down from the Sun, would be frozen tightly with, at best, only a comparatively thin layer of water above the enormous block of oceanic ice in the Tropics and a thinner layer in the temperate regions. The winds off the vast frigidity of the ocean would see to it that the land never warmed up very much either.

Obviously, this does not happen. Why not?

Because the density variation with temperature in the case of water does not work in the fashion just described. Water is exceptional in the way its density varies with temperature and it is the greatest good fortune (for us) that this is so.

Since water molecules are highly polar, they adjust themselves, in the solid state, in such a way that each negative end of a molecule is near the positive end of a neighbor molecule and that the whole arrangement is as symmetrical as possible. In order for this to happen most symmetrically, it turns out that the molecular arrangement must be very loose, considerably looser than is usual in solids. This, in turn, means that the molecules take up considerably more room than they might and that the density of ice is lower than it would be if less symmetry of position were required. The density of ice is, in fact, 0.917 grams per cubic centimeter, which is *less* than the 1.0 grams per cubic centimeter density of liquid water.

It is for this reason that pure ice floats in pure water, with 91.7 percent of itself submerged.

Nor is this all. As water cools, the tendency for the molecules to begin arranging themselves in the symmetrically solid fashion becomes more pronounced. When water is cooled to a temperature of 4 C. (or 3.98 C., to be more exact), the tendency toward the solid arrangement neutralizes the usual density increase with lowered temperatures. At 4 C., the density of water is at a maximum and it is then 1.00000 grams per cubic centimeter.

When water is cooled below 4 C., the density begins to decrease again and at 0 C., the freezing point, the density of water is 0.99987 grams per cubic centimeter. This is a decrease of only a little over a hundredth of a percent, but it is important.

Let's go back to our lake of liquid water which is cooling in the winter and see what happens under *actual* conditions. It cools down as before described, with the cool water on top sinking to the bottom and exposing fresh, warmer water to the cooling effect of winter temperatures—but only till the water in the lake is cooled to 4 C.

After that, as the water cools still further, the top layer, which experiences the cooling, grows slightly less dense and does *not* sink. The coldest water stays on top. When it freezes, the ice formed is considerably less dense than the liquid water and it stays on top, too. Even if the wind were to stir up the lake so that all of its water sinks to the freezing point, and if ice were to form somewhere below the surface, it would promptly rise to the surface and remain there.

After a while, the entire *surface* of the lake is coated with a solid layer of ice. Ice, however, does not conduct heat well and the water underneath the layer loses its heat only slowly. The result is that even in a cold winter, the ice layer does not grow very thick and almost all of the lake remains liquid under the ice layer throughout the season.

Furthermore, when the warmer weather comes, the ice layer on top of the lake is directly exposed to the heat of the Sun, quickly melts, and is gone.

As a result, entirely because the density of water *decreases* when cooling proceeds to temperatures very near the freezing point, and because ice is considerably less dense than water and is a poor conductor of heat, there is little tendency for bodies of water to freeze. The oceans and lakes and rivers over most of the Earth remain liquid at all times, and even though there is a tendency, in cooler places, for a scum of ice to form on the surface from time to time, that ice does not last.

It is this persistence of liquid water through the coldest winters that makes it possible for life to continue in lakes and rivers, let alone the ocean. Without that, land life could not exist either.

Sea Ice

Naturally, the tendency for bodies of water to develop ice on the surface becomes more pronounced the lower the average temperature in that part of the world. The colder the region, the sooner the icing begins in the fall and the later it lasts in the spring. If the region is cold enough, the ice remains throughout the year. The water of the polar regions, in particular, tends to be ice covered.

This is true not only of lakes and rivers, but even of the ocean. The use of the word "even" in connection with the ocean rests on the fact that the ocean is salty. The presence of dissolved solid matter interferes with the process of freezing, so that a liquid must be cooled to a lower temperature to make it freeze when it contains dissolved material than would be the case if it were pure.

Seawater freezes at a temperature of − 2 C., or 2 degrees below the freezing point of fresh water. Consequently, seawater will usually freeze later in the season than fresh water will.

If water containing dissolved matter is allowed to cool very slowly, the crystals of ice that slowly form and coalesce consist of water only. The ice, in other words, is fresh. The dissolved matter concentrates in what water is left unfrozen, which therefore becomes brinier and brinier.

In actual fact, though, as the sea freezes and forms "sea ice," the ice crystals trap some of this briny water between themselves, especially when conditions are such that the ice forms rapidly. Sea ice therefore ends by being quite salty.

The Arctic Ocean possesses sea ice the year round. In the winter, it is continuous and solid ("pack ice"), but no matter how frigid that winter is, the Arctic Ocean never freezes solidly, or comes even close to that. Thanks to the poor heat conductivity of ice, the Arctic Ocean remains liquid beneath a thin ice layer which has an average thickness of 1.5 meters, with occasional places where a thickness of 4 meters is reached.

The relative unimportance of the Arctic Ocean pack ice in terms of sheer bulk becomes evident when we realize that the average depth of the Arctic Ocean is 1800 meters (1.8 kilometers), and its greatest depth, 5300 meters (5.3 kilometers). If you imagine yourself dropping a line from the top of the Arctic Ocean ice cover to the sea bottom, that line would pass through ice for 0.08 percent of the distance and through water the remaining 99.92 percent.

In the depth of winter, when the Arctic Ocean pack ice is at its thickest, the continuous ice cover has a diameter of between 3000 and 4000 kilometers and covers an area of 13,000,000 square kilometers. Its most southerly penetration in winter lies along the eastern coasts of North America and of Asia. In North America it fills Baffin Bay and Hudson Bay and creeps down the coast of Labrador, even down to Newfoundland on occasion, reaching the vicinity of 50° N. In Asia it fills the Sea of Okhotsk, west of Kamchatka, and makes its way down the Siberian coast to the northernmost of the Japanese islands.

Because a current of warm water from the Gulf of Mexico (the famous "Gulf Stream") sends the last bits of its warmth up the Norwegian coast, the pack ice usually will not form in the vicinity of the northern shores of Scandinavia even when it is at its maximum extent. It is for that reason that, during World War II, Allied convoys could sail to the Soviet port of Murmansk around Norway's northern shore even in winter.

In the course of the spring and summer, the Arctic Ocean pack ice begins to melt and to retreat from those portions of the North Temperate Zone which it has invaded. By August, when the pack ice is at its minimum extent (it never disappears entirely, of course), it retreats beyond the Arctic Circle, and the sea is clear to Novaya Zemlya on the Asian side and to the northern reaches of Greenland and Ellesmere Island on the North American side. Almost all the northerly shores of the North American and Eurasian continents are clear (at least of solid pack ice), except for the more northerly reaches of Siberia.

What pack ice remains shrinks to about 10,000,000 square kilometers in area and ceases to be continuous. It becomes, instead, a conglomerate of large pieces of ice up to 8 kilometers across, with snaking, shifting lanes of open water all through what was once a solid tract of ice, right up to the North Pole. Near the fringes, the pieces are small ice floes, only a few meters across.

Then, as the weather begins to cool with the coming of winter, the lanes of open water thin, the separate ice floes coalesce and pack together. The ice grows thicker and winter conditions gradually prevail again.

The Arctic pack ice seems to drift slowly (even when it seems solid and firm) in a clockwise direction around the North Pole.

In the neighborhood of the Arctic shores, particularly of those of Greenland and of the islands of the Canadian Archipelago, pack ice may build up to great thicknesses, thanks to the fact that the continents are generally colder than the ocean in the winter. These built-up bits of pack ice may then break loose from shore and drift outward to form part of the general ice cover. Amid the thin portions of the oceanic pack ice, then, there may be chunks of ice that once adhered to the shore and that are up to 60 meters thick, and with areas of up to 800 square kilometers.

A piece of ice that is at least ten times thicker than most of the ice surrounding it naturally emerges from the water to a height at least ten times that of its surroundings. Aerial surveys after World War II discovered these flat stretches of ice prominently upraised and they are called "ice islands." Since that time, nearly a hundred ice islands have been observed, most of them in the regions between the islands of the Canadian Archipelago.

Ice islands, like the pack ice generally, move slowly through the Arctic Ocean and might make a complete circle in some 2000 to 3000 years, unless they collided with some land shore and remained there, or unless they blundered out of the Arctic Ocean through the channels southward and then slowly disintegrated in the warmer waters beyond.

In the Antarctic region, the situation differs from that of the Arctic in that there is no central ocean but a central continent. This means that most of the ocean water in the Antarctic region lies in the neighborhood of the Antarctic Circle and outside it in the South Temperate Zone.

Even so the frigidity of the continent of Antarctica spreads its icy hands over the neighboring ocean, and pack ice develops

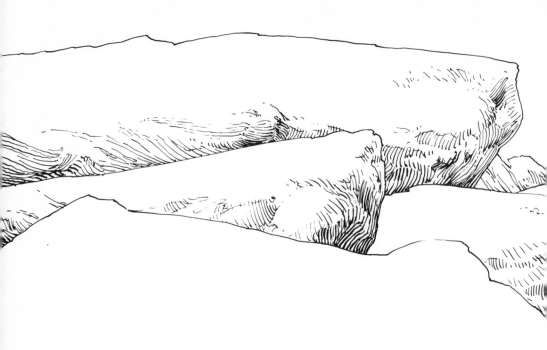

all along its shores and spreads outward in every direction. By the end of the Antarctic winter, the pack ice has stretched out for 1000 to, in some cases, 1500 kilometers from the Antarctica shores. It fills almost all the southernmost third of the South Temperate Zone and at its greatest extent covers 20,000,000 square kilometers, twice the area of the Arctic pack ice at its greatest.

In the course of the spring and summer, however, the Antarctic pack ice, which is mostly in the South Temperate Zone, is far more vulnerable to the warming effect of the Sun than the Artic pack ice, mostly in the North Frigid Zone, is. The Antarctic pack ice shrinks greatly and is down to 5,000,000 square kilometers at times, half the minimum area of the Arctic pack ice.

The seasonal variation of the Antarctic pack ice, 15,000,000 square kilometers, is five times that of the Arctic pack ice, 3,000,000 square kilometers.

The Tundra

Water will remain frozen much or all of the year on the land surfaces of the polar regions, too. This refers not only to such

Crabeater Seals and Skua (flying)

obvious cases as the surface layers of lakes and rivers, but to water on and in the soil as well.

If the temperature is cold enough, water vapor in the atmosphere will condense on the ground not as liquid dew but as fine, white crystals of ice called "frost." And if there is water already in the ground ("groundwater") that, too, can freeze.

Groundwater is to be found everywhere on the land portions of the Earth, even (if you dig deep enough) in those places where the surface is desert. Where the temperature remains at or below the freezing point of water through much of the year, the groundwater freezes and cements the soil and rock into a hard mass, and remains so, more or less, throughout the year.

Ground that is more or less permanently frozen in this way is referred to as "permafrost." It is estimated that up to 25 percent of the land areas of Earth contain some permafrost.

Permafrost is most noticeable, naturally, in the polar regions, where it can extend quite deep, and where it may exist unchanged, without melting, for thousands of years at a time. Even when the polar summer melts the ice near the soil, the soil, which is a poor heat conductor, prevents warmth from penetrating deeply so that the permafrost beneath remains untouched.

The maximum thickness of permafrost is in northern Siberia. At Nordvik, on the Arctic shore just east of the Taimyr Peninsula, the permafrost is reported to be over 600 meters thick.

Where permafrost exists, it becomes difficult for trees to grow, since these depend on a root system that gathers groundwater from considerable depths. As one goes toward the polar regions, then, there are fewer and smaller trees, until past a certain point (the "timberline," or "tree line") there are no trees at all.

The treeless areas fringing the Arctic Ocean are called "tundra." This comes from a Russian word, which was apparently taken in turn from a Lapp word. (The Lapps, after all, live on the tundra in northern Scandinavia.)

Tundra is to be found all along the shores of the Arctic Ocean, along the coasts of Siberia, Scandinavia, Canada, Alaska, and the various polar islands. Much of Iceland is tundra, for instance, as is the Greenland coastline. (The Greenland interior is something other than tundra, as we shall see later.)

For the most part, the tundra exists within the Arctic Circle, but it extends southward in Canada and along the west Alaskan shore. It is found along the shores of Hudson Bay as far south as 55° N., which is 1200 kilometers south of the Arctic Circle (see figure 28). The total area of tundra in the world is about 8,000,000 square kilometers, or roughly the area of the United States.

The tundra is treeless; there is only a short summer period in which the temperature rises above the freezing point of water, and even the warmest summer months have a temperature

Figure 28. The Tundra

average of no more than 10 C. Yet this does not mean that the tundra is barren.

It is a hard environment and there are relatively few species of organisms to be found there, pathetically few compared to the riotous proliferation of species in the warmer and more hospitable portions of the world. However, if relatively few species can adapt to polar rigor, those species seem to benefit from the lack of interspecies competition and multiply to unusually large numbers.

The tundra can, and does, support such plant life as does not require a deep root system. Some 900 species of grasses, sedges, moss, lichen, and even a few shrubs grow in the tundra during the warmer weather when the top few feet of the permafrost melts. Only a few of them grow as much as ankle high.

The growing season is very short, but the periods of light are very long. The plant life of the tundra is adapted to these long periods of light and by growing without rest, so to speak, manage to develop flowers and seeds, or to multiply asexually, with great rapidity. The flowers are often brightly colored and the drab desolation of the Arctic land turns briefly into a multicolored symphony during the short summer. Then, when that is over, the plant world manages to hang on under the snow, surviving the winter in one way or another and waiting for another short period of riotous growth.

Even on Peary Land, along the northern shores of Greenland, plant life of this sort thrives, and so it would do at the North Pole itself, if there were bare ground there and if the top foot or so of permafrost melted briefly during the summer.

Where one has plants, one has animals, and during the short growing season, insect life explodes into activity as well, all too often in the form of biting species that are the bane of man and other large animals. One might almost swear, after experiencing a polar summer, that the dominant form of animal life in the tundra is the mosquito.

Warm-blooded animals (birds and mammals) can thrive in the Arctic, since cold is no bother to them, provided they are well-enough insulated and can live on the food available there. To provide insulation, hair (or feathers in case of birds) is longer, more densely packed, more woolly than in similar species in warmer climates. Layers of fat under the skin act as further insulation.

Then, too, the shape of the bodies of polar animals tends to cut down the rate of heat loss. Polar animals are larger than similar species in temperate and tropic zones. As an animal increases in size, its bulk increases as the cube of its linear dimensions while its surface increases only as the square. This means that if an animal doubles its length, width, and height, but keeps its same shape and proportions, its weight increases $2 \times 2 \times 2$, or 8 times, while its surface area increases only 2×2, or 4 times. Every bit of its weight is manufacturing heat through various chemical reactions taking place within the body, but only the surface loses it to the outer environment. A large animal, therefore, loses a smaller proportion of the heat it generates than a small one does.

This was first pointed out by Carl Bergmann in the 1840s, and it is called "Bergmann's rule."

In addition, the various extremities of the body are reduced in size in polar animals as compared with similar species in

Willow Ptarmigan

warmer climates. Ears and snouts are smaller and blunter in polar animals, legs and tails shorter. This further cuts down on surface loss of heat, as was first pointed out by Joel Asaph Allen in 1877, so that it is called "Allen's rule."

The most characteristic birds of the tundra are various species of ptarmigan, birds of the grouse family which differ from nonpolar species in having their legs feathered right down to the claws—an obviously useful adaptation to the polar climate.

Their plumage is mottled brown, black, and gray in the summer, but as the winter approaches, these feathers are replaced by white ones and some species of ptarmigan are pure white in the winter.

Although a white coloration doesn't particularly help an organism keep warm, it is useful in another way. Since the dominant color of a polar winter is the white of snow and ice, white feathers or white fur serve as protective coloration, since white on white is difficult to see. An organism that is preyed on by others evades detection by potential predators, which is useful; while a predator, such as a fox or a weasel, that turns white in the winter also evades detection by potential prey, and that, too, is useful.

The typical ptarmigan is about 15 inches long and feeds not only upon the plant life characteristic of the tundra, but upon insects as well.

The small land mammals of the tundra are various rodents, which are too small to be efficient in retaining their body heat and therefore cannot brave the outside world very well in the winter months. Some, like the ground squirrels and marmots, defeat the winter by passive surrender and hibernate the cold

Arctic Fox (with white winter coat)

months away in a trancelike sleep, coming to life as the plants do for only the warmer part of the year.

Others, notably the lemmings, retreat beneath the snow, where at the snow-soil interface, it is considerably warmer than at the snow-air interface above. In the runways they manufacture, these rodents can remain active all winter long, feeding on the plant life that is likewise buried in the snow. These rodents serve as the chief food supply of the smaller predators, such as weasels, owls, and foxes.

Arctic Hares

The lemmings, which are small, short-tailed, mouselike organisms about 6 inches long, are perhaps the most characteristic small mammal of the tundra. Some species turn white in the winter, the only true rodents to do so.

Like many small creatures with high reproductive rates, there is a surging up and down in their numbers. A good year or two will lead to a wild increase in the lemming population, and this increase will inevitably bring about a shortage of food together with, apparently, psychotic reactions to crowding. The result is an enormous death rate and a precipitous drop in numbers.

This sort of wild up-and-down in population is more likely to take place in polar climates than in nonpolar ones, perhaps because the food base in the polar regions is more marginal and more likely to vary erratically even with normal weather variation.

The result of lemming overpopulation is particularly spectacular in Scandinavia. Generally, one of the results of such overpopulation is emigration, as starving lemmings strike blindly outward in search of food. In Scandinavia, the accident of geography funnels lemmings into narrow valleys where their densely packed numbers provide a rare feast for all the predators that feed upon them. Millions are killed, millions more die out of starvation or sheer excitement.

When they come to bodies of water, their blind forward surge continues and leads them even into open ocean where all will eventually drown. The idea that they are deliberately trying to commit suicide or that they are swimming toward some mysterious land that is no longer there is nonsense.

After the migration is over, there are always lemmings remaining behind to start the cycle over again.

The most characteristic large herbivorous animals of the Arctic are the musk-ox and the caribou.

The musk-ox, which is confined to northern Canada, some of the islands of the Canadian Archipelago, and some of the coastal areas of Greenland, looks like a small ox, but is more closely related to the sheep and goat families. It has a long, shaggy outer growth of hair that nearly reaches the ground. Beneath that hair is a dense, woolly undercoat that is shed in the spring but is so excellent an insulator during the winter that, when the musk-ox lies in the snow, its body heat does not

melt the snow beneath itself. It has a musky odor which gives it its name.

The musk-ox has two horns that are very broad at the base and meet at the midline of the skull. They curve down the side of the head, then upward and forward at the tip. When threatened by wolves, musk-oxen form a tight circle, heads outward, and against that unbroken row of horns, few wolves will venture. That instinctive defense is worse than useless against men with rifles, however, and the musk-ox has been decreasing rapidly in numbers. The Canadian government now forbids the killing of musk-oxen.

The musk-ox feeds on grass, sedge, and moss and scrapes snow away with its hooves to reach its food supply where that is necessary.

Norwegian Lemmings Migrating

Another animal living on the same kind of food supply in the same way is the caribou, a species of deer that lives in the Canadian tundra at least part of the year and that migrates from season to season in order to be as well-placed as possible with respect to its food supply. The caribou differs from other deer in that the female also bears antlers—the only doe to do so. The male is considerably the larger of the two, though, the buck weighing up to 160 kilograms, as compared to 90 kilograms for the doe.

Unlike the musk-ox, the caribou lives in the Scandinavian tundra as well and is there known as the "reindeer." The only difference between a caribou and a reindeer is that the former is wild and the latter is tame.

The chief food of the reindeer is "reindeer moss," which,

despite its name, is really a kind of lichen, tall and branching, which forms a dense mass that stands 6 to 12 inches high. (It is because Santa Claus has come to be associated with the polar regions that his sleigh is imagined to be drawn by reindeer.)

Musk-oxen and caribou form the chief food supply of the larger land carnivores of the tundra: the wolves and wolverines. These predators migrate with the caribou herds and so do human beings. In Lapland, the Lapps developed a culture that was virtually parasitic on the reindeer, which served as a draft animal and a source of meat, milk, and butter. The reindeer was to them horses and cattle combined.

Despite the plant and animal life supported by the tundra, it remains true that, compared to the warmer regions of the world, the land life of the Arctic regions is sparse and limited. And yet that is only looking at one side of the coin. Later, there will be occasion to look at the sea life and that will be another story.

If we turn from the Arctic to the Antarctic, we find that there is virtually no tundra in the Southern Hemisphere, largely because, except for Antarctica (which like the Greenland interior is something other than tundra), there is no land. The shores of southern Chile, of Tierra del Fuego, and of the various Antarctic islands are tundral in character.

The temperature drops, of course, not only as one goes toward the poles, but also as one travels higher above sea level. If mountains reach heights that are sufficiently far above sea level, a tree line is reached above which the ground has certain tundra-like characteristics. The farther from the pole, the higher one must climb to reach the tree line, but even at the

Musk-ox

Barren Ground Caribou

equator there are mountains high enough to rise beyond the tree line.

The most extensive area of "alpine climate" is in the Himalayan region and the Tibetan Plateau in central Asia where some 1,300,000 square kilometers are bleak and treeless. Smaller areas lie in the northern Rocky Mountains in North America and along the Andes Mountains in South America. The last is the most unusual, since there are sizable areas in Bolivia and Peru where there is a bleak climate reminiscent of the polar regions lying actually within the Tropic Zone and within 10 degrees of the equator.

These alpine environments have a plant and animal life reminiscent of the tundra, but differ from the polar environments in lacking a pronounced permafrost and in not having the large variations in the length of day and night, which means the seasons are not as extreme.

Snow

It is not only the liquid water on the surface of the Earth—in the oceans, in lakes, in rivers, and in the soil—that freezes. The water vapor in the air, when it condenses, need not condense to liquid water, but, if the temperature is low enough, can condense directly into crystals of ice, not merely on the ground as frost, but high in midair as well.

This formation of ice in air is more common than might be supposed, even in warm climates, as can be seen if we consider the properties of the atmosphere. On several occasions we have already made use of the fact that temperature drops with height, but let's see why.

The air, like any gas, can be compressed by its own weight. It is most compressed and densest at the Earth's surface, especially where the Earth's surface is as low as possible, for it is there that the amount of air above the sample being discussed is greatest and weighs the most and acts to compress the most.

Indeed, as one moves upward in the atmosphere, the amount of air still higher decreases and the amount of compression decreases. The air, therefore, gets thinner and less dense the higher we go. Nor is there any real boundary to the atmosphere; the air just gets thinner and thinner as one rises higher and higher from the surface of the Earth until it gets thin enough to fade into the general, very low density of matter in interplanetary space.

Nevertheless, about nine-tenths of all the weight of air and virtually all the water vapor are contained in the lowest layer of the air. This lowest layer rises to a height of 8 kilometers above the sea-level surface at the poles, and to progressively greater heights as one recedes from the poles. At the equator this lowermost layer rises to a height of 15 kilometers.

It is in this lowermost region of the atmosphere, in which the water vapor is to be found, that clouds form and from which there can be precipitation of water in some form. It is the portion that is involved in weather changes and has therefore been given the name of the "troposphere" ("sphere of change").

The troposphere is less thick in the polar regions than in the Tropics, in part at least because gases, like liquids and solids, increase in density as temperature goes down. For that reason the cold air in the polar troposphere takes up less room than the warm air of the tropic troposphere.

Sunlight, as it passes through the troposphere, is only slightly absorbed by the air. It is only absorbed sunlight that can exert a warming effect, so the air is very little warmed by the sunlight passing through. The sunlight, having passed through the troposphere, falls on the surface of the land and sea. It is there that it is absorbed, and there that it exerts its warming effect.

By night, the land and sea reradiate the energy they have gained from sunlight, but do so in the form of much less energetic waves than those of visible light. These long waves are "infrared radiation," and these are much more effectively absorbed by the troposphere than are the short waves of visible light from the Sun.

The atmosphere acts as a heat trap, therefore, and works most efficiently as such where it is densest. As one rises in the atmosphere and as the air grows thinner, it also grows colder, with the temperature dropping a degree about every 300 meters.

By the time the top of the troposphere is reached, the temperature is, on the average, about − 65 C., and the top of the troposphere is colder in the Tropics (where it is twice as high and therefore less dense) than at the poles.*

This means that, if clouds form high enough in the air, they are composed of ice crystals, even when the temperature below them on the surface is well above the freezing point of water. On the other hand, when clouds form sufficiently low in the atmosphere at times and in places where the surface is sufficiently warm, they are made up of tiny droplets of liquid water.

The tiny ice crystals that form the higher clouds (even in the warmer portions of the Earth) can conglomerate in loose and symmetrical fashion (something encouraged by the polar nature of the water molecule) to form six-sided structures of beautiful complexity. These are "snowflakes," and they can grow large enough to fall, despite air-resistance.

Falling snowflakes may melt as they pass into the warmer regions of the lower atmosphere and then they reach the ground as rain. If the temperature is below the freezing point all the way to the surface of the Earth, the snowflakes do not melt and it is snow that falls.

* In the regions of the atmosphere above the troposphere, the temperature changes are quite complicated and the temperature begins to rise again, but we need not be concerned about that in this book.

Where the atmosphere is near the freezing point, snowflakes may melt into small raindrops which may then refreeze into small bits of compact ice that fall as "sleet." Sometimes, turbulent air will drive raindrops upward, let them fall, drive them upward, and so on over and over. As the raindrops rise higher, they will freeze, and on each subsequent rise accumulate more ice. In the end, when they are too heavy to be lifted under the prevailing air conditions, the sizable pieces of ice ("hailstones") will fall as hail. Since hailstones are too large to melt in the short time they will pass through warm air, it may hail even in summer.

Sleet and hail are relatively uncommon, however, and on a global scale the only forms of precipitation that are important are rain and snow.

In a number of respects snow is crucially different from rain. Rain, being liquid, flows easily. It sinks into the soil, runs off the land, and returns to the sea relatively quickly. (Sometimes the runoff cannot keep pace with the rate of precipitation and enough water accumulates on land, locally, to produce flooding.)

Snow, on the other hand, is a solid that does not flow but tends to remain where it falls. It will melt, of course, more or less rapidly, when the temperature rises and it will then perform as a liquid. As long as the temperature remains low, however, snow will remain on the ground and will accumulate with further snowfalls. If enough accumulates, then even after the temperature rises melting can be a long-drawn-out affair.

In areas with a tropical climate, snow never falls, of course, but in the temperate regions, there is an alternation. In winter, precipitation is often in the form of snow, while during the rest of the year it is in the form of rain. In lands even as far south as the northern half of the United States, winter can present an Arctic aspect, if not quite in temperature, then certainly in appearance. (And sometimes in temperature, too.)

The fall of snow in temperate climates is by no means necessarily bad for life. Rather the reverse, in fact. Loosely packed snow is an excellent heat insulator, so that ground when covered by snow remains warmer than it would if bare and exposed to the low air-temperatures. Plants and animals can survive the winter, given the air and relative warmth beneath the snow, far more easily than they could on bare ground. Then, too, the slow melting of snow in the spring waters the ground and encourages plant growth far more effectively than a drenching and quick runoff of rain might.

It is characteristic of the temperate regions that the snow accumulation of the winter does melt in the spring and that the ground is bare of snow till the next winter. This happens in the tundra, too, even in the far-Arctic coast of northern Greenland; and, indeed, unless the ground were bare for at least part of the year and the upper layer of permafrost melted, plant growth could not take place and the animals that live on such plants, from lemmings to musk-oxen, together with their various predators, could not survive.

Yet one can see that if the temperature is low enough on the average and if the summer months are even cooler than they are in the tundra, enough heat will not be delivered in the spring and summer to melt all the snow of winter. The thickness of the snow layer may be thinner in midsummer than at the end of winter, but the snow will nevertheless not have entirely disappeared before the new falls of the next winter begin. When this is so, there is a perpetual snow cover.

It was not necessary for man to have penetrated the polar regions to know that a perpetual snow is possible. In western Europe, for instance, people could see a year-round snow cover on some of the peaks of the Alps.

It is not just the atmosphere that grows colder with height. This is true of the solid crust of the Earth as well.

Suppose we consider a plateau 2 kilometers high. It is exposed to precisely the same kind of sunlight as is a coastal plain at sea level and may absorb that sunlight as well. (In fact, the plateau is a trifle nearer the Sun and has less air above it to block some of the Sun's radiation, so that it should receive and absorb a tiny bit more of the Sun's radiation than the coastal plain does.)

However, the air is thinner 2 kilometers high and does not effectively absorb the long-wave radiation lost by the plateau's surface at night. The surface loses heat rapidly at night, therefore, and, from the low point reached, does not reach as high a temperature during the day as the plain would. In general, then, the average temperature drops with height for the Earth's surface.*

---

* It is the lack of an atmosphere on the Moon and the consequent high radiation loss from the Moon's nighttime

If we consider the upward slopes of a mountain range, we can see that the average temperature will drop steadily. The climate may be tropical at the foot, but it will become temperate as we climb, and then polar.

If a wind is blowing against the mountain and its current of air is lifted up its sides, that air becomes less capable of retaining water vapor. (The amount of water vapor the atmosphere can hold decreases with temperature.) Precipitation is much more likely to take place on the high mountain slopes than on the warm valley below.

Once the prevailing winds blow over the peaks of a mountain range, most of their water vapor has been precipitated out. As they descend the other side, the winds grow warm and dry, so that the land on the side of a mountain range opposite to the prevailing direction of the winds tends to be arid. It is constantly bathed in air that has lost its water vapor content in crossing the mountain range.

If the precipitation takes place high enough in the mountain range, it will be cold enough to fall as snow. Such snow as falls will melt more slowly the higher one goes. At certain heights the snow will melt slowly enough and the summer temperatures will be low enough to produce the tundra-like conditions mentioned in the previous section.

If the mountain is high enough, there comes a point where not enough heat is delivered in the summer to melt all the snow of the previous winter. Snow is then perpetual, and it is for that reason that high mountains are snow-capped the year round, even in the Tropics.

The "snow line" (above which a mountain peak is perpetually snow-covered) is higher in the Tropics, naturally, than elsewhere. A height of 5000 meters represents the snow line in the Tropics and the figure can be 6000 meters where climatic conditions are both hot and dry. Mount Kenya in Africa, however, and Mount Chimborazo in South America are both nearly on the equator, are both in well-watered regions, and both have peaks higher than 5000 meters. Both are perpetually snow-covered at the peak in consequence—equator or not.

The snow line grows steadily lower as one moves away from the equator in either direction. In the Alps, it is 2500 meters, and in Norway it is 1500 meters.

surface that is one of the reasons why the Moon grows colder
at night by far than the Earth does.

Glaciers

What happens to the snow on the mountaintop, as it accumulates from winter to winter, never melting in the summer as much as it receives in the winter? Surely, the snow layers cannot possibly grow thicker and thicker year after year without limit.

If snow had the consistency of sand, the added weight each year would push some of the snow down the mountain slope a way, and there it would melt in the warmer temperatures.

But snow is not sand and it doesn't work that way. Under the weight of upper layers of snow, the snowflakes of the lower layers are compressed. The added pressure encourages melting at temperatures that would not allow melting at normal pressures. The edges of the snowflakes melt, then refreeze, and the flakes stick together. Snow is sticky stuff, in other words, and unless strong winds constantly blow the uppermost, still loose layers off the ice altogether, it does indeed build up more and more thickly from year to year. Despite the fact that the ice on the mountaintop rests on an inclined slope, it remains in place because of its frozen hold on the rock beneath and because of the enormous friction that develops at the first beginnings of movement.

Yet as the load of mountain snow increases, it may eventually become too heavy for the slope to bear. The downward pull of gravity on the snow mass becomes great enough to overcome the friction of the slope, particularly in early spring when a sudden thaw combined with pressure at the bottom of the ice pack results in melting beneath. This would give the snow a foundation of moisture to slide upon. Large quantities of snow may then suddenly descend upon the valley below. This is an "avalanche" (from a French word meaning "to descend").

Avalanches scrape down with them considerable quantities of rock debris and can be an important agent in wearing down mountains. What is more important, from the human standpoint, is that the sudden descent of a large mass of snow, coming without warning, can bury whole villages. Such catastrophes sometimes take place in the Alps.

When an avalanche is on the point of beginning, a relatively small vibration may be enough to set it off—thunder, the rumble of a train or airplane, the blowing of a whistle, even a loud shout. In December 1916, during World War I, Austrian

Avalanche

troops stationed in the Alps started an avalanche when they began firing their cannon. Several thousand soldiers were buried.

Snow, however, does not always descend in the form of a catastrophic avalanche. A mountain slope may not be steep enough to make it possible for one to occur, or the snow may land in large hollows or depressions. In that case the snow accumulates to great amounts indeed. Under the pressure of its own weight, the snow presses together and compacts.

Snow, as it falls, consists of flakes of very loose construction. The density of a quantity of such flakes in light contact may be as little as 0.06 grams per cubic centimeter. This means that all but one-fifteenth of their bulk is air, this air being included in their own structure and in the spaces between adjacent flakes.

As the snow compacts, melts, and refreezes, the air is progressively squeezed out under pressure, and the snow that fell in the beginning of the year has been converted by the end of the year into minute ice crystals called "firn" (from a Swiss term for "last year's snow"). The firn has a density of 0.45 grams per cubic centimeter and is still half air. As pressure increases, the ice crystals, melting and refreezing, become larger and more compact, turning more and more into a solid, glassy transparent ice with a density at the 0.9-grams-per-cubic-centimeter mark.

As the snow continues to accumulate until thicknesses of over 15 meters are reached, the weight above finally forces the ice to flow. Ice, because of the looseness of its molecular structure, is not very strong mechanically, and if enough pressure is placed upon it, it will flow like extremely stiff toothpaste.

The ice on mountaintops may, therefore, eventually squeeze out of the depression in which it is accumulating over the lowest place (or break through) and proceed to work its way downward along the course of some groove in the mountain's side.

The result is a "glacier," from a French word for "ice." The Alps are rich in glaciers, some 1300 of them existing. This is not because they are mountains that are particularly high and cold but because they exist in a portion of the world that is high in precipitation.

A mountain glacier looks very much like a river of ice, frozen and motionless—except that it is not quite motionless. Very

Traleika and Muldrow Glaciers on Mt. McKinley, Alaska

slowly it is squeezing its way down the mountainside. The fact that this slow motion took place did not dawn upon men until mountain climbing became a sport (and that, oddly enough, was not until less than two centuries ago).

Objects, or even dead bodies, lost or abandoned at some upper portion of the glacier, would eventually be discovered some kilometers down-glacier. It might take a century for a piece of ice to travel from the top of the mountain to its bottom, though under particularly favorable conditions a glacier might move as much as 45 meters per day.

The glacier does not, of course, flow forever. As it flows, it moves steadily toward lower altitudes and, therefore, warmer temperatures. As it progresses, then, the rate of melting of its forward edge increases and finally overtakes the rate at which new ice is added from behind.

When that happens, the glacier seems to come to a halt, not because the ice is no longer moving, but because the lowermost edge, or "foot," of the glacier is melting as fast as new ice arrives.

If temperatures were more or less the same, year after year, the foot of the glacier would remain in place, moving a bit forward in winter and backward again in summer. If, however, there is a general cooling of the climate, the foot of the glacier will advance; in case of a general warming, it will recede.

In the warm regions of the Earth, the foot of mountain glaciers is far above sea level. In the Alps, for instance, the glaciers do not descend farther than 1000 meters above sea level. Above that height, however, there is a total area of about 7000 square kilometers of ice with thicknesses of up to 800 meters in places.

Nevertheless, the Alps are outdone in glacier formation by the southern Andes, the northern Rockies and, most of all, the Himalayas, where the total area of glaciers is ten times that in the Alps and where some glaciers curve and wind their way for a length of 80 kilometers. Even Africa, the most nearly tropical of the continents, has 13 square kilometers of glaciers high up on three of its highest peaks. Particularly mountainous islands such as New Guinea and South Island (of New Zealand) have glaciers. The largest body of land to be totally free of glaciers is relatively warm and nonmountainous Australia.

As one moves north or south toward the polar regions, the snow line is lower and lower, and mountain glaciers can descend more and more closely to sea level before they are brought to a halt by melting. If the region is polar enough, the glacier reaches the lowest part of the valley and then spreads out to either side, sometimes covering a large area. In Alaska there are glaciers that spread out at the foot of mountains to cover an area of 4000 square kilometers.

Under the proper conditions, glaciers can cover larger areas of generally nonmountainous territory, and then they are called "ice sheets." In the polar areas, where the average temperature the year round is low enough, glaciers do not have to form at mountain peaks but can form at or near sea level where depressions exist for the accumulation of snow.

Under polar conditions, where the temperature is particularly low the year round, there is a smaller tendency for ice particles to melt and refreeze so that ice does not tend to grow quite as compact as in less polar latitudes. Again since the polar glaciers tend to rest on flatter ground, there is even slower movement.

There are sizable ice sheets on many of the Arctic islands, such as Iceland, Spitzbergen, Severnaya Zemlya, Novaya Zemlya, Ellesmere Island, and Baffin Island. Dwarfing them all as far as the Arctic is concerned, however, is the ice sheet that covers the entire interior of the vast island of Greenland. This continuous ice sheet is about 2500 kilometers long, north and south, and, at its widest, is 1100 kilometers east and west. At its thickest point the Greenland ice sheet is about 3.3 kilometers thick.

The area of the Greenland ice sheet is just over 1,800,000 square kilometers, a single piece of ice, in other words, that is more than three times the area of the state of Texas. Surrounding the Greenland ice sheet is a fringe of bare land that, in places, is up to 300 kilometers wide.

In the Antarctic regions, the lack of land outside Antarctica means there is not much in the way of an ice sheet except on that continent itself—but that is enough.

Antarctica is covered by an ice sheet that leaves no coastal fringe of bare land at all, an ice sheet that is truly continental in size, that is so large it dwarfs the Greenland ice sheet (second in size) into near insignificance.

The Antarctica ice sheet is a roughly circular mass of ice with a diameter of about 4500 kilometers and a shoreline of over 20,000 kilometers. It has an area of nearly 8,000,000 square kilometers, over seven times the area of the Greenland ice sheet and nearly one and a half times that of the United States.

The average thickness of the Antarctica ice sheet is a bit over 2 kilometers. The South Pole is under 2.8 kilometers of ice, but the maximum ice thickness is, as one would expect, in the Pole of Cold region where the moderating influence of the ocean is least and the rate of melting is at the slowest. Consider, for instance, the "Pole of Inaccessibility," the point in Antarctica which, as the name implies, is the hardest to reach because it is most inland. Located at 78.4° S. and 87.6° E., it is 900 kilometers from the South Pole and the ice thickness there is 4.3 kilometers.

The volume of the Antarctica ice sheet is about 30,000,000 cubic kilometers, and it is because of the ice, piled high and higher, and not because of any plateaus or mountain ranges that Antarctica is, on the average, the highest continental mass in the world.

Altogether, nearly 10,000,000 square kilometers of the Earth's land surface lies under a permanent layer of ice. This represents just about 10 percent of the Earth's land surface. Of this area, the ice sheets of Antarctica and Greenland together make up about 92 percent (and Antarctica alone about 80 percent). The remaining 8 percent, about 80,000 square kilometers, is distributed among various polar islands and mountain peaks.

Ice on land, which is generated by snow, is solidified fresh water. It does not contain the brine that makes sea ice salty. The land ice, then, can be added to the Earth's total supply of fresh water. Even though most of it is not readily available for use by man, or by life-forms generally, it is there as a reservoir.

The total weight of permanent ice on Earth is about 23,000,000,000,000,000 (23 thousand trillion) tonnes. This reservoir of solid fresh water on Earth is nearly fifty times the size of the reservoir of liquid fresh water. Therefore, when we speak of Earth's freshwater supply, we are (in terms of bulk, at least, if not availability) speaking primarily of Earth's land ice. Indeed, we are speaking mostly of Antarctica, which, being not only larger but also thicker than the Greenland ice sheet, holds fully 90 percent of all the fresh water on Earth.

(Even so, the vast heap of ice on Earth is still less than one-fiftieth of the planet's total water supply. We mustn't forget that fully 98 percent of all the water on Earth is in its ocean.)

The vast weight of the Antarctica ice sheet presses down the Earth's crust beneath, and it is suspected that part of the crust of what seems a continent may be below sea level, either to begin with or as the result of the ice-sheet's weight. Most of the suspected below-sea-level land lies in Lesser Antarctica, and some of it (measured by detonating dynamite at the ice surface and measuring the time it takes for the sound waves to travel through the ice to the rocky crust beneath and return) may be as much as 2.5 kilometers below sea level.

If we were to imagine the ice removed from Antarctica, Greater Antarctica would be a landmass of continental size, but

Lesser Antarctica would prove to be an archipelago, a collection of islands. The exact size of the islands would depend on how far back the Earth's crust would spring once the weight of the ice was removed.

Once an ice sheet, such as those in Antarctica and Greenland, has formed, its mere existence cools the climate about it, prevents a rise in temperature that would accelerate its melting, and it therefore remains frozen. It is a kind of self-perpetuating mechanism which, by its very existence, produces conditions that favor its continued existence.

The melting of ice, like the vaporization of water, requires an input of energy. The attraction for each other on the part of the polar molecules arranged symmetrically in the ice must be overcome, and this takes energy. The amount of energy it takes to melt a quantity of ice would raise its temperature 80 degrees if none were required for melting. But the energy *is* required for melting, and, when the ice has melted, there has been *no* temperature rise; the water that is formed is still at 0 C.

It follows that all the radiation from the low-lying Sun of summer shining on the ice sheet of Greenland or of Antarctica for days and weeks at a time goes into melting some of the ice sheet and none of it into raising the temperature.

That is why, in northeastern Siberia, where the winter temperatures can drop lower than at any point on the Greenland ice sheet, and lower than in most of Antarctica even, the summer temperatures can nevertheless be tropical in intensity. The thin ice cover in Siberia melts in the spring, and the sunlight, shining down on the bare soil, supplies energy that goes into raising the temperature.

It is no puzzle then that the lowest *average* temperatures on Earth are (as pointed out in chapter 8) in the interiors of Greenland and Antarctica.

On the other hand, when liquid water freezes, the heat that had been absorbed in the melting process is given up again. This means that, all things being equal, a surface does not drop to as low a temperature as it otherwise would if there is water present to freeze and give up heat. That is why the temperature of even the interior of Greenland doesn't drop as low after having frozen the puddly water of summer as does northeastern Siberia, where water appears in solid form as already frozen snow.

Icebergs

Year after year, ice accumulates on the great ice sheets of Greenland and Antarctica.

It doesn't accumulate rapidly, for there is no great snowfall in the polar regions. The colder the air is, the less water vapor it can hold and the smaller the precipitation it can feed. In both the Arctic and the Antarctic, the total precipitation is about that which in more temperate places would be found in desert areas.

Thus, the tundra territories of Canada average about 20 centimeters of precipitation (measured as rain) per year, only a fifth as much as falls in New York City. The farther north, and the farther cold, the less precipitation there is. In Ellesmere Island, northernmost of the islands of the Canadian Archipelago, the annual precipitation is the equivalent of 4 centimeters of rain, less than falls in Death Valley. (Yet so little evaporates at the tundra's low temperature, and so difficult is it for water to drain away through the permafrost just under the surface, that the tundra, in summer, is littered with lakes.)

Since the Antarctic is colder than the Arctic, there is less precipitation in the former. In all of Antarctica, there is, on the average, an annual precipitation that is the equivalent of about 2 centimeters of rain. This makes Antarctica the largest and driest desert in the world. Only the Antarctic Peninsula, farthest from the South Pole, and washed by ocean on each side, gets a respectable amount of precipitation—ten times that of the rest of the continent.

To be sure, one hears much of "blizzards" in polar regions, particularly in Antarctica, but these are not blizzards in the ordinary sense of heavy snowfalls combined with great wind. They involve winds, to be sure, of up to 150 kilometers an hour, but there is no snow. Instead, it is the cold, dry, ice particles on the ice-sheet surface that are whipped about like sand in the sandstorms of the Sahara.

The small amount of precipitation in Antarctica does, however, suffice to keep the ice sheet in being, thanks to the negligible quantity of snow and ice lost through melting, evaporation, and wind blowing. Indeed, it has been calculated that the precipitation in Antarctica, if none were lost, would suffice to build up the Antarctica ice sheet from scratch in 9000 to 15,000 years.

Despite the desert conditions, then, whatever snow does fall in Greenland and Antarctica remains and the ice sheets grow higher and thicker. Yet surely they cannot do so forever.

Nor do they. As the weight increases, particularly in the center of either sheet, where the ice is thickest, the ice at the bottom of the ice sheet is forced outward.

In Greenland, for instance, there are glaciers that squeeze outward from the ice sheet along valleys toward the sea. Driven by the pressures behind, they move at rates of up to 45 meters per day, which is enormous by the standards of ordinary glaciers. Nor do these glaciers melt. When they reach the sea, they are still intact and there they "calve." That is, large pieces break off and float out to sea.

These lumps of floating ice are called "icebergs," the word "berg" being German for "mountain."

In Arctic waters some 16,000 icebergs are calved each year. About 90 percent of them originate from Greenland glaciers on the milder west coast. The largest glacier in the world, the Humboldt Glacier, lies far in the northwest at 80° N. It is 80 kilometers across at its coastal foot, but is too cold to break off icebergs at a record rate. Farther south, the Jacobshavn Glacier at 68° N. calves 1400 icebergs a year. That one glacier sends some 5.7 cubic kilometers of ice into the sea in a single year.

Some individual Arctic icebergs weigh over a million tonnes, are nearly a kilometer long, and tower 30 meters above the ocean surface. (The record height reported for any Arctic iceberg was a towering 170 meters above the ocean surface.)

Since ice has a density of 0.9, most of the iceberg is below the surface. The exact quantity submerged depends on how pure the ice is. The ice usually contains a great many air bubbles which give it a milky appearance rather than the transparency of true ice, and this lowers its density. On the other hand, in approaching the sea, the glaciers may well scrape up much in the way of gravel and rock, and this may break off with the iceberg and increase its overall density. On the whole, anything from 80 to 90 percent of the volume of an iceberg is submerged.

As long as icebergs remain in Arctic waters, they persist without much change. The freezing water of the Arctic Ocean will not melt them appreciably.

The icebergs that form off the western coast of Greenland linger in Baffin Bay for a long time, but eventually begin to move southward along the coasts of Labrador. Many are trapped along the shores, where they break up and slowly melt, but some persist, largely intact, as far south as Newfoundland, taking up to three years to make the 3000-kilometer journey. Some 400 icebergs, still massive and menacing, reach Newfoundland waters, on the average, each year. They are even more dangerous than they look, since the major portion of each is submerged and may jut outward considerably closer to some approaching ship than the visible upper portion is.

Once past Newfoundland, the icebergs find themselves in the Gulf Stream and that usually finishes them. Two weeks in that warm water and they are gone. Nevertheless, on occasion, icebergs can survive well down into southern waters. The remnants of one were sighted on June 2, 1934, in mid-Atlantic at the latitude of northern Florida.

In the waters off Newfoundland, there is grave danger to shipping, since this area happens to be on some of the most busily traveled ship lanes in the world. Between 1870 and 1890, for instance, fourteen ships were sunk and forty damaged by collision with icebergs.

The climax came on April 15, 1912, when the luxury liner *Titanic*, on her maiden voyage from Southampton to New York, collided with an iceberg 500 kilometers southeast of Newfoundland, and sank with the loss of 1500 lives.

As a consequence, an International Ice Patrol was established in 1914, and has been maintained ever since to keep watch over the positions of these inanimate monsters. It is supported by nineteen nations and is operated by the United States Coast Guard. It supplies continuing information on all icebergs sighted below 52° N. (that is, south of Labrador), with a prediction of the movements of each over the next twelve hours. During the years since this ice patrol has come into existence (and with the further development of aircraft surveillance and radio warnings), not one ship has been sunk by an iceberg. Indeed, modern liners stay so far away from them that passengers never see them—which is a shame, in a way, but the risks simply don't justify any attempt to close in on them for the sake of scenic delight.

Icebergs are lumps of fresh water immersed in the salt ocean. When they melt it is a matter of fresh water being wasted to no purpose. There are, therefore, periodic suggestions that icebergs somehow be towed to some shoreline where the human population is great and there be "mined" for fresh water. That fresh water would then be restored to the sea anyway, but only after being used. The thought of a captive iceberg in Long Island Sound or off Boston Harbor being pickaxed, loaded onto waiting boats, melted, and purified is a dramatic one.

But Arctic icebergs are miniature affairs compared with some of the huge monsters spawned by the enormous ice sheet of Antarctica. Where glaciers reach the shores in Antarctica, they calve and produce icebergs like those produced by Greenland glaciers. But what of the ice shelves?

The ice sheet of Antarctica, when it reaches the Ross Sea and Weddell Sea, which approach close to the South Pole, does not calve in the ordinary sense. It simply moves out, intact, over the seas for up to 1300 kilometers. This solid unbroken block of ice over each sea is 250 meters thick at its seaward edge and up to about 800 meters thick near the shore.

The seaward edges of these ice shelves break off periodically, forming huge "tabular icebergs," flat on top, with lengths that can be measured in hundreds of kilometers at times and reaching up to 100 meters above the sea's surface. In 1956, a tabular iceberg was sighted that was 330 kilometers long and 100 kilometers wide—a floating piece of ice with twice the area of the state of Connecticut.

Around Antarctica is the only stretch of open ocean (albeit often choked with pack ice) that can move about the Earth without interference by land. The movement of the surface current is from east to west in a great counterclockwise whirl (as viewed from an imaginary position above the South Pole) around Antarctica.

This section of the ocean about Antarctica is not a distinctly marked off portion of the ocean. It is, rather, the southern extension of the Pacific, Atlantic, and Indian oceans all meeting past the southernmost points of Africa and South America. It is convenient, however, to define that section of the ocean south of 55° S. (which is the southern tip of South America and south of which is no piece of considerable land other than Antarctica) as the "Antarctic Ocean." At least that is what it is called in the United States. The United Kingdom and the Soviet Union call it the "Southern Ocean."

The Antarctic Ocean, as so defined, is about 32,000,000 square kilometers in area and its narrowest portion is Drake Passage, between South America and Antarctic Peninsula. This is about 1000 kilometers wide.

For the most part, Antarctic icebergs drift in the Antarctic Ocean and are carried round and round Antarctica. There they are completely harmless and, although more numerous and larger than their Arctic cousins, scarcely impinge upon the consciousness of mankind, since they are well off the chief trade routes of the world.

As the Antarctic icebergs drift northward into warmer waters, they melt. In the Atlantic, however, it is not uncommon to sight the icebergs as far north as 40° S. In 1894, the last remnant of such an iceberg was sighted in the western Atlantic just south of the Tropic of Capricorn at 26° S.

There is talk of towing the large Antarctic icebergs northward so that they might serve as sources of fresh water. It would be a tremendous task and we might visualize such journeys as taking a few years. Some people have imagined icebergs covered with thin, plastic quilts, moving northward to southern California, and losing only 10 percent of their mass in a year as they crossed the tropic seas.

Planetary Ice Caps

At both polar ends, the surface of the Earth, whether land or sea, is covered by ice. In the north, there is the Greenland ice sheet plus the pack ice over the Arctic Ocean. In the south, there is the Antarctica ice sheet, plus the ice shelves and pack ice rimming that continent. We can therefore speak of the "polar ice caps of the Earth."

The Antarctic ice cap (if we can imagine ourselves viewing it from space and being able to penetrate through the veil of clouds and of night) is rather stable in size with the seasons. The Antarctic Ocean is, of course, more ice choked in winter than in summer, but the expansion and contraction with the seasons would be moderate.

The Arctic region is different in this respect. Its ice cap is as large at its summer minimum as the Antarctic ice cap would be, but is more asymmetrical. There is the pack ice of the Arctic Ocean forming a more or less circular patch, but then jutting out of it would be the large mass of the Greenland ice sheet.

What is more, there are large continental areas adjoining the

Arctic region (something not true of the Antarctic), and in the winter, a blanket of snow spreads southward over Alaska, Canada, Scandinavia, Siberia. To anyone viewing Earth from outer space through the aforementioned veil of clouds and night, the North Polar ice cap would seem to expand mightily in the northern winter (and asymmetrically, for the ice would spread out over the continents and not over the ocean) and shrink as drastically in the northern summer. Naturally, as one ice cap expanded the other would contract, and vice versa.

The phenomenon of planetary ice caps can occur elsewhere in the solar system (and perhaps in planetary systems generally, if our own is typical). Beyond the orbit of Mars, the radiation of the Sun is not strong enough to make any great difference in temperature between the equator and poles of any world. However, if there are volatiles, with lower melting points than water has, present on a world in quantity, the temperature difference may be great enough to establish ice-caps of something other than water-ice. In 1974, the Jupiter probe, Pioneer II, detected ice-caps on Callisbo, one of the large satellites of Jupiter. What the nature of the ice is, we do not know as yet.

But what of the five worlds in the inner solar system? Of these, the Moon and Mercury have no volatile content to speak of and have no ice anywhere. Venus has volatile matter forming a thick atmosphere, but the temperature of that planet is too high for any of the volatiles to exist as anything but gas.

We know about the situation on Earth, and now only Mars is left to consider.

Mars has volatiles, though by no means as large a content as Earth has. Mars is close enough to the Sun for an important temperature difference between equator and poles to exist, and its axis of rotation is tipped at an angle of 25.2 degrees, just slightly more than is the case for Earth. Seasonal phenomena should, therefore, be the same on Mars (allowing for its thinner atmosphere and its generally lower temperature) as on Earth.

Telescopic observation makes it quite clear that there are polar ice caps on Mars as well as on Earth. In fact, if the solar system were viewed from out in space, the Martian ice caps might be far easier to see than those of Earth, since the Martian atmosphere does little to obscure them.

In 1672, the Dutch astronomer Christian Huygens saw the South Polar ice cap of Mars and was the first to do so. At this time, very little was known about Earth's Arctic ice cap and nothing at all about Earth's Antarctic ice cap. We might almost say that the Martian ice caps were discovered by man before Earth's ice caps were.

The Martian ice caps, like those of Earth, grow and contract with the seasons, and do so in alternate fashion. This was first noted by the German-English astronomer William Herschel over a century after Huygens had first sighted them.

The Martian ice caps, however, expand equally both north and south, and do so more or less evenly in all directions. The difference lies in the fact that Mars has no ocean, but is all continent.

The southern hemisphere of Mars, which experiences its summer when Mars is in that portion of its orbit that brings it as close to the Sun as it ever gets, receives more radiation than the northern hemisphere does in its summer, when the planet is relatively far from the Sun. The result is that the southern ice cap shrinks more than the northern ice cap does.

The fact that the Martian ice caps shrink more in summer than Earth's do, even though Mars is considerably farther from the Sun than Earth is, and therefore considerably cooler, is not hard to understand. The frozen matter in the Martian ice caps is far smaller in quantity than is true on Earth, so there is less to melt. Then, too, the Martian ice caps are not entirely water, as is true on Earth, but seem to contain a large admixture of carbon dioxide, which sublimes into gas at a considerably lower temperature than ice melts into water.

10 THE POLAR OCEAN

The discussion of ice in the previous chapter inevitably makes the polar regions seem a scene of desolation and lifelessness and, to a certain extent, that is true. The tundra supports land life, but only tenuously. The musk-ox of the Canadian tundra is impressive but cannot be compared in numbers with the related bison that once roamed the American prairie. Nor can the caribou compare with the herds of antelope and zebras that fill the African veldt.

Still, the tundra has soil that is bare at least part of the year and permeated with liquid water. It can therefore support vegetation which can, in turn, support land life. But what of the ice sheets themselves, where there is neither soil nor liquid water?

Land Life on the Ice Sheets

Where soil is never exposed and where the average monthly temperatures are never above freezing, as on the ice sheet, it is next to impossible for life to exist, and the ice sheets are the most nearly sterile environments on Earth. There is no significant land life anywhere in the interior of Greenland, or anywhere in the vast area of Antarctica.

Greenland has, at least, vegetation along its coasts, even in the north, and a sparse animal (human, too) population. That is because so much of the coasts are bare.

Antarctica, however, is ice sheet to the very shores, and, in some places, well beyond the shores—and yet it doesn't lack bare soil altogether. There are bits of bare coast here and there, the largest patch being at McMurdo Sound at the eastern edge of the Ross Ice Shelf. The bare patch there is 150 kilometers long and 15 to 25 kilometers wide.

Strangely enough, there are ice-free "oases" in Antarctica's interior as well. Some of the mountaintops are blown free of snow and stand bare under the sky, but there are even ice-free spots here and there in the valleys.

The ice-free valleys must have held ice once, for there are unmistakable signs of the effect of scraping ice there. Something must have removed that ice to begin with. (Perhaps a slight local warming of the ground beneath, a leaking upward of Earth's internal heat?) Once it is removed, there is a tendency to stay ice free, since the annual snowfall is so meager, provided the situation is such that the prevailing winds blow the ice away faster than it can accumulate.

These ice-free valleys make up but a tiny fraction of Antarctica's territory. All the bare land put together comes to about 7500 square kilometers, or 0.06 percent of Antarctica's area. As a matter of curiosity, the southernmost bit of exposed land in the world is on Mount Howe, only 260 kilometers from the South Pole.

One indication that the ice-free valleys are ice free because of warmth from below is the fact that some of the valleys contain bodies of liquid water that stay liquid the year round. In 1947, for instance, an American survey plane discovered an oasis 175 kilometers inland that was about 800 square kilometers in area and contained 23 lakes.

Most Antarctica lakes are very small. One such body, San Juan Pond, is 600 meters above sea level, is about 2000 square meters in area, and has an average depth of about 0.15 meters. All the water in San Juan Pond comes to 300 cubic meters, or enough to fill six average-sized American living rooms.

The ice-free portions of Antarctica are desert in comparison to any other region of the world and yet are not entirely lifeless. Algae and lichens grow in the lakes. San Juan Pond, in addition to the utter bleakness of its surroundings, is thick with calcium chloride, a saltlike substance not favorable to life, yet it manages to harbor one species of bacteria. Only one.

The scattered ponds of Antarctica have the simplest life systems on Earth and perhaps nothing else on the planet so resembles what the Martian surface may be like. The study of such nearly totally sterile environments involves maximum efforts to avoid contamination.

Altogether some 200 species of freshwater algae grow in places in Antarctica where there is exposed water (and in some cases even on snow). Where there is exposed soil, some 400 species of lichens can be found and 75 species of moss. There are even two species of flowering plants on the Antarctic Peninsula (as compared with 900 species of flowering plants in the Arctic, to say nothing of 500 species of moss and 2000 species of lichens, all present in far greater mass). One of the Antarctic flowers is a variety of grass and the other a relative of the carnation.

Lichen have been detected on bare rock as close as 425 kilometers to the South Pole, a record approach for any form of life other than human beings, plus the other creatures brought by them closer to the South Pole, either deliberately or otherwise. And one other species which I'll mention later.

Where plants exist, animal life is bound to exist. However, the utterly insignificant plant cover of the utterly insignificant bare spots in Antarctica can support nothing larger than tiny animals. The *only* land animals native to Antarctica are 70 species of mites and primitive insects. The largest land animal native to Antarctica is a wingless fly, half a centimeter long. One species of mite has been detected only 680 kilometers from the South Pole.

Yet this picture of desolation is unfair because it deals with only a portion of the polar territory—the land and the life it supports directly. Actually, we can see that the polar regions are enormously rich in life, and in some ways support the life of all the Earth—the Antarctic even more so than the Arctic—if we consider not land but water. To see why this is so, we must consider the motions and circulation of Earth's atmosphere and ocean.

Air Circulation

The polar regions, with their load of ice, represent a general cold reserve for the planet as the Tropics, under the unslanted rays of the Sun, represent a general heat reserve. In the tropical regions, the air is heated, expands, and grows less dense, and consequently rises. In the polar regions, the air is cooled, contracts, and grows more dense, and consequently sinks.

In general, then, the overall circulation in the atmosphere is one in which the rising air in the Tropics spreads out toward the poles, north and south, at considerable heights, while the sinking air in the polar regions moves toward the Tropics nearer the surface.

Since it is the surface winds that affect us directly, let's concentrate on those. It would seem, from this first simple analysis of the situation, that there should be a constant surface wind from the north in the Northern Hemisphere and from the south in the Southern Hemisphere, and that every place should be swept by cold polar winds.

This is not so, however. The upper winds, moving from the Tropics poleward, cool sufficiently by the time they enter the temperate zones to enable some of them to sink and become still-warm surface winds. We might suppose then that in some region in the temperate zones—the United States, for instance —there are winds coming down from the north and up from the south and meeting head on.

This is not so either, for there is another complication. The Earth is rotating and this produces what is called the "Coriolis effect," since it was first described by a French physicist, Gaspard Gustave de Coriolis, in 1837.

The entire solid body of the Earth turns, naturally, in one piece, making one complete rotation about Earth's axis in 24 hours. As I explained earlier, the North Pole and the South Pole are the points where the axis intersects the Earth's surface, and therefore the poles do not move as the Earth turns. As one moves away from the poles, points on the Earth's surface make larger circles and therefore move faster in order to complete the turn in 24 hours.

The motion of the Earth's solid surface, as the planet rotates, increases its speed smoothly from a minimum of zero at either pole to a maximum of 1675 kilometers per hour at the equator.

Volumes of air in the neighborhood of the Earth's surface participate in this rotational motion and move at the speed that the surface does. If a volume of air moves northward or southward, it tends to retain its original speed, while the speed of the Earth's surface beneath it necessarily changes.

Imagine, for instance, air in that part of the Tropic Zone north of the equator. It is moving west to east quite rapidly, since the Earth's surface is moving roughly 1600 kilometers an hour west to east.

Suppose, next, that this air volume is moving northward. It is moving into regions where the motion of the Earth's surface west to east is slower. The air, retaining its original speed, outraces the surface and moves not only northward but eastward as well. To a person on the surface, in the United States, the wind from the warmer areas is moving from the southwest to the northeast, rather than from the south to the north. The farther north the observer is, the more pronounced is the eastward component of the wind.

Since the wind appears to be coming more or less from the west, the winds that are fairly characteristic of the United States and of the temperate zones generally are called the "prevailing westerlies." (Air from the southern portion of the Tropic Zone moving farther southward will also gain on the surface of the Earth and will also slip eastward, so that there are prevailing westerlies in the South Temperate Zone as well as in the North Temperate Zone.)

Because air moving from the Tropics northward and southward tends to slip eastward, there is a tendency to begin a clockwise whirl in the Northern Hemisphere and a counterclockwise whirl in the Southern Hemisphere. Friction against the soil and within the air itself tends to make the whirls spirals, and this is seen in typhoons, hurricanes, and tornadoes, all of which are whirling storms made possible by the Coriolis effect, and all of which turn clockwise in the Northern Hemisphere and counterclockwise in the Southern Hemisphere.

The situation is reversed for polar air drifting away from the poles. Thus, air moving from the North Pole southward is moving from a region where the Earth's surface is moving west to east very slowly into regions where the west-to-east motions are faster and faster. The southward flow of air lags behind the Earth's surface and flows southwestward farther than southward. Since the wind is coming more or less from the east, one speaks, therefore, of the "polar easterlies."

There comes a point where the polar easterlies, extending southward, meet the prevailing westerlies, extending northward. In general, the prevailing westerlies have the greater force and deflect the polar easterlies, making them move more or less from the west also.

Where the cold air from the north meets the warm air from the south, there are weather disturbances. The warm air has considerable water vapor which cannot remain in vapor form when that air is cooled by the cold air flooding down from the Arctic. The water vapor precipitates as rain and the place of meeting is therefore a place of storms.

Now, then, if the United States, for example, had its weather determined solely by the amount of sunlight it received through the year, there would be a slow but steady rise in the average daily temperature from winter solstice to summer solstice and then a slow but steady fall in average daily temperature from summer solstice to winter solstice again. Allowing for the lag as the Earth's surface continues warming for a while past the summer solstice and cooling past the winter solstice, we might make it a period of steady cooling from August 1 to February 1, and then steady warming from February 1 to August 1.

But now add the winds. Suppose the boundary between them remains steady, but moves generally southward as the North Pole tips away from the Sun and then generally northward as the North Pole tips toward the Sun again.

The boundary might sweep southward over New York City in mid-autumn and northward over it in mid-spring. It would then be generally cold from mid-autumn to mid-spring. Following a period of stormy weather it would be generally warm from mid-spring to mid-autumn. Following another period of stormy weather, the cycle would begin again.

There are places on Earth where the weather displays, in large part, a rather simple pattern like that with definite rainy seasons and dry seasons. That is not, however, characteristic of the temperate zones near the boundary between the prevailing westerlies and the polar easterlies.

There are many factors that modify the position of that boundary. There is the influence of the different rates of heating and cooling of land and ocean and, therefore, of the configuration of the shoreline, or even of the presence of large lakes. There is also the influence of mountains and plateaus and of the temperature change between day and night.

As a result, the flow of air responds to such a complexity of causes and modifications that the boundary between the cold and warm air masses shifts erratically, and areas near the average position are subjected to an extraordinary richness of storms and rapid weather changes. (New England and Scotland are notorious examples of this.)

Thus, it follows that polar air is not something that is far away in the haunt of ice. It comes to visit lands that consider themselves well removed from the frigid wastelands, doing so to the discomfort of millions when it brings winter storms and subzero temperatures, and to the great relief of equal millions when it breaks a summer heat wave and brings welcome cool breezes.

Surface-Ocean Circulation

The circulation of surface currents in the ocean resembles, in some ways, the circulation of surface winds in the air. Thanks to the Coriolis effect, the general circulation in those sections of the ocean north of the equator rims the continents in large clockwise circles, while in those sections of the ocean south of the equator, it does so in counterclockwise circles.

That part of each circle that moves from the Tropics to the poles is a warm current. The part that moves from the poles to the Tropics is a cold current.

Consider the northern half of the Atlantic Ocean, for instance. Here you have a surface current moving northward along the eastern coast of the American continents, along the coasts of Brazil and Central America, through and around the Gulf of Mexico and up the east side of the United States. Because, to Americans, the current seems to be coming primarily from the gulf, that portion off the East Coast of the United States is called the Gulf Stream.

The farther north the Gulf Stream moves, the more rapidly the speed of Earth's rotating surface falls off, and the more pronounced is the Coriolis effect. The slant of the East Coast of the United States encourages this, too, so that the Gulf Stream turns increasingly eastward as it moves northward until, south

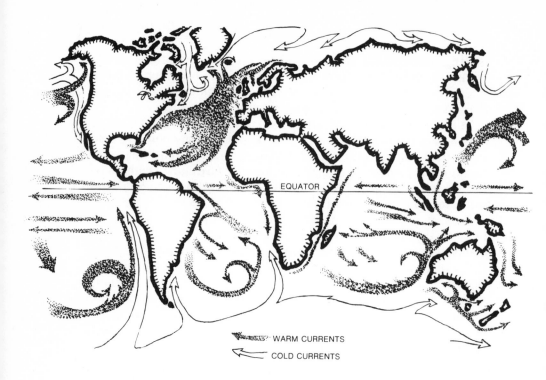

WARM CURRENTS

COLD CURRENTS

Figure 29. Water Currents of the World

of Newfoundland, it heads due east across the Atlantic (the "North Atlantic Drift"). Part of it is deflected by the European coast around the British Isles and up the Norwegian coast; the rest is deflected southward along the northwest shores of Africa. This last part, passing along the Canary Islands is called the "Canaries Current."

Again, the configuration of the African coast and the Coriolis effect combine to send the current westward across the Atlantic (the "North Equatorial Current"), and the circle starts all over.

In this clockwise circle, the Gulf Stream is a warm water current, the Canaries Current, a relatively cold one.

The Coriolis effect enforces a counterclockwise swirl in the South Pacific Ocean. There, the current skirting the continents moves northward from the Antarctic up the western coast of

South America, as far as Peru. This portion of the circle is the "Peru Current," or the "Humboldt Current" (named for the German naturalist Alexander von Humboldt, who first described it about 1810). It is a cold current, of course.

The configuration of the Peruvian coastline and the Coriolis effect combine to send this current westward across the Pacific, just south of the equator (the "South Equatorial Current"). Some of this flow finds its way through the waters of the Indonesian Archipelago into the Indian Ocean. The rest moves southward past the eastern coast of Australia and then eastward again.

These swirls of water help keep the temperature of the ocean equable. Most of the open ocean, well into what we would call the temperate zones on land, therefore, has a tropical distribution of fish.

Most of the ocean currents do not move very quickly, 1 kilometer per hour or less. The Gulf Stream is unusually rapid, however, with speeds of up to 8 kilometers per hour. Even these small speeds involve such areas of ocean that enormous volumes of water are moved. Off New York City, the Gulf Stream is moving water northeastward past some fixed line at the rate of about 45,000,000 tonnes per second.

If you follow the map and observe the clockwise swirls in the northern parts of the ocean and the counterclockwise swirls in the southern parts, you will see that the water that crosses the ocean on the poleward side in each case moves from west to east. Because they move in the same direction as the prevailing westerly winds in those latitudes, these portions of the currents are sometimes called the "West Wind Drift."

In the far south, the West Wind Drift in the Pacific rounds Cape Horn to join the West Wind Drift in the Atlantic which then moves past the southern edges of Africa and Australia to reach South America and past Cape Horn again. There, in the one place where the west-to-east movement is unrestrained by land, the ocean, freed from obstacles, forms the largest current on Earth. The volume of water moving endlessly around Antarctica past any given line is nearly 100,000,000 tonnes per second, which is roughly a hundred times the combined outflow of all the rivers of the world.

The cold polar waters that circle Antarctica have no land masses to deflect them northward into warmer regions in a massive flow. This is another way of saying that, outside

Antarctica, there is no land to be directly affected by the temperature of the current. Not directly.

The situation is different in the North Polar region. There the large landmasses of North America and of Eurasia approach the pole and separate the ocean into distinct halves, the North Pacific Ocean and the North Atlantic Ocean. Each has a West Wind Drift, which remain independent and are sometimes distinguished as the "North Pacific Drift" and the "North Atlantic Drift" respectively. These cross the oceans west to east in temperate latitudes and do not, as they do in the south, merge with cold polar waters.

Indeed, the cold polar waters in the north do not surround a land mass as they do in the south. In the north, they are penned in by broad landmasses and spill out into the temperate zone in only a few places.

From Greenland around to Norway, a stretch of 320 degrees, the Arctic Ocean is virtually landlocked. It is connected with the Pacific Ocean only by the relatively narrow Bering Strait. It is connected with the Atlantic Ocean, west of Greenland, by even narrower channels. It is only east of Greenland that the Arctic Ocean makes a broad linkage with any other section of the ocean—the Atlantic. Between Greenland and Norway is a 1450-kilometer-wide stretch of water, partly, but only partly, blocked by Spitzbergen and Iceland.

The current moving southward along the eastern shore of Greenland tends to hug the shore because the Coriolis effect causes it to move southwestward. It seems to swing around Greenland in part of a clockwise circle, moving round its southern tip and then northward along its western shore as the "West Greenland Current."

There, however, it meets a current moving directly southward through Baffin Bay and turns and joins it. The combined currents of frigid polar water move southward past Baffin Island, Labrador, and Newfoundland, and are called the "Labrador Current." The Labrador Current, moving south along the eastern shores of northern North America, and the Gulf Stream, moving north along the eastern shores of southern North America, have, as you might expect, distinctly opposing effects.

One dramatic example of this comes at the meeting place. South and east of Newfoundland, the Labrador Current (with its load of icebergs in the spring and early summer) meets the Gulf Stream. The warm winds blowing over the Gulf Stream cool rapidly as they pass northeastward over the cold water of the Labrador Current. The result is frequent fogs and storms.

Another example of opposed effect is the climate on opposite sides of the Atlantic Ocean. The frigid waters of the Labrador Current prevent the shores it passes from warming so that Greenland, Baffin Island, and Labrador are all Arctic lands without much in the way of population. Just across the ocean, however, Iceland and Scandinavia, which are in the same latitudes as Baffin Island and the southern half of Greenland, have comparatively large and certainly flourishing populations. The difference, of course, is that the North Atlantic Drift carries the cooling, but still warm, waters of the Gulf Stream to Europe.

Labrador, which contains 260,000 square kilometers that are mostly a desolation, with a total population of less than 25,000, stretches between 52° N. and 60° N. Great Britain, which is almost as large, stretches between 50° N. and 59° N.—but has a population of 55,000,000. Both areas get equal amounts of sunlight distributed in equal fashion; the difference is the Labrador Current in one case and the Gulf Stream in the other.

Another comparison might be between the generally nasty weather of Newfoundland and the generally smiling weather of northern France, which is in precisely the same latitude.

Cold Water

If we judge by the effect on adjacent land areas, it would seem that cold water currents are inimical to life. That would certainly be our first thought if we compare Labrador desolation with the climate of the British Isles. That, however, is only true if we confine ourselves to land life.

Remember that though the cold currents may encourage temperatures well below 0 C. on land, the currents themselves are at the freezing point or a little above—otherwise they could not be liquid and would not flow. The cold currents, therefore, are not really very cold by dry land standards, and sea life can exist in water at or near the freezing point without trouble. In fact, sea life can flourish in cold water to a greater extent than in warm water.

To see the reason for this, let us go back once more to the dissolved matter in water.

Most solid substances that dissolve in water can do so in amounts that vary with the temperature of the water. In almost every case, the warmer the water, the greater the extent to which it can dissolve a particular substance. Consider, for instance, a compound known as magnesium chloride. A hundred cubic centimeters of water at a temperature of 20 C. will dissolve 54 grams of magnesium chloride. Bring that same quantity of water to the boiling point, 100 C., and it will dissolve 73 grams of magnesium chloride, half again as much.

We might imagine a world in which the warm water of the Tropics might dissolve a great deal of magnesium chloride. Then, as currents carry the water poleward, the water would cool down and some of the magnesium chloride can no longer remain dissolved but must solidify and settle out, or "precipitate."

This doesn't happen in the actual world we live in, however, because the amount of magnesium chloride in our ocean is something like 0.5 grams per 100 cubic centimeters of seawater. This is far less than water can hold even at its coldest, so that the magnesium chloride never precipitates out of the ocean solution. (Of course, if shallow arms of the ocean are pinched off and evaporate, the salts will precipitate out. And if inland seas collect enough salts and shrink to a smaller area through evaporation, precipitated salts will line their shores— as is true around the Dead Sea, Great Salt Lake, and so on.)

The solid substance most common among the dissolved matter of the ocean is, of course, sodium chloride. The readiness with which sodium chloride is dissolved varies less with temperature than is true for most such substances. At 0 C., 100 cubic centimeters of water will dissolve 35 grams of sodium chloride, and at 100 C., it will dissolve 39 grams. However, 100 cubic centimeters of seawater only holds about 2.7 grams of sodium chloride so that again the problem of precipitation of the dissolved salts at any temperature and in any part of the ocean doesn't arise.

In fact, all the important solid materials dissolved in the ocean are at concentrations so far below the capacity of seawater to hold them (so far below "saturation") that the dissolved content of the ocean is not dependent upon temperature.

Are there any components of the ocean, other than the dissolved solids, that are held to the level of saturation; and if so, does this mean that some parts of the ocean can hold more than other parts because of temperature differences? Yes, and yes.

It is not solid materials alone that dissolve in the ocean, for the ocean does not merely make contact with the solid land, but also with the gaseous atmosphere. Gases dissolve in water just as solids do, some of them to a great extent, some to only a slight extent.

As it happens, the two gases that make up the bulk (99 percent) of the dry atmosphere, oxygen and nitrogen, both dissolve only slightly. For instance, at 0 C., 100 milliliters of water will dissolve only 0.007 grams of oxygen and only 0.006 grams of nitrogen.

The case of gases is, however, the reverse of that of solids. As the temperature of water rises, the extent to which it can dissolve gases *decreases*. At 100 C., 100 milliliters of water will only dissolve 0.003 grams of either oxygen or nitrogen.

The solution of oxygen and nitrogen in water takes place at the water surface, where ocean meets atmosphere, and where winds stir the top hundred meters or so and accelerate the process of solution.

If we consider the surface layers of the ocean, we find that they keep in solution about all the oxygen and nitrogen that they can. Since these gases dissolve to a greater extent in cold water than in warm water, the surface of the polar ocean contains more of these gases than does the surface of the temperate and tropic ocean. In fact the surface of the polar ocean contains some 60 percent more of these dissolved gases than the surface of the tropic ocean does.

The nitrogen dissolved in seawater is of little importance to life. Nitrogen, as such, is not directly utilized by any life form above the level of bacteria. The oxygen dissolved in seawater is another matter altogether.

Animal life in the sea depends on oxygen just as animal life on land does. A land animal (ourselves, for instance) breathes gaseous oxygen into its lungs. There the oxygen dissolves in the film of water that lines the surface of the lung, and it is the dissolved oxygen that crosses the lung membranes and ends up in the bloodstream.

In the ocean, the oxygen is already dissolved in the water,

and it is this dissolved oxygen that crosses the membranes of the gills of fish and other sea animals, or the cell membranes of simpler organisms, and makes the oxygen-using life processes possible.

On land, the oxygen content of the atmosphere is the same everywhere, so that whatever it is that makes some areas of land more favorable to life than others, it is never the variation of oxygen content of the atmosphere. In the ocean, however, the oxygen concentration *does* vary, and it does so chiefly because of temperature. The cold waters are richer in oxygen and can support, for this reason, heavier loads of life in general (though other factors may modify the situation here and there).

If all the currents of the ocean were strictly on the surface, then oxygen could penetrate the deeper layers only by diffusion, a slow process that would keep the lower layers very poor in oxygen—and therefore without any life to speak of.

This is not so. There is deep-sea life, less densely packed than nearer the surface, but still flourishing. In fact, man has penetrated to the very bottom of the very deepest part of the ocean and has found life in the water there and in the sea floor beneath. That fact alone is sufficient to show that there is considerable dissolved oxygen in the deepest parts of the ocean and that there must therefore be vertical currents carrying surface water (with its dissolved oxygen) downward and bottom water upward.

It is not hard to see why this must be so. The cold polar water, denser because it is cold, sinks downward and, with its oxygen content, spreads out slowly through the deep layers of the ocean equator-ward.

In the Arctic regions, polar water sinks downward chiefly in the North Atlantic Ocean, where alone it can spread southward into warmer seas. But just as the Greenland ice cap is dwarfed by that of Antarctica, so the polar water effect in the North Atlantic is dwarfed by the similar but much greater effect in the Antarctic.

Cold water from the melting ice around the rim of Antarctica spreads northward in all directions from the frozen continent. Since the ice melts into fresh water, that water is less dense than the salt-laden water of the ocean proper, even though it is cold water. As the water spreads northward, however, it slowly gains salt and becomes denser. What is more, it encounters masses of relatively warm water, eventually, which are less dense than the cold ocean it has been floating on up to that point.

At the point where the now-denser cold Antarctic water converges with the less-dense warmer water to the north, the cold water begins to sink and displace lower water upward. Where this happens is a region called the "Antarctic Convergence."

The Antarctic Convergence is a strip of water averaging 45 kilometers in width (north and south) and encircling Antarctica at a distance of from 500 to 2000 kilometers off-shore. It reaches to nearly 40° S. in the regions south of Africa.

From a biologic standpoint, the waters south of the Antarctic Convergence are markedly different from those to the north. The waters south of the Antarctic Convergence can be defined as the Antarctic Ocean, or the Southern Ocean. This biologic definition marks off a greater ocean than does the geographic one of south of 55° S. In fact, the portion of the ocean south of the Antarctic Convergence covers a surface area of 75,000,000 square kilometers, and such an Antarctic Ocean is some six times greater than the Arctic Ocean and makes up about 22 percent of the total oceanic area of the planet. (Yet it contains only 10 percent of the total oceanic supply of heat.)

If to the Antarctic Ocean, as defined in this way, is added Antarctica, the total area of the Antarctic region becomes 88,000,000 square kilometers, or one-sixth the total surface area of the world.

North of the Antarctic Convergence, the Antarctic water sinks to intermediate levels and continues to spread northward as "Antarctic Bottom Water" that cools all the oceans and helps regulate the world climate generally.

The northern portions of the ocean are least subject to the Antarctic influence, but the North Atlantic Ocean gets its own supply of bottom water from the Arctic. The North Pacific Ocean, which is far removed from the Antarctic and gets very little of the Arctic through the Bering Strait, is, of all parts of the ocean, the least influenced by polar bottom water.

There are places in the ocean where this polar bottom water rises to the surface again. Such "upwelling" takes place, for instance, in areas where surface currents diverge and move in opposite directions. This lowers the water pressure at the point of divergence and the lower water rises.

Then, too, at continental shores where winds are consistently blowing out to sea, the surface water is blown outward and lower water rises steadily to replace it. This is particularly true off the west-central coast of South America, where the cool Humboldt Current is further cooled by the upwelling of cold bottom water.

The bottom water brings up something of the greatest importance to life. At first thought, this seems an unlikely state of affairs because the lower reaches of the ocean are far less rich in life than the surface and would therefore seem to be less well adapted to life—but not so.

Life is richest in the upper layers of the ocean, not only because that is where oxygen enters the water and remains at the saturation level, but also because that is where the sunlight is.

Sunlight does not penetrate in significant quantities farther than about 150 meters below the surface, and it is only in this "euphotic zone" ("good light") that plant cells, which require light energy to convert carbon dioxide and water into their tissue substance, can grow. The plant cells that fill these upper layers of the ocean support a thriving animal population that feeds upon them.

Below the euphotic zone, there are no plants, only animals. There the ultimate life support must depend on forays upward into the euphotic zone, or else on the rain of life remains that sinks downward from the euphotic zone.

There is a constant rain of no longer living matter drifting downward through the water. Some can be snapped up, of course, en route, but some inevitably makes its way downward long distances. Then the life forms that are already living in the depths add to the rain when they die or are torn by a predator. In the end, the rain makes its way to the very bottom of the ocean and supports life (increasingly thinly) all the way down.

Living plants in the surface layers of the water incorporate into their tissues not only carbon dioxide and water, but also various groups of atoms (referred to usually as "mineral ions") present in the ocean in dissolved form. As a result, such mineral ions as are present in the surface water of the ocean are, in some cases, concentrated almost entirely in the living cells. Nitrate and phosphate, for instance, are not to be found in the water of the ocean, but only (in various forms) in living cells. When all the nitrate and phosphate have moved into the cells, it is clear that no further weight of life can form—there is lacking the raw material for it.

As living matter dies and sinks, the mineral ions it contains sink with it and eventually reach the sea bottom. If this alone is taken into account, there would be a slow but steady loss of these essential mineral ions from the surface to the depths with the result that the surface waters, then the ocean deeps, then the land and all the Earth, more or less, would become a desert.

It is the upwelling of cold, bottom water that brings mineral ions from the depths. Where upwellings exist, as in the Humboldt Current, there results the capacity for a particularly rich concentration of sea life. The best example of this is at the Antarctic Convergence. There, as the cold Antarctic water sinks and forces deep water upward, you have a region that is particularly rich in both oxygen and mineral ions. The result is that nowhere on Earth is life as rich and as concentrated as in the Antarctic Convergence.

In the absence of cold polar regions and of cold polar water, ocean life would be far less rich and abundant than it is now, and this would mean that life everywhere on Earth would be far less rich and abundant than it is now.

However much the polar regions seem inimical to life, then, their existence actually ensures that Earth is and remains a rich and lavish abode for living things—including man.

Polar Oceanic Life

The smallest living organisms of the ocean float passively in the surface layers. The German physiologist Viktor Hensen, in 1889, called this floating life of the ocean "plankton" from a Greek word meaning "wandering," and this expression has been used ever since. Most of the plankton are microscopic in size, but the name is used also for such large plant organisms as seaweed, and such large animal organisms as giant jellyfish.

The microscopic plant cells of the plankton ("phytoplankton," the prefix from a Greek word meaning "plant") are the basic food of all ocean animal life. All sea animals either eat phytoplankton or eat other animals that have eaten phytoplankton, or other animals that have eaten other animals that have eaten other animals—and so on, until we come to an animal that has eaten phytoplankton. This "food chain" can be of varying lengths.

The small animals of the surface ("zooplankton," the prefix from a Greek word meaning "animal") feed on the phytoplankton. The most common of the zooplankton are small crustacea called "copepods." There are 6000 species of copepods with lengths varying from 0.5 millimeter (barely visible to the naked eye) to 1 centimeter. They make up about 70 percent of all the zooplankton and can sometimes turn the ocean pink with their numbers. A somewhat larger variety of shellfish is the small, shrimplike "krill," which is up to 5 centimeters in length.

Larger animals, such as young fish, feed on the zooplankton and themselves serve as food for larger organisms.

Food is not converted into the tissues of the eater with perfect efficiency. There is, roughly, a 90 percent loss, so that, in general, the total mass of a species can only be about 10 percent that of the species it feeds upon.

Since plant life in general is the food of animal life in general, the mass of plant life on Earth must be ten times that of animal life, and the total mass of the phytoplankton in the ocean must be roughly ten times that of all the animal life there. (Animal life in the ocean exists at all levels, but plant life is confined to the euphotic zone and is all phytoplankton in nature.)

Because each step upward in the food chain means a decrease in total mass of the organism by a factor of ten, the actual number of larger and larger animals decreases drastically.

Thus, the white shark, which is the largest sea vertebrate with gills (12 meters long) that lives on other large organisms, is a relatively rare creature. The sea cannot support white sharks in the myriads that it can support herring, for instance —the herring live on plankton.

Large animals can be supported in larger numbers if they cut through the food chain by living on plankton directly. The whale shark and basking shark are even larger than the white shark (up to 15 meters long) but can be supported in surprising numbers because they live on plankton.

There are land animals that live primarily on sea life, and the distribution of these animals differs from that of land animals that live primarily on land life. Land plants grow stunted and sparse as one approaches the poles, and consequently land animals that live on them grow fewer, too. The sparseness of land life on the tundra and the virtual absence of land life in Antarctica have already been mentioned.

Sea life is, however, richer in the polar regions than in the Tropics, thanks to the greater supply of oxygen and nutrients in cold water than in warm water. As a result, the polar regions are rich in land animal life that finds its food in the ocean.

Land life that depends on the sea for its food must be adapted to ocean feeding and this takes place to a greater or lesser extent. In some cases, the adaptation is so extreme that the land animals are no longer really land animals, having adapted themselves to continuous life in the oceans, even to the point of developing the streamlined fish shape for more rapid motion.

The best known of the extremely adapted organisms are the whales and their smaller relatives, the dolphins, which breathe by means of lungs, bring forth living young, and are, by every criteria, as fully mammalian as we ourselves, but which spend all their lives in the water.

The smallest dolphins are about 1.2 meters long and weigh about 45 kilograms. The largest dolphin is the killer whale, with males as long as 10 meters. The killer whale is an example of an organism that is at the top of the food chain. There are no

Killer Whales

*White Whales and Glaucous Gull. Old
bull whales are pale brownish and often
scarred; cows and calves are white.*

other large organisms for whom the killer whale is a regular article of diet. A killer whale will die of disease, accident, or old age, not by ordinary predation.

The one exception to this in the case of the killer whale and of all other organisms that exist at the top of the food chain rests in the activity of man. In his natural physical state, man is no match for the larger animals, but armed with the products of the technology produced by his restless mind, he can destroy them all and is, indeed, in the process of doing so.

Another large dolphin, the narwhal, up to 5 meters long, is an Arctic animal. It inhabits the sea among the loose ice of the Arctic beyond 65° N., migrating farther northward as the pack ice melts and recedes in the polar winter. The most unusual characteristic of the narwhal is that one tooth on the left side of its jaw forms a straight, spiral tusk up to 2.5 meters long. Its appearance is exactly that of the fabled horn of the unicorn, which was supposed to have miraculous medical properties— and no wonder, since sailors brought home pieces of narwhal tooth and, claiming it to be unicorn horn, sold it for large sums.

The largest truly carnivorous whale is the sperm whale. The male sperm whale can be as long as 20 meters and may weigh as much as 60 tonnes. It lives largely on giant squid. It, too, is at the top of the food chain and is threatened only by man.

Still larger whales, like the largest sharks, must cut through the food chain if they are to be supported in any numbers. The largest of all whales (and, indeed, the largest animal that has ever lived) is the blue whale, which can be 30 meters long and weigh 135 tonnes. It feeds largely on krill, eating 3 tonnes per day. Whales that feed on plankton have fringes of horny plates, up to 3 meters long, extending down from the roof of the mouth and frayed and brushlike at the end. These, called "baleen," or "whalebone," trap and strain out the plankton.

Whales are worldwide in their distribution, but naturally they are most common where the food supply is richest, and this means the polar regions; and the Antarctic far more than the Arctic.

Whalers, hunting the whale for meat, oil, and whalebone, ventured into Arctic and Antarctic waters, and a great deal of the early exploration of the polar regions was performed by whalers and by those who hunted other sea mammals.

The search for whales was ruthless, however, and without any thought for preserving the species. In the eighteenth century, the large baleen whales of the Arctic were reduced to such small numbers that it was simply not worthwhile hunting them anymore.

With the passing of the baleen whales of the north, attention turned to the sperm whale when it was discovered that

Ross Seal

quantities of sperm oil could be obtained from the head of that organism and that such oil was particularly useful in oil lamps. The sperm whale was a more difficult and savage target (Moby Dick in Herman Melville's great novel was a sperm whale), but they would have been wiped out also if the electric light and the growing use of petroleum had not eased the need for sperm oil.

Whaling is now almost entirely confined to the Antarctic, where the food supply of the oceans is the richest in the world thanks to the Antarctic Convergence. Some 70 percent of the whales killed are hunted down in the Antarctic and of these 70 percent are the fin whale. Even now 35,000 whales are being killed each year, and these great animals will be wiped out if mankind does not manage to control the whalers.

Stepping down a notch in the extent of adaptation to the sea, we come to the seals. They, too, are typically polar in distribution because of the richness of the cold regions of the ocean.

Like the whales, the seals have been hunted down and slaughtered. Where the whales are bare-skinned and depend on

Alaskan Fur Seals: bull, cows, and pups

retaining warmth against the cold water of the polar oceans by thick layers of fat ("blubber") under the skin, seals have, in many cases, developed thick coats of hair. The coats of these "hair seals" have been coveted and have very nearly proved the doom of those animals.

The ones that yield the best "sealskins" are the Alaska fur seals, and these gathered in huge hordes on the Pribilof Islands (discovered by the Russian navigator Gerasim Pribilof in 1786) in the Bering Sea. At the time of the discovery some 5,000,000 seals formed the herd. They began to wither under the attack of the sealers until the Russian government exerted protection.

The Pribilof Islands, along with all of Alaska, passed to the United States in 1867, and at once the sealers began to make destructive inroads until only 125,000 seals remained in 1911. There seemed no way of making men forgo short-term profits in favor of a careful conservation that would, in the long run, yield greater returns.

Finally, when the United States and other nations imposed rigorous controls on sealing activities, the seal herds began to be restored. By now the herds are back up to 3,000,000 despite the fact that since 1911, under carefully rationed culling of the herds, 1,500,000 seals have been taken for their fur.

Walrus

Leopard Seal chasing Adélie penguins

The most northerly of the seals is the ringed seal, which lives almost exclusively on and under the ice of the Arctic Ocean.

The largest of the seals is the elephant seal, so called more because of its trunklike nasal protuberance than its size. Species are found in both the Arctic and the Antarctic, with the latter somewhat the larger. The Antarctic males reach a length of 6.5 meters and a weight of nearly 4 tonnes.

The next largest seal is the walrus, which can reach a length of 3.5 meters and a weight of 1.4 tonnes. It differs from the other members of the seal family in the possession of a pair of downward pointing tusks (the two upper canine teeth) which can be as long as 40 centimeters. The walruses are to be found only in the Arctic. Once 500,000 were to be found on the Arctic ice floes, but hunting has reduced their numbers to less than 50,000.

Of the forty-seven species of seals, five are native to the Antarctic. The largest of these (and third only to the elephant seal and the walrus) is the leopard seal. It is well named, for it is the most ferocious carnivore of the family. It needs to fear no other animal but the killer whale—and, of course, man.

The crab-eater seal, despite its name, lives on krill. It is the most common of the Antarctic seals and numbers 5,000,000 to 8,000,000.

The most thoroughly Antarctic of the seals, however, is the

Weddell Seal

Weddell seal. It sticks close to the shores of Antarctica, while the other seals range well out to sea. The Weddell seal finds safety beneath the coastal ice, breaking holes in it to breathe through. It can dive to a depth of 600 meters and can remain submerged for nearly an hour. Ordinarily, however, it comes up for air every 10 to 30 minutes. (The female spends considerable time on top of the ice, for only there can she feed her young.)

Another notch downward in adaptation to the sea and we come to what would seem so completely a land animal as the bear. Two species of bears are characteristic of the Arctic regions and they are the two largest: the Kodiak brown bear and the polar bear.

The more northerly of the two is the polar bear, creamy-white in fur, so that it is not noticeable against the snow and ice it lives among. It can be 2 meters or more in length and may weigh over 700 kilograms. The polar bear lives on fish and seals and is capable of swimming miles out to sea. It can also roam the Arctic ice all the way to the North Pole—followed by the Arctic fox, which scavenges the polar bear kills. (The polar bear's liver is so rich in vitamin A as to be actually poisonous to man.)

And while we're talking of land mammals adapted to seeking food by sea, we should mention man, too. The Eskimos, at least, live very well in the apparently bleak Arctic world by learning to turn to the rich sea for their food.

Polar Bear

There are important seabirds in the polar regions. In the Arctic, the most typical examples are the members of the auk family. These are not strong flyers, but are very well adapted to diving into water after the fish they eat. They are capable of swimming underwater by making the same wing movements they make in flight. One of the better-known auks is the puffin, which has a large head and a multicolored parrot-like beak.

The most tragic member of the family was the great auk, which stood about a meter high and was the most completely adapted to water life of any species of the family. It could swim underwater with complete expertise, but its wings were paddles only, and it could not fly with them.

What with its nonflight, its habit of congregating in great numbers on islands in the Atlantic section of the Arctic, its single egg laid on bare ground without protection, and its inability to recognize the presence of danger, the great auk was an easy prey. They were killed wantonly in huge numbers and the last members of the species were killed on June 4, 1844.

Not all polar seabirds are poor fliers. The gull-like Arctic tern is, in some way, a flying champion. It nests in the Arctic (as far north as 82.5° N.) but evades the winter by flying 17,500 kilometers to the Antarctic—then evades the Antarctic winter by flying back to the Arctic. It spends seven months of the year traveling and at each end of its journey experiences some two and a half months of continuous sunlight.

Arctic Tern

Another Arctic bird, the golden plover, also undergoes a long migratory flight, much of it being over the ocean and therefore nonstop, since the plovers don't swim well. A three-month-old golden plover can make it successfully from its birthplace in Alaska down to Hawaii (some 3500 kilometers) in two days of flying.

Although the Antarctic region has no mammals except for whales and seals which remain in the waters off the shores of Antarctica, there are birds that make their way across portions of the continent itself. Considering that the birds usually possess the ability to fly, this is perhaps not so unusual.

Of the fifteen species of flying birds that are found in the Antarctic region, the most southerly is a predatory gull-like bird called the skua. It seems very likely that skuas have ranged over all Antarctica and that they are the only species of living creature who have reached the South Pole independently of man.

There are two Antarctic petrels and one of these, the giant petrel, is the largest of the Antarctic flying birds—with a wingspread of 2 meters and a weight of over 4 kilograms.

The most characteristic birds of Antarctica, however, are

Antarctic Petrel

species incapable of flight, birds that actually walk extensively over the barren ice of that frozen continent. They are penguins, which adapted to the same kind of life and have developed a similar form to the great auk of the Arctic.

Penguins are as closely adapted to sea life as the great auk was, maybe more so. Their wings are paddles that are useless for flying but that give them an almost unmatched speed (almost 50 kilometers an hour) and turning ability underwater. Such is the force of their swimming that they can leap out of the water to twice their own height. On land, however, the best they can do is waddle in ungainly fashion. (Their upright posture, their humorous waddle, and their black and white coloration, as though they were wearing dress suits, have endeared them to men and spared them carnage.)

There are seventeen species of penguins altogether, all of them native to the Southern Hemisphere. Of these, two species actually live on Antarctica. The smaller of the Antarctic penguins is the Adélie penguin, so-called because it is found in Adélie Land. The Adélie penguins congregate in crowded nesting sites inland ("rookeries"). They are about 45 centimeters tall and weigh 6 to 7 kilograms.

The skua is always waiting to eat the eggs and the penguin chicks, while in the ocean the leopard seal waits for the adults.

Snow Petrel

As long as man does not interfere, however, enough survive to keep the species going.

More astonishing is the emperor penguin, the largest of all living penguins, standing over a meter high (twice the height of the Adélie) and weighing at times as much as 35 kilograms.

Adélie Penguins

(There are fossils of penguins, now extinct, that stood 1.6 meters high and weighed as much as 110 kilograms.)

Unlike the Adélie penguins, the emperors did not seem to possess rookeries. Edward Wilson, one of those fated to die later with Scott in the tragic attempt to reach the South Pole and return, was particularly interested in finding the eggs of the emperor penguin. He felt the emperor penguin to be the most primitive of all birds, and the species most closely related to the reptiles. (He was wrong in this.) He thought that a study of the embryos of these birds might clarify their position in the animal kingdom.

In 1902, he was the first to discover an emperor penguin rookery. (There are fourteen known rookeries now, sheltering perhaps 160,000 emperor penguins altogether.) For the first time, Wilson saw emperor chicks on the feet of adults. From their size, he realized the hatching of those chicks must have taken place quite awhile before during what was then winter.

In fact, it was discovered that the female emperor penguin laid her single egg in the depth of the Antarctic winter, so that the egg had to be incubated under worse conditions, by far,

Emperor Penguins

than those experienced by any other bird in the world. The emperor penguin is the only bird that does not nest on bare land. It nests on ice, and the emperor penguin may, indeed, never feel bare land but find itself always on or in water in liquid or solid form. (The Adélie penguin nests on exposed land along the rim of the continent and lays its eggs at the beginning of summer.)

The emperor penguin rookeries are located inland, some 80 to 130 kilometers from the coast. (Emperor penguins are occasionally found as far as 400 kilometers from the nearest coast, stubbornly trudging along—the farthest south any nonflying vertebrate has ever reached independently of man.)

It takes a month for the emperor penguins to travel from the shores of Antarctica, where food can be obtained, to the inland rookeries where no food exists (but where, except for man and skua, isolation and security are absolute). The emperor penguins fast during this trek.

There, in the interior, in winter, the female lays her single egg. There is no nest and no nesting territory, something that only the emperor penguin, of all birds, lacks. The single egg is taken by the male and placed on his feet immediately under a bare and unfeathered patch of the abdomen. A flap of skin covers the egg, which is then incubated against the father's body and on his feet, so that the nesting territory is, so to speak, the ground on which the bird stands.

The male emperor penguins can waddle about clumsily without losing the eggs, and most of them huddle together for warmth, which they need, for the icy Antarctic midwinter temperatures go as low as − 60 C. and the gales whistle past the birds at speeds of up to 150 kilometers per hour.

Once the egg is transferred, the female takes off for the sea again, and food—another month's journey. The male, however, stands his ground for sixty days, still fasting. Prior to the trek to the rookery, the male emperor penguin has eaten enough to lay by a sizable quantity of fat—attaining a weight of 35 kilograms—but this begins to melt away during the long fast.

Finally, when the chicks are near to hatching, the females return and take over. At last the males can head for the sea, which they finally reach after a four-month fast in which they lose 25 to 40 percent of their weight.

When the chick hatches, the mother feeds it with food it has stored in its crop, but this won't last. The father must return, and for a while the parents take turns walking to the sea, eating their fill, and returning to feed the chick. Fully one-quarter of the chicks don't survive the rigors of that first winter—but by the time the Antarctic summer arrives and the coastal ice begins breaking up, those that have survived can make it to the sea and go out to feed on their own.

11

THE GLOBAL MAGNET

So far, the discussion of the polar regions has involved, one way or another, the polar cold at every step: the reasons for it, the effects of it. It has dealt with the form water takes at low temperatures and the manner of life at low temperatures.

It is time to turn now, however, to important facts concerning the polar regions that have nothing directly to do with its temperature. Here we can begin with a phenomenon whose history dates back to ancient times, at least as far as it is connected with mankind, a phenomenon that, at first, seemed to have no connection with the poles.

Magnetism

The natural starting point for this part of the story is with the Greek philosopher Thales, who lived in Miletus on the Asian shore of the Aegean Sea about 600 B.C. He was the first, as far as we know, to study in systematic fashion certain minerals that had the power to attract iron, but not other materials.

According to legend, the first attracting mineral of this sort was brought to Thales' attention through the discovery of a shepherd lad of the nearby city of Magnesia, who found his iron-tipped staff sticking to a rock that was not otherwise sticky. The iron-attracting minerals were therefore called "magnetis lithos" ("magnesian stone"). The name has remained, for we now call such iron-attracting objects "magnets" and call the phenomenon "magnetism."

The magnesian stone nowadays is called "magnetite" and it is a compound of iron and oxygen. Atoms, generally, have magnetic properties associated with themselves and, in magnetite, the atoms happen to be arranged in such a way that the very weak magnetic properties of the individual atoms reinforce each other to the point where the sum of the force becomes detectably strong.

The atoms in iron itself are easily influenced by an outside magnetic force to take up an orientation that will produce a detectable magnetism in itself. In the close presence of magnetite, then, iron will itself become magnetic and the two magnets will attract each other. When the magnetite is removed, the atoms in the iron lose their special orientation and the iron no longer acts magnetically. Magnetite, in other words, is a permanent magnet, where iron is a temporary magnet, possessing that property only under the influence of a nearby permanent magnet.

Without understanding magnetism at the atomic level, the Greeks noticed the effects. In one of Plato's dialogues, Socrates is quoted as referring to magnets which not only attract iron rings, but allow those iron rings, while in contact with themselves, to attract still other iron rings.

It was only in later times that men discovered that magnetite could also produce other permanent magnets. Steel (which is iron mixed with a certain percentage of carbon) is much harder than iron itself, partly because the atoms within it cling together more tightly. These atoms are therefore more difficult to orient in such a fashion as to multiply their magnetic properties. Once oriented, however, they have little tendency to fall spontaneously out of order, and therefore remain magnetic even after the magnetite is removed. (They lose their magnetic properties if heated, however, since at higher temperatures atoms move more violently and can force their way out of orientation.)

Nor is the magnetic force always manifested as an attraction. In what must have seemed a paradox at first, it sometimes demonstrates itself as a repulsion, a fact first mentioned by the Roman poet and philosopher Lucretius about 60 B.C.

Nobody knows how mankind progressed from the study of the magnetic force to the discovery of one of its most notable uses. Perhaps it was through idle play; after all, it is difficult, once having obtained a magnet, to avoid playing with it.

The ability to attract or repel pieces of iron or other magnets is sufficiently unusual to allow endless amusements. One can imagine someone (perhaps the young son of a philosopher who had magnetized needles in his study) setting up a cork boat in a bowl of water and placing one of those needles upon it as cargo. The boy might then notice, and call to his father's attention, the fact that the boat always turned in such a way as to turn the ends of the needle in the same direction. A closer consideration by the surprised father may have shown him that that preferred direction was north-south.

This, or something like this, must have taken place first in China, which during the Middle Ages was the technological leader of the world. Discounting legends that seem to speak of north-south-seeking objects in the dim dawn of civilization, the first definite mention of determining direction by means of a magnetic needle comes in the eleventh century. Chinese entertainers would pretend to force a magnetic needle (apparently by their impressive mystical arts) to point out the north-south line.

Once that ability of a magnetized needle became common knowledge, it was not a huge step to take advantage of the property for navigational purposes.

In the open sea, out of sight of land, only astronomical objects could give a man a notion of direction (without which it is very difficult to navigate purposely). The Sun's position could give a general direction of east in the morning and west in the evening. In the North Temperate Zone, it will indicate south at midday. On a clear night, the stars (the Big Dipper, for instance) could be used to give a general notion of the north.

This sort of directional information, plus the nature of the wind and currents and the shrewd judgment of experienced navigators, made it possible for long sea voyages to be conducted out of sight of land in early times. The Phoenicians, as early as 1000 B.C., sailed fearlessly throughout the Mediterranean and even out into the Atlantic Ocean.

The Vikings, from A.D. 800 onward, sailed all round the coasts of Europe and ventured out into the Atlantic and through the sub-Arctic. Most remarkable of all were the Polynesian islanders of the Pacific, who, from A.D. 300 onward, sailed over the largest and emptiest ocean on Earth to hit their tiny island targets with astonishing precision.

Yet the remarkable success of some must not be allowed to obscure the difficulty involved. In cloudy weather, all the astronomical signs by day and by night fail. Clearly, navigation across the open sea could be conducted with greater confidence and with a smaller need for extraordinary talent if some device could be used that would unfailingly indicate direction regardless of the condition of the sky.

The magnetized needle was such a device. Whether floating on a piece of cork or, better yet, pivoted delicately on a needle, it indicated the north as easily by night as by day and as surely in cloudy weather as in clear. Such a device is called a "compass," and to distinguish it from the type of compass geometers use to draw a circle, it is called the "magnetic compass," or the "mariner's compass."

By 1100, Arab traders whose ships were plying the Indonesian islands had picked up knowledge of the north-seeking behavior of a magnetized needle and were using a compass to guide them. This much is reported by a Chinese writer of the period.

News of the compass drifted westward, and the first European to mention it, that we know of, was the English scholar Alexander Neckam. As early as 1180, he spoke of a compass as one of the essentials of the navigator's art.

Once the compass came into common use, there is no question but that ocean voyaging became less difficult. The age of exploration, into which Europeans plunged from 1400 on, led to a vast flowering of European technology and to a period during which Europe dominated the world. It would certainly not have taken place as quickly and as thoroughly as it did (and perhaps it would not have taken place at all) were it not for the compass.

The Magnetic Poles

Navigators could very well take advantage of the compass without knowing why it behaved as it did, but there was bound to be curiosity as to the cause. Since there was a force of attraction between a magnet and a lump of iron, it might be supposed that the magnetic compass needle was turning toward some distant lump of iron. The iron was too far off to see, and, since the attractive force clearly decreased with distance, the iron in question would have to be enormous in size to exert its effect.

The legend arose in the Middle Ages, therefore, that far in the north there was a huge magnetic iron mountain and that, attracted to this, the compass needle pointed yearningly northward. Naturally, tales arose of ships adventuring dangerously close to this vast magnet, which exerted such force at close quarters that the nails were pulled out of the ship. The planks then fell apart and the ship was wrecked. One such tale is found in the *Arabian Nights*, for instance.

This legend, which for the first time connected magnetism and the polar regions, was attractive partly because the Far North was a mysterious land which had not yet been penetrated by the civilized men of the south. Anything could be believed of that icy region near the poles.

In 1269, however, a French scholar, Peter Peregrinus, turned his attention to something closer to home, the actual magnet itself. At a time long before science had become experimental, Peregrinus began to observe and experiment.

He noted that parts of a piece of magnetite attracted a compass needle more strongly than other parts. It was as though the magnetic force was concentrated most strongly in two places on opposite sides of the magnetite. Those places were eventually called "magnetic poles."

Peregrinus found that the end of the compass needle that ordinarily pointed north was attracted to one of the poles of a piece of magnetite. It is naturally the "north magnetic pole." The other end of the compass needle pointed to the other pole, the "south magnetic pole."

Peregrinus also found evidence that all magnets had both north and south magnetic poles. If he broke a piece of magnetite in two, he found that he did not have two pieces that each possessed a single pole. The piece with the original north magnetic pole at once developed a south magnetic pole some-where on the broken edge, while the piece with the original south magnetic pole developed a new north magnetic pole.

He further found that the south magnetic pole of one magnet attracted the north magnetic pole of another. He did not seem to notice, however, that two north magnetic poles repelled each other, and that so did two south magnetic poles. Or if he did, he didn't mention it.

Unfortunately, Peregrinus reported his work in a letter to a friend, and the general scholarly world knew nothing of his findings until many years later.

Meanwhile, though, more was learned of the magnetic compass, including the fact that it was, in some respects, not altogether reliable. For one thing, it did not point exactly to the true north but a little to one side. (Of course, this could be allowed for as far as navigational requirements were con-cerned.)

However, when Christopher Columbus crossed the Atlantic Ocean westward, in 1492, he found, more than a little to his horror, that the direction indicated by the compass needle changed markedly as he traveled. It had been pointing some-what east of north when he left Spain, but it swiveled slowly westward and was eventually pointing distinctly west of true north. (This change could be detected by comparing the direction of the compass needle with that of the North Star.)

The danger here was that the laws of nature seemed to be changing, and in that case who could tell what dangerous and magical areas the ships might be approaching in these un-known waters? Columbus averted panic among his sailors by convincing them that it was the North Star that was shifting, not the compass needle. The sailors found irregularity in the sky less frightening than irregularity on the ship and remained calm.

The degree to which the compass points east or west of north is called the "magnetic declination," and before long mariners began to record the magnetic declination in various places as a guide to those who came after. The first important table of magnetic declination was drawn up by an English scholar, Robert Norman, in 1581.

Norman also studied a compass needle which was pivoted in such a way that it moved up and down rather than right and left. He found that such a needle pointed toward the ground at a rather large angle to the horizontal. This is called "magnetic dip," and the amount of magnetic dip also varies from place to place on Earth. In general, the end of the compass needle that ordinarily points north also points downward in the Northern Hemisphere—but points upward in the Southern Hemisphere.

Norman's contemporary, the English physician William Gilbert was, in the meantime, studying magnets in very much the fashion of Peter Peregrinus (whose work was now becoming known). Gilbert shaped a piece of magnetite into a sphere and studied the direction in which a compass needle pointed at various places in the neighborhood of the sphere. He found not only that the compass needle pointed north and south with reference to the spherical magnet, but that it also showed the property of magnetic dip.

Gilbert reported his results in a book, *De Magnete* ("Concerning magnets"), which was published in 1600. He suggested, for the first time, that the Earth itself was a huge magnet with a magnetic north pole and a magnetic south pole, and that it was this that explained the action of the compass, and not the existence of a magnetic mountain in the Far North.

About 1830, the German mathematician Carl F. Gauss showed that the actions of the compass needle, including magnetic declination and magnetic dip, could be explained by assuming the presence of a comparatively short but very powerful bar magnet at the center of the Earth. The axis of this hypothetical bar magnet would be set at an angle of about 12 degrees to the geographic axis of Earth's rotation.

These hypothetical "geomagnetic poles" are located at 78.5° N. and 70° W. in the Arctic and 78.5° S. and 110° E. in the Antarctic, so that a line connecting the two passes through the center of the Earth. The north geomagnetic pole is located on Hayes Peninsula, in Greenland, just about 35 kilometers north of Thule. The south geomagnetic pole is deep in Antarctica, quite near the regions of greatest cold, though that, of course, is coincidence.

After 1830, one of the objects of polar exploration was to check Gauss's theory and to locate the magnetic poles of the Earth, not as theoretically derived points, but as observed points, points where the compass needle pointed straight up and down. It was quickly observed that, in the Arctic at least, the magnetic pole as detected by the compass needle was *not* located at the theoretical position. Ever since, then, one speaks of the "geomagnetic poles" (theoretical) and the "magnetic poles" (observed).

The north magnetic pole was located in 1831 by James Ross (who was later to discover the Ross Sea in the Antarctic). He found it at 70.85° N. and 96.77° W., a site on the western shore of Boothia Peninsula, the northernmost extension of the North American continent. This point was fully 2100 kilometers from the geographic North Pole (equivalent to the distance from New York City to Dallas, Texas) and 450 kilometers southwest of the north geomagnetic pole.

Actually, there is strong reason to consider the geomagnetic poles the true magnetic poles. The observed location of the magnetic poles differs from the site of the geomagnetic poles because, apparently, of local irregularities produced by the uneven distribution of magnetic materials in the Earth's crust.

Since its discovery, the north magnetic pole has been moving slowly in a generally northward direction. In 1965, it was located at 75° N. and 101° W. on the southern shore of Bathurst Island in the Canadian Archipelago. It is now just over 1600 kilometers from the geographic North Pole, and only 330 kilometers west of the north geomagnetic pole.

Why it moves as it does and, indeed, why it moves at all is as yet completely obscure.

Naturally, the search was on for the south magnetic pole but, at first, without much chance of success. It seemed almost certain to be located somewhere in the Antarctic itself, and in the nineteenth century, explorers had only been able to nose about the limits of the pack ice.

In 1840, Dumont d'Urville ventured southward along unexplored longitudes, as mentioned in chapter 6, and discovered Adélie Land (and indirectly gave his wife's name to the Adélie penguins, too). His purpose was to watch the compass needle and try to decide if he was coming close to the south magnetic pole. He did come closer to it than he would have done along other sections of the Antarctica shores.

The south magnetic pole was actually located only after penetration of the continent began. In 1909, Edgeworth David and Douglas Mawson located it at 72.42° S. and 155.27° E., 250 kilometers inland from the western shore of Ross Sea. At the time it was located, it was just about 1600 kilometers from the geographic South Pole and was about 1400 kilometers northeast of the south geomagnetic pole.

Since then, however, while the magnetic north pole was moving northward toward the geographic North Pole, the magnetic south pole has moved northward *away from* the geographic South Pole. In 1965, it was at 66.30° S. and 139.53° E. The south magnetic pole is now almost exactly at the Antarctica shore and, by an ironic coincidence, almost exactly at the site reached by Dumont d'Urville in his search for it. The site came to the explorer—a century and a quarter too late.

The south magnetic pole is very nearly at the Antarctic Circle, about 2600 kilometers from the geographic South Pole and 1600 kilometers from the south geomagnetic pole. If it drifts a bit farther in the direction it has been drifting, it will move out of the South Polar region altogether.

The north and south geographic poles are at precisely opposite ends of the Earth. So are the north and south geomagnetic poles. A line drawn through the Earth from one geographic pole to the other, or from one geomagnetic pole to the other, will in each case pass through the center of the Earth.

This is not so for the north and south magnetic poles. Although generally on opposite ends of the Earth, this is not precisely true. A line drawn through the Earth from the north magnetic pole to the south magnetic pole (the "magnetic axis") passes about 1100 kilometers to one side of the center of the Earth.

If a circumference is drawn around the Earth, passing through both magnetic poles, then the distance from the north magnetic pole across North America and the South Pacific Ocean to the south magnetic pole is 38,000 kilometers. Continuing the circuit back to the north magnetic pole via the Indian Ocean, Africa, and Europe is 42,500 kilometers.

The Earth's Core

But why do the magnetic poles exist at all? And why is there magnetism associated with the Earth? Is the Earth really a magnet as Gilbert maintained nearly four centuries ago? Certainly the substance of the Earth that lies within our reach is not generally magnetic. The land and water surface of the planet, except for local bits of magnetite, shows no significant magnetic properties.

Can Gauss's suggestion be correct—that it is not the Earth

itself that is a magnet, but its core? Since magnetism seems to be associated with iron and with certain iron oxides, the suggestion that there is a bar magnet at the center of the Earth is equivalent to suggesting that iron, in some form or other, is present in considerable quantity at the core of the Earth.

This could be so. In 1798, the English scientist Henry Cavendish had made the first accurate estimate of the mass of the Earth. From that mass and from the Earth's known volume, it was possible to calculate the overall average density of the Earth, and this came out to be 5.5 grams per cubic centimeter. The density of the rocks of the Earth's crust, however, averages no more than 2.8 grams per cubic centimeter. To make up for that and reach the average, the density of the central regions of the Earth must be considerably more than 5.5. grams per cubic centimeter and should perhaps be 9 to 12 grams per cubic centimeter.

Even allowing for the increase in density that comes with the pressure of the rock layers above, it doesn't seem that any rocky substance could attain those densities. It would seem much more likely that there is some radical change in structure at some point within the Earth's formation and that there is a central core of high-density material—probably a metal or metal mixture, since these are the high-density materials with which we are most familiar.

A more direct piece of evidence came from meteorites, which scientists reluctantly accepted as something more than old wives' tales in the first decades of the 1800s. Those meteorites that were recovered were sometimes rocky in structure, but quite often were lumps of metal which were 90 percent iron and 10 percent nickel (an element closely related to iron and one which also shows magnetic properties).

There were many who suggested that the meteorites might be the remains of an ancient planet which had somehow broken up in a cosmic catastrophe. The fragments of the planet still circled the Sun, according to the theory, but occasionally a few pieces would be deflected into the neighborhood of Earth's orbit and eventually collide with us. If so, it was tempting to think that the rocky meteorites were fragments of the outer layers of the hypothetical planet, while the nickel-iron meteorites were bits of its core.

Even if such a dramatic theory were disallowed, the fact that so many of the meteorites were so largely iron could be used to argue that iron was a very common substance in the universe generally, and perhaps the most common metal and therefore the most common high-density material. Certainly, iron was by far the most common high-density metal in the Earth's crust. Therefore, if the Earth's core were indeed high density, it had to be made of iron, possibly of nickel-iron by analogy to the meteorites.

In 1866, the French geologist Gabriel August Daubrée was the first to argue in this fashion, and in the century since, nothing has come up to refute the argument, and much to support it.

More detail came from the study of earthquakes, for instance. Each earthquake sets up vibrations of several varieties, which travel partly along the surface of the Earth, and partly through its inner structure. By noting the times at which vibrations of each sort reach different parts of Earth's surface, the route followed by each through the Earth's depths can be calculated. At various depths below the surface, the vibrations seem to change their direction of travel suddenly. This is taken to indicate a sharp passage from layers of one chemical composition to layers of quite another chemical composition.

One of these changes in direction comes at a depth of about 2900 kilometers. In 1906, the Irish geologist Thomas Oldham suggested that this might be the boundary of the nickel-iron core, and this has been accepted ever since. It would seem, then, that Earth has a nickel-iron core that is a sphere of about 6900 kilometers in diameter, with a density varying from 9 grams per cubic centimeter at its outer boundary to 11 grams per cubic centimeter at its center. This core makes up about one-sixth the volume of the Earth and, because of its high density, fully one-third of its mass.

Could it be that this nickel-iron core of the Earth is a magnet? If so, the fact that it is a sphere raises a puzzling point. There does not seem to be any reason why the magnetic poles on the spherical core (and therefore on the Earth as a whole) should be on one set of opposite points rather than another. If the nickel-iron core is an ordinary magnet, the actual fact that the magnetic poles of Earth seem to be in the polar regions may be nothing but coincidence.

Yet even as the existence of the iron core came to be accepted, the possibilities of its being a magnet in the ordinary sense dwindled rapidly.

In 1845, the English scientist Michael Faraday had shown that many substances were very weakly attracted by a magnetic force. This ability to display a weak attraction is called "paramagnetism." The strong attraction displayed by iron (and to a considerably lesser extent by its sister metals, nickel and cobalt) is referred to as "ferromagnetism," the prefix coming from the Latin word for iron.

The response to the magnetic force, whether paramagnetic or ferromagnetic, decreases with rising temperature, and in 1895 the French physicist Pierre Curie discovered that, at a certain temperature, a ferromagnetic substance experiences a sharp loss of that property and becomes only paramagnetic.

Each substance has its own characteristic "Curie point." The Curie point for nickel is 356 C., for iron, 760 C., and for cobalt, 1075 C. It works the other way, too. Some substances are paramagnetic because their Curie point is well below the ordinary temperature of the environment. The metal gadolinium is a borderline case. Its Curie point is at 16 C., the temperature of a pleasant spring day. Below that temperature, it is ferromagnetic.

With this in mind, we must ask not only the composition of the Earth's core, but also its temperature. It is clear that the core is very likely to be hot, for even the most casual observations of mine conditions show that temperature goes up steadily with depth. The existence of volcanoes and hot springs, moreover, points to a reservoir of considerable heat under Earth's surface.

But just *how* hot is the core?

There is no way as yet of measuring the interior temperatures of the Earth with conclusive precision, but reasoning based on deduction from available data would seem to make the core hot indeed. At its boundary, it can scarcely be less than 2700 C., and the temperature of the innermost part at Earth's center may reach 5000 C. There seems no question that the temperature of the core is far above the Curie point of any known ferromagnetic substance, so that there is no chance of its being a magnet in the ordinary sense of the word.

The best evidence for the heat of the core rests again upon

earthquake waves. Some varieties of these waves are deflected at the outer boundary of the core and some are stopped cold. Those waves that are stopped are precisely the kind that can travel through solid matter but not through liquid. It would seem, then, that the nickel-iron core of Earth is hot enough to be liquid.

Since the melting point of iron is 1535 C. under ordinary conditions and should be higher under the great pressures at the core boundary, that alone should remove any question as to whether the core is above the Curie point or not. It is. (In 1936, the Danish geologist Inge Lehmann deduced from certain properties of earthquake waves that at the very center of the liquid core there might be a solid "inner core" with a diameter of about 2500 kilometers. This inner core is solid, however, only by virtue of the great pressures on it. Its temperature is even higher than the liquid outside it and it cannot be an ordinary magnet.)

The presence of a liquid core, however, opens new possibilities. It is possible to produce magnetic effects by means of an electric current. In 1820, the Danish physicist Hans Christian Oersted discovered, quite by accident, that a copper wire carrying an electric current could attract a compass needle, while that same copper wire without an electric current passing through it could not. This represented the discovery of "electromagnetism."

If electricity passes through a wire helix (shaped more or less like a bedspring), the result is a magnetic effect very much like that which would originate from an ordinary bar magnet which we could imagine was placed along the axis of the helix.

With this in mind, the German-American geophysicist Walter Maurice Elsasser has suggested that the rotation of Earth may set up eddies in the liquid core: vast, slow swirls of molten iron. Atoms are made up of electrically charged subatomic particles, and, because of the particular structure of the iron atom, such swirls in the liquid core might produce the effect of an electric current moving round and round.

If so, such a swirl would act as though it were a bar magnet at right angles to the direction of movement of charge, and, what's more, such an electromagnetic duplication of the properties of a bar magnet does not fade with rising temperature. Since the Earth rotates west to east, the swirls of iron would be west to east, too, or possibly east to west, and in either case, the imaginary bar magnet would extend along a north-south line.

If this were so, then it is necessary that the magnetic poles be in the neighborhood of the geographic poles after all, and it is no coincidence that the magnetic poles are phenomena of the Arctic and Antarctic. (Of course, it doesn't explain why the geomagnetic poles are not closer to the geographic poles than they are.)

If Elsasser's suggestion is correct, then in order for a planet to behave as a magnet, two criteria must be met. There should be a liquid core of some substance which, like iron, can create magnetic effects if it is set to swirling; and second, there should be a reasonably rapid rotation that will serve to initiate the swirling.

Thus, the Moon has an overall density of 3.4 grams per cubic centimeter (as compared with the 5.5 figure for Earth) and is therefore not likely to have much of an iron core—or its overall density would be higher than it is. Even if it had an iron core, and if the Moon's inner temperature were high enough to keep it liquid, the Moon rotates only once in 655 hours, rather than once in 24 hours as the Earth does. This very slow lunar rotation is not likely to set up swirls. As a result, the Moon does not meet either criterion, and we might argue that the Moon would therefore show little or no magnetic effects, certainly nothing like those displayed by the Earth.

Mars rotates once in 24.6 hours, nearly as rapidly as the Earth does, but its density is 4.0 grams per cubic centimeter so that it is not likely to have very much of a liquid iron core, if any. Since Mars meets the second criterion but not the first, it should show little or no magnetic effects.

Venus has nearly the size of the Earth and nearly the density, so we might argue that Venus does have a liquid iron core, though probably not one as large as Earth's. But Venus rotates only once in 5834 hours, and that surely is not fast enough to set up swirls. Venus meets the first criterion but not the second, and it should show little or no magnetic effects.

And, as it turns out, planetary probes show that, indeed, the Moon, Mars, and Venus all show very little in the way of magnetic effects, which is a point in favor of the Elsasser theory.

What about Mercury? It is as dense as Venus and Earth, and

possibly even a bit denser, so it should have an iron core, perhaps one larger in proportion to the planet than Earth's iron core is. On the other hand, Mercury rotates only once in 1368 hours, four times as fast as Venus, but surely not fast enough to set up swirls. It was therefore pretty confidently thought that Mercury would not show any magnetic effects.

In early 1974, however, the Mariner 10 probe passed by Mercury and detected magnetic effects about a thousandth as strong as those associated with Earth. This is a weak effect, indeed, and yet it is more than was looked for and presents a puzzle. Mercury is, of course, a small world with less than half Earth's diameter. Perhaps its small size keeps its internal temperature low enough to keep the iron core solid and below the Curie point. Mercury might then be a permanent magnet and not an electromagnet. As a permanent magnet, Mercury's core would not depend upon swirls and would not be dependent on the speed of rotation.

Another puzzle of the sort is to be found among the planets beyond Mars. Jupiter was found in 1955 by the American astronomer Kenneth Franklin to emit radio waves, and the best explanation for this was to suppose Jupiter displayed magnetic effects. The space probe Pioneer 10, which passed near Jupiter in December 1973, corroborated this and showed that Jupiter did indeed behave as a magnet, and one that was 250,000 times as strong as the Earth. Jupiter's magnetic axis, like that of Earth, is tipped with respect to the planet's geographic axis. The tipping in Jupiter's case is about 15 percent.

It is not surprising that Jupiter displays magnetic effects so much stronger than those of Earth, since it not only turns more rapidly than Earth does, but is also larger and more massive so that its core temperatures are higher than Earth's. There must be far more material to swirl in Jupiter's interior than in Earth's, and the swirling must be far more energetic. (The other outer planets, Saturn, Uranus, and Neptune, which are also large and rapidly rotating—though not as large and as rapidly rotating as Jupiter is—ought therefore also to have large magnetic fields.)

The mystery is, however, what it may be that swirls in the outer planets. Jupiter's average density is only a quarter that of Earth, so it must be far richer in the light elements such as hydrogen and helium. It cannot possibly have as much iron proportionately as Earth does. Does it nevertheless have enough iron at the core to set up the magnetic effects? Or is Jupiter's core completely different in structure from Earth's and yet capable of giving rise to magnetic effects? There is no answer, as yet, to such questions.

12

THE MAGNETIC FIELD

The association of the magnetic poles with the Arctic and Antarctic may not seem to be of the same order as the other phenomena associated with them. Anyone who penetrates the polar regions cannot be oblivious to the behavior of the Sun and of the odd nature of day and night; nor can he ignore the cold and the ice.

The magnetic poles, however, would seem to be detectable only to the compass needle. Surely a traveler could walk right over either magnetic pole or either geomagnetic pole and be quite unaware of the fact.

And yet might there be some visible effect, characteristic of the polar regions, that is related to the magnetic poles rather than to the geographic ones?

Yes, indeed! There is!

The Aurorae

In the polar regions, there is commonly seen (almost every night, in fact) a beautiful atmospheric phenomenon marked by soft, shifting, colored lights—green, yellow, orange, and red, sometimes violet, rarely blue. They appear in arcs or bands, and sometimes resemble giant drapery hanging in the sky.

Since these lights are closely associated with the polar areas and are seen only occasionally in the temperate zones—the farther south, the more rarely—the ancient Greeks and Romans had very little occasion to note or discuss them.

In medieval times, the centers of scholarship moved farther north and the lights were seen more often. They are occasionally visible in northern France as a dim glow on the northern horizon. About 1620, a French scholar, Pierre Gassendi, called this light the "northern dawn," since it looked very much like the first flush of dim light on the eastern horizon that marked the true dawn. Naturally, Gassendi used the Latin language for the name so he called it the "aurora borealis." The equivalent phenomenon in the Antarctic is the "aurora australis" ("southern dawn"), and the two can be lumped together as the "aurora polaris."

In the 1700s, attempts were made to judge the height of the aurora by observing it simultaneously from two widely separated points and noting the change in position with reference to the stars. As a result of those and later efforts, it became apparent that the aurora was located high in the atmosphere.

Measurements by the Norwegian physicist Fredrik Carl Störmer, beginning in 1911, showed that, at the very lowest, aurorae appear 75 kilometers above the surface of the Earth, while some faint streamers may reach up as high as 1000 kilometers above the surface. Of all visible atmospheric phenomena, the aurora is the highest.

Because of the frequency with which the aurorae are seen in the polar regions, it might be assumed there was a connection with the poles. It was not at the poles that aurorae were most frequently seen but in a doughnut-shaped band well away from the poles. At the center of the doughnut is *not* the geographic pole but the geomagnetic pole. This immediately connected the aurorae with Earth's magnetism and not with (for instance) the low temperature of the polar atmosphere, the reflecting effect of snow and ice, or anything else.

The aurorae are most frequently seen from 20 degrees to 26 degrees away from the geomagnetic poles. Since the north geomagnetic pole is located in northwestern Greenland, it means that the aurora borealis is better seen in the Western

Aurora Borealis

Hemisphere than in the Eastern. Whereas northern Canada is bathed in aurorae nearly every night, Europe sees them only rarely and then only when the zone is extended because of unusual activity. On those occasions, aurorae are visible far south in the Western Hemisphere and can be seen in much of the United States. I, myself, for instance, witnessed a gorgeous display in New York City, on September 18, 1941.

The auroral zone of the aurora australis spreads out over no populated areas, and only those who are for any reason in

Antarctica or in certain Antarctic waters are likely to see it.

When the auroral displays spread out over a wider area than ordinarily, there is simultaneous erratic behavior of the magnetic compass, which shifts from side to side by several degrees. The intensity of Earth's magnetism fluctuates by a few percent as well. Such "magnetic storms" are another indication of the connection between the aurorae and the Earth's magnetism.

For the cause of magnetic storms we must seek beyond Earth itself.

In 1826, a German amateur astronomer, Heinrich Samuel Schwabe, began a daily observation of the spots on the solar surface. By 1843, he was able to announce that the sunspots were cyclic; that is, that the number increases and decreases regularly with maxima coming at 11-year intervals. By 1873, it had become plain that periods of magnetic storms and high auroral activity seemed to be much more common at times of sunspot maxima than at times of sunspot minima. For the first time, the Sun was found to have an effect on Earth that involved something other than its radiation of light and warmth.

A closer tie between the Sun and Earth's magnetism came through another line of investigation that began with an observation by an English astronomer, Richard Christopher Carrington. He was keeping painstaking track of sunspots over prolonged periods of time, and in 1859 he noted a short-lived, brilliant flare-up on the face of the Sun. It was as though a tiny star had made itself visible on that face for some five minutes. Carrington thought that this had been caused by the collision of a meteorite with the Sun and that the substance of the meteorite had vaporized and flared. He turned out to be wrong in this explanation but the phenomenon is now called a "solar flare."

In 1889, the American astronomer George Ellery Hale invented the "spectroheliograph," a device whereby the Sun could be photographed by the particular wavelengths of light connected with a single chemical element. He could photograph the Sun by the light put out by the hydrogen in its glowing surface and atmosphere, or by the calcium.

In 1926, Hale modified the instrument in such a way that the Sun could be photographed over a period of time in hydrogen light, for instance, so that any changes in its structure could be watched second by second. Through this "spectrohelioscope" it could be seen that there were occasional flashes of hydrogen, usually near active sunspot groups. The flashes would flare up to maximum brightness for five to ten minutes, then be utterly gone after half an hour to an hour. It was one of these hydrogen explosions and a particularly large one, too, that Carrington must have seen.

When a solar flare is well within the face of the Sun, there's not much to be seen by spectrohelioscope except a brightening and spreading patch of light (and usually hardly anything at all by ordinary telescope). Occasionally, though, one catches a flare coming into being near the edge of the Sun. Then one can see, in profile, a huge surge of brilliant gas climbing at a rate of 1000 kilometers or so per second, and reaching a height of some 8000 kilometers above the Sun's surface.

Small flares are quite common, and, in places where there happen to be large complexes of sunspots, as many as a hundred a day can be detected, especially when the spots are growing. Very large flares of the kind that can be seen even without a spectrohelioscope (as Carrington did) are rare, however; only a few occur each year.

On occasion, a large flare occurs in the very center of the solar disk (as seen from Earth), and when that happens a vast quantity of matter rises from the Sun in a direction aimed right at us. And when that happens, there invariably occurs, within a day or so, a magnetic storm and brilliant and widespread auroral displays. Thus, the great aurorae of September 18, 1941, so clearly visible in New York City, followed the crossing of the center of the Sun by a large group of sunspots, and undoubtedly a large flare had burst out at the crucial moment.

Since flares are commonly associated with sunspots, it is not surprising there should be more flares altogether at times of sunspot maxima than at times of sunspot minima. More flares would then, by chance, happen to be aimed in our direction at sunspot maxima, and that would, in turn, explain why the frequency of occurrence of magnetic storms rises and falls with the sunspot cycle.

Ions

How, then, do we explain the aurorae? What are they? Why are they connected with Earth's geomagnetic poles? What is their connection with the Sun? What reaches across space from the solar flares to ourselves?

The beginnings of a solution came through studies of the Earth's atmosphere in the light of new findings as to the nature of matter.

In the 1880s and 1890s it became clear that atoms were not indivisible, featureless objects, but were made up of more fundamental particles, far smaller still, some of which were electrically charged. The outer regions of the atom contain electrons, which carry a negative electric charge, while the inner core (or "atomic nucleus") contains a number of particles, including protons, which carry a positive electric charge.

An ordinary atom has the negative and positive charges balanced so that the atom as a whole is electrically uncharged. It is possible, however, to knock one or two electrons (or in extreme conditions, even more) out of an atom, or group of atoms. In that case, the positive charge on the atomic nucleus is not entirely neutralized by the electrons that are left and the atom, or group of atoms, carries, as a whole, a positive electric charge.

In reverse, additional electrons can be added to an atom or group of atoms, and in that case the atom or group of atoms has an overall negative charge.

Such charged atoms, or groups of atoms, whether positively charged or negatively charged, are called "ions."

In the 1860s, the Scottish physicist James Clerk Maxwell had worked out a theory (which has since been firmly established and universally accepted by scientists) that demonstrated the close connection between electricity and magnetism, a connection so close as to be indissoluble. One invariably implies the other.

There is nothing strange, then, in the suggestion that the presence of electrically charged ions in Earth's atmosphere might influence its magnetism, and that the aurorae might have a connection with both.

But are there indeed ions in the atmosphere? Some evidence toward that had already come in 1901, when the Italian inventor Guglielmo Marconi sent the first radio signal across the Atlantic Ocean from England to Newfoundland.

The puzzle there is that radio waves travel in straight lines, and to get from England to Newfoundland the radio waves had traveled around the bulge of the Earth. Between England and

Newfoundland, the terrestrial bulge reaches to about 320 kilometers above the true straight line. If we imagine ourselves trying to send a beam of straight-line radiation over it, we can see that the only way of doing it is to bounce that radiation off some reflecting layer in the upper atmosphere.

But what could possibly make up such a reflecting layer?

As long before as 1882, a Scottish physicist, Balfour Stewart, had suggested there might be electric currents in the upper atmosphere, moving around the Earth. He suggested this in order to explain the daily variations in Earth's magnetism, since the electric current would produce magnetic effects that would be added in different ways to the basic magnetism of the Earth.

In 1882, of course, there was no way of explaining why such an electric current could exist, but if it did exist it could serve to reflect radio waves.

Once the nature of ions was understood, it was a different matter. In 1902, two British electrical engineers, Oliver Heaviside and Arthur Edwin Kennelly, independently suggested the presence of comparatively high concentrations of ions in the upper atmosphere. Their charges and movements would be equivalent to Stewart's suggested electric current and they would act to reflect radio waves and make it possible for Marconi to send beams across the Atlantic.

Those atmospheric regions rich in ions proved to exist and came to be referred to as the "Kennelly-Heaviside layer" in consequence.

In 1924, the English physicist Edward Victor Appleton attempted to measure the height of this layer by sending a radio beam upward and allowing it to be reflected to a receiver on the ground a short distance away. From the lapse in time, and knowing that the beam traveled at the speed of light (but allowing for the slowing effect of ions on the radio beam), Appleton demonstrated that the Kennelly-Heaviside layer was about 80 to 100 kilometers above Earth's surface.

Appleton then worked with shorter radio waves capable of penetrating the Kennelly-Heaviside layer and found that these were reflected by another layer far higher—at heights of from 200 to 400 kilometers. This was the "Appleton layer."

Actually, these layers are not sharp and there are a number of sub-layers. In effect, a whole section of the atmosphere from 100 kilometers above the surface to 1000 kilometers can be considered as rich in ions. At the suggestion of the Scottish physicist Robert Alexander Watson-Watt, the entire region was given the name of "ionosphere."

It seems reasonable to suppose that if anything disturbed the nature, motion, or concentrations of ions in the ionosphere that might be responsible for magnetic storms and might also affect any devices that depended on radio-wave transmission. (And, indeed, after radio and allied devices were invented, it became clear that during magnetic storms they behaved erratically.)

There are, indeed, influences upon the ionosphere. The Sun affects it, for instance. It was quickly discovered that the lower level of the ionosphere lifts at night and that the number of ions and electrons in it falls. In short, the ionosphere intensifies during the day and weakens at night.

There is no mystery here. The Sun's radiation includes very energetic ultraviolet light that does not reach Earth's surface (fortunately for ourselves since it would be harmful to living tissue) precisely because it interacts with the upper atmosphere. The ultraviolet light is absorbed by atoms and molecules there, and these become energetic enough in consequence to eject electrons and become ions.

At night, the ions tend to reunite with the electrons and, in some cases, with each other, and release the energy they had absorbed during the day. This released energy is the "night glow" and lends a very faint luminosity to the night sky, far too faint to be observed without special instruments.

Might it be that the aurora is a very bright night glow produced by unusual activity in the Sun?

Yes, but surely not the kind of activity that is responsible for the ordinary day-night variation in the properties of the ionosphere. The variation produced by the energetic ultraviolet radiation of the Sun cannot possibly have anything to do with the aurorae.

Ultraviolet radiation, like other forms of light, streaks across space in the form of a particle-like wave packet called a "photon." Photons travel at the speed of light (300,000 kilometers per second) and are not affected by magnetic fields so that they approach Earth in straight lines. They bombard those portions of the atmosphere facing the Sun and do not pay special attention to the polar regions where the aurorae are to be observed. Indeed, since it is the tropic regions that face the Sun most directly, and the polar regions the least, the regions of the aurorae receive least energy in the way of photons and should be least affected by solar ultraviolet radiation.

Whatever it is that produces the aurorae must be connected with something that is produced in solar flares and shoots upward from the Sun in our direction. Those flares do not brighten the Sun perceptibly, and the rain of photons upon the Earth is not increased; yet the aurorae brighten enormously. Furthermore, while photons, traveling at the speed of light, take only 8 minutes to reach the Earth, whatever emerges from the Sun takes 20 to 30 hours to reach the Earth and travels at only about 1000 kilometers per second, 1/300 the speed of light.

Something *other* than photons, something other than visible light and related radiations, must be bombarding the Earth.

Cosmic Rays

The first hint that something other than light and related radiations might be bombarding the Earth came in 1911. At that time, the Austrian physicist Victor Franz Hess was studying faint traces of radiation so energetic that it could not be shielded by lead sheathing capable of blocking off very energetic forms of photons such as those making up X rays or even the gamma rays produced by radioactive materials.

Hess thought the radiation was coming from the Earth, and he sent detecting devices high in the atmosphere by balloon, expecting the intensity of the radiation to fall off. He demonstrated precisely the reverse. The radiation became more intense the higher the balloon lifted, so that the radiation must originate from somewhere in outer space.

In 1925, the American physicist Robert Andrews Millikan named this radiation "cosmic rays." He believed it to be a lightlike radiation, consisting of very energetic photons, making a new member of the series which, in order of increasing energy, would be radio waves, microwaves, infrared waves, visible light, ultraviolet rays, X rays, gamma rays, and finally (in Millikan's view) cosmic rays.

Others, notably the American physicist Arthur Holly Compton, felt that the cosmic rays might be streams of very energetic electrically charged particles. Scientists had been studying streams of electrically charged particles since "cathode rays" had begun to be intensively observed in 1876.

Cathode rays, produced when an electric current was forced

through a vacuum, proved, however, to be streams of electrons. These are very light particles, and it was difficult to suppose that they could display the vast energies of cosmic rays. If cosmic rays were streams of electrically charged particles, those particles would have to be more massive than electrons.

Somehow it was necessary to distinguish between very energetic photons and very energetic charged particles, and the method of doing so involved Earth's magnetism.

When Peter Peregrinus was first experimenting with magnets, he sprinkled iron filings on a piece of paper held over a magnet. When the paper was tapped, the filings moved slightly and adjusted their positions in such a way that they seemed to line up in a series of curves leading from one magnetic pole to the other.

In the 1820s, Michael Faraday repeated the experiment and said there were "lines of force" leading from one magnetic pole to another. These are imaginary curved lines (actually curved surfaces when considered in three-dimensional space) along which a magnetized particle can move freely without losing or gaining energy. To cross lines of force *does* involve an energy change.

The lines of force fill all of space, though they are strong enough to be detected only in the neighborhood of the magnetic source. The volume over which the lines of force make themselves evident is a "magnetic field." (You can speak similarly of other attracting forces and have an "electric field" and a "gravitational field.")

When a metallic wire is forced across magnetic lines of force, the energy required to do so shows up as an electric current in the wire. In the 1830s, Faraday made use of this phenomenon to convert mechanical energy into electricity. Once the mechanical energy was produced by steam, the energy of burning coal could be turned into electricity and the modern electrical age was born.

This connection between magnetism and electricity was formalized by Maxwell, who showed that every electric field was associated with a magnetic field at right angles to itself, and vice versa. Properly one should speak neither of an electric field nor of a magnetic field, but of an "electromagnetic field."

It follows that an electrically charged particle is affected by a magnetic field. A magnetized particle would move directly along the magnetic lines of force. An electrically charged particle, controlled by the electric field at right angles to the magnetic, spirals about the magnetic lines of force, and travels in this spiral from one magnetic pole to the other. (This was made clear, eventually, in 1957, by a Greek engineer named Nicholas Christofilos.)

The Earth, being a magnet, has a magnetic field. Its magnetic lines of force reach far out into space, looping from one geomagnetic pole to the other. As the lines approach the Earth's actual surface, the uneven distribution of magnetic material in the Earth's crust diverts the lines of force and brings them down to the actually observed magnetic poles. This deviation from the ideal is a matter of the last few kilometers only. As measured from any point beyond those few kilometers, it is clear that the lines of force would, if allowed to curve smoothly, end at the geomagnetic poles, which may thus be viewed as the true magnetic poles.

Any effect, then, related to Earth's magnetic lines of force beyond the immediate neighborhood of the surface would center about the geomagnetic poles, not the magnetic poles. This would certainly make it appear that the aurorae had something to do with the Earth's magnetic lines of force.

Given the Earth's magnetic field, it might seem that we can now decide whether the cosmic rays were photons or charged particles. Photons, being neither electrically charged nor magnetized, would be totally unaffected by the Earth's magnetic lines of force, would pass through them as though they weren't there, and would hit all parts of the Earth's surface. Charged particles, on the other hand, would be trapped in the magnetic field and would go spiraling back and forth along the lines of force and would reach the Earth's surface only in the polar regions.

Since cosmic rays could be detected everywhere on Earth, that seemed to be a score in favor of photons.

The trapping of an electrically charged particle by a magnetic field depends, however, on how much energy the particle has and on how strong the magnetic field is. The less energetic the particle and the stronger the field, the more likely it would be that the particle would be trapped by the field and would go spirally along the lines of force.

If the particle were very energetic, or if the field were weak, or both, the particle would be able to force its way across the lines of force without being trapped. In doing so, however, it would be deflected northward or southward toward the geomagnetic poles. The more energetic the particle, the smaller the deflection, but that deflection would never be zero. It *would* be zero for photons, however.

In the 1930s, Compton traveled over the Earth, testing the intensity of cosmic rays here and there to see if the intensity increased as one approached either geomagnetic pole; if, in other words, cosmic ray bombardment were heavier in high latitudes north and south than in low equatorial latitudes. He was able to show definitely that this "latitude effect" did, in fact, exist, and that the cosmic rays were composed of very energetic electrically charged particles.

By 1935, furthermore, it was possible to show, from the nature of another kind of deflection, that the charged particles that make up the cosmic rays are positively charged and not negatively charged.

Since then, it has been established quite definitely that the cosmic rays are streams of positively charged atomic nuclei, some of which are far more energetic than any streams of charged particles mankind has yet produced in the laboratory. Since most of the atoms in the universe (as many as 90 percent of them) are hydrogen, it is not surprising that the overwhelming majority of the cosmic ray particles are hydrogen nuclei.

(The most common positively charged particles known to scientists are the protons, and these occur in all atomic nuclei. A proton is 1836 times as massive as an electron, and, if the two are moving at equal velocities, the proton is correspondingly more energetic. Atomic nuclei may contain many protons, and many neutrons, too, where the neutron is a particle as massive as a proton, but without an electric charge.)

The hydrogen atom is the simplest of all atoms and has a nucleus containing the fewest particles. The nucleus of the hydrogen atom can consist of either a proton and nothing more, a proton plus a neutron, or a proton plus two neutrons. More than 99.9 percent of hydrogen atoms are "hydrogen-1," which contains as its nucleus a proton only. It follows then that cosmic rays are essentially streams of protons, with more massive nuclei present as minor constituents.

We must ask, then, whether it is cosmic ray particles, deflected toward the geomagnetic poles by Earth's magnetic field, that give rise to the aurorae and to magnetic storms.

For this to be so, there ought to be some connection between cosmic rays and the Sun, since there is no question but that magnetic storms are the result of solar activity. And, as a matter of fact, the Sun *is* a source of cosmic rays, although the vast majority come from space beyond the Sun. A rise in cosmic ray intensity was measured after a large solar flare was detected on February 28, 1942.

We might imagine that cosmic rays from outside the solar system produce the aurorae from night to night, while an occasional burst of cosmic rays from the Sun produces strengthened aurorae and magnetic storms. But no, this is not so!

The cosmic rays are simply too energetic. Even solar cosmic rays (which are about as unenergetic as cosmic rays can be) are too energetic to be the source of the aurorae. The trouble is that they are not sufficiently deflected by the Earth's magnetic lines of force. More cosmic rays end up in the polar regions than elsewhere but only by a relatively small amount. All parts of the Earth's surface get some share of the cosmic ray bombardment and if the cosmic rays caused the aurorae, aurorae would be visible everywhere on Earth.

We must look elsewhere.

The Solar Wind

If cosmic rays are made up chiefly of very energetic protons, might there not be streams of less energetic protons in space, too? Being less energetic they would be more easily produced by milder phenomena and they would exist in much greater quantity than cosmic ray particles would. They might also be so unenergetic as to be completely trapped by the lines of force of Earth's magnetic field; they would all be decanted into the polar regions where alone the aurorae are to be seen night after night.

An extremely energetic solar flare might produce a stream of protons so energetic as to count as cosmic rays, but milder solar flares might produce milder protons.

And why not? The Sun is, after all, mostly hydrogen; at least 85 percent of its atoms are hydrogen-1. It is, moreover, surrounded by a "corona," a very thin atmosphere extending outward from the Sun in all directions in sufficient density to be detectable for millions of kilometers.

Apparently, energetic processes on the Sun's surface spray

atoms outward in all directions to form this corona, and most of these atoms must be hydrogen which, under the energetic conditions of the corona, break up into protons and electrons. The protons must continue to expand outward, with the corona growing less and less dense with distance from the Sun. Eventually, the corona becomes so rarified it cannot be detected by the usual astronomical methods, yet it may remain denser than the matter in interstellar space for hundreds of millions of kilometers.

By this view, the inner planets, certainly including Earth, would be revolving within the Sun's corona. Moreover, the corona would not consist of a mere static assemblage of atoms and charged atom fragments, but would be a dynamic system of moving particles, traveling constantly outward from the Sun in all directions, past the planets, till they lose themselves in the depths of interstellar space.

In 1958, the American physicist Eugene Norman Parker was able to show from his studies of the corona that all this was indeed so. From the Sun, emerging in all directions, was a constant stream of speeding protons, moving outward at speeds of from 350 to 700 kilometers per second. Particularly energetic protons, originating from the violent activity of a solar flare, could reach speeds of 1000 kilometers per second. (And very occasionally, a batch of protons could reach speeds much higher still and attain the cosmic ray level of energy.) Parker called this steady outward flow of protons the "solar wind."

Though the ordinary protons of the solar wind are not energetic enough to be cosmic rays, they are energetic enough to produce noticeable phenomena. It had been thought for half a century that comets' tails (which always face away from the Sun) were driven outward by the "radiation pressure" of the photons of the Sun's light. As more came to be known about the structure of comets, it came to be increasingly certain that radiation pressure wasn't strong enough to accomplish the feat. The particles of the solar wind *were* strong enough, however.

What's more, since the particles of the solar wind are much less energetic than the cosmic rays, many of them cannot force their way through the Earth's magnetic field but are trapped by the lines of force.

Dramatic evidence in favor of this came soon after the solar wind was first recognized.

The very first American satellite to be launched, Explorer I, carried devices intended to measure the number and intensity of charged particles immediately beyond the atmosphere. It was launched on January 31, 1958, and its orbit carried it as far as 2525 kilometers above Earth's surface.

The data it sent back concerning the particle concentration over the first few hundred miles above the surface were about what scientists had expected. But then, the data it sent back from still higher levels dropped off, to everyone's surprise, to zero.

Instruments on later satellites, including the American Explorer III launched on March 26, 1958, and the Soviet Sputnik III launched on May 15, 1958, yielded the same results.

The American physicist James Alfred Van Allen, who was in charge of this part of the American space program, came up with a possible explanation. The count fell virtually to zero, he decided, not because there was little or no radiation, but because there was too much. The instrument could not keep up with the particles entering it, and it blanked out in consequence. (This would be analogous to the blinding of our eyes by a flash of too-bright light.)

When Explorer IV went up on July 26, 1958, it carried special counters designed to handle heavy loads. One of them, for instance, was shielded with a thin layer of lead (analogous to dark sunglasses intended to protect eyes from too-bright light) that would keep out most of the radiation.

This time the counters did tell another story. They showed that the too-much-radiation theory was correct. Explorer IV, reaching a height of 2200 kilometers at the far end of its orbit, sent down counts which, allowing for the shielding, disclosed that the number of charged particles up there was far higher than scientists had imagined.

There were indeed vast concentrations of protons and other charged particles moving along the lines of force of Earth's magnetic field. The Earth, well outside its atmosphere, was surrounded by a region of concentrated charge, which was first referred to as the "Van Allen belts," but later came to be called the "magnetosphere."

The particles in the magnetosphere, spiraling back and forth along the lines of force, were farthest from the Earth's surface in the region of the magnetic equator, and closest to the Earth's surface at those points where they spiraled in toward the geomagnetic poles. It was in the neighborhood of the geomagnetic poles that the charged particles of the magnetosphere interacted with the molecules of Earth's upper atmosphere and produced the aurorae.

What's more, the solar flares pumped an unusually high concentration of protons into that section of the solar wind emerging from that part of the Sun. This meant a local intensification of the solar wind, sometimes a large one. If the flare were pointed in our direction, the temporarily intensified solar wind would pump an unusually high quantity of charged particles into the magnetosphere. That unusual quantity would reach the atmosphere above the magnetic poles, producing vividly intensified aurorae and so affecting the Earth's ionosphere as to produce magnetic storms.

Not all the particles of the solar wind that reach the neighborhood of the Earth's magnetic field are trapped along the lines of force. Some are diverted to such a degree that they slide around the Earth altogether.

The Earth's magnetic field is distorted under the pressure of the solar wind, compressed on itself in the direction of the Sun, until there is a relatively sharp line between open space, where there isn't much in the way of magnetic effects, and the interior of the magnetosphere, in which magnetic effects are pronounced.

This line of demarcation, which is particularly sharp on the side toward the Sun, and pushed relatively close to the Earth's surface, bellies outward to either side, following the lines of the diverted particles of the solar wind, and extends outward in a long "tail" on the nightside of Earth. The magnetosphere is rather tear-shaped, in other words.

The push of the solar wind, which distorts the shape of the magnetosphere, also distorts the auroral zone at times of flare-induced high intensity. The auroral zone is forced farther into whichever hemisphere is experiencing night at the time, so that the auroral displays (only visible at night, of course) are seen farther south than they would otherwise be.

The outer boundary of the magnetosphere is the "magnetopause," and in the direction of the Sun it is from 650 to 950 kilometers above the Earth's surface, or a distance equal to from 0.1 to 0.15 times the Earth's radius.

Jupiter's magnetic field is more complicated in shape than Earth's according to the findings of Pioneer 10 in December 1973. As is not surprising, in view of the large size of Jupiter's magnetic field, its magnetopause was detected over 6,500,000 kilometers from its surface, a distance rather better than a hundred times Jupiter's radius.

Evolution

It might seem that these discoveries concerning the Earth's magnetic field, the solar wind, and the magnetosphere don't really have much to do with mankind. After all, the aurorae are beautiful but are just something to look at, it might seem, and if they were to disappear altogether, we might be sad, but we would go on living. It might also seem that magnetic storms might be inconvenient while they last, but that they are only temporary, and if we are not involved in radio-wave communication or in navigation by magnetic compass, we would not even know such a storm were taking place, or care if we did know.

Yet this is not so! Earth's magnetic field, the existence of magnetic poles, the fact that the magnetic poles are located near the geographic poles would all seem to be of extreme importance to life generally.

To see why this should be, let us consider living tissue, which is made up of large and complex molecules to a certain extent. The two chief classes of these are the proteins and the nucleic acids. The protein molecules include the enzymes, which control all the chemical reactions in the body. The nucleic acids include those molecules in the genes which control the manufacture of specific enzymes.

These large and complex molecules, essential to life, tend to be rickety and are easily altered or even broken down by the impingement upon them of energetic particles.

The energetic protons sprayed out by the Sun in the solar wind, and some of the more energetic photons of the Sun's radiation, can damage or destroy these large molecules and are, for that reason, dangerous to life. Or, at least, they would be dangerous to life if they could reach living things.

In order to reach the world of life, the energetic photons and protons from the Sun must penetrate Earth's magnetic field and its atmosphere. The photons pass through the magnetic field as though it weren't there, but the more energetic photons interact with the atmosphere. What reaches the surface is visible light, which is composed of photons without the kind of energy level that would enable them to interact with the molecules of the atmosphere. The atmosphere is therefore transparent to visible light—which is why life has adapted itself to make use of it in vision, and why such light is visible.

Fortunately, the photons of visible light are sufficiently low in energy to present no danger to our complex molecules, though they are energetic enough to affect the retina of our eyes and the chemicals on a photographic plate.

As for the charged particles from the Sun, they are shunted aside by the magnetic field. Some move around the magnetosphere and miss the Earth altogether; some enter the magnetosphere and are then trapped by the lines of force and are decanted into the upper atmosphere in the polar regions. There, most of their energy is expended in those upper regions and little, if any, reaches the Earth's surface to damage life. The aurorae are the visible indication of the protective role of our atmosphere.

And even if the protons did reach the surface in the auroral zones, they would do so in precisely that portion of the Earth where land life is least rich. (Sea life is rich in the polar regions, but water is a more effective filter of energetic particles than air is, so sea life is not as likely to be affected.)

The chief source of energetic particles capable of affecting life on Earth's surface generally is the cosmic ray particles. These are energetic enough to force their way through both the magnetosphere and the atmosphere and, in one way or another, to reach the surface of the Earth.

Occasionally, a cosmic ray particle, in passing through a living organism, may strike a nucleic acid molecule directly, or create high energy molecules which react with nucleic acid molecules, thus changing them indirectly.

In either case, the nucleic acids are changed, and since each one controls the formation of a particular enzyme which, in turn, controls a particular chemical reaction, the chemical nature of the cell in which the nucleic acid is contained is changed. If the cell happens to be an egg cell or a sperm cell that goes toward the formation of an offspring, that offspring will have the chemistry of all its cells somewhat different from that of its parents.

Such a sudden difference in cell chemistry from one generation to the next is a "mutation." The constant appearance of mutations means that organisms of somewhat different types can compete for survival. Most mutations produce changes for the worse, but occasionally one happens, by chance, to produce a change that is useful under certain conditions, and the changed organism flourishes and produces many offspring which flourish in their turn.

It is mutation building on mutation in a random way—and then the useful ones being culled out by natural selection—that represents the driving force behind evolution.

Cosmic rays are not the only causes of mutation. The radiation given off by radioactive substances in the Earth's crust can produce mutations. Energetic photons, certain chemicals, and even the random motions of atoms and molecules within the body can cause mutations, too. There is no question, though, that cosmic rays are an important cause and, in the long run, may be the steadiest and most important driving force behind evolution.

If, in other words, there were no cosmic rays, evolution would, at best, proceed more slowly, and the chances are that something with as highly specialized a brain and nervous system as man would not now exist on Earth.

If, on the other hand, cosmic rays struck the Earth with considerably greater intensity than they do now, the incidence of mutations would go up. Since most mutations are for the worse, the "genetic load" of unfavorable mutations might increase to the point where some species would not produce sufficient numbers of unmutated or favorably mutated forms to survive.

There have been times in Earth's history when large numbers of species seem to have become extinct in a relatively short time for no reason we know. About 75,000,000 years ago, for instance, all the dinosaurs died out, though various species of them had thrived for 150,000,000 years before that. There is some speculation that a sudden rise in cosmic ray intensity was responsible.

But how would such a rise come about?

The one object we know for certain as a cosmic ray source is our Sun. When a particularly large flare explodes on the Sun, the protons it produces are energetic enough to qualify as rather weak cosmic ray particles.

A star more energetic than the Sun, larger and hotter, would produce more energetic cosmic ray particles and do so oftener. In particular, this may happen if a whole star explodes into one huge flare, so to speak, and produces a temporary surge of energy enormously greater than is produced in the day-to-day operations of a stable star. An exploding star would produce, in the course of its explosion, a surge of cosmic ray particles, the extent of which would depend on the force of the explosion.

The most energetic star-explosions known are produced by "supernovae," and it is thought that these supernovae, exploding in a way that virtually destroys almost their entire structure, produce most of the cosmic ray particles in existence. Every time a star explodes in supernova fashion and releases energy at as much as a hundred billion times its former rate, a vast surge of cosmic ray particles is hurled outward in every direction.

If, indeed, life evolves primarily because of mutations induced by cosmic ray particles we might say that the development of life depends on the death of stars.

If cosmic ray particles traveled in straight lines, they would reach us mostly from those directions in space in which a supernova had exploded. They do not travel in straight lines, however, because they are electrically charged. They curve in their travel paths in response to the magnetic fields of any stars they may pass and also in response to magnetic fields that belong to galaxies of stars generally. Eventually, the particles diverge in their paths and separate as each is affected slightly differently. Finally, they end up all traveling in different directions, and it is for this reason that Earth finds cosmic ray particles hitting it, more or less evenly, from every direction.

Supernovae are not a very common phenomenon, but it is estimated that there are three every thousand years in every galaxy (on the average). If that is so, there may have been 30,000,000 supernovae in our own galaxy so far in its history.

The cosmic ray particles they supply are produced fairly evenly over time and space, and it is very unlikely that the quantity reaching Earth in a given period of time would ever fall below a certain level, at least over those billions of years that the galaxies will maintain their present level of structure.

On the other hand, there may be temporary upsurges in the unlucky chance that a supernova exploded in the Sun's neighborhood of the galaxy. For a period of time, the cosmic ray intensity in our solar system would rise above the normal level, and this could be a period of high mutation rates and the extinction of many species too specialized to bear an increased genetic load.

Magnetic Field Reversals

Yet we must not underestimate the protective effect of the Earth's magnetic field and atmosphere. The magnetosphere shunts some of the weaker cosmic ray particles to one side. Many of the less weak are deflected to the higher latitudes where they have less capacity to do harm. The molecules of the atmosphere interact with cosmic ray particles, too, so that few of the original "primary radiation" particles actually reach the surface. Instead, "secondary radiation" produced from the atoms into which the primary radiation has smashed reaches the Earth.

Even if cosmic ray production increased in the neighborhood of the solar system, these protective influences would still be in play.

Is there any chance, though, that Earth's magnetic field might fail for some reason so that part, at least, of Earth's protection may disappear?

Certainly, the magnetic field hasn't failed at any time since the magnetic compass came into use—but that is only a matter of 700 years or so, and in speaking of life we must consider stretches of millions and, indeed, billions of years. Is there any way we can check the behavior of Earth's magnetic field for times long before the magnetic compass was used and, for that matter, long before mankind existed on this planet?

Oddly enough, there is. Volcanoes spew out molten rock (lava) which contains among its components various weakly magnetic minerals. The molecules of these minerals have a certain tendency to orient themselves along the magnetic lines of force.

While they are in liquid form, this tendency is overcome by the random motion of the molecules in response to the high temperature. As the volcanic rock cools down slowly, however, the random motion of the molecules slows down, too, and eventually they orient themselves with the magnetic lines of force of the Earth and lock into place. Molecule after molecule does so and, finally, whole crystals exist in which we can detect magnetic poles, the north pole pointing northward and the south pole pointing southward, just as is true of a magnetic compass.

These crystallized minerals are, in fact, compasses of the past that have been fixed in place. They mark out the nature of the magnetic field at the time of their solidification (and that time can be determined by measuring how much radioactive breakdown has taken place in the rock generally since solidification). If the magnetic field has changed its nature after the rock was solidified, that would not affect the orientation of the crystals. The Earth's magnetic field is strong enough to line up molecules in a cooling liquid, but not to change that alignment against the much stronger forces holding the molecules in a solid crystal.

In 1906, a French physicist, Bernard Brunhes, came across samples of volcanic rock-crystals that were magnetized in the direction opposite from normal. Their north magnetic poles pointed south and their south magnetic poles pointed north. Brunhes suggested that, at the time those crystals formed, the direction of the Earth's magnetic field was opposite to that of today.

How can that be? We know that the north magnetic pole and the south magnetic pole are drifting. Can it be that they drift all around the Earth's surface until finally the north magnetic pole has drifted into the Antarctic and the south magnetic pole into the Arctic? And do they continue to drift in this manner so that the Earth's field is oriented first one way and then the other, then the first and then the other, over and over?

This does not seem reasonable. If the magnetic poles drifted around the world, there would be times when the magnetic axis was east-west, or northeast-southwest, northwest-southeast, and all directions between. There should be crystals oriented in all possible ways.

In the years since Brunhes' original discovery, however, large numbers of volcanic rocks have been studied, and the alignment is always either north-south or south-north. Nothing else. There is no inbetween.

Is it possible that some particular minerals simply align themselves in a direction opposite to that of Earth's magnetic field owing to some peculiarity in their structure? Yes, this can happen, in some cases, but minerals that do so form only a tiny minority of the total, whereas the reverse orientation is found in all kinds of minerals.

Can it be that the reverse orientation is produced by purely local conditions and has nothing to do with the general magnetic field of Earth? This apparently is not so. If the minerals are dated, it turns out that minerals from a certain period in Earth's history are all north-south ("normal") or are all south-north ("reversed").

No, it seems that Earth's magnetic field reverses itself periodically in a rather sudden shift.

For the last 700,000 years, the magnetic field has been in its present "normal" orientation. (This is no more normal than the other, but it is the one we are used to.) For about 1,800,000 years before that it was "reversed" almost constantly, although there were two 100,000-year periods within that time when it was "normal."

On the whole, over the last 76,000,000 years, no fewer than 171 reversals of the magnetic field have been identified. The average length of time between reversals is about 450,000 years, and the two possible alignments, normal and reversed, take up equal lengths of time in the long run.

The length of time between reversals varies widely from the average, however. The longest measured lapse of time between reversals is 3,000,000 years, the shortest 50,000. (Jupiter's magnetic field, by the way, is at present in the reversed position, compared to that of the Earth.)

How does one account for such reversals without moving the magnetic poles from the polar regions (allowing for some minor wandering)?

One way is to suppose that the magnetic field gradually weakens until it becomes zero. Then it begins to increase in strength again but in the opposite direction. It gets stronger and stronger, reaches a maximum and declines in strength to zero again, then begins to strengthen in the first direction.

Something like this seems to happen in the Sun. The number of sunspots increases and decreases in an 11-year cycle. In one cycle, however, the spots are associated with magnetic effects that are normally oriented and in the next with magnetic effects that are reversely oriented. It would seem that the Sun's magnetic field therefore reverses every 11 years.

But *why* do magnetic fields reverse?

The best current explanation for the existence of Earth's magnetic field lies in the possibility of swirls or eddy currents in the molten iron interior of the planet. These eddies move a little faster than the Earth rotates. We would have to suppose that the swirls decrease in speed until, finally, the core is, for a brief period, moving at just the speed of the Earth's rotation. Then it begins to lag behind more and more—and then begins to speed up again.

Relative to the Earth's surface, in other words, the eddies are moving west to east faster and faster, then slower and slower. They stop, then move east to west faster and faster, then slower and slower. They stop, then—

As to why the molten core might act that way and why the reversals come at such widely irregular intervals as compared with the quite regular reversals in the Sun, nobody knows.

Still, whatever the reasons for the reversals, the fact seems to be that the intensity of the Earth's magnetic field increases and decreases, and with it, its efficiency in deflecting cosmic rays.

From the standpoint of the cosmic ray particles, it doesn't matter in which direction the Earth's magnetic field is oriented. The cosmic ray particles are equally deflected in either case. It is the intensity of the field that matters. As the field grows more and more intense, the cosmic ray particles are deflected more and more. More and more of them land in the polar regions, where they are relatively less effective in producing mutations; fewer and fewer arrive in the tropic and temperate regions. The reverse is true as the field grows less and less intense.

It just may be, then, that these reversals of Earth's magnetic field affect the history of life on the planet. The rate of evolution may be faster or slower depending on whether the field is feeble or strong. The rate of species' extinctions may also be faster or slower.

At the moment of reversal, when the magnetic field is absent (or so feeble as to be virtually absent), there may be a period of some thousands of years when cosmic ray particles fall on Earth virtually unobstructed and those areas of the surface that are richest in life are exposed to higher intensities of radiation than they get at other times in Earth's history.

And what if, at just the time when a field reversal is taking place, radiation from a relatively nearby supernova reaches the solar system? There might then be a combination of an unusually high concentration of cosmic ray particles and an unusually low ability of the Earth's magnetic field to ward them off.

There's no way in which we can know whether, about 75,000,000 years ago, there was a brilliant supernova shining in Earth's skies or not. Nor can we tell, specifically, whether a field reversal came at precisely the time of the extinction of the dinosaurs, for instance.

But it may be, at any rate.

And what of the future?

Although the Earth's magnetic field has been in existence in the normal direction ever since the magnetic compass has been in use, its intensity seems to be weakening, and it is possible that the current normal period, which has already lasted some 700,000 years (considerably longer than the average duration between reversals) may be coming to an end.

The magnetic field seems to have lost about 15 percent of the strength it had in 1670 and, at the present rate of decrease, it will reach zero by A.D. 4000. About that time there will be a period when the cosmic ray particles will not be warded off. Even if there is no overall increase in those particles through any nearby supernova explosion, the number hitting the Earth's surface will be double what it is now.

This, perhaps, may not affect life (or mankind, in particular) too badly in itself, but what if a supernova *does* let loose within a few thousand light-years of ourselves at that time—

Of course, mankind may have destroyed itself in other fashions by then.

13

THE ICE AGES

The fact that the magnetic field of Earth changes intensity with time, and that the magnetic poles flip-flop, can't help but cause one to wonder if other aspects of the polar regions may not change drastically with time, too.

Can there be periods in Earth's history when the most characteristic properties of the polar regions—their frigid cold and their vast fields of ice—are more intense than now, or possibly less intense?

Actually, there can. At least for more than a century now, it has been known that Earth has experienced periods when the ice sheets had spread out far over the temperate zones.

The Glaciers of the Past

The first indications that something unusual might have taken place in the past arose in the late eighteenth century, when modern geology was coming into being. Some aspects of the

Earth's surface began to seem puzzling and paradoxical in the light of the new geology. Here and there, there were boulders of a nature unlike the general rocky background around them. In other places, there were deposits of sand and gravel that didn't seem to fit the background.

You might imagine, of course, that a race of giants once existed on Earth that used boulders as weapons, or that tossed boulders about for amusement. Indeed, there were tales of giants in the myths of various nations. There is mention of giants in the Bible, and the Greeks have legends about wars between the gods and the giants, with both sides throwing huge boulders.

Geologists of the eighteenth century could scarcely accept this as an explanation, but what about the great Flood mentioned in the Bible? Right into the nineteenth century, very few Europeans doubted the literal truth of the Bible, and the fact of the Flood was generally accepted. Very naturally, the vast surges of moving water in a worldwide flood would push boulders around and leave deposits of sand and gravel here and there.

Yet there were some geological features of the environment not so easy to explain in terms of a flood, however vast. In many places rock was exposed that was covered with parallel scratches, ancient weathered scratches that might have been caused by the scraping of rock on rock. In that case, though, something would have to hold two rocks together with great force and yet have the additional force to move one against the other. Water alone could not do that, but if not water, what?

In the 1820s, two Swiss geologists, Johann H. Charpentier and J. Venetz, noted that isolated boulders that were scattered over northern Switzerland had no apparent connection with the geologic background of the area, but *were* characteristic of the mountainous areas farther south.

Anyone familiar with the glaciers of the Alps knew that, when they retreated somewhat in the summer, they left behind deposits of sand and gravel. Could it be that the sand and gravel had been carried down the mountain slopes and that the glacier accomplished the task because it moved like a very, very slow river? Could glaciers carry large boulders as well as sand and gravel? And if glaciers were once much larger than they are now, could they have carried such boulders and then melted backward for many miles, leaving those boulders isolated and far from the rocky structures of which they had once formed a part?

Charpentier and Venetz maintained that this was what happened. They suggested that the Alpine glaciers had been much larger and longer in times past and that the isolated boulders in northern Switzerland had been carried there by the enormous glaciers of the past and were left there when the glaciers retreated and dwindled.

The Charpentier-Venetz theory was not taken seriously at first. The thought of huge glaciers in the past seemed fanciful. In fact, the suggestion that the ice of the glaciers moved at all seemed equally fanciful. There were always tales of people who had been swallowed up in crevices near the mountaintop and had then appeared in the valley, perfectly preserved, years later, but dramatic stories of this kind seem notoriously unreliable to men of science.

One of those who doubted was a young Swiss naturalist, Jean Louis Rodolphe Agassiz. He was a friend of Charpentier, who presented his views cogently. Agassiz finally determined to study glaciers for himself.

Once he did so, it seemed to him that it made sense after all to suppose that the glaciers crept their slow way downhill, scraping off large and small rocks as they moved and scraping them against the solid rock below, forming those parallel scratches that puzzled geologists. What was necessary, though, was to get some hard evidence that glaciers did indeed move and that was something that would take time.

He began a series of unprecedented experiments with glaciers. He drove stakes in a straight line across the width of a glacier, driving them deep, for in one experiment where he drove them in only 2 meters or so, the surface melting in the summer loosened them and let them fall flat.

In 1839, he hammered stakes 6 meters into the ice and by the summer of 1841, he found that they had moved a substantial distance. What's more, those in the center of the glacier had moved considerably farther than those near the sides, where the ice was held back by friction with the mountainside. What had been a straight line of stakes became a shallow U shape with the opening uphill.

This showed that the ice did not move all in one piece. Instead, there was a kind of plastic flow as the weight above forced the ice slowly to extrude, like toothpaste out of a tube.

Agassiz' experiments roused a veritable flood of interest in glaciers, and many others performed experiments and made observations of their own. The conclusion was inescapable that glaciers did move and that the Alpine glaciers were much more extensive in the past.

Agassiz then traveled the world over, finding signs of glacier scrapings on rocks here and there. He found boulders and detritus in odd places that marked forward push and retreat of glaciers. He found depressions of "kettle holes" that seemed to have the characteristics one would expect if they had been dug out by glaciers. Some of them were filled with water, and the Great Lakes of North America are particularly large, water-filled kettle holes.

Agassiz' conclusion was that the time of extended glaciers in the Alps was a time of vast sheets of ice in many places. There was an Ice Age when ice sheets like those that now cover Greenland and Antarctica covered large areas of North America and Eurasia as well, so that musk-oxen which are now the characteristic fauna of northern Canada were at one time common in Kentucky.

In fact, the Earth may now be as it is only because the Ice Age is not yet over. The ice sheets in Greenland and Antarctica may not be characteristic of Earth in its normal state but may be the last great remnants of the Ice Age. The permafrost in Canada and Siberia is, on the whole, considerably thicker than would be expected under climatic conditions. Perhaps it, too, is a lingering unmelted remnant of the Ice Age.

But how can there have been an Ice Age? What can have happened to the Earth to account for so extreme a condition so different from that which exists today? Must we search for some substantial astronomic or geologic change? Would the Earth have to be considerably farther from the Sun than it now is to produce an Ice Age? Would its axis have to be differently tipped by a considerable amount? Would the Sun itself have to be markedly cooler?

None of these things, it would seem, can possibly have been so. The Sun, Earth, and solar system are too stable in their properties to have changed in any of these ways in the past few billions of years. And if that is so, must we conclude that the evidence for an Ice Age, however conclusive it may seem, must be an illusion?

Not at all. It is possible to reason out the production of an Ice

Age (or the disappearance of one) as the result of only a *small* change, but a long-continued one.

Under ordinary conditions, snow falls in the winter. It spreads out to cover a certain amount of land and places an additional weight of ice on those glaciers that exist. Then, in summer, that amount of snow and ice melts. If the balance is good, then the snow comes and goes, season after season, while the glaciers advance and retreat slightly, season after season. In the long run, the glaciers remain the same size and so do any continental ice sheets that exist.

But suppose that, for some reason, the average temperature of the Earth goes down by a small amount, a degree or so. This would not be very noticeable, but it would mean that in the course of each winter (which, on the whole, would be slightly colder on the average than winters had been earlier) snow would fall a bit sooner in the season and remain on the ground longer than it ordinarily would in the spring. Each summer (cooler than average) there would be less melting of the winter accumulation. Of course, there would be variations in average temperature from winter to winter and from summer to summer, but on the whole, over the centuries and millennia, the snow would accumulate a little each year, and the glaciers would extend themselves.

This change would feed on itself. Ice reflects light more efficiently than bare rock or soil does. In fact, ice reflects some 90 percent of the light that falls on it, while bare soil reflects less than 10 percent. This means that when there is a slightly larger than average ice cover on Earth, more sunlight is reflected and less is absorbed. The average temperature of the Earth would drop a little further and more ice would begin to persist.

As a result of a very small cooling trigger, then, the glaciers would grow and turn into ice sheets, which would slowly advance, year by year, until finally they would cover vast stretches of ground.

Similarly, if the Earth's average temperature went up by a small amount, perhaps no more than a degree or so, a little more snow would melt each somewhat warmer summer than would be delivered by each previous, somewhat milder winter. What ice sheets there were would begin to retreat. As they retreated, less sunlight would be reflected and more would be absorbed; the warming trend would be accelerated.

The vast changes in climate that accompany the appearance and disappearance of an ice age, in other words, are produced by the triggering of a small change. The problem rests chiefly on what the initial trigger might be—but that is something that will concern us later. For the moment we will simply assume that a trigger exists.

Advances and Retreats

Whatever the trigger may be, it went off about a million years ago, and in much of the time since the Earth has been familiar with ice. These last million years make up the geologic period known as the Pleistocene epoch, the period during which Homo sapiens has evolved.

The "Pleistocene glaciation" is now the term usually used for what was previously called the Ice Age, since it has turned out that there were ice ages before the Pleistocene, too. There was one about 250,000,000 years ago and another about 600,000,000 years ago. There may also have been still another in between, about 400,000,000 years ago. Little is known of these earlier ice ages since the great time lapse has wiped out much of the geologic evidence.

It is clear, then, that ice ages are, on the whole, uncommon and take up only a few tenths of a percent of Earth's total history. A million years ago, when the trigger was pulled and the ice sheets began to form and advance, there came to an end a quarter of a billion years of nonglaciation, a quarter of a billion years during which the dinosaurs had come into being, expanded, and then become extinct, and in which the mammals and birds had come to take over the land areas of the Earth. During all that time, Earth was largely, or even, perhaps, entirely ice free.

It seems rather odd, then, that Homo sapiens should have developed in just one of those rare periods of glaciation. Is that purely coincidence, or did the harsh environments of the Ice Age stimulate human development and might we not be here in our present advanced form were it not for the ice sheets? It is difficult to tell.

In any case, whatever theory is used to explain periods of glaciation must also explain why they are so rare and why one might start after a vast stretch of time in which there were none. In other words, we must decide not only what the Ice Age trigger might be, but also why it works so infrequently.

Again leaving theory to one side, we can consider the situation as it was about a million years ago. The infrequent trigger was pulled and the glaciers began to grow. Since the land formations at that time were very much as they are now, we can suppose, without fear of being wrong, that the initial growth took place on the two landmasses nearest the poles, where even now there are large ice sheets: Antarctica and Greenland.

The Antarctic ice sheet, though the largest by far now, cannot have had an interesting history in the Pleistocene epoch, for it can have had little influence on the rest of the world. It can grow until it covers Antarctica as it does now, but then it can do very little more than that. When the Antarctica ice sheet expands into the sea, it breaks off and fills the surrounding ocean with large pieces of floating ice. Sea ice itself would also develop, but even at the worst of the Ice Age, there would be no chance of freezing any sizable portion of the ocean.

Though the Antarctic Ocean might exert its cooling influence more thoroughly during an Ice Age, it would remain liquid. The land areas of the Southern Hemisphere were too far from Antarctica to be affected to the point of growing ice sheets of their own, protected as they were by ample stretches of open water.

Quite otherwise is the case in the Northern Hemisphere, where great stretches of land crowd close about the pole. It is there that the expansion of the ice sheets is most dramatic, and, when the Ice Age is discussed, it is almost exclusively in connection with the Northern Hemisphere.

There the glaciers of Greenland choked the narrow straits that separated it from the northern islands of the Canadian Archipelago. These islands iced up one by one as the years progressed until the Canadian mainland was reached. On that mainland, glaciers were also expanding, and from the Hudson Bay area, the ice advanced southward and westward.

Meanwhile, the glaciers turned into ice sheets on other Arctic islands such as Iceland, Spitzbergen, and Novaya Zemlya, as well as in Scandinavia. From Scandinavia, the ice sheets spread out over northern Europe, including much of the British Isles. From Novaya Zemlya, they spread out over parts of north-central Siberia.

Mountain glaciers in the Alps, the Caucasus, the Rockies, the Himalayas all expanded also. In the Southern Hemisphere the mountain glaciers of the southern Andes expanded.

In addition to the single northern ice sheet (Greenland) that now exists, there were three more ice sheets that were over 2,500,000 square kilometers in area—Canada, Scandinavia, and Siberia.

Perhaps because Greenland was the seed land of the northern glaciation, nearby Canada was far more glaciated than more distant Scandinavia or still more distant Siberia. In fact, considering Siberia's present reputation for frigidity, it is odd to discover that comparatively little of it was glaciated during the Pleistocene.

The Canadian ice sheet, growing from the northeast, left much of Alaska and the Pacific slope unglaciated, but extended southward until the rim of the ice stretched from the Pacific Ocean to the Atlantic Ocean over a stretch of territory that is now part of the United States. At its maximum southern extension, the boundary of the ice stretched from Seattle, Washington, to Bismarck, North Dakota, then veered southeastward, following very much along the line of the modern Missouri River, past Omaha and St. Louis, then eastward past Cincinnati, Philadelphia, and New York. The southern boundary seems to have been right along the full length of what is now Long Island.

The North American ice sheet stretched as far south as 38° N. in places and at times. The Scandinavian ice sheet stretched southward no farther than 50° N. As a result, less damage was done to the soil in the Eastern Hemisphere than in the Western. The Soviet Union has more than a million acres of land under cultivation north of 60° N., while Canada has scarcely a thousand.

All in all, when the ice sheets were at their farthest extent, they covered over 45,000,000 square kilometers of land. This amounts to over 30 percent of Earth's present land surface as compared with the 10 percent now covered by ice.

Careful examination of the layers of sediment in the soil of areas where the ice sheets existed show that it was not just a matter of the ice sheet advancing and then retreating. Rather, the ice sheet advanced, retreated, advanced, retreated, and so on.

In the million years of the Pleistocene epoch, the ice sheets advanced four times so that there were four periods of glaciation. These are given names (in the Western Hemisphere) in accordance with the areas where the evidence for the particular glaciation is most clear-cut.

The oldest of the four periods of glaciation is the "Nebraska glacial," then the "Kansas glacial," the "Illinois glacial," and finally the "Wisconsin glacial." (In Europe, the four periods of glaciation receive different names, all of which are German in origin.)

Each of the four glacial periods endured from 50,000 to 100,000 years. Between them were three "interglacial periods" which were mild, even warm, and in which the Earth's iceload was reduced to less than what it is now. The interglacial periods can also be very long. The one between the Kansas and Illinois glacials may have been 200,000 years long.

There is thus a kind of pendulum swing back and forth between glacial and interglacial, powered by whatever the trigger may be, as it dips the Earth's average temperature a little below normal and a little above normal to set off, in either case, the big swing.

Nor can we really consider the Pleistocene glaciation to be necessarily over and done with. We are now in a fourth interglacial period and, as a matter of fact, we are not yet all the way into it. Greenland and Antarctica are still fully within the Wisconsin glacial.

Will there be a fifth glacial period in the future? This is something we will consider later.

The most recent period of glaciation, the Wisconsin, is known in better detail than the three earlier ones. It is the most recent, and techniques developed over the last twenty years have enabled geologists to pinpoint the times of advance and retreat with an accuracy that earlier would have been undreamed of.

Timing the past is an intricate art. Prior to the twentieth century, only the very roughest guesses could be made. With the discovery of radioactivity in 1896, the way was opened to something better. The heavy radioactive metals, uranium and thorium, break down very slowly to lead, so slowly that in all the history of Earth only about half the uranium has had a chance to break down and only about a fifth of the thorium.

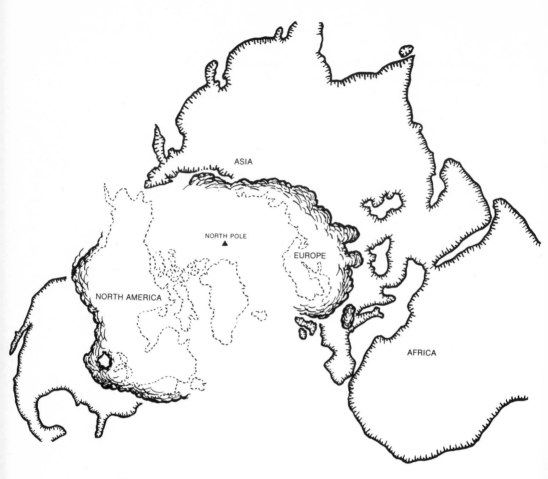

Figure 30. Maximum Glaciation, Northern Hemisphere

In 1905, an American chemist, Bertram Borden Boltwood, pointed out that, in rock containing uranium or thorium, there should also be present lead that had arisen from the radioactive breakdown of those metals. By measuring the quantity of lead present, the length of time during which that rock had been solid could be determined.

It was as a result of the use of this "radioactive clock" that the measurement of ancient times ("archaeometry") first began to have reasonable validity. Eventually, rocks were discovered that were some 3,300,000,000 (3.3 billion) years old, and it was first clearly established that the Earth's age could indeed be measured in the billions of years (something like 4,600,000,000 [4.6 billion] years, it is now believed).

The use of uranium or thorium breakdown was excellent for timing great ages, but would not do for such comparatively short periods of time as the million years of the Pleistocene.

Other archaeometric methods were evolved for shorter periods of time, such as noting the patterns of tree rings. By matching patterns, the age of old pieces of wood (and the human remains associated with them) could be traced back for thousands of years. A similar system can be applied to layers of sediment, or "varves," which are laid down summer after summer by melting glaciers in such places as Scandinavia. In Sweden, varves can be used to trace back events as long as 18,000 years ago.

The use of tree rings and varves, however, is effective only for periods too short to matter as far as the Pleistocene glaciations are concerned. Something is needed that is of intermediate length: shorter-ranged than uranium, longer-ranged than varves.

The beginning of an answer came in 1939, when an American physicist, Serge Korff, showed that cosmic rays, when striking the atmosphere, collided with various atoms found in the atmosphere and induced various changes in the nuclei of those atoms. As a result of a certain type of change, small quantities of carbon-14 were produced.

Ordinary carbon is made up of two varieties, carbon-12 and carbon-13, both of which are stable and endure indefinitely, if left to themselves. Carbon-14, however, is radioactive and breaks down at a certain definite rate. Breaking down at that rate it takes 5600 years for half of a given quantity to break down, then another 5600 years for half of what is left to break down, and so on. (The "half-life" of carbon-14, in other words, is 5600 years.)

Naturally, once carbon-14 is formed in the atmosphere, it starts breaking down at once. Since more is always being formed, thanks to the continuing steady bombardment of the atmosphere by cosmic ray particles, an equilibrium is established and the atmosphere always has a certain content of carbon-14. It is found as part of the carbon dioxide molecules that make up 0.03 percent of the atmosphere. (The total amount of carbon-14 in the atmosphere is almost vanishingly small, but the particles produced when carbon-14 breaks down can be detected easily even so.)

In 1946, an American chemist, Willard Frank Libby, pointed out that the carbon dioxide in the atmosphere is made use of by plants which incorporated it into the carbon-containing compounds of their own tissues. Animals, in turn, ate plants and incorporated the carbon atoms into their own tissues.

Some of the carbon atoms that passed from tissue to tissue, Libby stated, had to be carbon-14. Small quantities of carbon-14 should therefore make up a part of the tissues of every living organism on Earth. Naturally, the carbon-14 within living tissue breaks down and the atoms change into other kinds of atoms at a fixed rate. More carbon-14 is, however, forever being introduced from the food in the case of animals or from the atmosphere in the case of plants. An equilibrium is established in tissue, too, then, and it follows that living creatures have, at all times, some fixed and small percentage of carbon-14 within their tissues.

What happens when an organism dies? The carbon-14 continues to break down, but now no new carbon-14 is added. This means that the carbon-14 content of a dead organism or of its remains is less than the corresponding content of a living organism of the same type. The longer the time lapse since it has been alive, the smaller the quantity of carbon-14 in the dead organism. Since the rate of breakdown of carbon-14 is known accurately, it is possible to tell from the carbon-14 content how long it has been since the organism died.

Dating by carbon-14 in this way can fix time lapses up to 30,000 years quite accurately, and this enables geologists to date events in the last of the four periods of glaciation in any case.

This is done chiefly by measuring the carbon-14 content of ancient wood. Some of the wood is the remains of forests that had been mowed down by the slow advance of glaciers, or bits of driftwood from the lakes that formed south of the glaciers as they melted and retreated, or peat that accumulated in the damp fields that had been ice covered and were now ice free.

As a result of work of this sort, it appears that the Wisconsin glaciation, the last of the four, was creeping southward across Canada 30,000 years ago or so. (Carbon-14 measurements showed it was also expanding in Eurasia—thus supplying us with definite evidence that glaciation proceeded simultaneously on both sides of the pole and not on one side, then the other, alternately.)

The Wisconsin glaciation reached the region of what are now the Great Lakes 25,000 years ago, and by 18,000 years ago had spread still farther southward to the region of the Ohio River. The glaciation then stood at its maximum extent.

Slowly, the ice then began to retreat. An idea of the slowness of this retreat comes from the time it seems to have taken to retreat from the position of Hartford, Connecticut, to St. Johnsbury, Vermont—a distance of 300 kilometers. This retreat took 4300 years, or about 70 meters a year, on the average.

Nor did the retreat continue at a steady pace. There were periods when it slowed to a halt and when the ice even began to advance again, first about 12,500 years ago, and then again about 10,500 years ago. Forests would grow after the retreat of the ice and then be destroyed as the ice returned. In the second reexpansion, the ice reached down as far south as Buffalo and northern New England.

About 10,000 years ago, the glaciers began their final retreat. By 8000 years ago, the Great Lakes were clear and, for the first time in some 25,000 years, Canada began to lose its ice cover. By 5000 years ago, the ice had retreated to about where it is today.

The carbon-14 dating showed that the last of the glaciation had taken place considerably later in time than had been thought. At the time the glaciers were beginning their last retreat, agriculture had already been developed in the Middle East. Five thousand years ago, when the ice had finally retreated to its present position, writing had been invented and the pyramids were soon to be built.

Sea Level

The coming and going of the ice had to have a profound effect on the Earth generally.

Consider first that all that ice must have come from somewhere, nor is the source a mystery: it had to come from the ocean. Every tonne of ice that rests on the land surface of the globe represents a tonne of water that was in the ocean at one time when there was no ice on the land at all. (Of course, there is water on the land, too, fresh water in the form of lakes, rivers, and so on. This cannot be the source of the ice, however, since fresh water makes up but a small proportion of the volume of the ice fields of a glacial age. Besides, the fresh water on land also originates in the ocean.)

At the present moment there are some 24,000,000 cubic kilometers of ice resting on land, but, at the height of a glaciation, the total amount of ice on land may have been triple that amount. Perhaps 50,000,000 cubic kilometers of water, now in the ocean, was locked into the ice sheets resting on Canada, Scandinavia, and Siberia.

This is only about 0.35 percent of all the water in the ocean, so that even at the height of the glaciation, the ocean was not seriously affected as far as its total size was concerned. Sea life would continue relatively undisturbed during all the comings and goings of the ice.

Still, there would be a little less water in the oceans and the ocean would therefore not be quite as deep as it is today; the sea level would drop. When the glaciation was at its maximum, the sea level may have been as much as 100 meters lower than it is right now.

This isn't much considering that the average depth of the ocean is something like 3600 meters, but it is still enough to bring about some important changes. Not all sections of the ocean are kilometers deep. On the borders of the continents, there are shallow sections of the ocean where the water is less than 180 meters deep. The sea floor under these shallow sections, extending outward some 600 kilometers in places, makes up the "continental shelves."

From a geological standpoint, the continental shelves seem to be part of the continents in structure and makeup. At the end of the shelves, the sea bottom falls off more or less sharply (the "continental slopes") and takes up a structure that is quite distinct from the continents geologically.

About 7 percent of the ocean area covers the continental shelves rimming the continents. Part of this would be exposed as the sea level drops. Although perhaps as much as 25,000,000 square kilometers of land that is now exposed was covered by deep ice sheets at the height of glaciation and was as barren as Antarctica now is, perhaps 12,000,000 square kilometers of continental shelf, now under the sea, was exposed and made available to land life.

In addition, the Earth as a whole was cooler, with the tropic ocean waters anywhere from 2 to 5 degrees under what they are now. The ocean therefore contained more oxygen, so that sea life may well have been richer than it now is. The rain belts in advance of the glaciers were farther south than they now are, so that the American Southwest was a land of lakes, and what is now the Sahara Desert was a lush grassland.

Nor need we imagine that the advance of the ice sheets was a great calamity to life in the north. Remember that the advance was a very slow one. Plant life was destroyed in the glaciers' path, but spread southward at least as fast as the ice did. Animals had plenty of time to migrate and were not even very likely to be trapped against the sea, since the dropping sea level resulted in the formation of land bridges between islands and continents that did not exist before the coming of the glaciers. In the depth of a glacial period, the British Isles are connected to Europe, while Japan and much of Indonesia are connected to Asia.

Some of the animals who roamed the plains ahead of the very slowly advancing (and later the very slowly retreating) glaciers adapted to the greater cold by developing thick coats of fur (like the musk-oxen today). Woolly rhinoceroses and woolly elephants were characteristic of what was then the Arctic.

The human population of the Earth, which had been evolving from apelike ancestors since well before the Pleistocene epoch, had reached the point in the course of the last glaciation when it could pursue these large animals for food. In fact, it was as they followed the herds northward during the slow retreat of the ice that human beings may have entered the Arctic for the first time.

The woolly elephants, called "mammoths," were particularly abundant in Siberia during the period of glaciation. We know what they looked like because of the paintings made of them by the primitive hunters who pursued them. Their tusks were larger and more splendid than those of modern elephants and their ears were smaller. They had thick coats of shaggy hair and humps of fat on top of the skulls and sometimes on their shoulders.

They were so numerous that, for thousands of years after

Mammoths

they were finally extinct (partly from the effects of the retreat of the glaciers and the warming of the climate, and partly from the effects of human hunting), the ivory of their tusks, found here and there, remained an important Siberian export.

Indeed, it is not just bone and ivory that remain of the mammoths, and it is not just primitive paintings that need serve as evidence as to their appearance. Life was risky for them, and falling into a cold bog just before a cold air mass swooped down could mean death and entrapment in ice. Under proper conditions, the carcass might be buried in ice and in frozen earth and remain, undecayed for thousands of years, in that deep freeze.

Some frozen mammoths have actually been dug out of the Siberian ground, and the very word "mammoth" is supposed to be from an old Tatar word meaning "to dig." The Siberian natives of today apparently have no trace of legend concerning the Homeric struggles between their ancestors and the mammoth, and have completely forgotten the true nature of the beast. They therefore suspected the occasionally exposed mammoths to be giant moles who dug their way underground and who died instantly when exposed to air.

In 1899 an intact mammoth was found in the Siberian ground, so unspoiled that its stomach contents could be studied and used to show that the tundra vegetation had not changed, noticeably, over the last 25,000 years. So unspoiled was the mammoth, indeed, that dogs ate some of the carcass before they could be stopped and, to all appearances, enjoyed it.

What with animal adaptation and migration, the opening of new lands by the falling sea level, and the southward swoop of the rain, there is no need to think of the glacial periods as a time of great hardship for life. Living organisms, even on land, may have been better off at the height of the glaciation than they are now.

Even man himself owed a remarkable expansion to the glaciation. The falling sea level produced a land bridge, some 2000 kilometers wide, between Siberia and Alaska. Since this was an area relatively free of ice, Siberian tribesmen, in their hunt for mammoths, crossed over into the North American continent about 25,000 years ago. These migrants spread gradually over the entire continent and into South America down to its Patagonian tip, filling the land with a population we now refer to as "Indians." No human beings had existed in the American continents prior to that migration.

By the time of that migration, modern man was the only form of mankind existing. All earlier forms, from the Neanderthal on backward, have left traces in the temperate and tropical zones of the Eastern Hemisphere only.

And what of the interglacial periods, when the ice cover had receded to where it is now, and perhaps farther?

It has been commonly felt that at the height of the interglacial periods, all the snow and ice on Earth might vanish and even Antarctica might lie exposed. Perhaps this is not so, however. In 1973, reports from vessels exploring Antarctic waters were to the effect that the Antarctica ice cap is at least 20,000,000 years old (and reached a maximum size, extending out over the surrounding continental shelf, about 5,000,000 years ago). If this is so, Antarctica is relatively unaffected by the coming and going of glaciation but remains steadily frozen and icebound through it all.

Assuming that the Antarctica ice cap remains in the interglacial, even considerable melting of Arctic ice would not add much to ocean water, and the sea level might not be more than 6 meters higher than it is today. The continents would shrink a bit at their rims, but not very much land would be lost. What is lost would be more than made up for by the increased hospitability of the Arctic.

What's more, the fact that continents would be somewhat smaller in area with somewhat more generous ocean inlets here and there might mean that the land surface would be, on the average, better watered than it is now, so that a smaller percentage of the land would be desert.

We might even argue that we live now in a period in which the Earth is least favorable to land life. There is still enough ice cover to make large areas of northern lands relatively inhospitable to life, and there is neither enough ice nor enough ocean to keep large tracts of the subtropical sections of the world from turning into deserts through lack of rainfall.

Dust Clouds and Sunspots

But now we must consider the possible causes of these periods of glaciation. What is the trigger that produces the small drop in Earth's average temperature that is enough to set the glaciers to advancing—or the small rise that is enough to set them retreating?

A variety of explanations have been advanced, none of which has as yet been accepted by scientists generally. We can begin with the one that is farthest from home and which we can call the "cosmic explanation."

After all, Earth's temperature depends just about entirely on the amount of radiation it receives from the Sun, and something may occur in deep space to reduce that amount.

Consider the possibility that cosmic clouds, volumes of dust and gas in open space, may be involved. Such dust clouds do indeed exist and we can see them among the stars as "nebulae." Where the clouds have stars immersed in themselves, they are lit to a faint glow. Some clouds do not surround stars and so are nonluminous and invisible except when they happen to be between ourselves and bright clusters of distant stars. The clouds then block our vision and appear to us as "dark nebulae" surrounded, beyond their borders, by bright stars shining past them.

Might it not be, then, that the Sun and its attendant planets are traveling through the midst of a thin dust cloud, which varies in thickness from place to place? Now and then the Sun passes through a thicker portion which absorbs a little more of its light and cuts the amount falling on Earth by just enough to lower the temperature a degree or two and set off the glaciation trigger. When the Sun passes through a thinner section, the Earth's temperature rises and sets off the glacial-retreat trigger.

If this were true, there might be minor variations here and there which cause the periodic minor advances of the ice during deglaciation and the periodic minor retreats of the ice during glaciation. What's more, we might have entered the cloud only at the start of the Pleistocene epoch. Prior to that, the Sun may have traveled through clear space for 250,000,000 years so that in that period of time there was no Ice Age at all. The early ice ages may have come when the Sun was passing through other dust clouds.

This explanation can account for everything, if we imagine a dust cloud (or clouds) with the proper increases and decreases in dust concentration. The trouble is, though, that such a cloud cannot be detected in space and there is no evidence for its existence except for reasoning backward from the ice ages.

The result is that, except for the necessity of explaining the ice ages, no one would ever have occasion to think there might be dust clouds in our neighborhood of space. A theory that serves to explain one particular phenomenon, without any outside evidence to support it, is an ad hoc theory, from a Latin term meaning "for this."

Scientists find themselves uncomfortable with ad hoc theories, and when only such a theory is available, they must continue to try out other theories, too.

For instance, why postulate a cosmic cloud to account for varying quantities of solar radiation over the history of the Earth, if the variation may be accounted for by the internal workings of the Sun itself? Working from this viewpoint, we could devise a "solar explanation."

The Sun does, indeed, vary in its energy output—not by much, but certainly by a little. The reason for that rests in the sunspots. Sunspots, it would seem, appear as local areas of expansion of the solar substance. As the gases in the outer layers of the Sun expand, their temperature must drop and the sunspots are, indeed, cooler than the surrounding unspotted sections of the Sun. It is because the spots are cooler than the surrounding material, and therefore give off less radiation, that they seem dark in comparison to the glow around them.

The Sun, when its face contains many spots, is slightly cooler than it would be if it were free of spots. The number of spots present at any one time increases, then decreases, in a fairly regular way, with sunspot maximum and minimum alternating with a period, from maximum to maximum, of about eleven years.

The difference in the extent of solar radiation between maximum and minimum is not really very much, and the shift back and forth between them is sufficiently rapid so that neither a higher-than-average radiation nor a lower-than-average one has a chance to establish itself at an extreme enough level or for a long enough time to initiate either glaciations or deglaciations.

It might be, however, that there are times when the Sun is considerably spottier than it is now, or considerably clearer. When it is considerably spottier, the Earth would receive a less-than-normal quantity of radiation over a long enough period of time to initiate a glaciation. If, afterward, the Sun became less spotty, a deglaciation could be initiated.

It might also be that these periods of super-spottiness were rare in the history of the Sun, and that for hundreds of millions of years at a time it might shine unspotted, keeping Earth steadily warm and steadily free of ice.

In fact it is even possible to work out a scheme that would account for glaciation both as the Sun warmed and as it cooled.

Let's connect the present level of spottiness of the Sun with the present interglacial period, and suppose that the Sun is never spottier than this, but can become freer of spots.

Let us imagine, then, that a time comes when the sunspot level begins to decline and the amount of solar radiation reaching us begins to rise slightly.

In that case, there is more evaporation of water from the oceans, more clouds, and more precipitation. The precipitation falls as snow in the polar regions, and in the generally cloudy summer, there is insufficient heat reaching the polar surface to melt all that snow, so that the glaciers would spread southward from the Arctic.

In the long run, however, the increasing heat reaching the Earth over thousands of years would finally make its effect felt and the glaciers would begin to melt and recede. There would follow an interglacial period under a virtually spot-less Sun.

But then the tendency to spottiness would establish itself and the Sun would begin to deliver less and less heat. As the heat delivered very slowly declines, the snow falling in polar regions is not entirely melted in the summer and the glaciers form and expand. As the heat continues to decline, however, the ability of the Sun to evaporate the ocean declines also, and the amount of precipitation is lowered—which means less snow in winter. With lessened cloudiness, the Sun, though cooler, can get in more work in the summer, and the glaciers begin to recede.

In this way, we can argue that when the Sun goes through a period of first losing, then regaining its spots, there is a pair of glaciations with a warm interglacial period. In between two such pairs of glaciations, there would be a relatively cool interglacial period in which the Sun is more or less substantially spotted. Our own interglacial is of this latter variety.

The trouble with this theory is that it also is ad hoc. We have no direct evidence that the Sun's general spottiness varies in this way, nor would we have reason to suggest that it happens except out of the necessity of explaining the ice ages. We know of the 11-year cycle of sunspots, which can't cause ice ages, and we know of nothing else.

A very recent version of the solar explanation involves the interior of the Sun. Ordinarily, the theory explains, the different materials within the Sun's core are separated into onion-like layers, and when that is so, the Sun produces a certain quantity of subatomic particles called "neutrinos."

There is a mixing tendency, however, and every 250,000,000 years or so, this tendency results in a more or less complete mixing of the materials in the solar core, at which time the amount of solar radiation drops 5 percent and the neutrino production falls to almost zero. After about a million years of this mixed state, the materials separate out again and the Sun's normal rates of radiation and of neutrino production are restored.

This would account for the million-year on-and-off glaciation of the Pleistocene, preceded by a long period of no ice at all. It may also account for the earlier periods of glaciation of which we find dim records. And, as a matter of fact, astronomers have in recent years detected far fewer neutrinos from the Sun than they felt they ought to detect, under the assumption that the materials in the solar core are not completely mixed.

Unfortunately, we don't know enough about the solar interior to make this theory, ingenious though it is, anything more than speculation.

The Changing Orbit

If we ignore the possibility of dust clouds in space and assume the Sun and its spots to behave in a perfectly regular manner, can we find possible causes of the ice ages closer to home?

What about the behavior of the Earth itself? After all, the amount of radiation it gets from the Sun depends on Earth's distance from the Sun and on the manner in which the Earth's axis of rotation is tipped. Even if the Sun were rock-steady with respect to the radiation it emits, the Earth would get varying amounts if its distance or its axial tip or both were to change.

Such orbital changes can't possibly take place to any large extent, but they can take place to a minor extent—enough to give rise to a possible "orbital explanation."

To begin with, Earth's orbit is such that its distance from the Sun varies over a yearly period. The orbit is not a circle with the Sun at the center—in which case the Earth would be always at the same distance from the Sun as it moved in its circular path.

Instead, the Earth's orbit is an ellipse, with the Sun at one focus. An ellipse always has two foci, one to either side of the center, so that each focus is closer to one end of the ellipse than to the other. The Sun, being at one focus of Earth's elliptical orbit, is closer to one end of that orbit than to the other.

Fortunately, Earth's orbit is not very elliptical but is quite close to circular so that the distance of the Sun does not vary much in the course of a year. Even so, when the Earth is at the end of the orbit closest to the Sun ("perihelion"), it is only 147,000,000 kilometers from the Sun. When the Earth is at the end of the orbit farthest from the Sun ("aphelion"), it is 152,000,000 kilometers away. These two points are at opposite ends of the orbit, so that for six months of the year the Earth is slowly but steadily increasing its distance from the Sun, and then for the remaining six months it is just as slowly but steadily decreasing that distance.

The extreme difference in distance is only 3.5 percent, but it means that, on the day of perihelion, the Earth, as a whole, is getting 7 percent more heat than on the day of aphelion.

The day of perihelion happens (by coincidence) to be January 1, and the day of aphelion, July 1. This means that from October 1 to March 1 the Earth is getting more-than-average heat, and from March 1 to October 1, less-than-average heat.

Since the October-to-March period includes the northern fall and winter and the southern spring and summer, while the March-to-October period includes the northern spring and summer and the southern fall and winter, it means that fall and winter in the Northern Hemisphere, coming as they do when Earth is closer to the Sun, are warmer than the fall and winter in the Southern Hemisphere, when the Earth is farther from the Sun. For similar reasons, the spring and summer in the Northern Hemisphere are cooler than the spring and summer in the Southern Hemisphere.

Another way of putting it is to say that the seasons are less extreme in the Northern Hemisphere than in the Southern.

It might be argued, now, that the less extreme the seasons, the more likely there is to be glaciation. If the winters are generally milder, for instance, the milder air will hold more water vapor and there is likely to be a greater fall of snow (always supposing that the mildness is not so great as to lift the winter temperatures above the freezing point). Then the cooler summers will not deliver enough heat to melt that snow and the glaciers will grow and expand.

Although the Earth's axis of rotation remains steadily tipped by a certain amount, the whole axis can slowly turn in a period of 26,000 years so as to form a double cone, or an hourglass-shaped figure called the "precession of the equinoxes." This means that 13,000 years ago, or, for that matter, 13,000 years from now, the axis is tipped in the direction opposite to that in which it is tipped now (but, of course, by the same amount).

At the present moment, the North Pole is tipped most directly away from the Sun on December 21, when the Earth is quite near perihelion, and the South Pole is tipped most directly toward the Sun. At the other extreme of the cycle, 13,000 years ago or 13,000 years from now, the South Pole will be tipped *away* from the Sun at perihelion and the North Pole toward it. Under such conditions, it would be the Northern Hemisphere that would have the more extreme seasons and the Southern that would have the less extreme.

There would be a cycle, then. Beginning from a period such as now, when the southern seasons are at their most extreme and the northern seasons at the least extreme, the slowly precessing axis would reduce the extremeness of the southern seasons and increase the extremeness of the northern seasons. Some 6500 years from now, both hemispheres would have seasons that would be equally extreme. Then 13,000 years from now, the northern seasons would be at their most extreme and the southern at the least extreme. After that, the changes would reverse and we'd get back to the present situation after 26,000 years.

If lack of extreme seasons, mild winters and cool summers, brings on the period of glaciation, you might suppose there would be an ice age every 13,000 years, alternating in the Northern Hemisphere and the Southern Hemisphere.

This, however, is not so. Glaciations are not that frequent and regular. Besides, we are presently at a time when there should be glaciation in the Northern Hemisphere and there is not.

This difference between perihelion and aphelion, and the effect of the change in the direction of the tipped axis brought on by the precession of the equinoxes, is not enough by itself, apparently, to make the Earth's temperature vary sufficiently to set off the glaciation trigger. There are, however, other changes in the Earth's orbit.

If the Sun and Earth were the only objects in the solar system, then the Earth's orbit, whatever it was, would remain constant from revolution to revolution over long periods of time. The other planets, however, exert small and shifting gravitational pulls on Earth (and Earth on them), and, as a result, there are small changes in Earth's orbit, all of them cyclic.

For instance, the eccentricity of Earth's orbit changes through a slow cycle. The Earth's orbit is sometimes a bit less eccentric than it is now so that the difference in distance from the Sun between perihelion and aphelion is less than it is now;

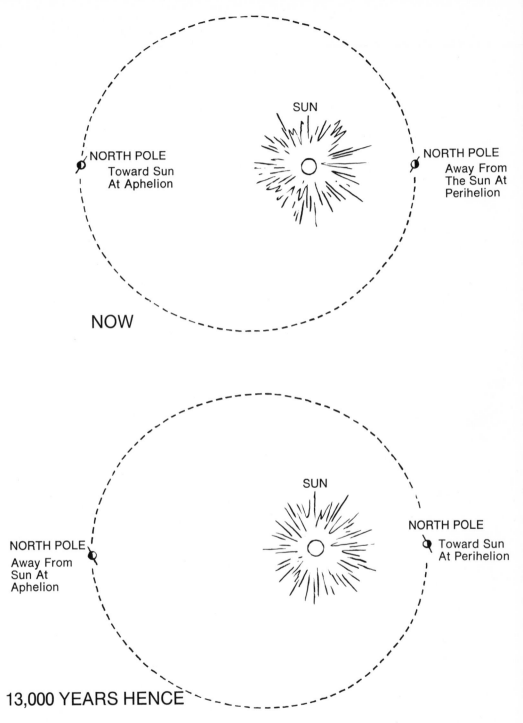

Figure 31. The earth at perihelion now and 13,000 years from now

and it is sometimes a bit more eccentric so that the perihelion-aphelion difference is greater than it is now. Then, too, the positions of the perihelion and aphelion slowly move about the orbit. And again, the degree by which the axis tilts oscillates slightly and is a bit larger at times than it is at others.

If these variations in eccentricity and axial tilt are combined with the precession of the equinoxes and the positions of perihelion and aphelion, the amount of heat received by the Earth varies in a regular, but longer cycle than if the precession is considered alone.

In 1920, a Yugoslavian physicist, Milutin Milankovich, suggested a cycle of this sort that was 40,000 years in length, with a "Great Spring," "Great Summer," "Great Fall," and "Great Winter," each 10,000 years long. (We are now in a "Great Summer.")

The Earth would, by this theory, be particularly prone to glaciation in the time of the "Great Winter" and would actually undergo it when other factors were favorable as well. Once glaciated, the Earth would undergo deglaciation most likely in the "Great Summer" if other factors were favorable.

This longer cycle would make it still seem as though ice ages ought to occur in the Northern and Southern hemispheres alternately, yet the evidence makes it quite clear that the Pleistocene glaciations affected both polar regions each time.

A second difficulty is that these orbital variations have been proceeding regularly, in the present fashion as nearly as we can tell, for all the billions of years of Earth's history. Why is it, then, that glaciations were frequent in the last million years, but nonexistent in the 250,000,000 years preceding?

Here a possible answer lies in the fact that it is not entirely the rise and fall of heat delivered from the Sun that accounts for glaciation. There must exist regions on Earth that are particularly sensitive to glaciation—plateaus and mountain ranges, for instance, where the temperature is always lower than it is at sea level at similar latitudes.

Perhaps it is only when the land areas are generally mountainous (as is true now) that the glaciers get a chance to start in the course of a Great Winter. Then, by serving to cool the Earth further, they advance into the lowlands, too. When the land areas are generally low-lying (as they have been most of the time during Earth's history), there is no place for the glaciers to get a good start and glaciation does not take place even in the Great Winter.

Then, too, once glaciers start in either polar region, the Earth's average temperature may decline to the point where they start also in the other polar region—thus accounting for the simultaneous glaciations.

The "orbital explanation" has the advantage over the "cosmic explanation" and the "solar explanation" in not being ad hoc. The orbital cycles and the changes in heat received from Earth really exist and arise out of observations and reasoning that have nothing to do with the ice ages.

What's more, the "orbital explanation" can be applied with interesting results to at least one other planet—Mars.

Mars has an orbit that is somewhat more eccentric than that of Earth and an axis that is just as tipped. Cyclic changes in its orbit and axial tilt cause the solar radiation it receives to vary by about 1 percent in a 95,000-year cycle.

Mars, too, may have "ice ages" as a result. Of course, Mars has less water by far than Earth does, so it cannot have ice sheets to anything like the extent on Earth. On the other hand, its atmosphere is chiefly carbon dioxide, and, at the lower temperature of Mars, this atmosphere can freeze during an ice age.

At the present moment, Mars may be in an ice age, with all its water and almost all its carbon dioxide in its polar ice caps. Only enough carbon dioxide remains gaseous to make up a very thin atmosphere, perhaps 1 percent as dense as ours.

Thousands of years from now, perhaps, as the cycle turns, deglaciation will set in. The ice caps will slowly disappear, a fairly thick carbon dioxide atmosphere will appear and liquid water (in small quantities, by Earth's standard) will exist. Perhaps Mars, in its deglaciated stage, is fairly hospitable to life and perhaps some native Martian life is now hibernating through its planet's Ice Age.

Carbon Dioxide

The "orbital explanation" offers an uncomfortable regularity, however, for what seems such an irregular phenomenon as the ice ages. In order to convert the regularity into irregularity, other somewhat more ad hoc effects must be added—such as the mountainous nature of Earth's land areas.

Can we find another characteristic of the Earth itself that could have an influence—perhaps all by itself?

After all, the average temperature of the Earth depends not only on the amount of radiation reaching its dayside from the Sun, but on the amount of radiation escaping into outer space from the Earth's nightside. The Earth's temperature can rise either because it receives more radiation or because it loses less. The Earth's temperature can fall either because it receives less radiation or because it loses more.

So far the various explanations of the ice ages which we have considered dealt entirely with variations in the amount of radiation received from the Sun. Now what about the amount of radiation the Earth gives off to space?

One factor that can alter the manner in which Earth radiates heat into space rests on the nature of the atmosphere through which such radiated heat must pass. We come, therefore, to what we might call the "atmospheric explanation."

Air is not equally transparent to all radiation. It does, as a matter of fact, happen to be quite transparent to those forms of radiation with the wavelengths of visible light. That is why life forms have evolved sense organs capable of responding to those particular wavelengths that penetrate the atmosphere and reach the surface, and why the light is therefore *visible*. To most types of radiation with waves longer or shorter than those of visible light, the atmosphere is more or less opaque.

The radiation given off by the Earth at night is not in the form of visible light, but appears as the much less energetic infrared radiation which has wavelengths considerably longer than those of visible light. The major components of the atmosphere are transparent to the infrared radiation, but carbon dioxide, which is a minor component (making up 0.03 percent of the whole), is not. It tends to absorb the infrared radiation, instead of letting it pass unaffected.

The result is that some of the infrared radiation given off by the Earth does not escape but serves, instead, to warm the carbon dioxide in the atmosphere, and through that (by collision of carbon dioxide molecules with the other molecules in the air) to warm the atmosphere and the Earth generally.

Small though the quantity of carbon dioxide in the air is, it has a perceptible effect. If there were no carbon dioxide in the atmosphere at all, infrared radiation would escape more easily, and without warming the atmosphere appreciably so that the Earth's average temperature would drop a bit. The presence of carbon dioxide in the atmosphere, in other words, suffices to keep the Earth's surface a little warmer than it would otherwise be.

The carbon dioxide in the atmosphere acts like the glass in a "greenhouse" which allows the short waves of sunlight to penetrate and warm the greenery within, but which does not allow the infrared radiation produced within to pass out again. This conserves the heat and keeps the interior warmer than it would be if glass were transparent to infrared radiation. (You will also notice this effect in an automobile that has been sitting with closed windows in the sun.)

The action of carbon dioxide to conserve heat, first pointed out by the British physicist John Tyndall in 1861, is therefore called the "greenhouse effect."

The greenhouse effect can be enormous, though, fortunately, it does not display its full strength on Earth. On Venus, however, the atmosphere is some ninety-five times as dense as it is here and is almost entirely carbon dioxide. That vast amount of carbon dioxide traps enough heat to raise Venus' surface temperature to a fiercely high level.

Astronomers, before they learned the nature of Venus' atmosphere, had expected Venus to be warmer than the Earth, since it is closer to the Sun than Earth is—but only moderately so, particularly in view of the fact that Venus' unbroken cloud layer reflects some 60 percent of the sunlight falling upon it, whereas Earth's less solid cloud layer reflects only 30 percent. Nevertheless, various Venus probes, beginning with Mariner 2 in 1962, have made it plain that Venus' surface temperature is an astonishing 470 C. The planet suffers from a "runaway greenhouse effect."

On Earth, the influence of the carbon dioxide content of the atmosphere is very small compared to that on Venus, but it is not nil. Small variations in the carbon dioxide content of Earth's atmosphere may suffice to trigger glaciations or deglaciations.

But how can the carbon dioxide content be made to vary? Some carbon dioxide is dissolved in ocean water; indeed there is about fifty times as much dissolved carbon dioxide in the ocean as there is gaseous carbon dioxide in the atmosphere. Very tiny changes in the capacity of the ocean to retain carbon dioxide in solution may result in larger percentage changes in the atmospheric content of gaseous carbon dioxide.

Again, plant life incorporates gaseous carbon dioxide into its tissues. Generally, this is restored to the atmosphere because animals eat the plants, oxidize their tissues, and breathe out carbon dioxide, or because bacteria decay the plants and produce carbon dioxide. On the other hand, there are periods in which large quantities of plant life are buried and decay in such a way as to produce layers of coal (mostly carbon) underground; or in which animal sea life is buried and decays in such a way as to produce pools of petroleum (mostly carbon and hydrogen). In either way, carbon dioxide is removed from the atmosphere, if not quite permanently, at least for long periods of time. Similarly, carbon dioxide can combine with minerals freshly brought to Earth's surface at times of mountain building, forming carbonates that remain out of the atmosphere for long periods of time.

On the other hand, volcanic eruptions are continually producing quantities of carbon dioxide (produced by the breakdown of carbonates or the burning of coal and oil) which are discharged into the atmosphere.

The amount of carbon dioxide leaving the atmosphere and the amount entering the atmosphere may not always balance even over long periods of time. In periods of high volcanic action, the balance may swing toward an increase of the carbon dioxide content of the atmosphere; in periods of low volcanic action, the balance may swing toward a decrease.

It may be, then, that a period of little volcanic action on Earth may see a slow decrease in the carbon dioxide content of the atmosphere and a slow decrease in the average temperature of the Earth (as more infrared radiation escapes into space). Eventually, the decrease in temperature is sufficient to trigger a glaciation.

Again, a period of high volcanic action on Earth may see a slow increase in the carbon dioxide content of the atmosphere and a slow increase in the average temperature of the Earth (as less infrared radiation escapes into space). This would prevent a glaciation, or, if one already exists, it would eventually trigger a deglaciation.

And yet the difficulty here rests in the fact that scientists are not actually sure how the atmospheric content of carbon dioxide varies with volcanic activity, or how it has varied in the past, or how the extent of volcanic activity has varied in the past. So far we can't tie in changes in carbon dioxide content or in volcanic activity with the actual periods of glaciation and deglaciation.

We must look further.

14 THE DRIFTING CONTINENTS

All the theories concerning the cause of the ice ages, as outlined in the previous chapter, are really unsatisfactory. Even if they can be used to explain the events of the Pleistocene epoch, they fall afoul of earlier glaciations.

Some 600 million years ago, in what is known as the pre-Cambrian era, there seem to have been (judging from scrapings on rocks of known age) periods of glaciation that took place simultaneously in equatorial Brazil, in South Africa, in India, and in western and southeastern Australia. None of the theories described in the previous chapter can possibly explain how glaciation could have taken place in tropic and near-tropic areas. Could the entire land surface of Earth have glittered in a mantle of ice? That isn't possible, since other places show no signs of glaciation for that period.

To explain the early ice ages, something new is needed; and, indeed, in the last two decades a new look has been worked out in geology, one which may explain not only this puzzle but many others as well. Let us begin by taking another look at the Pleistocene glaciation.

The Arctic Ocean

The most dramatic aspect of this last Ice Age is not so much the existence of the great glaciers as their slow coming and going. Is there any way we can explain this alternation of glacial and interglacial periods as a matter of geography alone?

Thus, suppose the polar region consists of an unbroken stretch of water with no land within some thousands of miles. We can assume there will be a slowly rotating mass of sea ice around the pole. This is bound to be relatively thin and, in terms of mass, inconsequential. Furthermore, warmer currents entering, uninterfered with, from lower latitudes may break it up nearly as fast as it is formed. It would not be difficult to imagine such polar waters as ice free even at present global temperatures.

Naturally, the open or nearly open sea will be a great source of water vapor, to say nothing of water vapor that sweeps in from warmer stretches of ocean. This water vapor, cooled in the upper atmosphere, will fall as snow in the polar region, but falling into the ocean, it will melt. It is unlikely that, considering the high heat capacity of water, enough snow will fall to freeze the ocean surface beyond some minimum quantity of sea ice in the winter—at least under present climatic conditions.

Even if the Earth's temperature drops slightly for any reason, enough to serve as a trigger for glaciation, the sea ice may only expand its area by some modest amount. No glaciers will form, since there is no neighboring land to be affected by the snowfall.

The vast expansion and contraction of glaciers characteristic of the Pleistocene in the Northern Hemisphere would then not take place.

Suppose, on the other hand, we had a polar region that consisted of an unbroken stretch of land, with a surrounding ocean outside the polar region. The surrounding ocean would serve as a source of water vapor which would precipitate as snow. The snow, falling on the water, would have little effect, though there might be considerable sea ice clinging to the rim of the polar continent. The snow falling on the land, however, would quickly cool the land (with its heat capacity so much smaller than that of the ocean) to the point where the snow would not melt. It would accumulate and eventually form a vast ice sheet covering the continent.

Such an ice sheet would have very little opportunity to expand if the Earth's temperature drops a little, since it already covers the entire continent, and the surrounding ocean can at best offer an opportunity for an ice shelf if a large inlet exists in the continent.

The ice shelf pushes out a bit farther and the sea ice increases moderately in area as the temperature drops. On the other hand, if the temperature rises moderately, the sea ice and the ice shelf may retreat somewhat, but it is unlikely that the continental ice cap will suffer much. In fact, one can argue that it may grow thicker, since a warmer temperature on Earth generally will increase water vapor in the air and therefore increase the quantity of snow falling on the continent.

On Earth, of course, the situation just described actually exists, since the Antarctic is virtually filled with a land area that is surrounded by ocean.

Neither a polar continent nor an unbroken polar sea would undergo glacial oscillations—but our Northern Hemisphere does.

In 1953, the American geologists Maurice Ewing and William L. Donn suggested that this might be the result of the peculiar geography of the Northern Hemisphere. The Arctic region is almost entirely oceanic, but the Arctic Ocean is not free and open. Rather, it is landlocked, with large continental masses hemming it in on all sides.

Consider what would happen in such a case. Imagine the Earth's temperature to be a trifle warmer than it is today so that there is little or no sea ice in the Arctic Ocean and so that it is an unbroken stretch of liquid surface.

The Arctic Ocean would then serve as a source of water vapor which, cooling in the upper atmosphere, would fall as snow. The snow that fell back into the Arctic Ocean would melt, but the snow that fell on the surrounding continental masses would accumulate. Year after year the snow would accumulate, little by little, and the glaciers would form and expand.

The existence of the glaciers would lower the average temperature of the Earth by reflecting back much of the sunlight that fell on them, and slowly sea ice in the Arctic Ocean would form and expand.

Although ice also yields water vapor, it does so in smaller quantities than liquid water does. This means that the more sea ice there is and the smaller the area of open water, the less water vapor is lifted into the atmosphere.

In the Antarctic, even if the sea ice rimming Antarctica expands, there is always a vast free ocean beyond to serve as a vapor reservoir. In the Arctic, however, when the Arctic Ocean freezes, there is comparatively little other ocean in the neighborhood to serve as an alternate reservoir that can supply water vapor that will reach the northern landmasses before precipitation elsewhere.

Therefore, as the Arctic Ocean freezes, the quantity of snowfall over Canada, Scandinavia, and Siberia decreases. This means that even though little of the ice melts in the summer, still less ice will form in the increasingly snowless winters—and the glaciers start to retreat.

As the glaciers retreat, the temperature of the Earth rises slowly and the glaciers retreat still faster (as long as the Arctic Ocean remains frozen). Finally, North America and Eurasia are free of the continental ice sheets while the Arctic Ocean is *still* covered with sea ice—and that is the situation today.

Greenland, which is a small Antarctica, a polar landmass entirely surrounded by water, has an ocean to the south that remains as a vapor reservoir even when the ocean to the north freezes, so it retains its ice cap. Its ice cap may survive the interglacials, as it seems to be surviving the present one.

In the course of an interglacial, however, as the temperature continues to rise, the sea ice in the Arctic Ocean begins to shrink in area (already it only covers some four-fifths of the ocean) and eventually disappears altogether, leaving the Arctic Ocean unbroken liquid surface once more.

As the Arctic sea ice melts, the water vapor delivered into the atmosphere increases in the polar region, and so does the snowfall, so that the whole thing starts over again.

In other words, it is, paradoxically, a warming trend that initiates a glaciation, and a long enough period of cooling that heralds the start of a deglaciation.

This might well account for the four glacial advances and retreats in the last million years. The minor irregularities are not unexpected, since weather is a complicated thing and there may well be minor warming and cooling trends, minor shifts in wind patterns, minor changes in the carbon dioxide content of the atmosphere, or in volcanic activity, or in sunspots, and so on.

But why only in the last million years? Why was there no period of glaciation in North America and Eurasia for 250,000,000 years before the Pleistocene epoch?

Could it be that the general temperature of the Earth was so high prior to the Pleistocene that there was insufficient precipitation *in the form of snow* to start the glaciers going even when the Arctic Ocean was free of sea ice? Actually, there are ways of testing this that involve the element oxygen.

Oxygen, as it occurs on Earth, is in the form of three varieties, or "isotopes." These are oxygen-16, oxygen-17, and oxygen-18. Oxygen-16 is by far the most common, making up 99.635 percent of all the oxygen atoms. Oxygen-18 makes up 0.204 percent, and the tiny quantity left over is oxygen-17.

The ratio of oxygen-16 to oxygen-18 is just about the same in all oxygen-containing compounds found on Earth, but in 1947, the American chemist Harold C. Urey and his co-workers showed that this ratio varies very slightly, depending on the temperature at which the compound was formed. By 1950, Urey and his group had developed the technique to so fine a point that by analyzing the isotope ratio in the shell layers of a millions-of-years-old fossil squid, they could follow the rise and fall of temperature with the seasons. They could show that the squid had been born in summer, had lived four years, and had died in spring.

By using such a "thermometer," it has been established that, 100,000,000 years ago, the average worldwide ocean temperature was about 21 C. It cooled slowly to 16 C. over the next 10,000,000 years and then rose again to 21 C. in 10,000,000 years more. Since then, the ocean temperature has cooled steadily (and oddly enough the onset of this long cooling trend was at the time when the dinosaurs began to die off). By 30,000,000 years ago, the temperature of the ocean was 10 C.; 20,000,000 years ago, it was 6 C., and now it is about 1.5 C.

It is reasonable to argue, then, that as the temperature of the ocean and (presumably) of the Earth, generally, fell, there was first an icing up of Antarctica and then, eventually, the beginning of the glacial oscillations in the Northern Hemisphere.

The Shifting Poles

The combination of ocean-temperature studies and the Ewing-Donn reasoning would seem to account both for the events in the Pleistocene and for the long period of nonglaciation before the Pleistocene. It leaves unexplained, however, the queer distribution of tropic and near-tropic glacial areas in the ice ages prior to the Pleistocene.

Perhaps one should look for some other way of accounting for the long, long interglacial period before the Pleistocene, and see if that will do better.

Let's ignore the fact that the Earth may have been warmer than it is now prior to the Pleistocene and ask if there is any other reason why there might have been no glaciations then.

Since the glacial oscillations depend on the fact that the North Pole is located in a nearly landlocked ocean, it might be that prior to the Pleistocene, the North Pole was located elsewhere; in open water, perhaps. Not only would that explain why there were no glaciations in the long period prior to the Pleistocene, but it might explain why earlier glaciations took place in the Tropics. Perhaps those regions were not located at the Tropics at that time but happened to be near the shifting North Pole (and South Pole).

This is a startling possibility indeed, and geologists are not likely to accept it as a purely ad hoc explanation. They would want some evidence, independent of the ice ages, that there can be such a shifting of the poles.

To begin with, for instance, we might ask whether the North and South poles have shifted in any way during the period in which scientists have been making careful measurements of the position of parts of Earth's surface with respect to the stars.

Yes, they have, but the shift is small.

The actual precise position of the North and South poles at any moment of time, the actual northern and southern ends of the axis around which the Earth rotates, are the "spin poles" and they are not stationary.

The spin poles move in a roughly circular path, shifting rather erratically, at a rate of some 3 to 6 meters a year, over a patch of ground some 20 meters across. Each makes a complete circle in about 435 days, and it is the average position of the spin poles, somewhere in the center of the circle, that is accepted as the geographic poles.

If the material making up the Earth stayed put, the spin poles would remain stationary and would be identical with the geographic poles. Actually, however, the material making up the Earth shifts. Ice forms in winter and accumulates in places, then melts in spring and is redistributed. Silt is brought down from mountaintops to deltas by rivers. Tides shift the ocean back and forth, while earthquakes shift the inner layers of rock. This redistribution is tiny on a whole-Earth scale, but it is enough to keep the spin poles moving.

The tiny shiftings of the spin poles, however, cannot possibly alter the nature of the glacial oscillation, but this is only what has been observed in the last century or so.

Who can tell what might have happened in the vast ages when scientists were not around to make observations? Might not the Earth have in some way become unstable as the result of weight shiftings within itself and, so to speak, turned over a bit into a stable position and begun to spin about a different axis? Could this happen, little by little by little, so that the North and South poles would slowly migrate out of the positions they are in now and eventually be in radically different positions, and, of course, with different degrees of tipping?

On theoretical grounds this seems very unlikely. The Earth, as it spins about its axis, possesses something called "angular momentum," the quantity of which depends on its mass and on the speed with which it is spinning. The speed of the spin isn't much—it takes a full 24 hours for the Earth to turn once—but the vast mass of the planet is sufficient to make the angular momentum enormous.

A fundamental law of physics is "the conservation of angular momentum," which states that the angular momentum of an isolated body cannot change. This would mean that if the Earth were considered all by itself, it would be completely impossible for its angular momentum to change; that is, for the Earth to spin more slowly, more quickly, or about a different axis than it does now.

The Earth cannot be considered alone, of course. The gravitational effect of other bodies in the solar system does result in tiny shifts of angular momentum from Earth elsewhere. The Moon's pull and the tides it produces bring about, for instance, a tiny shift of angular momentum from Earth to Moon, so that the Earth's speed of rotation is very, very slowly slowing down—1 second every 100,000 years.

To shift the position of the axis appreciably is more than the known gravitational effect of other bodies in the solar system can do. We might imagine some cataclysmic effect, the passing of some planetary body near the Earth, that might produce such results (effects such as those imagined by Immanuel Velikovsky in his popular but scientifically worthless book *Worlds in Collision*). There is no evidence, however, that such a thing has happened, and if it did, the results would be so cataclysmic as to leave drastic evidence in the fossil record.

Perhaps, though, one might opt for a lesser effect. Is it possible that it is not the entire Earth that shifts, but only the outer crust? The Earth's crust, which is 15 to 65 kilometers thick, makes up only about one-third of 1 percent of the Earth's mass, and has much less angular momentum than the Earth as a whole.

Consider, next, that it is well known that the temperature of the Earth goes up with depth. Could the crust, then, be resting on a lower layer which is hot enough to be plastic and which offers little friction? Could weight shifts on the Earth's surface produce an asymmetry that would finally force the crust to shift, perhaps only slowly, until a new position of stability is found?

If this is the case, then, the bulk of the Earth, well over 99 percent of its mass, would still be rotating about the same axis as before. The axis would remain oriented as it was before and there would be comparatively little change in the angular momentum. However, the crust, with everything on it, including the continents, the seas, and the planet's load of life, would move. With respect to the crust and the continents and oceans, it would seem that the North and South poles were shifting.

This suggestion, first advanced in 1886 by a German nobleman, Carl Löffelholz von Colberg, also runs into difficulties. Is there, in actual fact, a plastic layer underneath the crust over which it could easily slide? In 1958, satellite measurements of the exact shape of the Earth showed there were large-scale bumps and hollows; not large ones, but still bumps and hollows that would not be there unless the Earth's interior was stiff and rigid. Given that fact, it seemed quite unlikely to suppose the crust could shift.

Then, too, neither the rolling of the globe as a whole nor the sliding of the crust could account for the early tropical glaciations. In either case, the North and South poles must move together, since the two must always remain on opposite sides of the globe. There is no way in which we can arrange the North and South poles of the Earth so as to account for all the places that were glaciated 600 million years ago. If any of those are imagined to be straddling one of the poles as a result of crustal shiftings, other places would be temperate or even tropical. Thus, if you placed the North Pole in the bulge of Brazil to account for the glaciation there, the South Pole would be in the western Pacific. India, which was also glaciated, would then be in the Tropics.

No, as long as the Earth's continents have their present relative positions, there is no way of explaining early glaciations by any amount of rolling of the globe as a whole or by any amount of sliding of the crust as a whole.

The Shifting Plates

But then, do the Earth's continents always maintain their present relative position? Is it possible that the Earth's crust shifts but not all in one piece? Do the continents themselves move, rather than the crust to which they are attached? Does one continent move here and another move there, and can we so arrange them that all the parts that show the early glaciation are clumped together—and if they can be located in one polar region or the other can they all have experienced glaciation? Can the fact be puzzling now only because the glaciated region has broken up and drifted apart every which way?

Actually, the notion of moving continents is attractive and arose first of all not too long after the discovery and exploration of the American continents.

Anyone looking at a map of the Atlantic Ocean is bound to be struck by the similarity of the coastlines of South America and southwestern Africa. The Brazilian bulge just fits neatly into the Gulf of Guinea and the coastlines to the south seem to fit like a jigsaw if only you move South America and Africa together and turn them a little.

The first person we know of who mentioned this in writing that survives was the English statesman and writer Francis

Bacon, who in 1620 pointed out the similarity in the shape of the coasts.

Could it be that Africa and South America were once joined, that they split apart along the line of the present coasts and then drifted apart? It seemed very easy to think so and occasionally people did speculate in that fashion.

Biologists studying fossils of living creatures of the far past came across similar species in far separated parts of the world. Sometimes they assumed that land bridges had existed over vast parts of the ocean and gave fanciful names to huge continents of the past. The Austrian geologist Edward Seuss suggested in 1880 that there had once been a large supercontinent stretching around the Southern Hemisphere, including South America, Africa, India, and so on, plus the land bridges in between. This he called "Gondwanaland," after Gondwana, a region in central India which he thought to be characteristic, geologically, of this supercontinent.

There was a difficulty, though, in assuming that the continents had always been in their present position and that they were either connected or separated according to whether land bridges rose or sank. Such massive risings and sinkings were hard to account for geologically. Thus, evolutionary considerations and not geographic ones alone drew men to the thought that the continents wandered and did not require land bridges to be connected.

The first person to deal thoroughly with the notion of "continental drift" was a German geologist, Alfred Lothar Wegener, who published a book on the subject, *The Origin of Continents and Oceans*, in 1912.

The continents are made up of less dense rock than the ocean floor. The continents are chiefly granite, the ocean floor chiefly basalt. Might not these granite continental blocks slowly drift about on the underlying basalt? It was something like the notion of the slipping crust, but instead of the entire crust slipping, it was only the continental blocks that were doing so.

The continental blocks covered only one-quarter of the Earth's surface, and their moving about involved even less question of angular momentum. Then, too, if the continental blocks moved independently, all difficulties in evolutionary detail and in primordial glaciations could be removed. One just rearranges the continents to account for similar species in different landmasses, or glaciations.

Indeed, Wegener suggested that all the continents at one time existed as a single vast block of land which was set in a single vast ocean. The supercontinent he called "Pangaea" (from Greek words meaning "all-Earth") and the superocean he called "Panthalassa" ("all-Ocean").

For some reason, Pangaea broke up into several fragments which drifted apart until we ended with the continental arrangement of today.

Wegener's book aroused considerable interest but it was difficult to take it seriously. The same objections to the shifting of the entire crust seemed to work against the shifting of individual continents. The underlying layers of the Earth's structure were simply too stiff to allow drift, and for nearly half a century the theory of continental drift was considered as one of those interesting notions one need not pay attention to.

Nevertheless, the more the continents were studied, the more it seemed they must once have fitted together. If one considered the edge of the continental shelf as the true edge of the continent, the fits were even better. Not only did South America fit southwest Africa nearly perfectly, but North America fit into Europe and northwest Africa equally well. In 1966, intimate details of geology were found to correspond from one continental shore to another across an ocean.

Scientists could eventually fit all the continents together into a Pangaea as Wegener had suggested. (Wegener died at the age of fifty in the winter of 1930 while exploring the Greenland ice cap and did not survive to see any of the exciting developments of his theory.) In fact, judging from the fossil record, one could reason that Pangaea still existed as late as 225,000,000 years ago, at the time when the dinosaurs were just beginning to develop.

Then, too, geologists could reason as follows: Assuming that Pangaea split up and the fragments drifted apart, the floor of the oceans that formed between the fragments would have to be relatively young. Fossils from continental rocks were as old as 600,000,000 years, but fossils from sedimentary rocks from the sea bottom couldn't possibly be that old unless they were from places that had never been passed over by a continent in all that time.

As a matter of fact no fossils older than 135,000,000 years have ever been located from rocks at the sea bottom, which means that the sedimentary layers lining the top of the ocean

Figure 32. Continental Drift

floor are much younger than the continental rocks, and that is what would be expected if two continents drifted apart, creating an ocean between them.

In short, numerous lines of evidence converged to indicate that the continents drifted, and in the early 1950s (when all these lines of evidence had not yet been worked out) the great problem was *how?* Continents, it would seem, must drift, but there was no way in which they could.

Perhaps some evidence could be found through studies of the sea bottom. Perhaps if the newest portions could be found, they might be illuminating.

Nothing was known of the sea bottom until modern times, of course, since miles of water effectively hid it. If anyone thought of the sea bottom at all, it seemed natural to suppose that it was flat and relatively featureless, as one would expect a water-holding basin to be.

The first hint to the contrary came in 1853, when it proved necessary to make some soundings so that the Atlantic cable could be laid, and Europe and America, for the first time, could be connected by electric signals. At that time, it was reported that there seemed signs of an undersea plateau ("Telegraphic Plateau" it was called) in the middle of the ocean. At least, the Atlantic Ocean seemed shallower in the middle than on either side.

In those days, soundings could only be made by dropping a long, weighted line overboard and few such soundings could be made, so that the shape of this plateau in midocean could be given only in the sketchiest possible fashion.

During World War I, methods for telling distance by the speed with which ultrasonic sound echoes (sound too high in frequency to be heard) returned from some reflecting surface were worked out. In 1922, a German oceanographic vessel began to make soundings in the Atlantic Ocean in such a way, and by 1925 those aboard could report a vast undersea mountain range winding down the center of the Atlantic Ocean.

The undersea mountain range (with its highest peaks breaking through the water surface to form islands such as Ascension, Tristan da Cunha, and the Azores) was called the Mid-Atlantic Ridge, but continuing investigations showed that it was not confined to the Atlantic Ocean.

At its southern end, it curves around Africa and up the

western Indian Ocean to Arabia. In mid-Indian Ocean, it branches so that the range continues south of Australia and New Zealand and then works northward in a vast circle all around the Pacific Ocean. One must refer to it, therefore, as the Mid-Oceanic Ridge.

Part of the Mid-Oceanic Ridge is to be found in the Arctic Ocean, too. There the Lomonosov Ridge (named for an eighteenth-century Russian scientist, Mikhail Vasilievich Lomonosov) extends some 14,500 kilometers across the Arctic Ocean, from Ellesmere Island to Siberia, dividing the ocean basin into two parts. The Lomonosov Ridge has peaks rising about 1000 meters above the general Arctic sea bottom, but none is high enough to have its top rise above a sea level which rolls another 1000 meters above the highest reach of the ridge. (The greatest known depth in the Arctic Ocean, measured in 1955, is 5400 meters.)

The Mid-Oceanic Ridge may well represent the youngest part of the sea bottom since, in general, the farther from the ridge a fossil is found, the older it is. It is reasonable, then, to suppose that careful studies of the ridge might help yield information on continental drift. After World War II, Ewing (while he was working out his theory of glacial-interglacial oscillations) was particularly interested in such research.

He and Bruce Heezen discovered, in 1953, that running down the length of the ridge, right down its long axis, was a deep canyon. This was eventually found to exist in all portions of the Mid-Oceanic Ridge, so that sometimes it is called the "Great Global Rift."

Figure 33. Oceanic Mountain Ridges

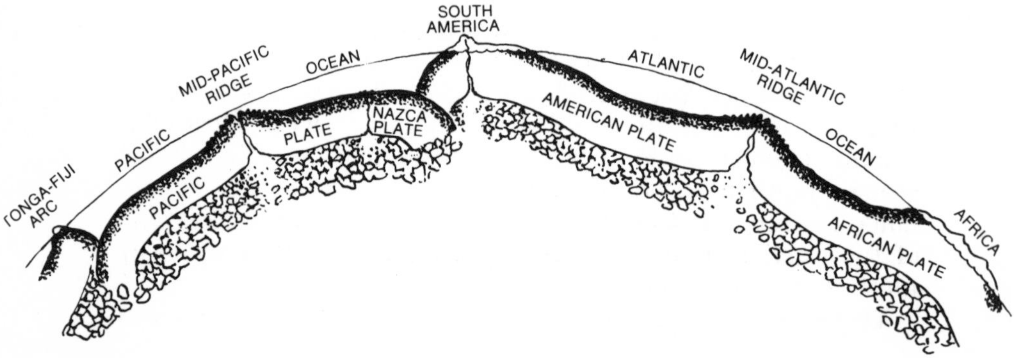

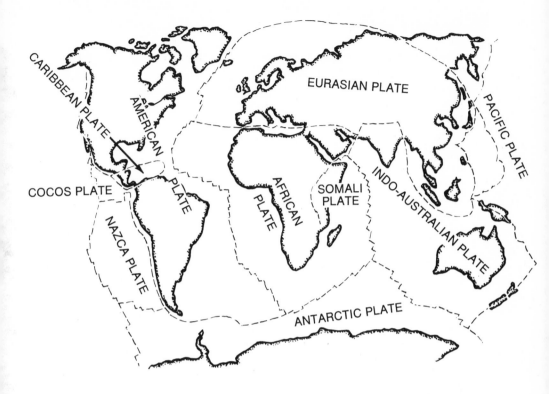

Figure 34. Continental Drift: The World Today

There are places where the rift comes quite close to land; it runs up the Red Sea between Africa and Arabia, while an offshoot runs southward through the Great Lakes area of southeastern Africa. Another portion of the rift skims along the western coasts of South and North America and actually cuts across the length of western California.

It appeared at once that the Earth's crust was divided into large plates, separated from each other by the Great Global Rift. These were called "tectonic plates," with "tectonic" coming from a Greek word for "carpenter," since it almost seemed as though the plates were cleverly joined together to make a seemingly unbroken crust. The study of the evolution of the Earth's crust in terms of these plates is referred to by these words in reverse as "plate tectonics."

There are six large tectonic plates. There is the American

plate, including North and South America from the western coast of the continents to the Mid-Atlantic Ridge. East of the Mid-Atlantic Ridge are the Eurasian and African plates, separated from each other by a line running along the Mediterranean and Red seas. The Australian plate and the Antarctic plate are centered on Australia and Antarctica and include the neighboring waters. The sixth is the Pacific plate, which includes most of that giant ocean.

There are also smaller plates, lying between the larger ones. Lying between the southern part of the American plate and the Pacific plate, just off the western coast of South America, is the "Nazca plate." There is also a small "Caribbean plate" south of the West Indies and north of South America, and so on.

It was at once apparent that earthquakes commonly take place along the boundaries of the tectonic plates. The boundaries of the Pacific plate include the earthquake zones in the East Indies, in the Japanese islands, in Alaska, in California, and so on. The Mediterranean boundary between the Eurasian and African plates is second only to the Pacific rim for its well-remembered earthquakes.

Indeed, the Great Global Rift is not a continuous crack. Closer examination showed it consisted of short, straight sections that were set off from each other as though earthquake shocks had displaced one section from the next.

Then, too, the "faults" that had been detected in the Earth's crust as deep cracks where the rock on one side could, periodically, slide against the rock on the other to produce earthquakes were extensions of the rift. The most famous of all such faults, the San Andreas Fault, which runs the length of California from San Francisco to Los Angeles, represents part of the boundary between the American plate and the Pacific plate.

In one way, the discovery of the tectonic plates put an end to any notion of the Wegener type of continental drift. The continents were not floating and drifting on the rock of the sea bottom. Each was an integral part of one plate or another and could not move independently of the plate. Since the plates were tightly joined, they could not move, it would appear, except in the way of an occasional earthquake slip by at most a fraction of a meter.

The answer came from another consideration. The plate boundaries were places where not only earthquakes were common but volcanoes, too. Indeed, the shores of the Pacific are so marked by volcanoes, both active and inactive, that they have been referred to as the "circle of fire."

Could it be then that liquid rock ("magma") welled up from the hot layers deep in the Earth through the cracks between the tectonic plates, these cracks representing weaknesses in the otherwise solid crust of the Earth? Specifically, magma might be welling up very slowly through the Mid-Atlantic Rift and, freezing as it did so, accumulating on either side of it to form the Mid-Atlantic Ridge.

We can go further. Perhaps as the magma welled up and solidified, it pushed the plates apart. If it did that, it would succeed in pushing Africa and South America apart on the south, and Europe and North America apart on the north, forming the Atlantic Ocean and making it ever wider. Europe and Africa would be pushed apart, too, with the Mediterranean and Red seas forming.

Because the sea floor would grow wider as a result, this effect was called "sea-floor spreading," something that was first proposed by the American geologists Harry H. Hess and Robert S. Dietz in 1960. By this theory, Wegener was held to be essentially correct, but his theory was modified in that the continents weren't viewed as floating and drifting apart, but as solidly based and yet being *pushed* apart.

How could sea-floor spreading be demonstrated? The rocks obtained from the ocean floor on either side of the Mid-Atlantic Ridge were tested for their magnetic properties, beginning in 1963. It turned out that there were strips of rocks on either side of the ridge that were, alternately, of normal polarity and reversed polarity. The pattern was a mirror image on both sides. Apparently, as the magma solidified it took on the polarity that the Earth was experiencing at the time. It was clear that the rocks were youngest at the ridge and older and older as one moved away from it on either side.

By measuring the width of the strips, it could be clearly shown not only that the Atlantic sea floor was spreading, but the rate at which it was spreading (about 2 centimeters per year at the moment), and therefore the time when the Atlantic Ocean first began to open up, could be roughly determined.

The study of the movement of these tectonic plates has completely revolutionized the study of geology in these last two decades.

Thus, when two plates are forced apart, then somewhere else on Earth two plates must be forced together. If land surfaces are pushed together, as a result, at a rate of less than 6 centimeters per year, the land buckles both upward and downward, forming mountain ranges with deep roots of relatively light rock. This explains why the Earth's crust is thicker in mountain areas than anywhere else, and why it is thinner at the sea bottom than anywhere else—thick where plates come together, thin where they are pushed apart.

If two plates come together at a rate faster than 6 centimeters per year, there is no time to buckle. One plate slips under the other and begins to melt in the great heat beneath. In this process whereby one plate moves downward, the sea floor is pulled downward, too, and thin ocean trenches are formed which are much deeper than the average depth of the ocean. The trenches, together with parallel lines of islands, and volcanoes, too, tend to appear at the boundaries of the plates.

Presumably, there has been a long, very slow cycle of magma welling up to push plates apart in some places, and plates coming together, pushing crust downward and converting it to magma. In the process, the continents come together into a single landmass and then split up. This may happen many times, with the Pangaea of 225,000,000 years ago only the most recent of such landmasses.

Geologists can now even follow the course of the breakup, though still only in a rather rough manner. An early break came in an east-west line. The northern half of Pangaea, including what is now North America, Europe, and Asia, is sometimes called "Laurasia" because the oldest part of the North American surface rocks, geologically speaking, are those of the Laurentian Highlands north of the St. Lawrence River.

The southern half, including what is now South America, Africa, India, Australia, and Antarctica, is called "Gondwana-land," thus preserving Suess's old name. This is not a bad idea, since it is just like Suess's supercontinent minus the land bridges.

About 200,000,000 years ago, North America began to drift away from Eurasia, and 150,000,000 years ago, South America began to drift away from Africa, the two Americas eventually connecting narrowly at Central America. The landmasses were pushed northward as they separated, until the two halves of Laurasia clasped the Arctic region between them. This, together with the generally dropping temperature on Earth, set up the conditions a million years ago for the beginning of the alternation between glacial and interglacial periods.

About 110,000,000 years ago, the eastern portion of Gondwanaland broke into several fragments: Madagascar, India, Antarctica, and Australia. Madagascar stayed fairly close to Africa, but India moved farther than any other landmass in the time since the most recent Pangaea. It moved 9000 kilometers northward to push into southern Asia. In doing so it produced the buckles that represent the vast Himalayan Mountains, the Pamirs, and the Tibetan plateau—the youngest, greatest, and most impressive highland area on Earth.

Antarctica and Australia may have separated only 40,000,000 years ago. Antarctica moved southward to its frozen destiny. Australia is still moving slowly northward today.

And, of course, continental drift continues today. The Atlantic Ocean is still widening, and Iceland, which straddles the ridge, is being slowly torn in two. The plate boundary which runs down the Red Sea and through east-central Africa along the line of such long deep lakes as Tanganyika and Nyasa is also widening. The Red Sea is thus the nucleus of a new ocean which will eventually separate east-central Africa from the rest of the continent.

Fossils in Antarctica

The question of continental drift received, as it turned out, its strongest support and what many consider its final proof from Antarctica.

Antarctica is frozen now and has been frozen for millions of years. It has been frozen for so long, perhaps, that no native mammalian life may ever have existed there, so that, when Captain Cook and his crew first crossed the Antarctic Circle, they may not merely have been the first men, but the first land mammals *ever* to cross that imaginary line.

But fossils show that complex life forms have existed on Earth at least 600,000,000 years, and it is quite likely that Antarctica has not been frozen all that enormous length of time. If that is so, there might be evidence of that fact available to those who search for it.

If Antarctica had once not been frozen, but had possessed a mild climate, surely it would have had a rich plant and animal life. The first indication that this was so came in the Antarctic summer of 1892–1893, when a piece of fossil pine tree was discovered. Not much, but it was as good a piece of evidence of past life as the finding of a whole forest would have been. There wasn't even any chance that the fossil remnant had been brought there from somewhere else, since in Antarctica in those days, wherever man placed his foot was a first and nothing could be in place but what had been there for millions of years.

If there was any doubt, that ended in 1903 when the Antarctic explorer Scott came upon a deposit of coal in Victoria Land. Since then signs of surprisingly extensive deposits of coal have been located. This showed that not only did forests once grow in Antarctica, but they must have done so luxuriously and over many years, since some of the coal deposits are 13 feet thick.

Trunks of petrified trees have been found, too, as well as imprints of leaves on rocks. Some of these imprints are detailed enough to allow the leaves to be identified as those of "Glossopteris," a plant that flourished in tropical jungles of Africa and South America 250,000,000 years ago.

Where plant life exists, animal life does, too. There is no known exception to this rule on Earth today, and that has probably held true for many hundreds of millions of years. We can assume, then, that in a plant-rich Antarctica, animals existed, too. In 1903, fossil shells of ammonites were discovered in Antarctica.

How do we account for a mild Antarctica? If Antarctica had always been in its position at the South Pole, could there have been a time when the temperature of the Earth, the world over, was mild? We would have to suppose that, long before the Pleistocene epoch and its glaciations, there must have been long periods when life flourished everywhere and did so in the polar regions on equal terms with life in lower latitudes. The polar regions must have had the same odd arrangement of day and night they have now, but the consequences, ice and low temperature, did not follow.

How that could be is difficult to see—luxurious, coal-producing forests only a few hundred kilometers from the South Pole. Once the notion of tectonic plates and continental drift arose, however, the difficulty disappeared.

Antarctica did not necessarily have its fossils because the

South Pole once had a pleasant climate; it might have them because it was not always at the South Pole. Once, when it was part of Pangaea, it might have had a temperate or even a tropical climate, while whatever land might then have been at the South Pole was as frozen as it would be today. Or, if there were only water at the South Pole, as was more likely, the sea ice would have swirled there as it swirls now in the Arctic Ocean.

The problem is, though, how one can tell from a fossil whether the land that gave it birth had been at the South Pole at a time when that area had an unusually mild temperature or had been elsewhere, where mild temperature was not unusual. In short, could a fossil remnant indicate whether Antarctica had changed position, geographically, or not?

The answer came, quite surprisingly, in December 1967, when the New Zealand geologist Peter J. Barrett came across something that looked like a pebble, but that caught his eye and turned out to be a fragment of bone. The find was made on Graphite Peak in the Transantarctic Range on the western coasts of the Ross Ice Shelf.

At once, paleontologists (whose field of study is ancient fossils) began to investigate the region. The fragment of bone was identified as a piece of a skull of a long-extinct amphibian called "labyrinthodont," and in March 1968, the American paleontologist Edwin H. Colbert discovered the lower jawbone of such a creature.

The jawbone was found in a cliff about 520 kilometers from the South Pole, and it was surrounded by fossils of swamp plants about 200,000,000 years old. By the continental-drift theory, the labyrinthodont and the swamp plants lived when Antarctica was still part of Gondwanaland and when Pangaea was just in the earliest stages of its breakup. The labyrinthodont was the first vertebrate fossil ever found in Antarctica.

The labyrinthodont was quite like known fossils of this type of organism in Africa, Madagascar, and Australia. They are so similar in these various places that it doesn't seem likely that they arose independently here and there. It is much more likely that they arose in one center and then spread out. The point is, though, that the labyrinthodonts are freshwater creatures and could not survive in the ocean; they cannot be visualized as swimming miles across the ocean to establish themselves on islands.

*Lystrosaurus, 28,000,000 years old
(dragonfly for size comparison)*

Assuming Africa to be the point of origin of the organism, it is not impossibly difficult to see it as maneuvering its way to Madagascar and Australia. Madagascar is less than 500 kilometers from Africa at its point of closest approach, and one can dream of a land bridge, perhaps. Again, one can imagine the labyrinthodonts making their way across the African and Asian landmasses over millions of years and finally reaching Australia by way of the Indonesian islands. The widest water passage would be less than 400 kilometers and maybe that could be done, too.

To be sure, it is much easier to assume that Africa, Madagascar, and Australia were once part of a single body of land and that the labyrinthodonts waddled their way from one body of fresh water to another without any problem of the salt sea at all—but the alternative can't be ruled out entirely.

However, with labyrinthodonts in Antarctica, the case is entirely different. If present-day geography is the permanent state of affairs on Earth, then the nearest approach of

Antarctica to the Africa/Madagascar/Australia home of the labyrinthodonts is nearly 5000 kilometers. Surely that width of sea water is prohibitive. It becomes so much easier to see Antarctica as part of the same landmass as Africa, Madagascar, and Australia, something so many other lines of evidence support that the discovery can be considered as establishing continental drift beyond a reasonable doubt.

At the time the labyrinthodonts flourished and Pangaea was in the early stages of its breakup, the amphibians that had been the most highly developed forms of vertebrate life were being replaced by the reptiles that were the first vertebrates to be truly adapted to land life. They had been in existence for 100,000,000 years, and the earliest dinosaurs were beginning to appear.

Even supposing that the dinosaurs appeared first on those parts of Pangaea other than the fragment that eventually became Antarctica, Antarctica should surely have carried some reptiles with it as it moved slowly toward the South Pole and death.

In 1969, fossil fragments of another 200-million-year-old vertebrate was discovered, this time at Coalsack Bluff in the Transantarctic Mountains, about 650 kilometers from the South Pole. It proved to be that of a small hippopotamus-like reptile called "lystrosaurus"—and it was the first reptilian fossil to be discovered.

Skeleton of Thrinaxodon

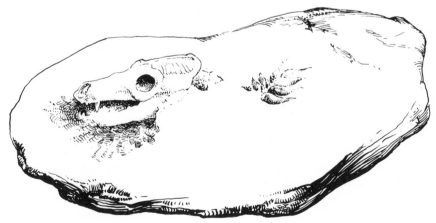

Then, on November 10, 1870, James Colinson discovered the first *complete* vertebrate fossil ever found in Antarctica. It was that of a foot-long "cynodont," which in the evolutionary scale seems to have been a contemporary of lystrosaurus.

Perhaps the most exciting part of this last discovery is that the cynodont is a mammal-like reptile, the member of a group which became extinct only after some of its descendants had accumulated enough mammalian characteristics to become entitled to the name of mammal.

As far as we know, the first mammals appeared 180,000,000 years ago at most, or at least 20,000,000 years after the time of the amphibian and reptilian fossils discovered in Antarctica. However, it took many millions of years for Antarctica to move from its position in Pangaea to the South Pole, and in that time some primitive mammals may have been developed from the mammal-like reptiles of which we now have some evidence.

At the present moment, the fossil search in Antarctica is proceeding at top speed, or at least at as great a speed as is possible in that frozen waste.

The Future

Where does Earth stand now and what does it face in the future? We are, after all, still in the Pleistocene. Whatever conditions have brought about four gigantic oscillations of ice cover, four enormous advances and retreats of the great glaciers—those conditions still exist. The Arctic Ocean, for instance, if it is the key to the situation, is still where it has been. It is at the moment iced in, but it may not remain so.

For how long will the Earth stay at its present temperature and in its present situation as far as ice cover is concerned? Will the trigger be pulled? If so, when? And in which direction?

The question as to the direction is to remind us that we face a double-barreled danger. If the temperature drops and allows the glaciers to advance (or, for that matter, if the temperature rises sufficiently to melt the Arctic sea ice and if *that* allows the glaciers to advance), we have one variety of danger. It will be a bad one, too, for the prospect is for a much worse glaciation than ever before, at least as far as man is concerned.

The glaciers themselves may, possibly, not advance as far or be as thick as in earlier periods of the Pleistocene, but that is not the point. In the four earlier glaciations, the Earth was thinly inhabited by human beings (or their prehuman ancestors) who lived in a mobile hunting economy and with no possessions they could not carry. They could drift southward or northward, with the glaciers, without much trouble. If northern land disappeared, under the ice, coastal land was uncovered by the dropping sea level, and vice versa. What's more, the disappearance of land, and its appearance, was excessively slow. In the lifetime of individual human beings, no perceptible change took place.

How different the situation is now. The Earth is full of human beings—four billion of them right now and with the figure still going up. Millions live in the areas that were covered by glaciers the last time, and this time (it is possible) there are reasons to suppose the glaciers may move more quickly than ever before. Even if the glacial advance is slow enough to keep the refugee situation from becoming overwhelming, consider that there are cities, farms, and mines in these regions that cannot be moved. Moreover, the glaciers will exert their effect far ahead of their actual presence, and, as the weather cools and farms grow less productive, starvation may face mankind's swollen numbers even at a time when the advance of the glaciers has scarcely begun.

If, on the other hand, the Earth's temperature warms *past* the glaciation trigger to the point where Earth will no longer retain *any* load of permanent ice, that is also bad. It is the other half of the double-barreled danger.

In fact, we might argue that a too-great warming trend can be more dangerous than a too-great cooling trend. After all, in a glaciation the first regions affected will be lands where human population is relatively thin—Canada and Siberia. If the Earth grows warm enough to melt what ice now exists, however, the sea level will rise, and the encroaching ocean will invade the lowland rims of the continents, precisely where the greatest densities of population, and where man's largest cities and most thriving centers of commerce and industry, exist.

If all the ice melts, even the Antarctica ice cap, the sea level will rise some 60 meters and will cover New York City, for instance, to the height of the twentieth story of the Empire State Building. All of Long Island and Cape Cod will be underwater; all of Delaware and Florida, most of Maryland

and New Jersey, half of Alabama and Mississippi. Abroad, all of the Netherlands and Denmark will be gone, half of England and so on, and so on, and so on.

Remember, it doesn't take much of a change in temperature to start things off in either direction, so how stable is Earth's temperature right now?

From what evidence climatologists have been able to gather, it would seem that, since the end of the last glaciation, Earth's temperature has oscillated both above and below the present normal.

Between 4000 B.C. and 3000 B.C., when civilization was first being established in Egypt and in the Tigris-Euphrates valley, the Earth warmed steadily, until by 3000 B.C. the climate was markedly warmer and drier than today. During this thousand-year interval, the Arctic Ocean may have been fairly open in the summer (but, apparently, not for long enough to set off the glaciation trigger); the alpine glaciers may have retreated to some 300 meters above their present level. As a result of melting ice, the sea level may have risen 12 or 13 centimeters each year over periods of time. (Some speculate that the effect of this on coastal areas helped give rise to the flood legends that have appeared in so many different places.)

This warm temperature did not remain. Eventually, the temperature dropped, then rose, then dropped, then rose, in a slow swing.

Between A.D. 1000 and 1200, the temperature was warmer than it is today, though not as warm as at the 3000 B.C. peak. It was in this warm interval that the Vikings colonized Greenland, and in those days parts of the coast may even have been green enough to warrant the name.

By A.D. 1450, however, the climate had cooled off to the point where the Viking colony was destroyed, and it continued to go down into what is sometimes called the "Little Ice Age." Temperature was at a minimum about A.D. 1600, and it stayed cold throughout the eighteenth and nineteenth centuries.

We don't know what caused these swings in temperature—slow cycles in volcanic action, perhaps, or something else. We are on firmer ground when we consider the last century.

Toward the end of the nineteenth century, the Little Ice Age came to a sudden end, and from 1889 onward the average temperature of the Earth began a steady half-century rise, sharper than anything that has happened in recent centuries.

It seems certain that humanity was involved by now. Mankind has been burning coal at a more and more rapid rate, and in this way producing carbon dioxide which was added to the atmosphere. What's more, the forests were cut down and grain fields substituted. All green plants withdraw carbon dioxide from the air and convert it into plant tissue, but a given area of forest does this to a greater extent than does that same area of grain. The two effects taken together have reached the point where, nowadays, there is a human-caused input of 8 billion tonnes of carbon dioxide into the atmosphere each year.

All told, mankind has added some 325 billion tonnes of carbon dioxide to the atmosphere in the past century. Not all has remained, but enough has to increase the carbon dioxide concentration in the air by 13 percent. The temperature of the Earth was 0.6 C. higher, on the average, in 1940 than in 1900. As a consequence, glaciers retreated and the sea level rose. The sea level rose over 6 centimeters between 1900 and 1940.

If all the coal and oil in the ground were burned, it is estimated that the carbon dioxide of the atmosphere would be increased to four times what it is today and that the Earth's temperature would rise 7 C. over what it is now. That would certainly suffice to melt the ice caps and, moreover, might do it with considerable speed. One can visualize the ice caps melting in a century and, in that time, drowning the Earth's lowlands, where half the population lives and where most of the fertile farming areas are to be found.

Yet this prospect seems to have receded. The Earth's temperature, which had risen inexorably and with disquieting speed till 1940, suddenly did an about-face and began dropping again.

Apparently, this, too, is the result of human activity. Man's burning of fuel and his industrial activity generally have added not only carbon dioxide to the atmosphere but also dust as well. The dust acts to cool the Earth's temperature, and by 1940 the dust effect had overtaken the greenhouse effect of the carbon dioxide and now dominates the situation.

For the last third of a century, the Earth's overall temperature has dropped precipitously by nearly a degree—and remember that a single degree is enormous when it represents a global average. The temperature has dropped even more rapidly since 1940 than it had risen before 1940, and we are now nearly at the Little Ice Age level and the temperature seems still to be going down.

It is amazing by how narrow a thread man's comfort hangs, and in the last century, which has seen man's numbers swell explosively and depend ever more heavily on an expanding technology, the consequences of the breaking of that thread have grown steadily more formidable.

Of course, it may be that the current fall in average temperature may turn as quickly as did the previous rise in 1940. And it may not. If, as a result of human activity, rises and falls in Earth's average temperature take place more sharply than ever before, it seems we are going to face icing or drowning sooner or later.

What we need is more information, more details, about what is going on with respect to temperature fluctuations on Earth, and, in particular, with respect to the polar regions, which have a great influence on those fluctuations.

There have been attempts to learn the nature of the globe generally, its properties, its stabilities, and its instabilities.

In the winter of 1882–1883, for instance, the First International Polar Year took place, with eleven nations establishing twelve stations in the Arctic. It was the first time a concerted effort had been made for a concerted scientific study of the polar region, as opposed to individual exploratory assaults— modern war, so to speak, rather than knight-errantry.

The most important result of that winter of work was the discovery that the aurorae were most frequent in a doughnut-shaped ring about the magnetic poles.

A half century later, a much larger effort, the Second International Polar Year, was conducted in the winter of 1932–1933. Some twenty nations set up about 120 stations in the Arctic and sub-Arctic and, for one thing, studied the ionosphere in great detail.

The next such study, which followed a quarter century later, was far larger and more intensive still. It might have been called the Third International Polar Year, but the research aims had so broadened that it could not be named in such a way as to suggest that it was confined to polar phenomena. It was called the "International Geophysical Year" (IGY) instead. Originally it was planned for an 18-month period but it was extended to a 30-month period from July 1, 1957, to December 31, 1959.

The findings of the IGY, to which 70 nations and 30,000 scientists at thousands of stations contributed, were broad indeed. To mention perhaps the most glamorous consequence, it marked the opening of the space age, when the Soviet Union, as part of its contribution, launched the first artificial satellite on October 4, 1957.

The most notable discovery in the Arctic was that of the existence of the Lomonosov Ridge.

The IGY was the first to set up a massive research program for the Antarctic as well as the Arctic. In frozen Antarctica, which now saw scientists swarming over its ice by the hundreds, and even thousands, the weather was, for the first time, closely studied and the subfrigid lows to which the temperature dropped were for the first time recorded. The rather basic difference between an East Antarctica, continental in nature and made of ancient rock, and a West Antarctica, an archipelago in nature and built up of recent sedimentary rock, was established. The thickness of the Antarctic ice was measured and in one place was found to be over 4 kilometers thick. What's more, the total quantity of ice covering Antarctica was found to be about 18,500,000 cubic kilometers, about 40 percent higher than had been estimated previously.

The IGY did not, however, establish the exact pattern of temperature fluctuation in the world. It did not even indicate in which direction we are moving and reports ever since have been contradictory.

Some estimates are to the effect that the Antarctic ice cap is growing at a rate of about 293 cubic miles a year, while others state that the Greenland ice cap is losing about 22 cubic miles of ice a year.

Toward the end of 1973, T. Hughes of Ohio State University argued that though East Antarctica's ice load may be stable, that of West Antarctica is melting rapidly because it is based on a sub-sea-level foundation and because it includes the two great ice shelves which are less stable than land-based ice. Hughes estimates that, in the last 4000 years, this part of the Antarctic ice cap has lost 1,500,000 cubic kilometers of ice and has thinned by 400 meters. If it all melts, the sea level will be 4 meters higher than it is now.

But either way, up or down, it seems we face catastrophe. Is there nothing we can do?

Well, *if* our technological civilization survives the dangers that press upon it now, and if the level of technological expertise continues to rise, perhaps all is not hopeless. After all, it is a question not of controlling huge mountains of ice or vast floods of water, but only of controlling the relatively tiny triggers.

We may learn to control the carbon dioxide content of the air, and the dust content, keeping each in careful balance. We may learn to melt ice when necessary by spreading carbon black over its surface, or to influence climate by diverting rivers this way and that to suit the circumstances. Or perhaps we may learn useful tricks that are now undreamed of.

If so, we might envisage a future in which the Earth is carefully "air-conditioned" and will never again be at the mercy of either the advancing ice or the rising ocean. That is, if all goes well.

INDEX

Absolute zero, 144
Adélie Land, 129
Adélie penguin, 242
Africa, 38, 71
African plate, 336
Agassiz, Jean L. R., 291
Alaska, 93, 94
Albedo, 165
Aleutian islands, 61, 93
Alexander I, 127
Alexander I Island, 127
Allen, Joel A., 187
Allen's rule, 187
Alpine climates, 193
Altitude, temperature and, 157
Aluminum, 170
Amber, 41
American plate, 335, 336
Ammonia, 138, 145, 147, 150
Amundsen, Roald, 101, 109, 131
Amur River, 81

Ångular momentum, 10, 327
Antarctica, 134
  area of, 136
  coal in, 340
  continental drift and, 339, 343
  discovery of, 129
  fossils in, 339ff.
  ice age and, 295
  icebergs and, 210
  ice sheet on, 204ff., 305, 349
  interior of, 130ff.
  land animals in, 217
  mild past of, 340
  oases in, 216
  plant life in, 217
  snowfall in, 207
  temperatures in, 157
Antarctic bottom water, 229
Antarctic Circle, 57
  crossing of, 124
Antarctic Convergence, 229

Antarctic Ocean, 210, 229
Antarctic Peninsula, 126
Antarctic plate, 336
Antarctic region, 57
  population of, 136
Aphelion, 310
Appleton, Edward V., 269
Appleton layer, 269
Aquarius, 53n.
Arabian Nights, 251
Archaeometry, 298
Arctic Archipelago, 86
Arctic Circle, 57
  crossing of, 60, 69, 75, 88
Arctic fox, 239
Arctic Ocean, 81
  area of, 135
  depth of, 180
  exploration of, 105, 110
  ice ages and, 322ff.
  pack ice and, 179, 180
Arctic region, 56
  animals in, 186ff.
  ice age in, 295
  population of, 136
  temperatures in, 158
Arctic tern, 240
Argentina, 114, 117
Aries, 47, 53n.
Aristotle, 47
Arkhangelsk, 76
Arnarson, Ingolfur, 65
Astrology, 53n.
Atlantic cable, 333
Atlantic Ocean, 339
Atmosphere, carbon dioxide in, 347
  circulation of, 218ff.
  development of, 141
  dust in, 347
  heat-trap properties of, 195
  ions in, 269
  man-made changes in, 347
  planetary, 140
  temperature change in, 192
  water vapor in, 163
Atoms, 268
Auks, 240

Aurorae, 264
  solar flares and, 267
  solar wind and, 276
Australia, 118
Australian plate, 336
Austria-Hungary, 95
Autumnal equinox, 30
Avalanche, 199
Axis of rotation, 10, 20, 24

Bacon, Francis, 329, 330
Baffin, William, 90
Baffin Bay, 90
Baffin Island, 85, 86, 88, 90
Baleen, 235
Banks Island, 100
Barents, Willem, 78
Barents Sea, 78
Barrett, Peter J., 341
Barrow, 136
Barrow, John, 97
Bear Island, 78
Belle Isle, Strait of, 84
Bellingshausen, Fabian G., 127
Bellingshausen Sea, 128
Bennett, Floyd, 110
Bennett, James G., 106
Bergmann, Carl, 186
Bergmann's rule, 186
Bering, Vitus J., 93
Bering Island, 93
Bering Sea, 93
Bering Strait, 81, 93, 95
Big Diomede, 93
Big Dipper, 55
Biscoe, John, 129
Black Death, 67
Blubber, 237
Blue whale, 235
Boiling point, 143
Bolshevik Island, 97
Boltwood, Bertram B., 298
Booth, Felix, 98
Boothia, Gulf of, 98
Boothia Peninsula, 98, 99
Borchgrevink, Carsten E., 131
Bouvet de Lozier, Pierre, 123

Bouvet Island, 123
Bransfield, Edward, 126
Bransfield Strait, 126
Brunhes, Bernard, 284
Buoyancy, 171
Button, Thomas, 90
Byrd, Richard E., 110, 134

Cabot, John, 83
Callisto, 146
Canada, 85
Canaries Current, 222
Cancer, 32, 47
Cape Agulhas, 112
Cape Bismarck, 103
Cape Chelyuskin, 94
Cape Columbia, 105
Cape Dezhnev, 93
Cape Farewell, 66
Cape Horn, 116
Cape Morris Jesup, 105
Cape of Good Hope, 112
Cape of Storms, 112
Cape York, 102, 118
Capricorn, 32, 47
Carbon, 138
Carbon-14, 299
Carbon dioxide, 145
    atmospheric, 142n.
    Earth's temperature and, 316
    ice ages and, 317, 318
    man-made, 347
Caribbean plate, 336
Caribou, 191
Carrington, Richard C., 266
Cartier, Jacques, 84
Caspian Sea, 169, 170
Catherine I, 93
Cathode rays, 271
Cavendish, Henry, 256
Celestial equator, 46
Celestial sphere, 45
Celsius scale, 2n.
Centimeter, 8n.
Chancellor, Richard, 76
Charpentier, Johann H., 290

Chelyuskin, S., 94
Chile, 114, 117
China, 81
Christofilos, Nicholas, 273
Civilizations, ancient, 40
Cimmerians, 41
Circle of fire, 337
Circumpolar stars, 54
Clouds, 164, 195
Coal, Antarctica and, 340
Coalsack Bluff, 343
Cobalt, 139, 258
Colberg, Carl Löffelholz von, 328
Colbert, Edwin H., 341
Coleridge, Samuel T., 125n.
Colinson, James, 344
Columbus, Christopher, 59, 72
    compass and, 252
Comets, 146
Compass, magnetic, 249
    aurorae and, 266
Compton, Arthur H., 271, 274
Constellations, 32
Continental climates, 156
Continental drift, 330
Continental shelves, 302
Continental slopes, 302
Cook, James, 95, 118, 119, 124
Copepods, 232
Coppermine River, 92
Core, Earth's, 255ff.
Coriolis, Gaspard G. de, 218
Coriolis effect, 218
Corona, solar, 275
Corte-Real, Gaspar, 83
Cosine, 7
Cosmic rays, 271
    life and, 280
    nature of, 273, 274
    supernovae and, 282
Crab-eater seal, 238
Cubic centimeter, 170n.
Cubic kilometer, 149n.
Cumberland Sound, 88
Curie, Pierre, 258
Currents, ocean, 221ff.
Cynodont, 344

Da Gama, Vasco, 71, 149
Dalrymple, Alexander, 123
Dark nebulae, 306
Daubrée, Gabriel A., 257
David, Edgeworth, 254
Davis, John, 88, 127
Davis Strait, 88
Daylight saving time, 28n.
Dead Sea, 170
Declination, magnetic, 252
Degrees of arc, 4
Del Cano, Juan S., 74
De Long, George W., 106
De Magnete, 253
Demeter, 36
Denmark, 65, 66
    Greenland and, 87
Density, 170, 172
Desolation Island, 124
Devon Island, 90
Dezhnev, Semyon I., 81
Dias, Bartholomeu, 71, 112
Dietz, Robert S., 337
Dinosaurs, 281
    continental drift and, 343
Diomede Islands, 93
Dip, magnetic, 253
Discovery, geographic, 59
Dmitri Donskoi, 77
Dolphins, 233
Donn, William L., 323
Draco, 53
Drake, Francis, 116
Drake Passage, 116
Drake Strait, 116
Duarte I, 71
D'Urville, Jules D., 129, 254
Dust, atmospheric, 347
Dutch East Indies, 117n.

Earth, 2
    age of, 168, 299
    albedo of, 165
    atmosphere of, 141
    circumference of, 14, 49
    circumnavigation of, 74
    core of, 255ff.
    density of, 256
    diameter of, 51
    flat, 3, 4
    formation of, 139
    ice caps of, 211ff.
    inner core of, 259
    magnetic properties of, 253, 259, 273
    magnetosphere of, 277
    mass of, 10, 256
    Moon and, 327, 328
    nickel-iron core of, 257
    orbit of, 23, 310ff.
    recent temperature changes of, 346
    revolving, 23
    rotating, 10ff.
    seasons of, 30, 311, 361
    spherical, 8ff., 46
    tilted, 4ff.
    zones of, 32ff.
Earthquakes, 336
    Earth's core and, 257, 259
East Antarctica, 132
East Falkland, 115
East Indies, 117
Edward VII Land, 131
Egede, Hans, 87
Egerton, Francis, 91
Eielson, Carl B., 110
Electric field, 272
Electromagnetic field, 272
Electromagnetism, 259
Electrons, 150, 268, 272
Elephant seal, 238
Ellesmere Island, 91
Ellipse, 23
Ellsworth, Lincoln, 109, 134
Elsasser, Maurice, 259
Emperor penguin, 243ff.
Enderby Land, 129
England, 75, 85
Equator, 14, 23, 27
Equatorial bulge, 51
Equatorial diameter, 51

Equinox, 30
  precession of, 311
Eratosthenes, 49
Eric the Red, 66
Ericsson, Leif, 67
Eskimos, 62, 239
  in Greenland, 68, 87
Ethiopia, 40
Euphotic zone, 230
Eurasian plate, 336
Europe, ice age in, 296
Everest, Mount, 59
Ewing, Maurice, 323, 334
Explorer I, 276
Explorer III, 277
Explorer IV, 277

Faeroe Islands, 63ff.
Fahrenheit scale, 2n.
Falkland Islands, 115
Falkland Sound, 115
Faraday, Michael, 258, 272
Faults, geologic, 336
Ferdinand II, 72
Ferromagnetism, 258
Filchner, Wilhelm, 132
Filchner Ice Shelf, 132
Firn, 201
First International Polar Year, 348
Fixed stars, 44
Flare, solar, 266
Floating, 172
Flood, Biblical, 290
Fool's gold, 86
Fossils, Antarctican, 229ff.
Fram, 107
France, 84
Franklin, John, 99
Franklin, Kenneth, 261
Franz Josef Land, 96
Fresh water, 162, 165ff.
  ice as, 205
  salt in, 168
Frobisher, Martin, 85
Frobisher Bay, 85
Frost, 183

Fuchs, Vivian, 134
Fury and Hecla Strait, 98

Gadolinium, 258
Gas giants, 144
Gassendi, Pierre, 264
Gauss, Carl F., 253
Genetic load, 281
Geographic poles, shift of, 326
Geomagnetic poles, 253, 273
  aurorae and, 264
George III, 98
George IV, 98
Germania Land, 103
Germany, 103
Gilbert, William, 253
Glaciers, 201ff., 290
  calving of, 208
  movement of, 291
Glossopteris, 340
Golden plover, 241
Gondwanaland, 330, 338
Graham, James R. G., 126
Graham Land, 126
Gram, 153n.
Graphite Peak, 341
Gravitational field, 272
Great auk, 240
Great Britain, 127
Great circle, 14
Greater Antarctica, 132
Great Global Rift, 334
Great Lakes, 292
Great Salt Lake, 170
Greeks, 40
Greely, Adolphus W., 106
Greenhouse effect, 317
Greenland, 66
  exploration of, 101ff.
  final discovery of, 87
  ice sheet on, 204
  interior of, 103
  temperatures on, 160
Grinnell, Henry, 100
Grinnell Peninsula, 100
Groundwater, 183

Gulf Stream, 180, 209, 221
  speed of, 223

Hades, 36
Hail, 196
Hale, George E., 266
Hall, Charles F., 102
Hammerfest, 136
Hayes Peninsula, 102
Hearne, Samuel, 92
Heaviside, Oliver, 269
Hebrides, 63
Heezen, Bruce, 334
Helium, 136, 144
Henry IV, Part One, 55
Henry the Navigator, 71
Hensen, Matthew, 108
Hensen, Viktor, 231
Herald Island, 106
Herodotus, 38
Herschel, William, 213
Hess, Harry H., 337
Hess, Victor F., 271
Hibernation, 187
Himalayan Mountains, 339
Hipparchus, 48
Homer, 41
Hooper, Calvin, 95
Hudson, Henry, 88
Hudson Bay, 89
Hudson River, 89
Hudson's Bay Territory, 90
Hudson Strait, 85, 89
Hughes, T., 349
Humboldt, Alexander von, 223
Humboldt Current, 223, 231
Humboldt Glacier, 208
Huygens, Christian, 212
Hydrogen, 136
  atom of, 274
  boiling point of, 144
  density of, 176
Hyperborea, 40

Ice, 177, 178
  ocean and, 179ff.
  quantity of, 204, 205

Ice Age, 292
  animals of, 303
  causes of, 292ff., 306ff.
  early, 321
  future, 344ff.
Icebergs, 64, 208ff.
  Antarctic, 210, 211
  dangers of, 209
  fresh water nature of, 209ff.
  tabular, 210
Ice cap, Antarctic, 211
Ice islands, 181
Iceland, 42, 64, 65, 66
  continental drift and, 339
Ices, 146
Ice sheets, 203
  Pleistocene, 2
  temperature and, 206
IGY, 348
Illinois glacial, 297
India, continental drift and, 339
Indians, American, 67, 305
Indonesia, 117n.
Infrared radiation, 195
Inland seas, 169
Inner core, 259
Insects, Antarctican, 217
Interglacial periods, 297
International Geophysical Year, 348
International Ice Patrol, 209
Ionosphere, 270
Ions, 161, 268
Ireland, 63
Iron, 138
  Curie point of, 258
  density of, 172
  magnetism and, 248
  melting point of, 259
Isabella I, 73
Isotopes, 325
Ivan III, 77
Ivan IV, 76, 77

Jacobshavn Glacier, 208
James I, 89
James Bay, 89
Jan Mayen Island, 88

Jensen, Jens A. D, 103
John II, 112
Jones Sound, 91
Jupiter, 139
   magnetic field of, 261, 278
   satellites of, 146

Kamchatka, 93
Kane Basin, 102
Kane, Elisha K., 102
Kansas glacial, 297
Kennelly, Arthur E., 269
Kennelly-Heaviside layer, 269
Kerguelen Island, 123
Kerguelen-Tremarek, Yves J. de, 123
Kettle holes, 292
Kiev, 77
Killer whale, 233
Kilometer, 2n.
King William Island, 99
Kodiak brown bear, 239
Kola peninsula, 68
Koldewey, Karl C., 103
Kolyma River, 80
Komandorskie Islands, 94
Komsomoletz Island, 97
Korff, Serge, 299
Kotelny Island, 95
Krill, 232
Kristenson, Leonard, 131

Labrador, 83, 85, 225
Labrador Current, 224
Labyrinthodont, 341
Lachine, 84
Lancaster Sound, 90
Lapps, 61, 192
Latitude, degrees of, 15
Latitude effect, 274
Latitude, parallels of, 13
Laurasia, 338
Lead, 298
Lehmann, Inge, 259
LeMaire, Jakob, 116
Lemmings, 188, 189
Lena River, 80

Leopard seal, 238
Lesser Antarctica, 132
Libby, Willard F., 300
Libra, 47
Lichen, 217
Light, refraction of, 21n.
Lines of force, magnetic, 272
Little America, 134
Little Diomede, 93
Little Ice Age, 346
Lomonosov, Mikhail V., 334
Lomonosov Ridge, 334, 349
Lucretius, 249
Lyakhov Islands, 95
Lyra, 53
Lystrosaurus, 343

Macquarie Islands, 120
Madagascar, 117
Magellan, Ferdinand, 73, 113
Magellan, Strait of, 114
Magma, 337
Magnesium, 138
Magnesium chloride, 226
Magnetic axis, 255
Magnetic compass, 249, 250
Magnetic declination, 252
Magnetic dip, 253
Magnetic field, 272
   evolution and, 286, 287
   reversals of, 283ff.
Magnetic lines of force, 272
Magnetic poles, 251, 254
Magnetic storms, 266, 267
Magnetism, 248
Magnetite, 248
Magnetopause, 278
Magnetosphere, 277, 283
Magnets, 248
Mammoths, 303
Marconi, Guglielmo, 268
Marcus Aurelius, 40
Mariner 10, 261
Mariner's compass, 249
Markham, Albert H., 106
Mars, 260
   atmosphere of, 141, 142

carbon dioxide on, 315
ice age on, 315
ice caps on, 212-213
water on, 146
Mass, 170
Mawson, Douglas, 134, 254
Maxwell, James Clerk, 268, 272
McClure, Robert J., 100
McClure Strait, 98
McMurdo Bay, 130
Melting point, 143
Melville, Herman, 236
Melville Island, 98
Mercury (element), 172
Mercury (planet), 141, 165, 260, 261
Meridians of longitude, 46
Meteorites, 256
Methane, 138, 145, 150
Metric system, 2n.
Mid-Atlantic Ridge, 333
Mid-Oceanic Ridge, 334
Milankovich, Milutin, 314
Millikan, Robert A., 271
Mineral ions, 230
Minutes of arc, 5
Mithras, 37
Moby Dick, 236
Molecular weight, 150
Molecules, 138, 149
Mongols, 70, 77
Moon, 140
    albedo of, 165
    Earth and, 327, 328
    magnetic properties of, 260
    temperature of, 156, 197n.
Mountains, 338
    snow and, 198
Mount Erebus, 130
Mount Fridtjof Nansen, 134
Mount Howe, 216
Mount Terror, 130
Murmansk, 136, 180
Muscovy, 77
Muscovy Company, The, 76
Musk ox, 189, 190
Mutation, 280
Mylius-Erichsen, Ludvig, 103

Nansen, Fridtjof, 103, 107
Nares, George S., 105
Narragansett Bay, 84
Narwhal, 234
Nautilus, 110
Nazca plate, 336
Nebraska glacial, 297
Nebulae, dark, 306
Necho, 38
Neckam, Alexander, 250
Neon, 138
Neptune, 139, 261
Nerchinsk, Treaty of, 81
Netherlands, 78, 89
Neu Schwabenland, 132n.
Neutrino, 309
Neutron, 274
New Columbia, 95
Newfoundland, 67, 83, 84
New Guinea, 117
New Siberian Islands, 95
New York Bay, 84
New Zealand, 119
Nicholas II Land, 97
Nickel, 139, 258
Nickel-iron core, 259
Night glow, 270
Nitrogen, 138, 145, 227
Nonpolar molecules, 151
Nordenskjöld, Nils A. E., 96, 103
Norman, Robert, 252
Normans, 69
North America, 67, 73
    ice age in, 296
North Atlantic Drift, 222, 224
North Cape, 68
North Celestial Pole, 45, 50, 53
    motion of, 52
Northeast Foreland, 103
Northeast Passage, 70, 81
North Equatorial Current, 222
Northern Hemisphere, 14
North Frigid Zone, 33
North geomagnetic pole, 253
North Island, 119
North magnetic pole, 254
North Pacific Drift, 224

North Polar region, 22, 24
North Pole, 1, 11
　days and nights at, 25ff.
　Peary and, 108
　tipped axis and, 20
North Star, 51
North Temperate Zone, 33
Northwest Passage, 73, 83, 96, 97
　navigation of, 100
Norway, 65, 66, 128
Novaya Zemlya, 68, 78
Novgorod, 76
Nucleic acids, 279
Nucleus, atomic, 268

Oases, Antarctican, 216
Ob River, 80
Ocean, ancient temperatures of, 325
　area of, 148
　circulation of, 221ff.
　depth of, 149
　Earth's size and, 149
　floor of, 331ff.
　gases in, 227ff.
　ice age and, 301ff.
　interglacial periods and, 305
　land temperature and, 153-155
　light and, 230
　parts of, 148
　planetary temperature and, 166
　salt in, 161, 169
　sea-floor spreading and, 337
　solids in, 161
　temperature of, 153
　vaporization of, 162
　volume of, 149
Ocean currents, 173
Oceanic climates, 156
October Revolution Island, 97
Odyssey, 41, 56
Oersted, Hans C., 259
Oldham, Thomas, 257
Olekminsk, 158
Orkney, 63
Ottar, 68
Oxygen, 137
　boiling point of, 145

isotopes of, 325
ocean content of, 227, 228
solubility of, 227
Oymyakon, 158
Ozone, 142

Pacific Ocean, 73
　islands in, 120
Pack ice, 179
　Antarctic, 181, 182
　Arctic, 179, 180
Palmer, Nathaniel B., 126
Palmer Land, 126
Pangaea, 331, 338
Panthalassa, 331
Parallels of latitude, 13
Paramagnetism, 258
Parker, Eugene N., 276
Parry, William E., 97, 105
Parry Islands, 98
Patagonia, 114
Payer, Julius von, 95, 103
Peary, Robert E., 103, 107, 108
Peary Land, 104
Penguins, 242
Peninsula de Brunswick, 114
Peregrinus, Peter, 251, 272
Perihelion, 310
Permafrost, 184
Persephone, 36
Peru Current, 223
Peter I, 92
Peter I Island, 127
Petrels, 241
Phaethon, 41
Philip II, 74
Philippine Islands, 74
Philolaus, 47
Phoenicians, 38, 41, 56, 250
Photon, 270
Photosynthesis, 142
Phytoplankton, 231
Pioneer, 10, 261, 278
Pisces, 53n.
Planets, 44
　formation of, 139

Plankton, 231
Plant life, 142
Plate tectonics, 335
Platinum, 170
Plato, 248
Pleistocene glaciation, 294
Point Barrow, 94, 97
Polar bear, 239
Polar diameter, 51
Polar easterlies, 220
Polaris, 51, 53
Polar molecules, 151
Polar regions, 135, 220
Polar Years, 348
Pole of Cold, 157
Pole of Inaccessibility, 204
Poles, Celestial, 45
Poles, geographic, 11
Poles, geomagnetic, 253
Poles, magnetic, 251, 254
Poles, spin, 326
Pole Star, 51
Polo, Marco, 70
Polynesians, 123, 250
Portuguese Timor, 117n.
Portugal, 71
Posidonius, 49
Precession of the equinoxes, 53, 311
Prevailing westerlies, 219
Pribilof, Gerasim, 237
Pribilof Islands, 237
Primary radiation, 283
Prince Albert Mountains, 129
Prince of Wales Strait, 100
Prince Regent Inlet, 98
Proteins, 279
Protons, 274, 275
Ptarmigan, 187
Ptolemy, 48
Puffin, 240
Pytheas, 42

Queen Elizabeth Islands, 86

Radiation pressure, 276
Radioactive clock, 298

Radio waves, 268
Rae, John, 99
Rain, 164, 165
Rasmussen, Knud J. V., 104
Red Sea, 339
Refraction, light, 21n.
Reindeer, 191
Reindeer moss, 191, 192
Reykjavik, 66
"Rime of the Ancient Mariner," 125n.
Ringed seal, 238
Rio de Janeiro, Bay of, 114
Rio de la Plata, 114
Roman Empire, 63
Roosevelt Island, 130
Ross, James Clark, 129, 254
Ross, John, 97, 129
Ross Ice Shelf, 130
Ross Island, 130
Ross Sea, 129
Russia, 79
    Antarctic and, 127
    Arctic and, 76, 92

Sahara Desert, 41
Saint Brendan, 63
St. Lawrence, Gulf of, 84
Salt, 161
Salt mines, 169
Samoyeds, 61
San Andreas Fault, 336
San Juan Pond, 216
Santa Claus, 1
Satellites, artificial, 349
Saturn, 139, 261
Saturnalia, 37
Scandinavia, 42, 64
Schouten, William C., 116
Schwabe, Heinrich S., 266
Scoresby, William, 97, 105
Scoresby Land, 97
Scoresby Sound, 97
Scott, Robert F., 131, 132, 340
Scurvy, 124n.
Sea-floor spreading, 337
Sea ice, 179

Seals, 236
  Antarctic exploration and, 125
Seawater, freezing of, 179
Secondary radiation, 283
Second International Polar Year, 348
Seconds of arc, 5
Seuss, Edward, 330
Severnaya Zemlya, 97
Shackleton, Ernest, 131
Shakespeare, William, 55, 90
Sharks, 232
Shetland Islands, 42, 63
Siberia, 60
  ice age in, 296
  permafrost and, 184
  Russians in, 79
  temperatures in, 158
Sibir, 79
Silicates, 138
Silicon, 138
Silicon dioxide, 138
Skua, 241
Sleet, 196
Smith, William, 125
Smith Sound, 92
Snow, 195ff., 199
Snowball effect, 140
Snow line, 198
Socrates, 248
Sodium chloride, 161
  solubility of, 226
Solar flare, 266
Solar wind, 276, 279
Solstice, 29
Solubility, temperature and, 226
South Africa, 112
South America, 73
Southampton, Earl of, 90
Southampton Island, 90
South Celestial Pole, 45, 52
Southeast Cape, 118
Southeast Passage, 70
South Equatorial Current, 223
Southern Hemisphere, 14
Southern Ocean, 210, 229
South Frigid Zone, 33

South geomagnetic pole, 253
South Georgia Island, 125
South Island, 119
South magnetic pole, 254
South Orkney Islands, 126
South Polar region, 232, 241
  international character of, 128
South Pole, 11
  days and nights at, 25ff.
  first men at, 132
  tipped axis and, 22
South Sandwich Islands, 125
South Shetland Islands, 125
South Temperate Zone, 33
Southwest Passage, 75
Soviet Union, 95
Spain, 75
Specific heat, 153
Spectroheliograph, 266
Spectrohelioscope, 266
Sperm whale, 234
Spin poles, 326
Spitzbergen, 68, 78
Sputnik III, 277
Square kilometer, 63n.
Standard time, 28n.
Stars, 44
Steel, 248
Stefansson, Vilhjalmur, 108
Stewart, Balfour, 269
Störmer, Fredrik C., 264
Stroganov family, 79
Sublimation, 145
Summer solstice, 29
Sun, 2
  composition of, 275
  corona of, 275
  cosmic rays from, 275
  flares on, 266
  ice ages and, 307
  ionosphere and, 270
  motion in sky of, 16, 20, 25,
    28, 31ff., 47ff.
  position in sky of, 16ff.
  protons from, 275
  sunspot cycle of, 266

Sunspots, 266, 307
Supernovae, 282
Svalbard, 68

Taimyr Peninsula, 94
Tasman, Abel J., 118
Tasmania, 119
Tectonic plates, 335
Telegraphic plateau, 333
Temperature, 152, 153, 159
  height and, 197
  measurement of, 172
Terra Australis, 120
Thales, 247
Third International Polar Year,
  348
Thorium, 297
Thorvaldsson, Eric, 66
Thuban, 53
Thule (legendary), 42
Thule, 102
Thule Island, 125
Tides, 42
Tierra del Fuego, 115
Timberline, 184
Timofievich, Yermak, 79
Timor, 117n.
Tin, 41
Titan, 141
Titanic, 209
Tonne, 10n.
Torres, Luis Vaez de, 118
Torres Strait, 118
Torrid Zone, 33
Transantarctic Mountains, 134
Tree line, 184
Tree rings, 299
Tropic of Cancer, 32
Tropic of Capricorn, 32
Tropics, 31
Tropic Zone, 33
Troposphere, 194
Tundra, 184, 185
  snowfall on, 207
Tungus, 61
*Twenty Thousand Leagues Under
  the Sea*, 110n.

Twilight, 22n.
Tyndall, John, 317

Ultima Thule, 42
Ultrasonic sound, 333
Ultraviolet radiation, 141, 270
Unicorn, 234
United States, 85
  Alaska and, 94
  Antarctic exploration and, 127
  Arctic exploration and, 100, 102
  Greenland and, 87, 102
Universe, atomic makeup of, 136
Upwelling, 229
Ural Mountains, 79
Uranium, 297
Uranus, 139, 261
Urey, Harold C., 325
Ursa Major, 56
Ursa Minor, 56

Van Allen, James A., 277
Van Allen belts, 277
Van Diemen, Anton, 118
Van Diemen's Land, 119
Varves, 299
Vega, 53
Velikovsky, Immanuel, 328
Venetz, J., 290
Venus, 260
  albedo of, 165
  atmosphere of, 141, 142
  temperature of, 317
  water on, 146
Vernal equinox, 30
Verne, Jules, 110n.
Verrazano, Giovanni da, 84
Vespucius, Americus, 73
Victoria Island, 99
Victoria Land, 129
Vikings, 64, 250
Vilkitski, B., 96
Vilkitski Strait, 97
Vinland, 67
Vitamin A, 239
Volatile materials, 139, 140

Volcanoes, 318, 336, 337
Von Wrangel, Ferdinand P., 95
Vostok, 158

Waldseemüller, Martin, 73
Walrus, 238
Water, 137
  boiling point of, 144
  density of, 170, 172, 178
  distilled, 168n.
  electron distribution of, 152
  freezing of, 144, 175, 176
  fresh, 167
  ocean formation and, 146
  solvent properties of, 161
  specific heat of, 153
  vaporization of, 162, 166
Water vapor, 162
Watson-Watt, Robert A., 270
Weather, 220
Weddell, James, 128
Weddell Sea, 128
Weddell seal, 239
Wegener, Alfred L., 330
West Antarctica, 132
West Falkland, 115
West Greenland Current, 224

West Passage, 70
West Wind Drift, 223
Weyprecht, Karl, 95
Whalebone, 235
Whalers, 235
Whales, 233
  Antarctic exploration and, 125
  Arctic exploration and, 97
White Sea, 68, 77
Wilkes, Charles, 129
Wilkes Land, 129
Wilkins, Hubert, 110, 134
Willoughby, Hugh, 75
Wilson, Edward, 244
Wind, 219ff.
Winter solstice, 29
Wisconsin glaciation, 297, 300, 301
Worlds in Collision, 328
Wrangel Island, 95, 106

Yakuts, 61
Year, beginning of, 37
Yenisei River, 80

Zodiac, 32
Zooplankton, 232